CREAM farewell show at Royal Albert Hall, London, November 1968
Photo © 2001 Barrie Wentzell/Star File

DEREK AND THE DOMINOES, November 24, 1970
Photo © 2001 Elliot Landy/Star File

E.C. 1971 Photo by Adrian Boot
London Features International, LTD

Rainbow Theater, London, January 13, 1973

New Jersey Arena, February 22, 1983
Photo © 2002 Michael Brito/Star File

Nassau Coliseum, April 6, 1990
Photo © 2002 Michael Brito/Star File

Madison Square Garden 1996
Photo © 2002 Jim Cummins/Star File

from Eric Clapton - *Another Ticket*

Another Ticket

Words and Music by Eric Clapton

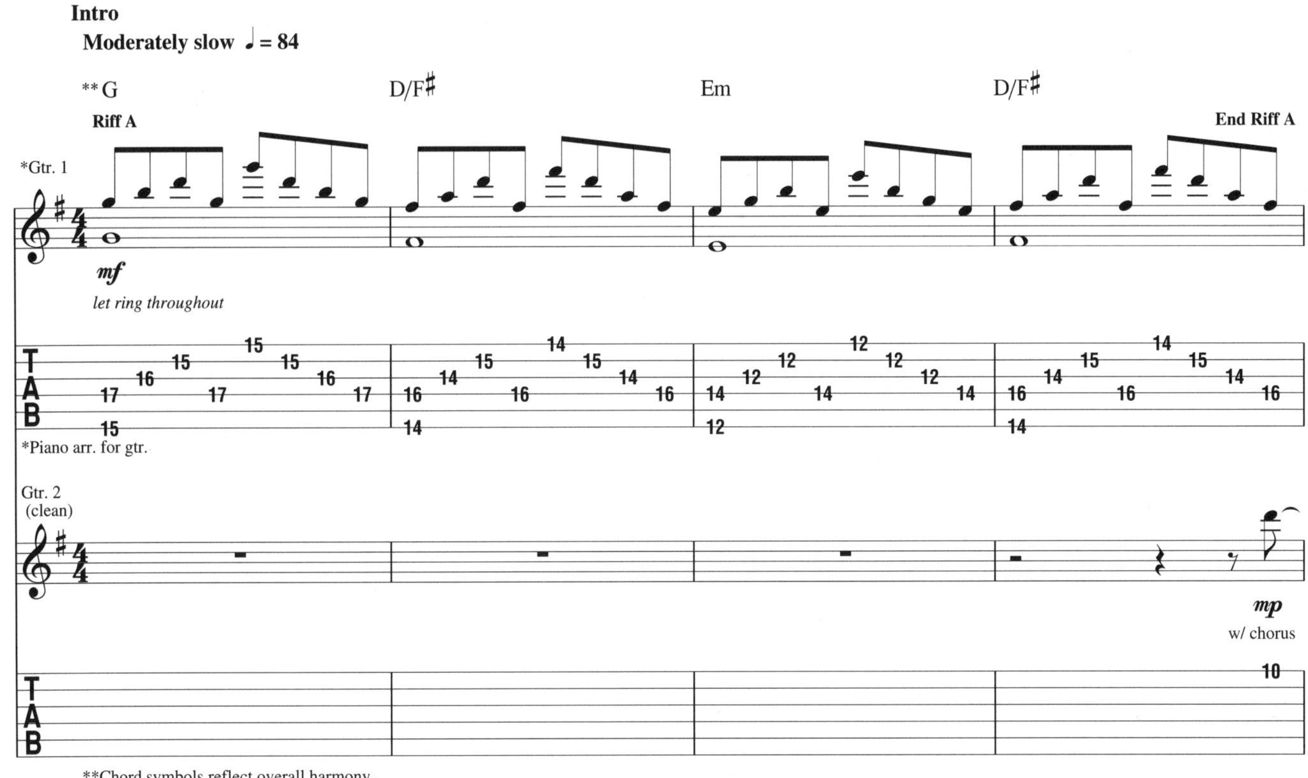

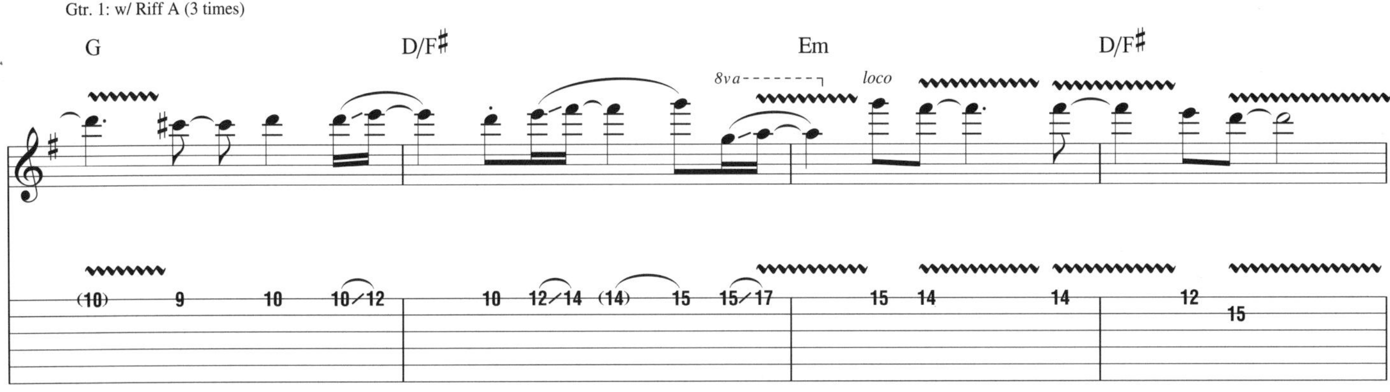

Dsus2/G
Dsus2/F♯
Dsus2/E
Dsus2/F♯
A/G
Riff B
D/F♯
Em7
D/F♯
End Riff B
Verse
Gtr. 3: w/ Riff B
A/G
D/F♯
Em7
D/F♯
1. Why can't it stay like this for - ev - er?
2. Why must we wait un - til to - mor - row?
A/G
D/F♯
Em7
Why does it al - ways have to change?
When we al - rea - dy know the score.
Gtr. 3
D/F♯
Chorus
G5
D/F♯
Ev - 'ry - time you think you've paid the price,
Riff C

To Coda
Em7
D/F♯
G5
seems you've al - ways got to pay it twice.
Ev - 'ry - time you think you're
End Riff C
D/F♯
Em
A5
near the end, you turn a - round and find an - oth - er tick - et.
And
Bridge
D
E9/D
Gmaj7/D
D
oh, my love, time is run - ning out.
D.S. al Coda
E9/D
Gmaj7/D
D
Oh my love, time is run - ning out.

Coda
G5
D/F♯
Em7
Ev - 'ry - time you think you've got it made,
seems you're on - ly ly - ing
Riff D
in the shade.
Ev - 'ry - time you think you've run the course,
seems you've got to ride an - oth - er horse.
Ev - 'ry - time you think you're
near the end,
turn a - round and find an - oth - er tick - et.
A5
End Riff D

Bridge
D
E9/D
Gmaj7/D
D
Oh my love, time is run - ning out.
E9/D
Gmaj7/D
D
Oh my love, time is run - ning out.
Guitar Solo
Gtr. 3: w/ Riff B (1 3/4 times)
A/G
D/F♯
Em7
D/F♯
Gtr. 2
A/G
D/F♯
Em7
Gtr. 3: w/ Fill 1
D/F♯
Fill 1
Gtr. 3

Chorus

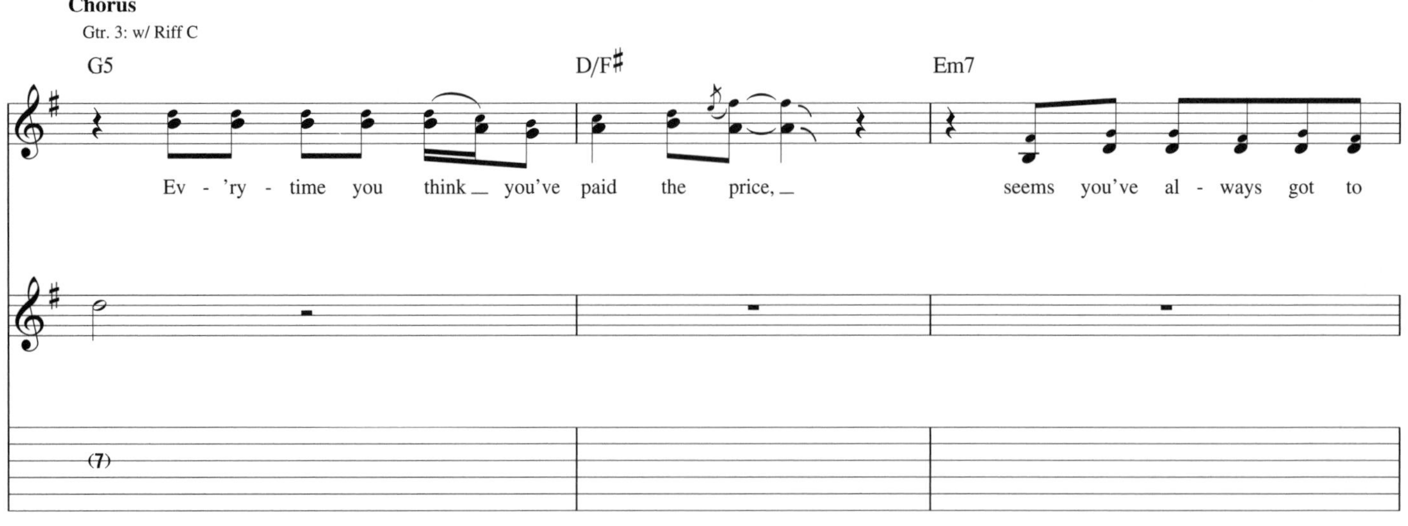
Gtr. 3: w/ Riff C
G5
D/F♯
Em7
Ev - 'ry - time you think _ you've paid the price, _
seems you've al - ways got to
(7)

Gtr. 3: w/ Riff D
D/F♯
G5
D/F♯
pay it twice. _
Ev - 'ry - time you think _ you've got it made, _

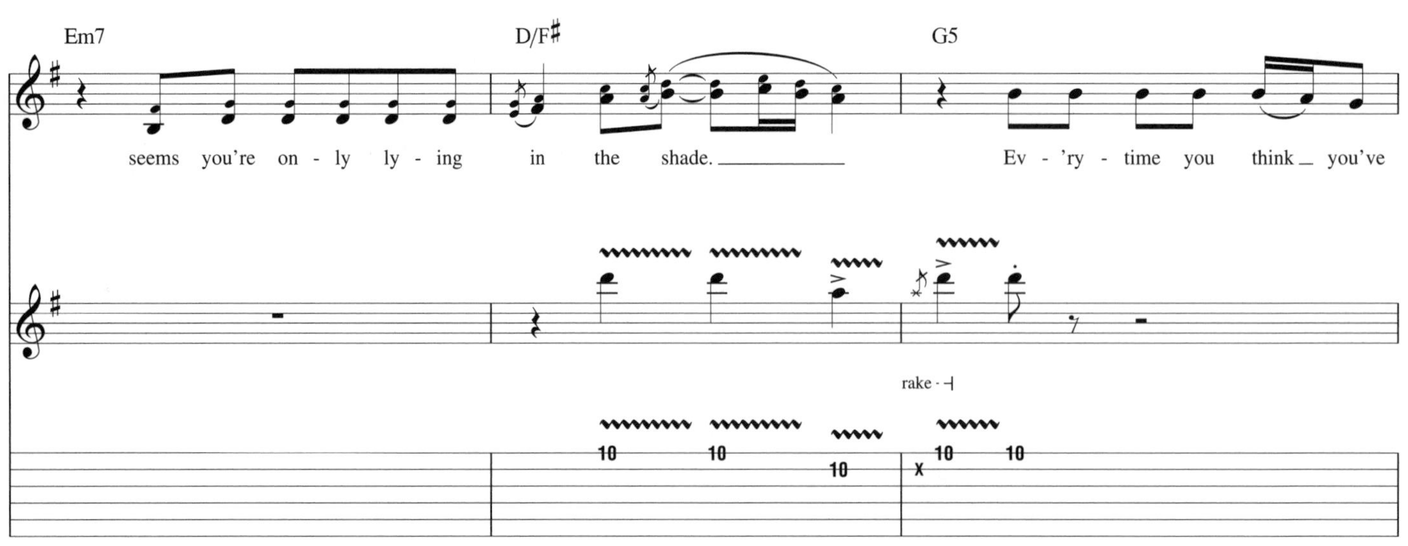
Em7
D/F♯
G5
seems you're on - ly ly - ing in the shade. _
Ev - 'ry - time you think _ you've
rake

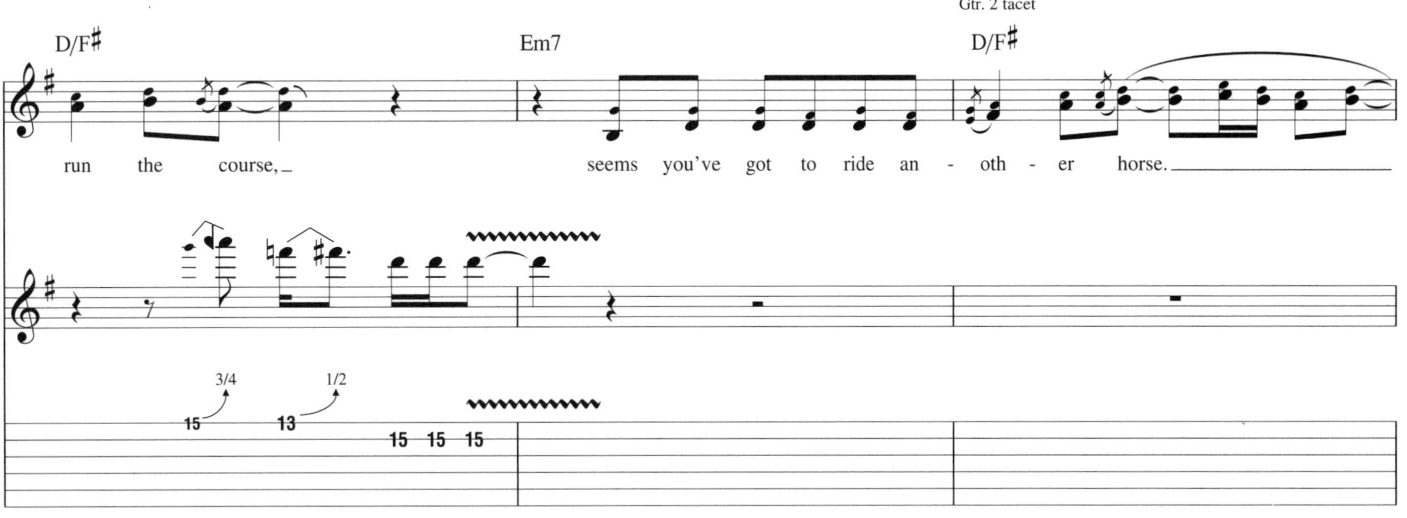
Gtr. 2 tacet
D/F♯
Em7
D/F♯
run the course,
seems you've got to ride an - oth - er horse.
3/4
1/2
15
13
15 15 15

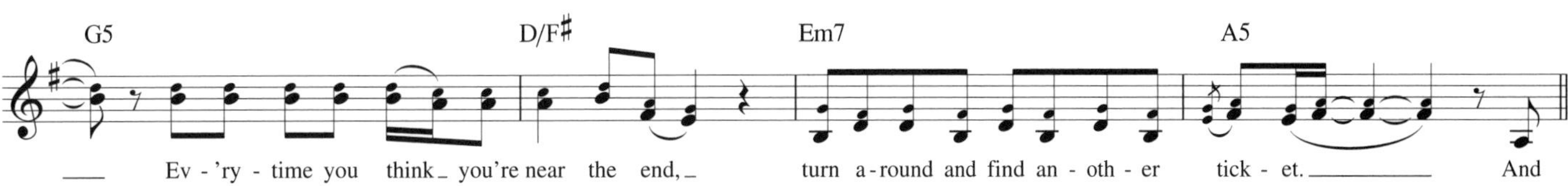
G5
D/F♯
Em7
A5
Ev - 'ry - time you think you're near the end,
turn a-round and find an - oth - er
tick - et.
And

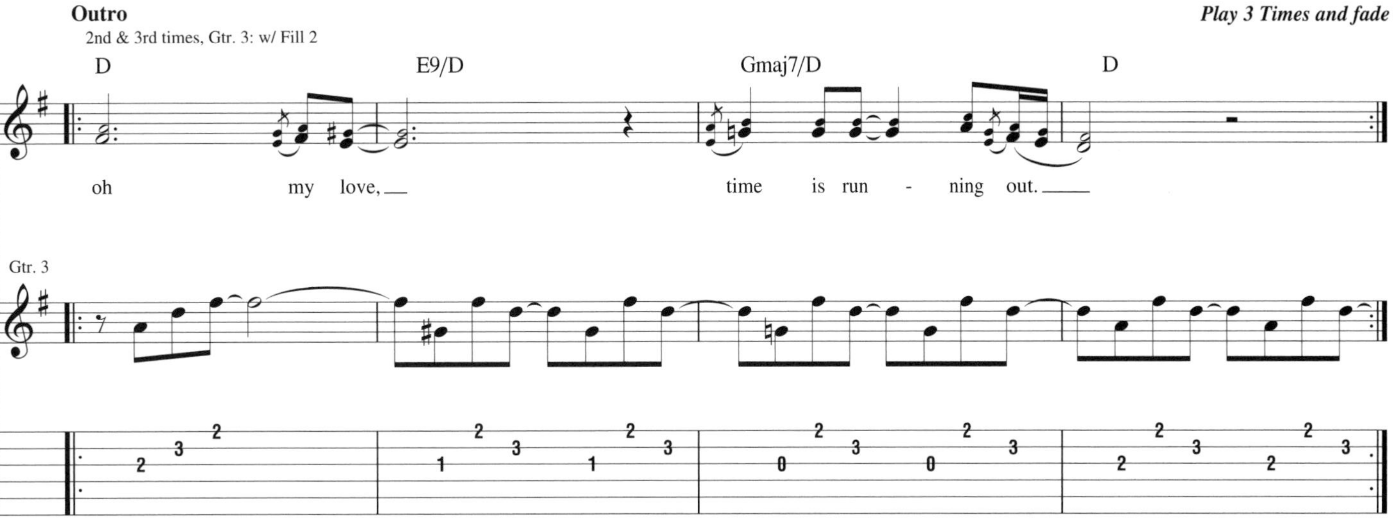
Outro
2nd & 3rd times, Gtr. 3: w/ Fill 2
Play 3 Times and fade
D
E9/D
Gmaj7/D
D
oh
my love,
time is run - ning out.
Gtr. 3

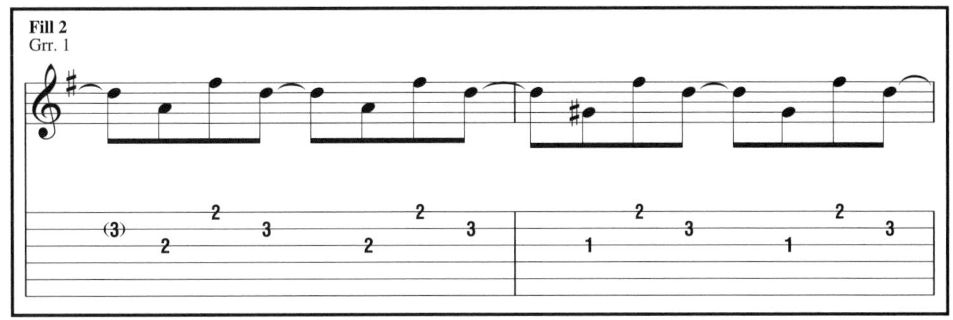
Fill 2
Grr. 1
(3)

from Eric Clapton - *Journeyman*

Bad Love

Words and Music by Eric Clapton and Mick Jones

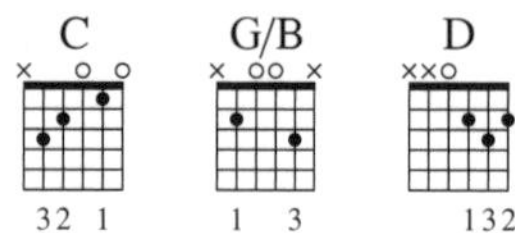

Gtrs. 1 & 2: Drop D tuning:
(low to high) D-A-D-G-B-E

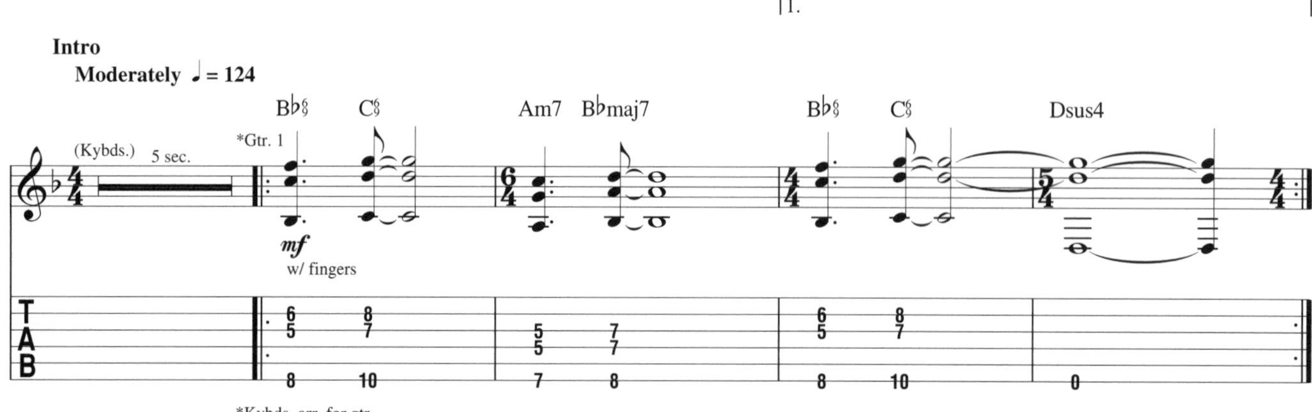

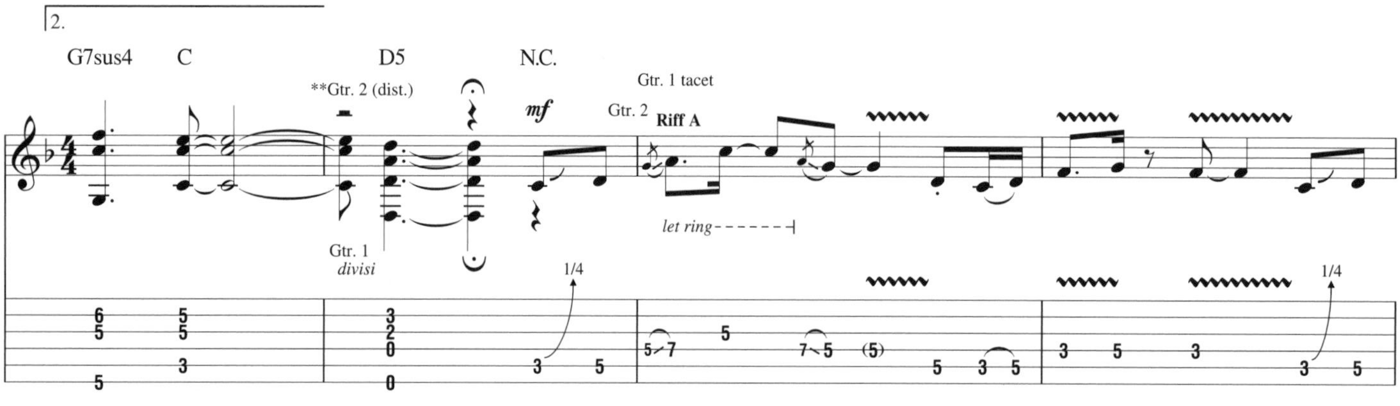

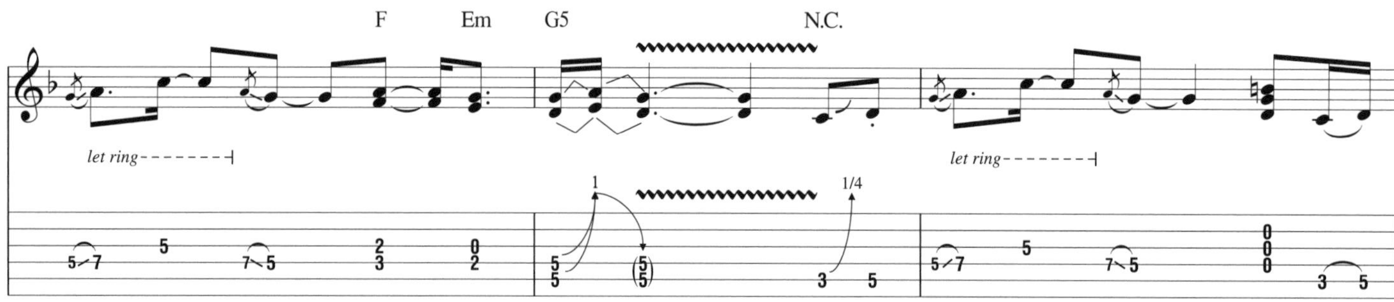

Gtr. 2: w/ Riff A
4th time, Gtr. 6: w/ Fill 2

Dm7 C G7 Dm7 C

Gtr. 3

Gtr. 4
(clean)

Riff B

mp

P.M.

Gtr. 5
(clean)

Rhy. Fig. 1

mp

let ring

let ring

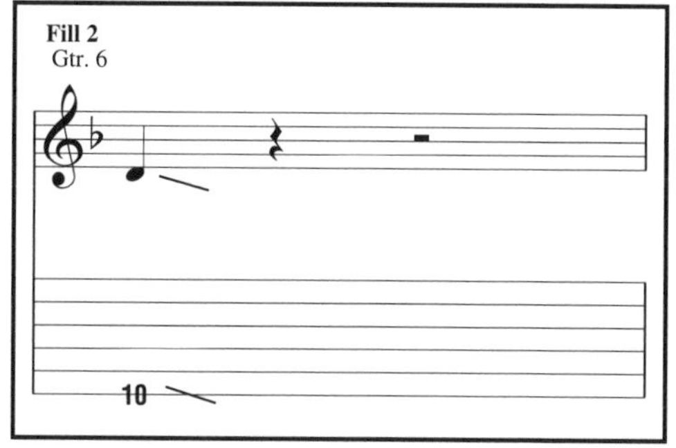

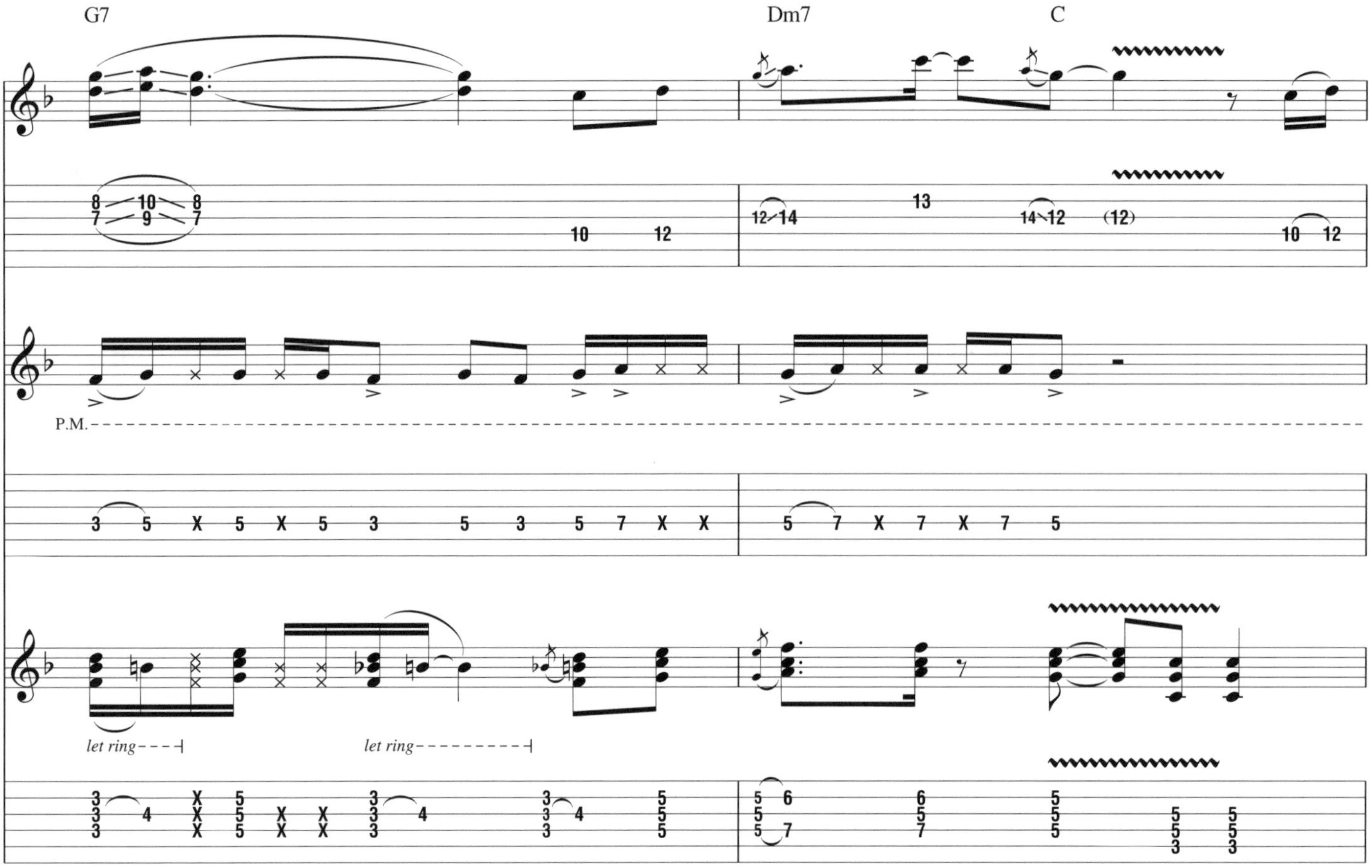

G7 Dm7 C

P.M.

let ring

let ring

To Coda 1

To Coda 2

G7 Dm7 C B♭sus2

Gtr. 3

Gtr. 2
divisi

End Riff B

P.M.

End Rhy. Fig. 1

let ring

let ring

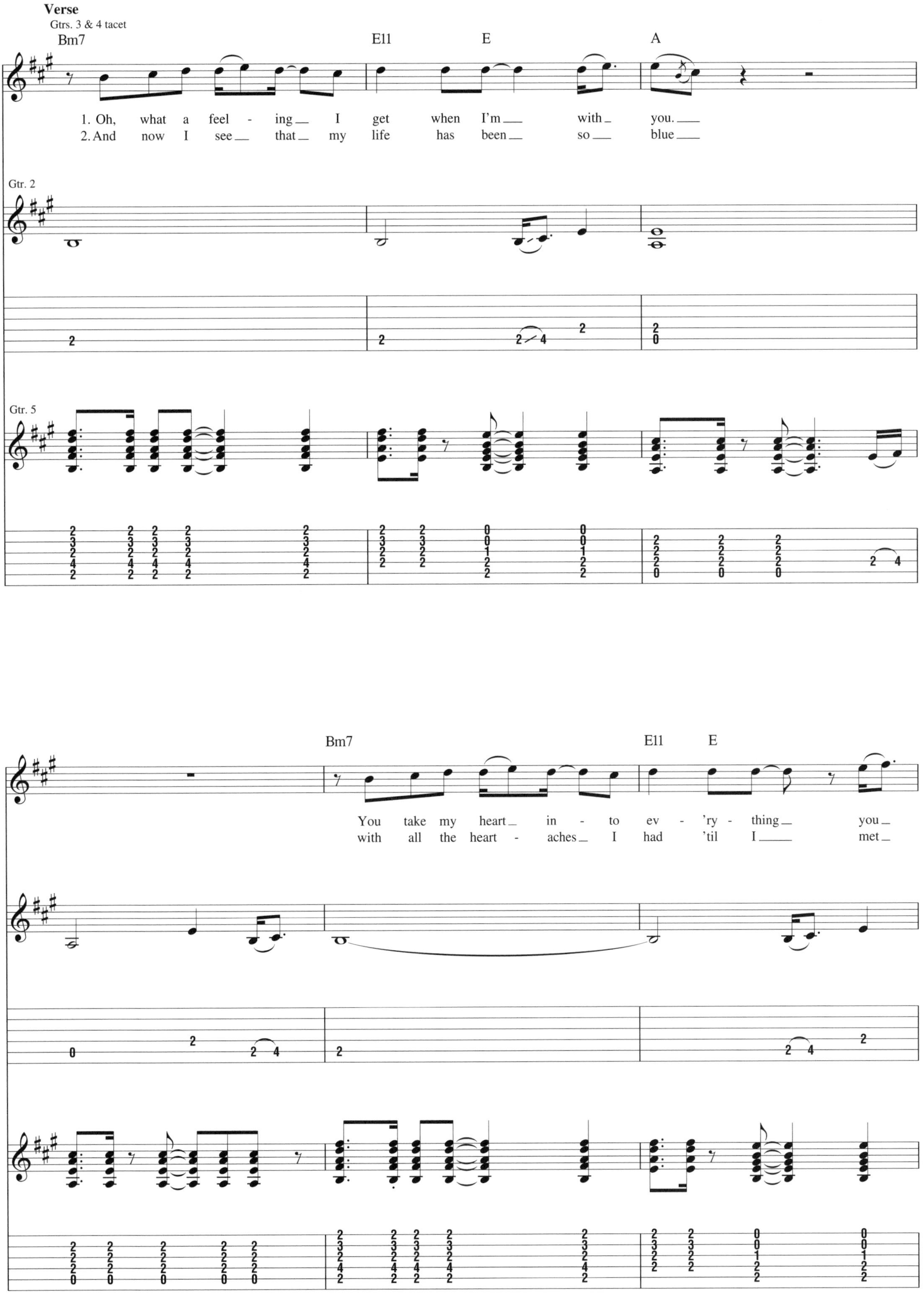

Verse

Gtrs. 3 & 4 tacet

Bm7 E11 E A

1. Oh, what a feel - ing I get when I'm with you.
2. And now I see that my life has been so blue

Gtr. 2

Gtr. 5

Pre-Chorus

A | | B♭ C

do, ___ | and ___ it | makes me sad ___ for the
you. ___ | But ___ I'm | glad to say ___ now that's

Am7 B♭ | Gm7 C | Dm

lone - ly peo - ple, | I walked that road for ___ so ___ long. ___ | Now I
all be - hind ___ me | with you here by ___ my ___ side, ___ | and there's

let ring

B♭
C
Am7
B♭
Gm7
C
Gm
N.C.
know that I'm one of the luck - y peo - ple. Your love is mak - ing me strong.
no more mem - o - ries to re - mind me. Your love will keep me a - live.
Had e -
(cont. on lower staff)
Chorus
Gtr. 4: w/ Riff B
Gtr. 5: w/ Rhy. Fig. 1
Dm7
C
G7
nough bad love, I need
Gtr. 3
Riff C1
Gtr. 2
Riff C

Dm7 C G7 Dm7 C

some - thing I can ___ be ___ proud of. ___ Had e - nough bad

2nd time, D.S. al Coda 1

G7 Dm7 C B♭sus2

love. No more ___ bad ___ love. ___

End Riff C1

End Riff C

*Tacet on last beat during recall.

Coda 1

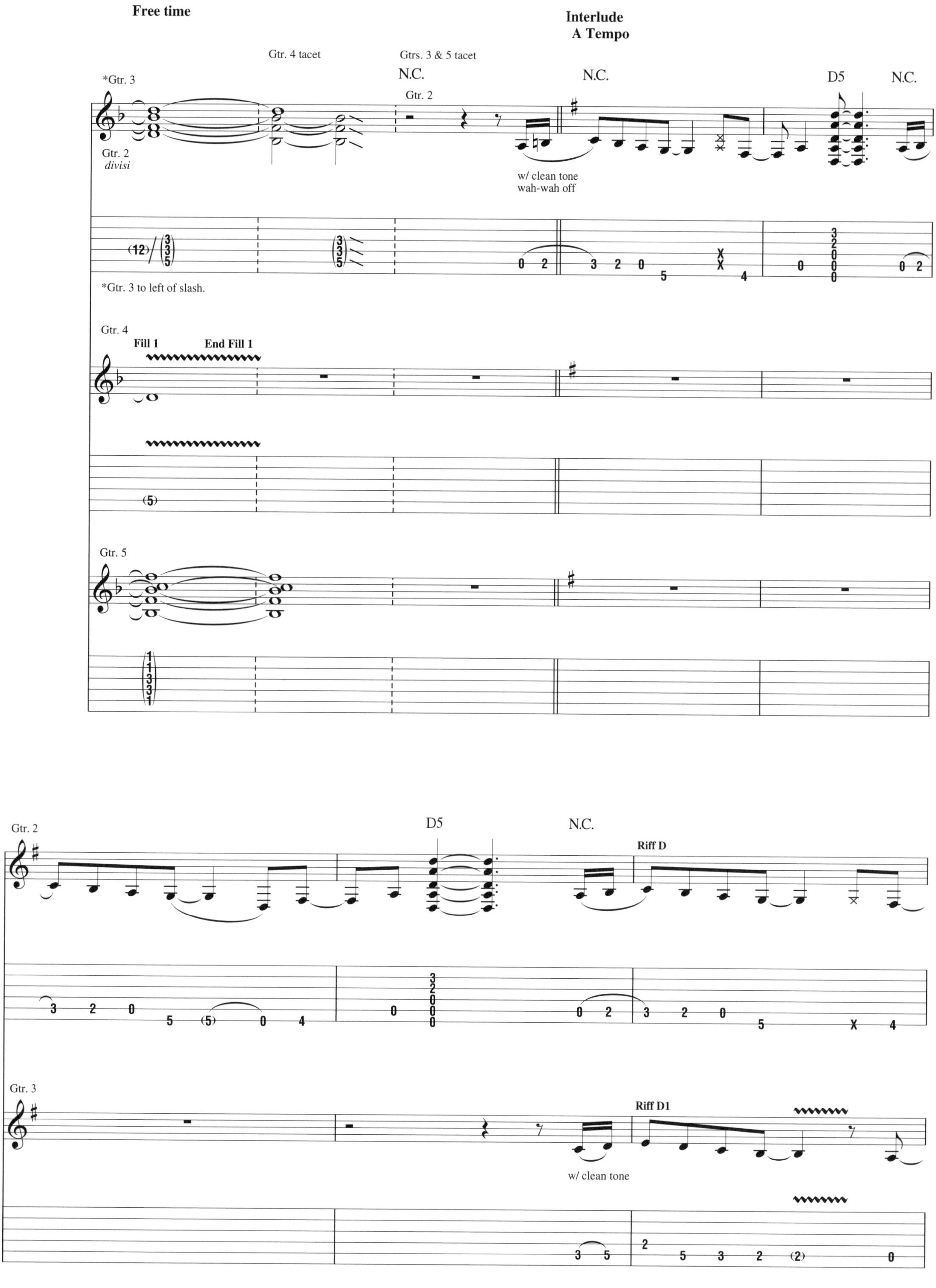

Free time

Interlude
A Tempo

Gtr. 4 tacet

Gtrs. 3 & 5 tacet

N.C.

N.C.

D5

N.C.

*Gtr. 3

Gtr. 2

Gtr. 2
divisi

w/ clean tone
wah-wah off

*Gtr. 3 to left of slash.

Gtr. 4

Fill 1

End Fill 1

Gtr. 5

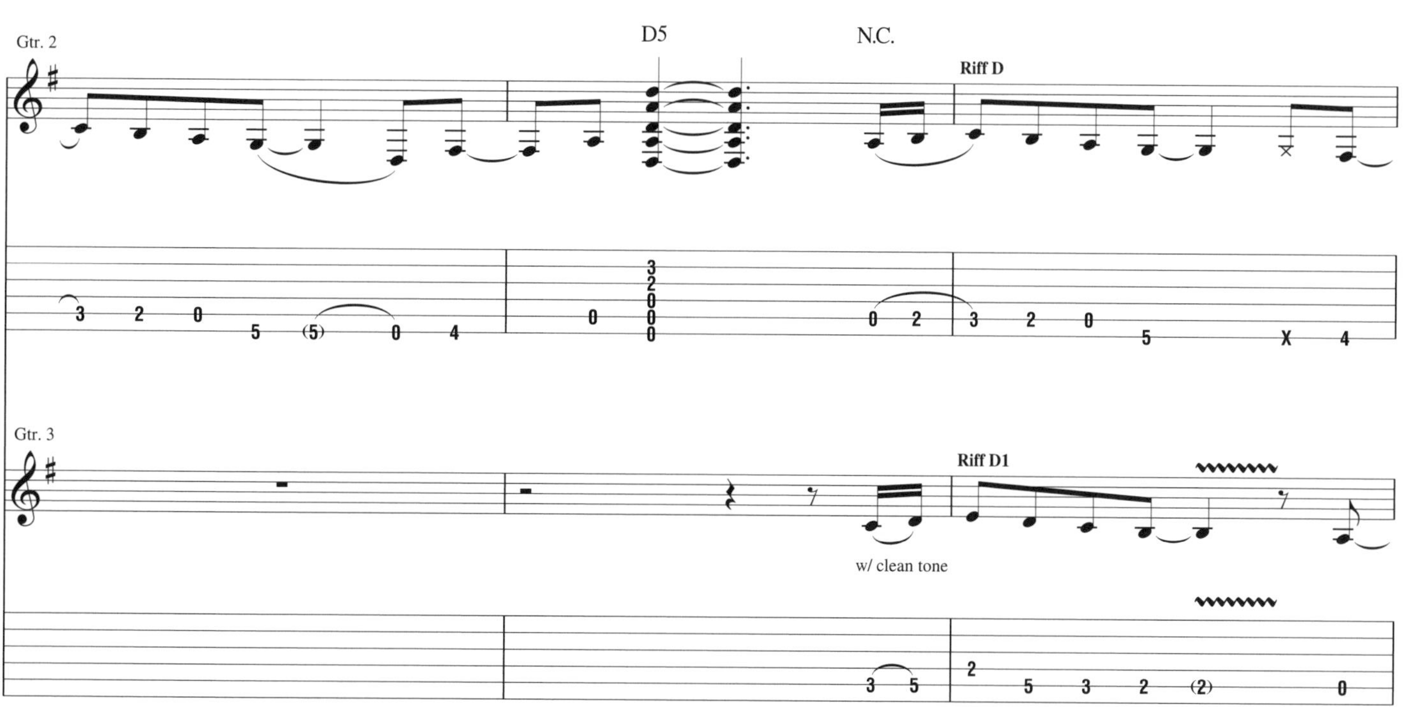

D
End Riff D
End Riff D1

Guitar Solo

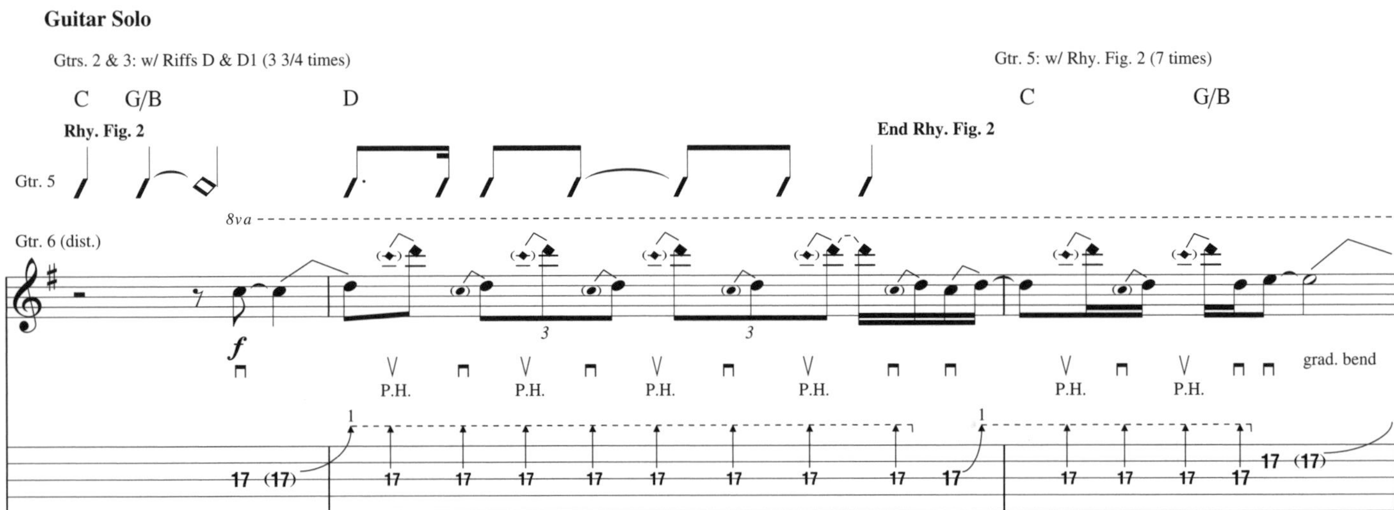
Gtrs. 2 & 3: w/ Riffs D & D1 (3 3/4 times)
Gtr. 5: w/ Rhy. Fig. 2 (7 times)
C G/B D C G/B
Rhy. Fig. 2
End Rhy. Fig. 2
Gtr. 5
Gtr. 6 (dist.)
8va
P.H.
grad. bend

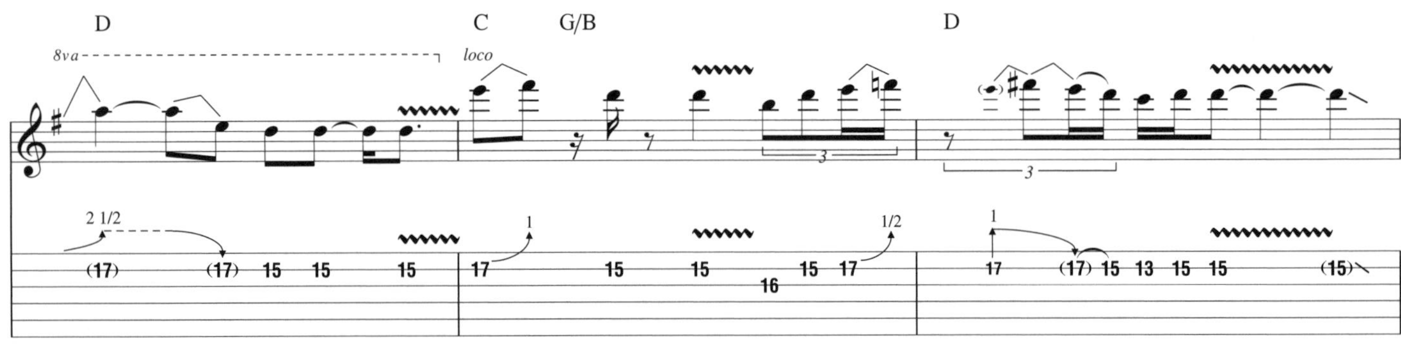
D C G/B D
8va
loco

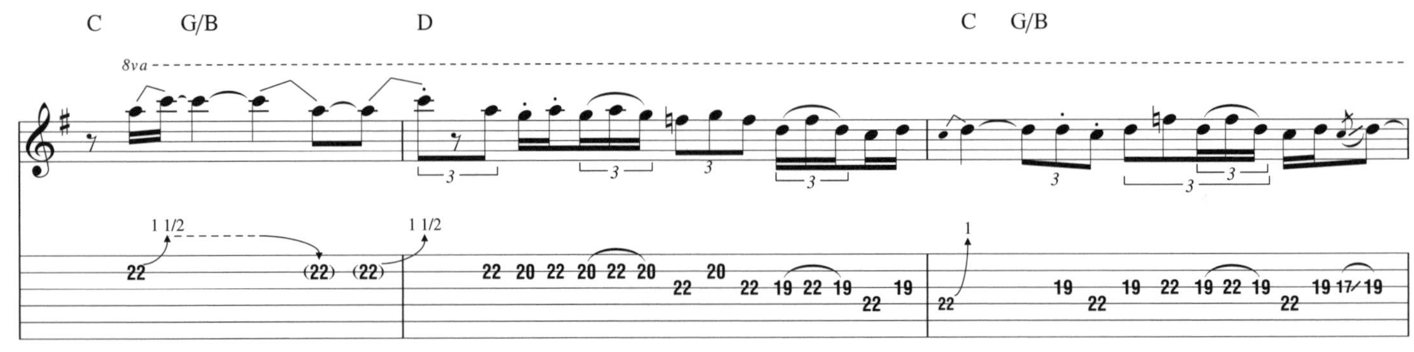
C G/B D C G/B
8va

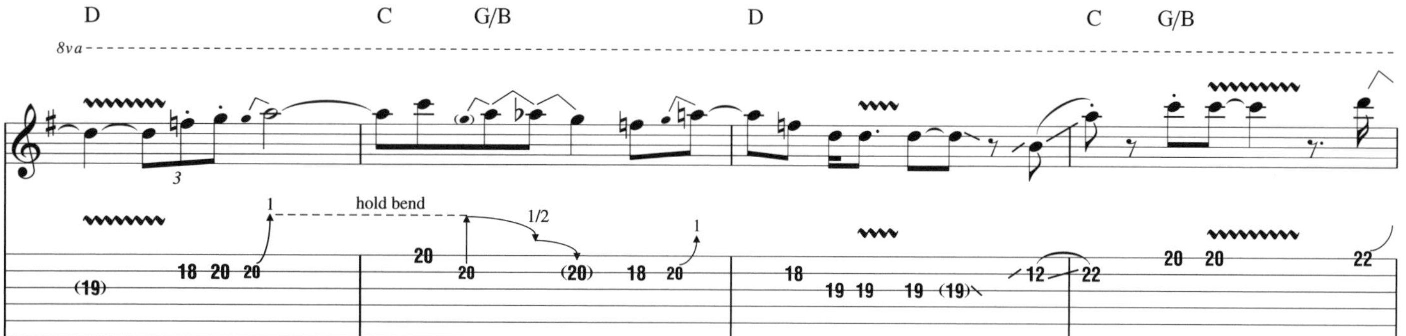
D
C
G/B
D
C
G/B
8va
hold bend
1/2

D.S. al Coda 2

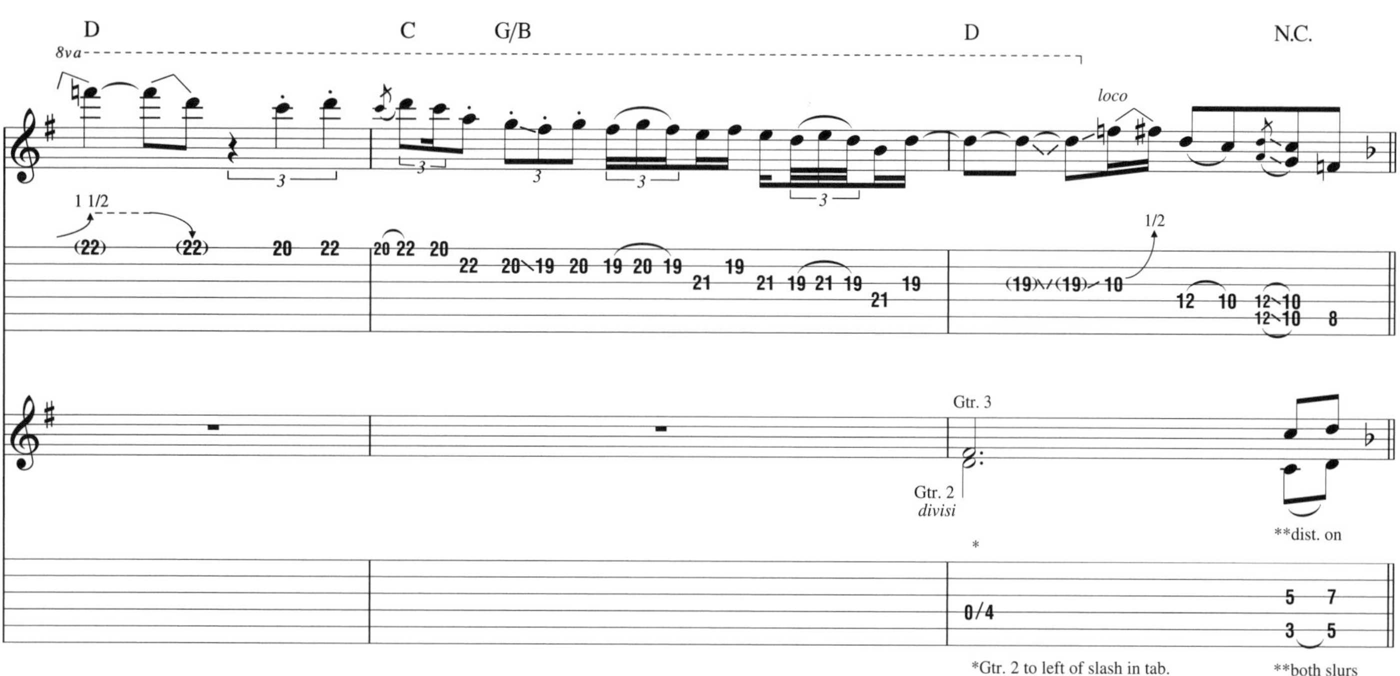
D
C
G/B
D
N.C.
8va
loco
1 1/2
1/2
Gtr. 3
Gtr. 2
divisi
**dist. on
*Gtr. 2 to left of slash in tab.
**both slurs

Coda 2
Outro-Chorus
Gtr. 4: w/ Fill 1
Gtrs. 2 & 3: w/ Riffs C & C1 (till fade)
Gtr. 4: w/ Riff B (1st 4 meas.) (till fade)
Gtr. 5: w/ Rhy. Fig. 1 (1st 4 meas.) (till fade)
Dm7
C
G7
I've had e - nough bad love. I need
Gtr. 3
Gtr. 6
8va
Gtr. 2
divisi
Gtr. 5

Dm7 C G7 Dm7 C
some - thing I can ___ be ___ proud of. ___ I've had e - nough bad
Gtr. 6 8va
G7 Dm7 C G7
love. No more ___ bad ___ love. ___ Had e -
loco
8va
Dm7 C G7 Dm7 C
nough bad love. I need some - thing I can ___ be ___ proud
8va
G7 Dm7 C G7
of. ___ I've had e - nough bad love.
loco
grad. bend

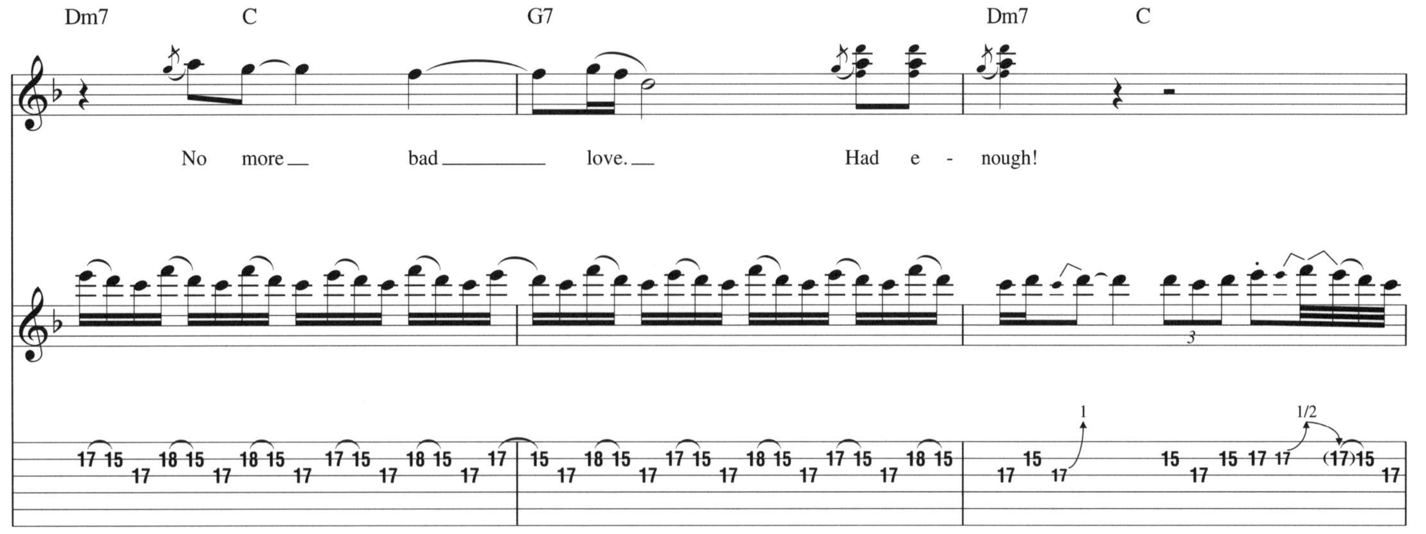

Dm7
C
G7
Dm7
C
No more bad love. Had e - nough!

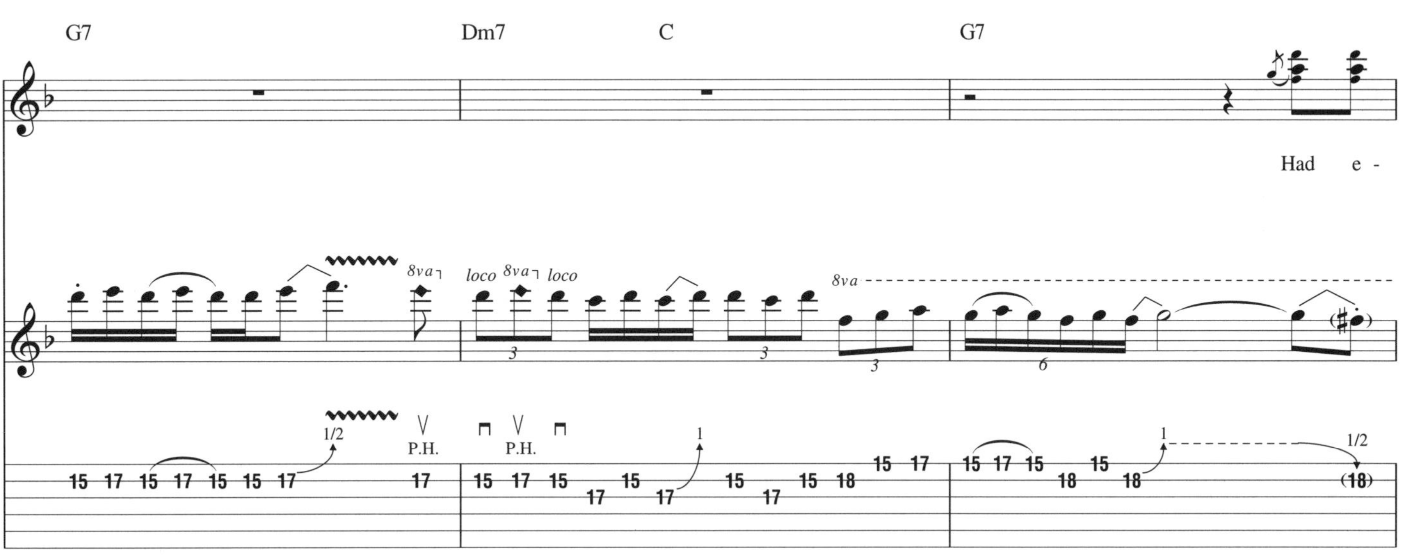

G7
Dm7
C
G7
Had e -
P.H.
P.H.
loco
loco

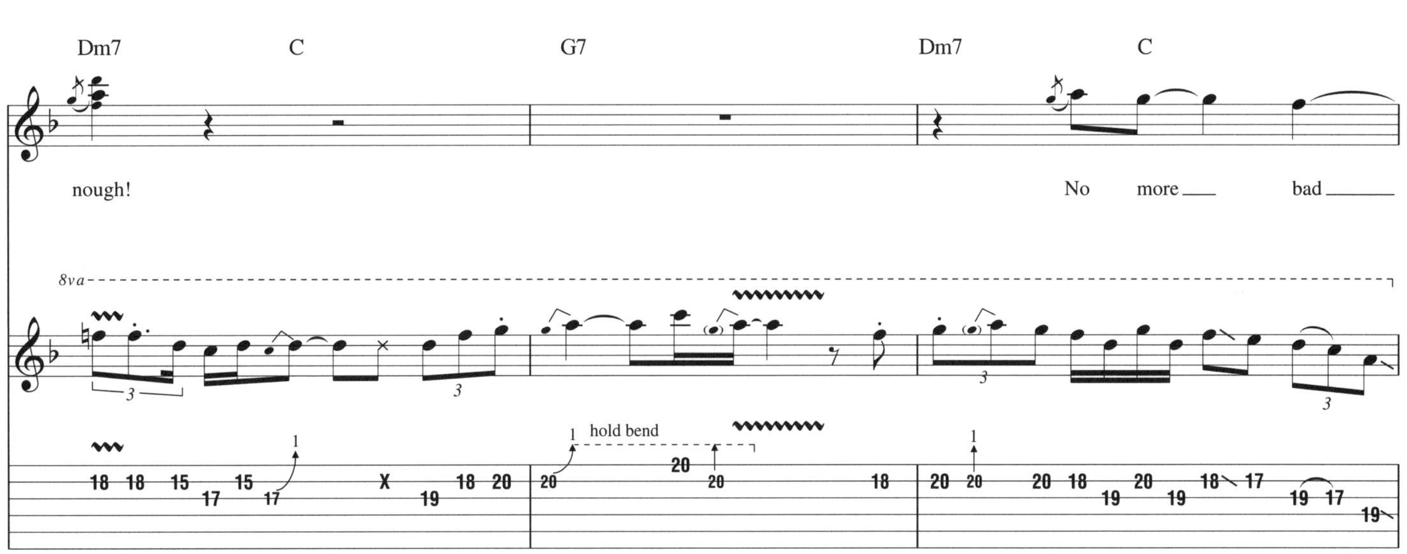

Dm7
C
G7
Dm7
C
nough!
No more bad
hold bend

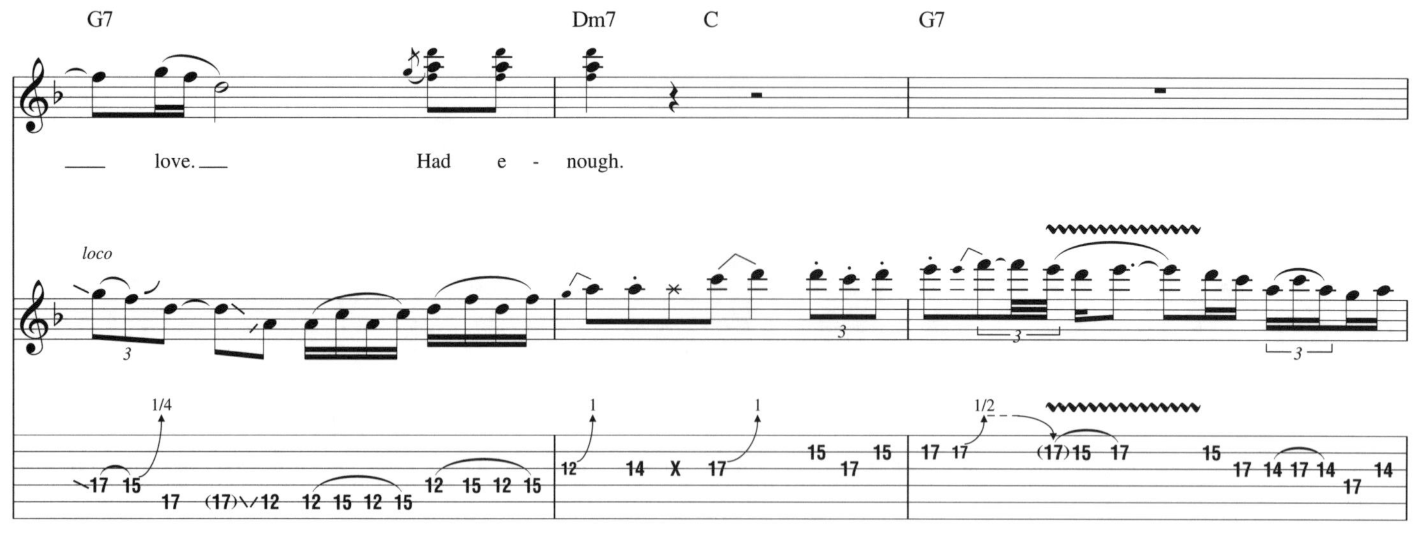
G7
Dm7
C
G7
love.
Had
e -
nough.
loco
1/4
1
1
1/2

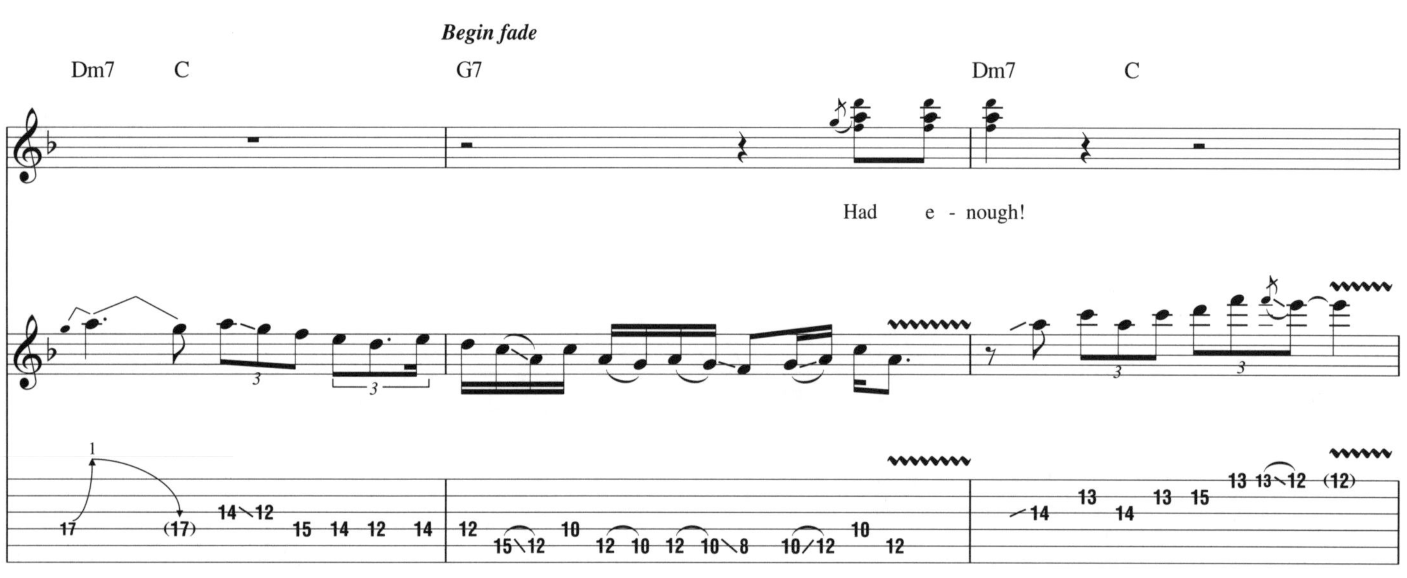
Begin fade
Dm7
C
G7
Dm7
C
Had
e - nough!
1

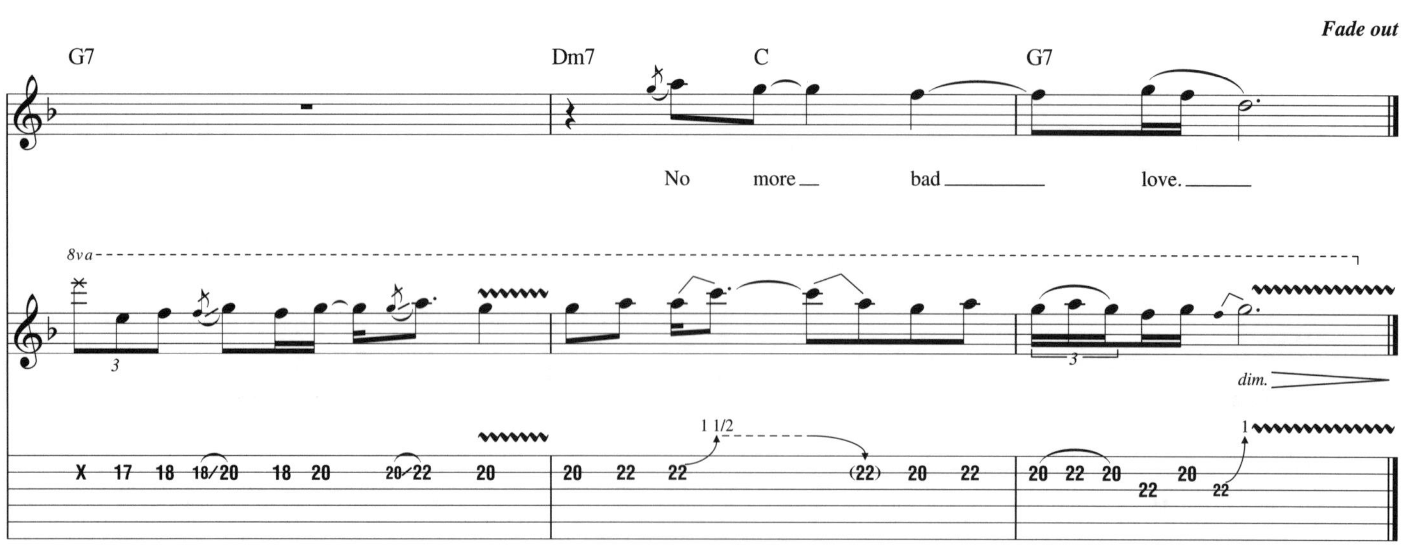
Fade out
G7
Dm7
C
G7
No
more
bad
love.
8va
1 1/2
1
dim.

from Cream - *Goodbye*

Badge

Words and Music by Eric Clapton and George Harrison

2.
C
Am
Bm
Am(add9)
Then I told you 'bout our kid now he's mar-ried to Ma - ble.
Gtr. 1 tacet
* D
Cmaj7(sus2)
G/B
G
D
Cmaj7(sus2)
G/B
G
Rhy. Fig. 2
Gtr. 1
Gtr. 2
Gtr. 2
divisi
mf w/ chorus & delay
let ring
* Chord symbols reflect implied tonality.
Bridge
Gtr. 2: w/ Rhy. Fig. 2, 2 1/2 times, simile
D
Cmaj7(sus2)
G/B
G
D
Cmaj7(sus2)
Yes, I told you that the light goes up and down. Don't you no -
Gtr. 2
End Rhy. Fig. 2
let ring
Gtr. 1
G/B
G
D
Cmaj7(sus2)
G/B
G
D
Cmaj7(sus2)
- tice how the wheel goes 'round. And you bet - ter pick your-self up from the ground be - fore
Rhy. Fig. 3
Gtr. 1
End Rhy. Fig. 3

G/B G D Cmaj7(sus2) G/B G
they bring the cur - tain down.
Yes, be - fore they bring the cur - tain down.
P.M.
Guitar Solo
Gtr. 2: w/ Rhy. Fig. 2, 3 1/4 times, simile
Gtr. 1: w/ Rhy. Fig. 3, 3 1/4 times, simile
D Cmaj7(sus2) G/B G D Cmaj7(sus2)
Woo.
Gtr. 3 (dist.)
Gtr. 1
G/B G D Cmaj7 G/B G
Gtr. 3
D Cmaj7(sus2) G/B G D Cmaj7(sus2)
Yea, yea, yea.
8va

G/B G D Cmaj7(sus2) G/B G

8va

1/4 full hold bend full 1/2

Gtr. 2: w/ Rhy. Fill 3
Gtr. 1: w/ Rhy. Fill 4

D Cmaj7(sus2) G/B G D

Yeah, yeah, yeah.

8va loco

full 3/4 1/2 1/2 1/2

let ring

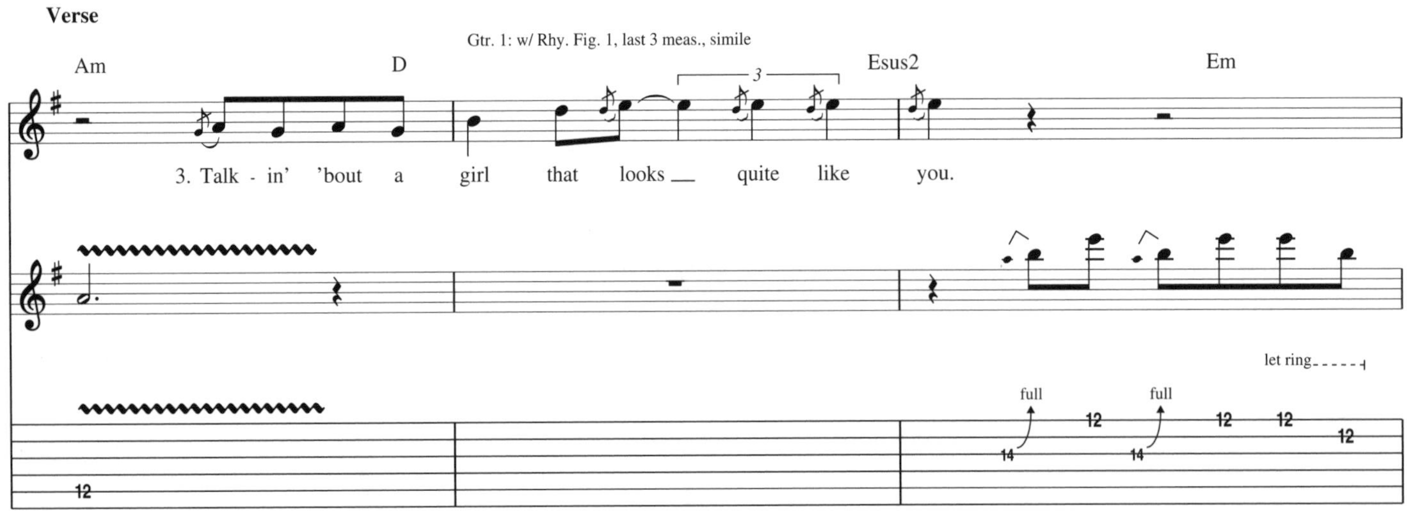

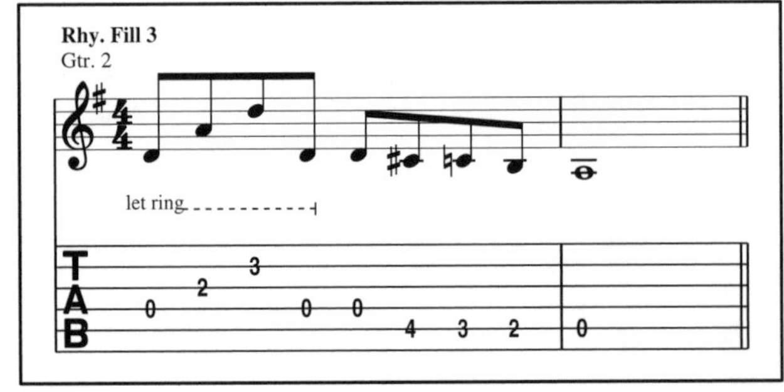

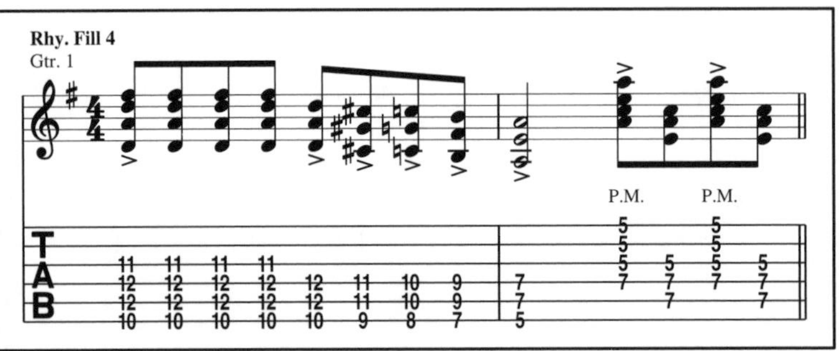

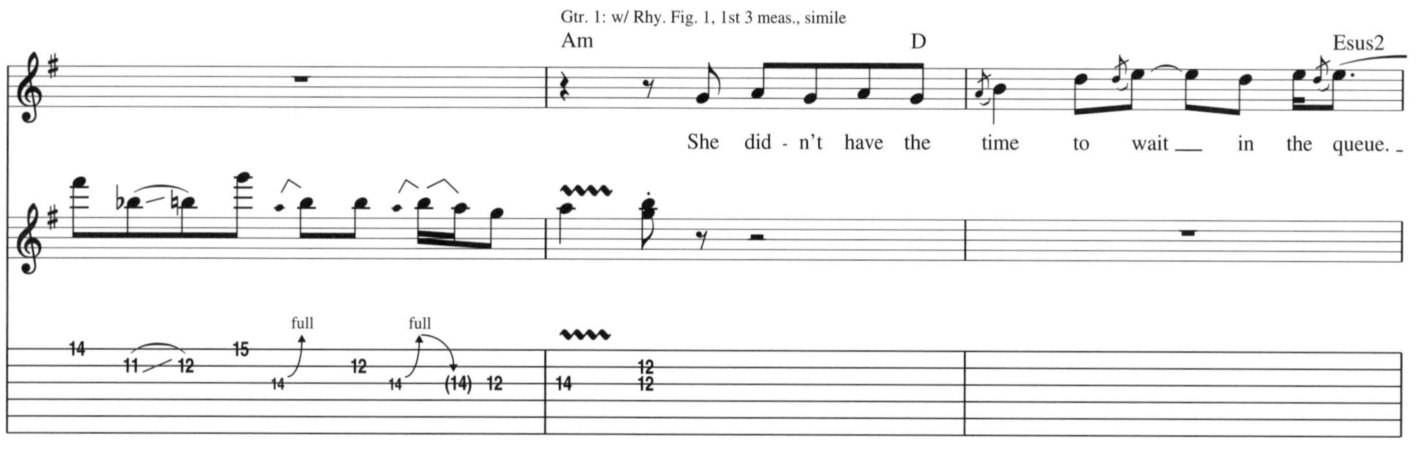
Gtr. 1: w/ Rhy. Fig. 1, 1st 3 meas., simile
Am
D
Esus2
She did - n't have the time to wait in the queue.
full
full

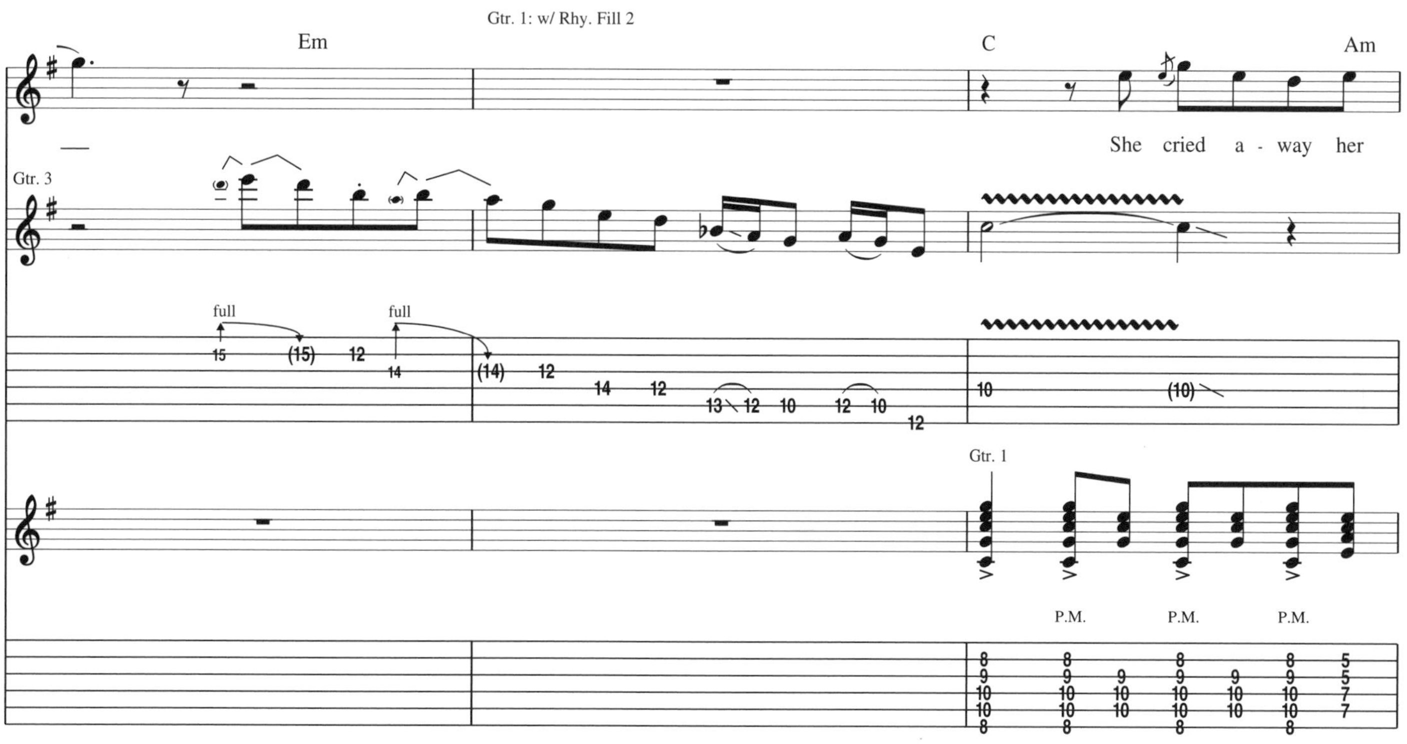
Gtr. 1: w/ Rhy. Fill 2
Em
C
Am
She cried a - way her
Gtr. 3
full
full
Gtr. 1
P.M.
P.M.
P.M.

Bm7
Am(add9)
life since she fell off the cra - dle.

from Eric Clapton - *Journeyman*

Before You Accuse Me (Take a Look at Yourself)

Words and Music by Ellas McDaniels

Intro
Moderately ♩ = 106
*E7
B7
Gtr. 1 (slight dist.) Eric Clapton
f
1/4
1/4
1/4

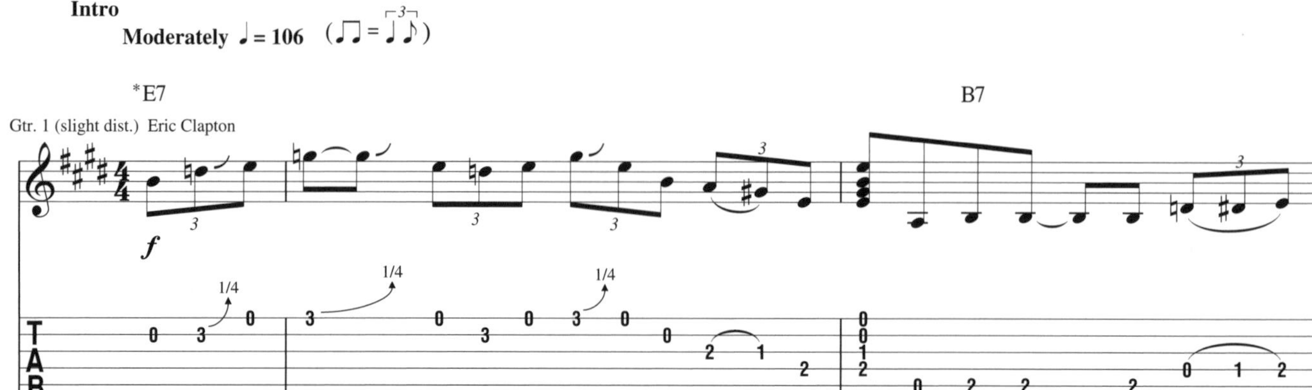

*Chord symbols reflect basic harmony.

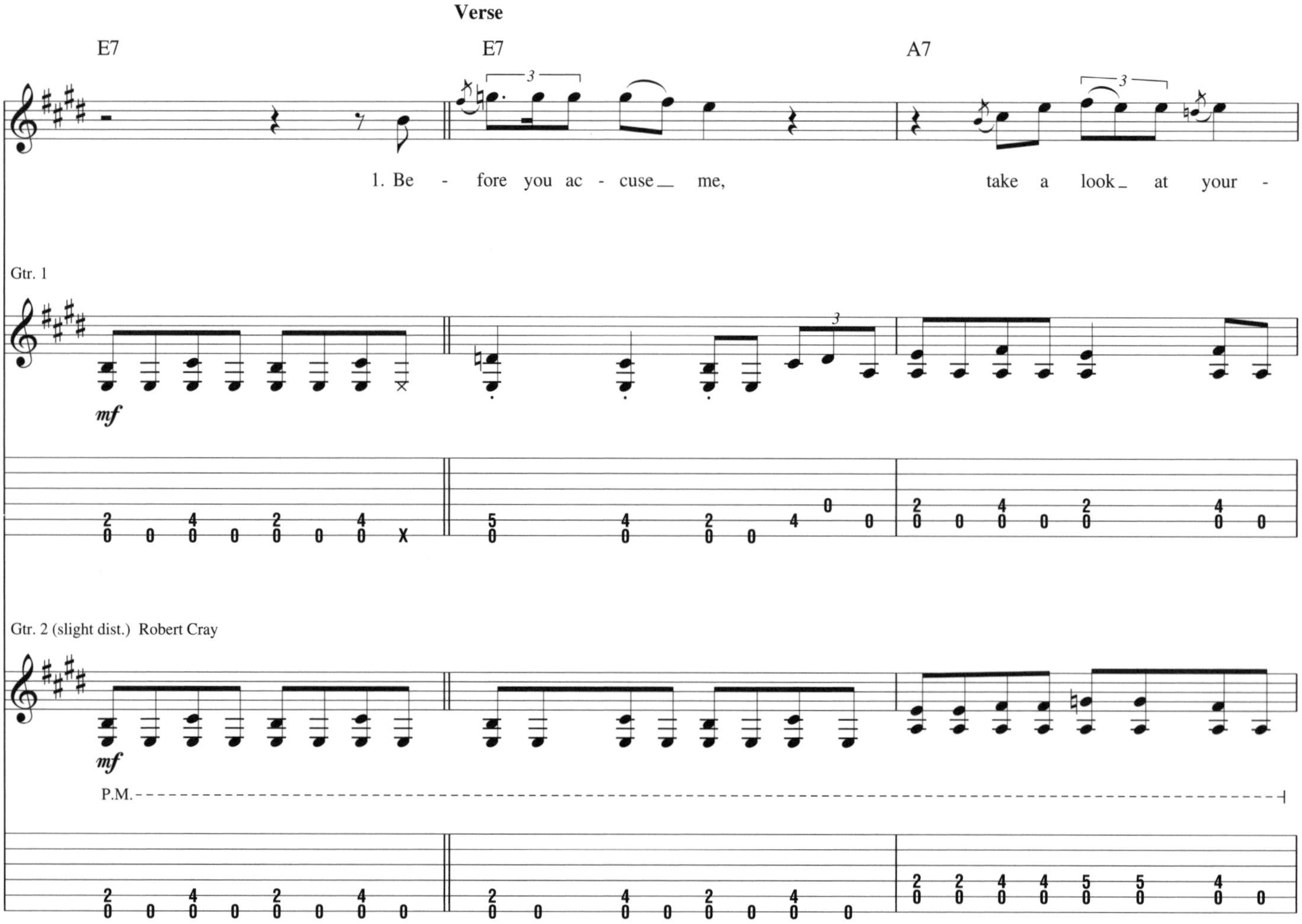

Verse
E7
E7
A7
1. Be - fore you ac - cuse me, take a look at your -
Gtr. 1
mf
Gtr. 2 (slight dist.) Robert Cray
mf
P.M.

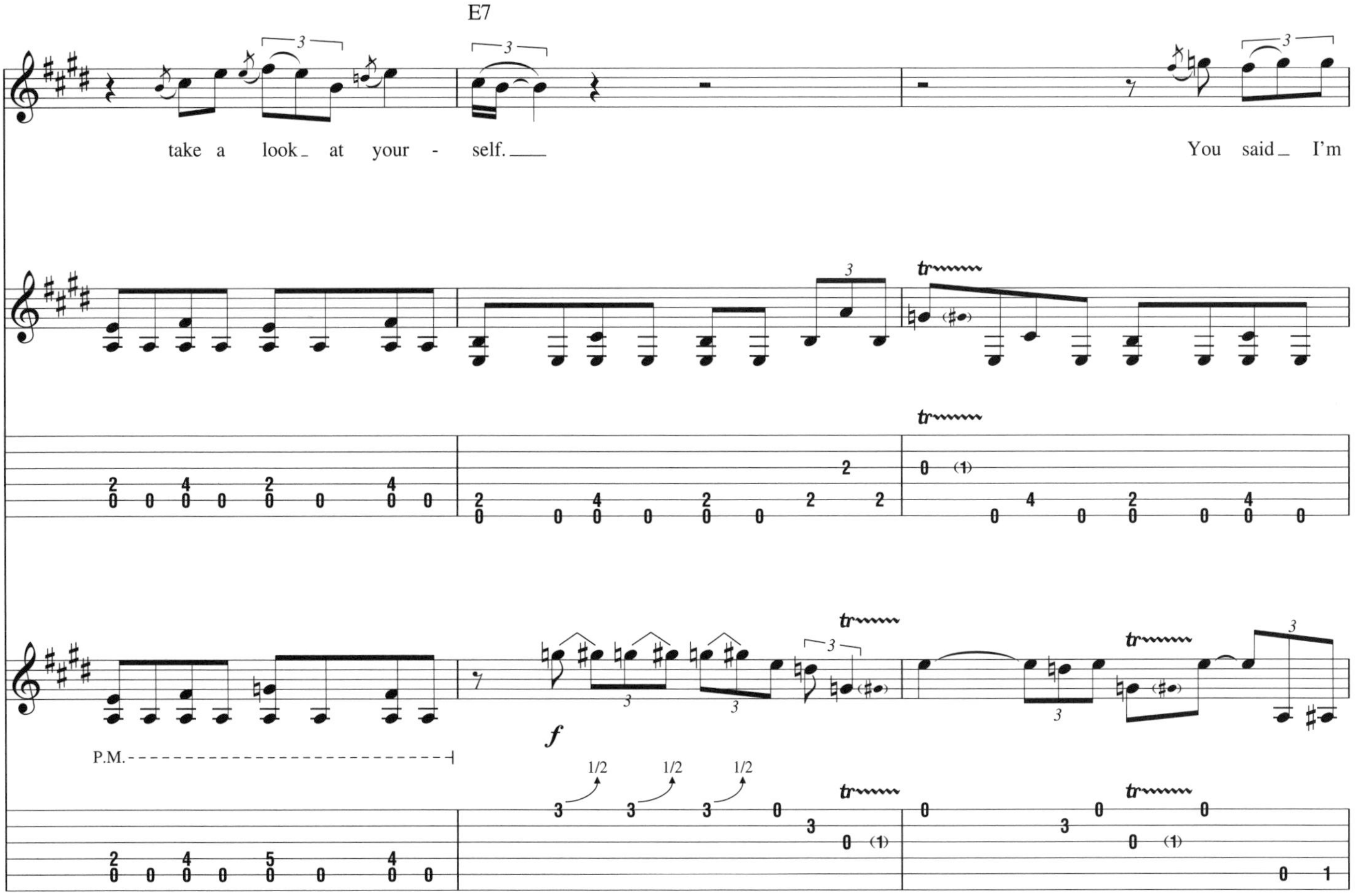

E7

take a look at your - self. You said I'm

tr

P.M.

f

1/2 1/2 1/2

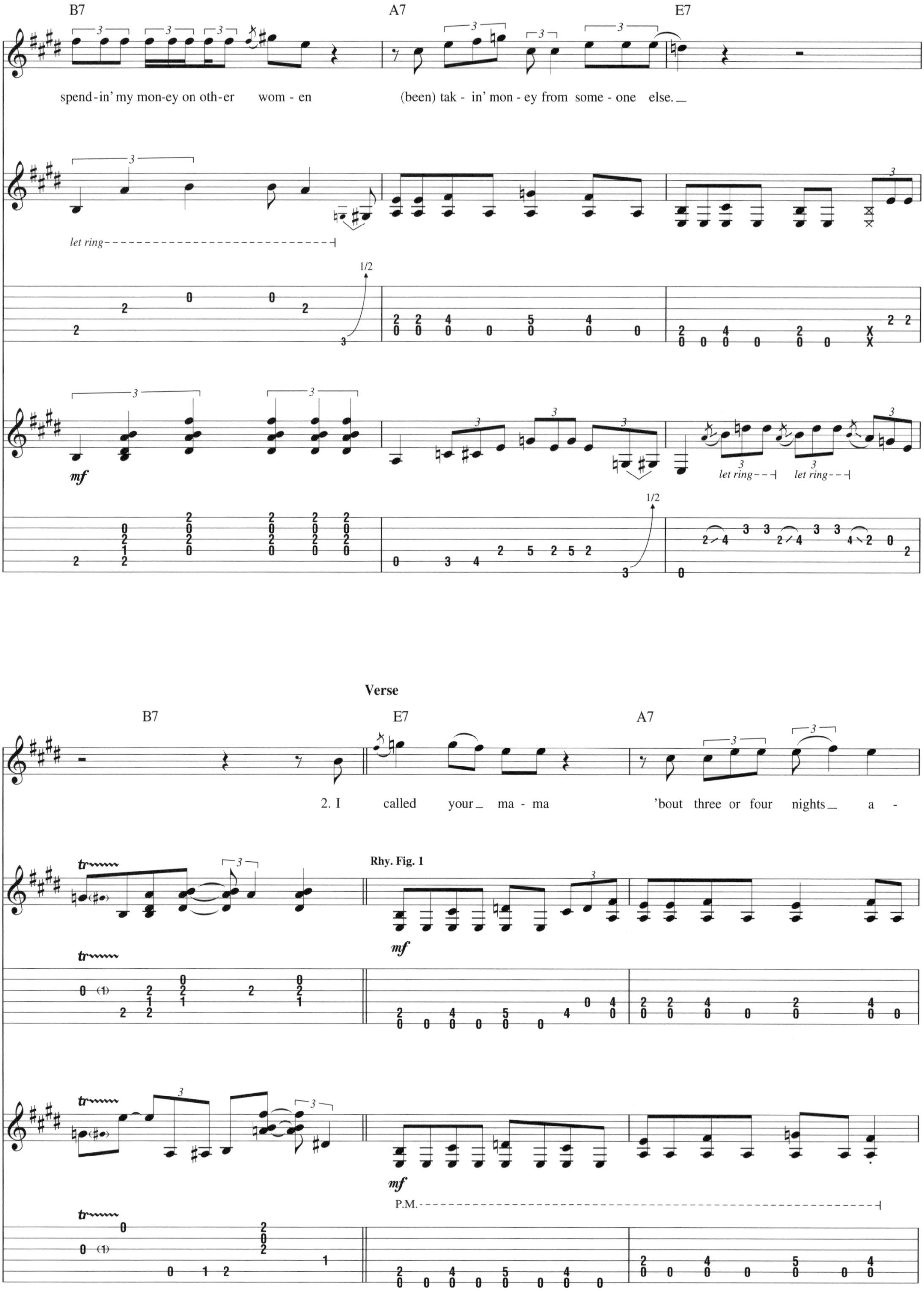

Verse

B7
E7
A7

2. I called your ma - ma 'bout three or four nights a -

Rhy. Fig. 1

mf

mf

P.M.

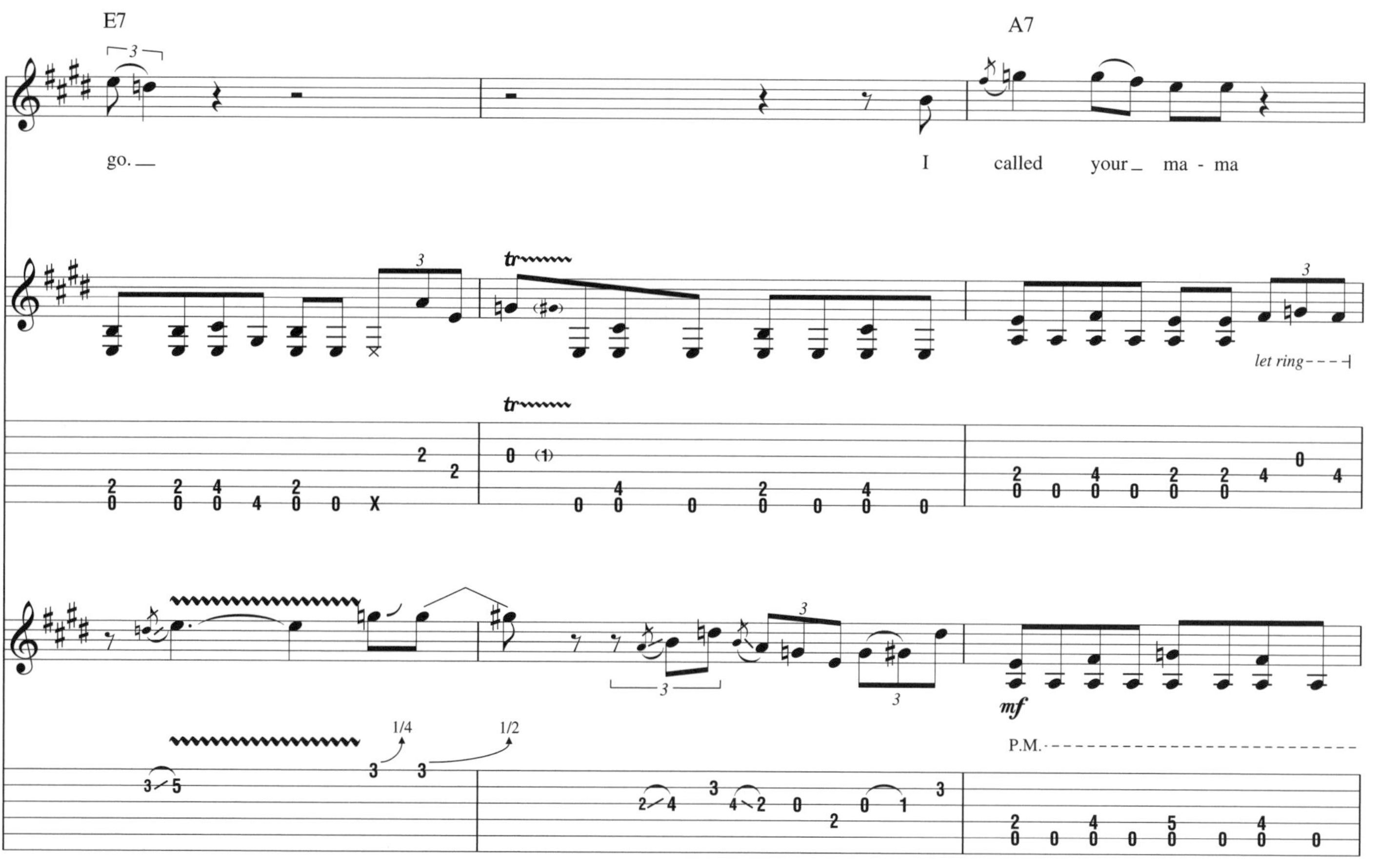
E7
A7
go. ___
I called your ___ ma - ma
let ring
P.M.
mf

E7
'bout three or four nights ___ a - go. ___
(Your)
P.M.
f

B7
A7
E7
B7
ma-ma said, "Son, don't call my daugh-ter no more!"
3. Be-
End Rhy. Fig. 1
let ring
P.M.
let ring
let ring
let ring
let ring
1/2
mf

Verse
Gtr. 1: w/ Rhy. Fig. 1 (1st 11 meas.)
2nd time, Gtr. 2: w/ Fill 1
E7
A7
E7
fore you ac - cuse me,
fore you ac - cuse me,
take a look at your - self.
Gtr. 2
mf
f
P.M.

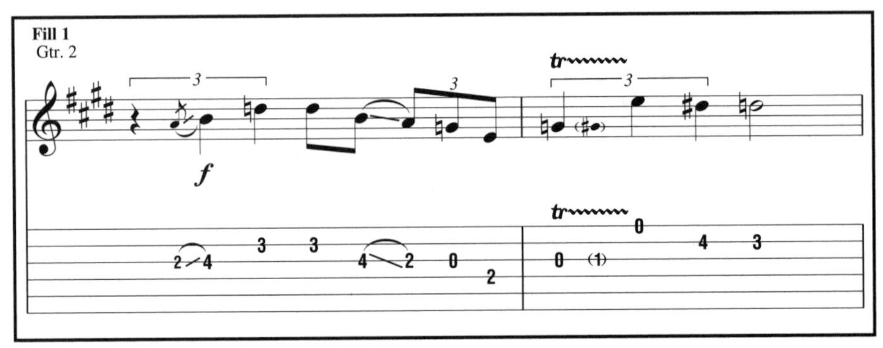
Fill 1
Gtr. 2
f

A7
Be - fore you ac - cuse me, take a look at your -
Gr. 2
let ring
mf
P.M.
2nd time, Gtr. 2: w/ Fill 2
E7
B7
self. You say I'm spend-in' my mon-ey on oth - er wom - en
f
P.M.
*Harm.
mf
1/2
1/4
*Harmonic is a result of slightly touching first string while fretting the second string.
To Coda
A7
E7
B7
(you) been tak - in' mon - ey from some - one else.
Gtr. 1
Gtr. 2
Rhy. Fill 1
End Rhy. Fill 1
let ring
Fill 2
Gtr. 2
f
let ring

Guitar Solo
Gtr. 1
E7
A7
E7
f
Rhy. Fig. 2
P.M.
A7
*Played behind the beat.
P.M.
E7
B7
rake
P.M.
let ring

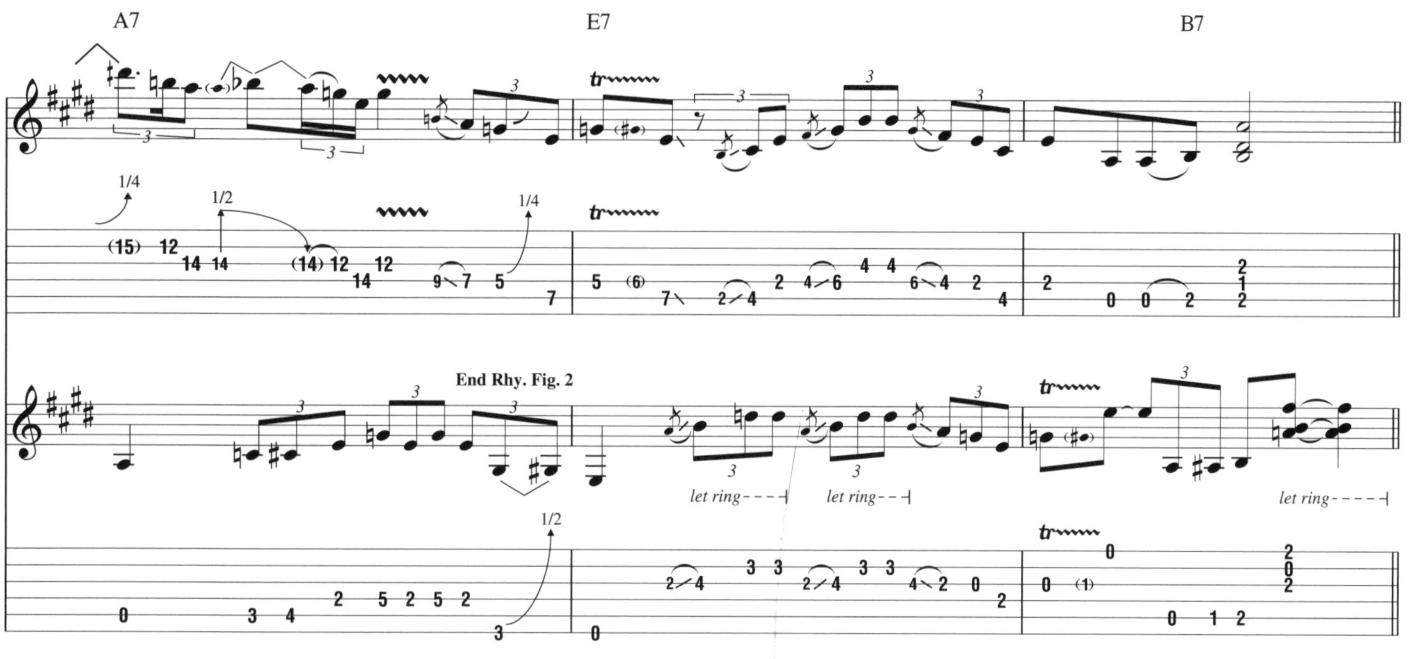

Verse

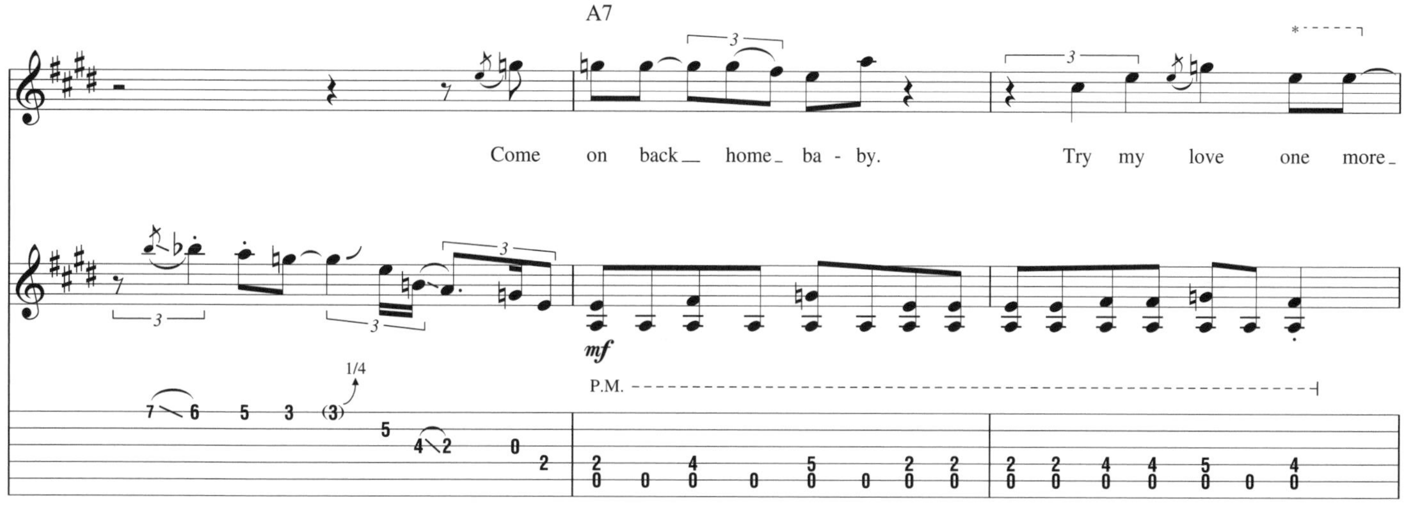

*Sung as even eighths.

E7
B7
time.
You know I don't know when to quit you.
f
mf

*Played as even eighths.

Guitar Solo

Gtr. 1: w/ Rhy. Fig. 1

**Played behind the beat.

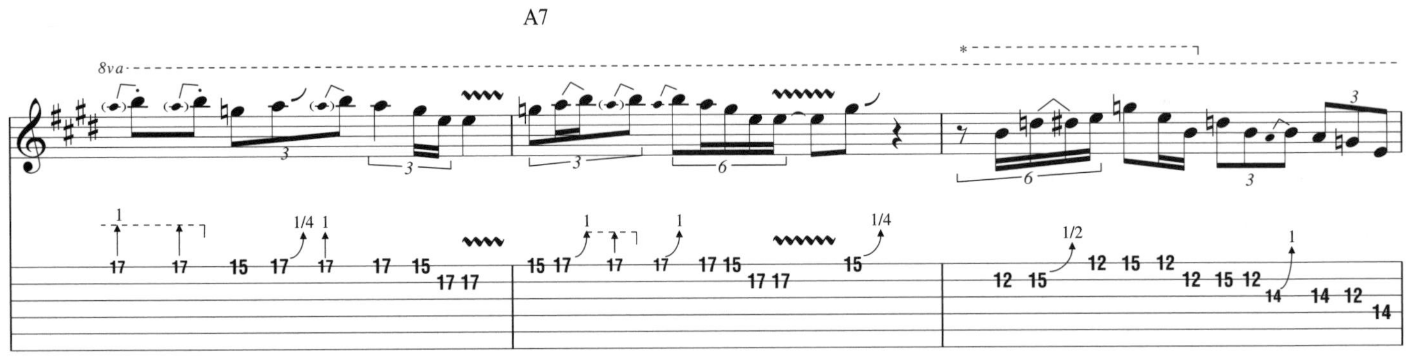

*Played as even eighths.

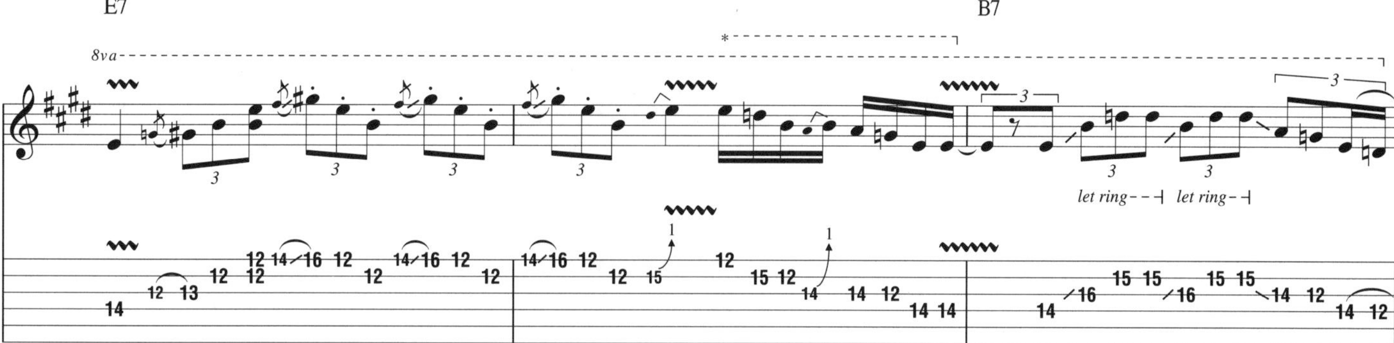

*Played as even eighths.

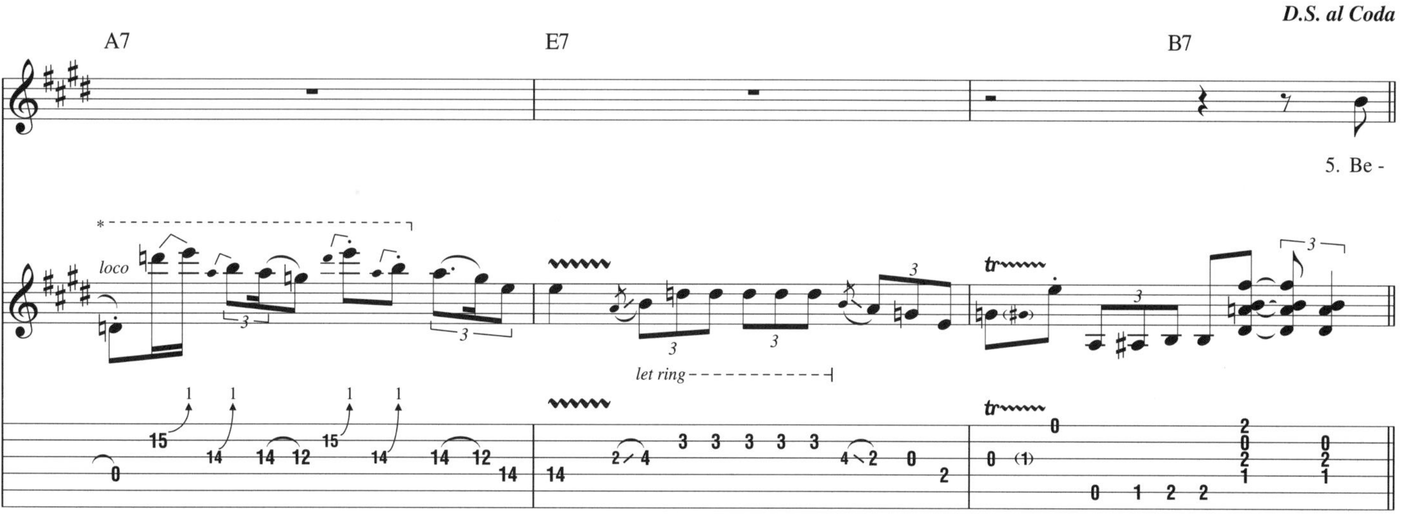

Coda

Guitar Solo

*Played as even eighths.

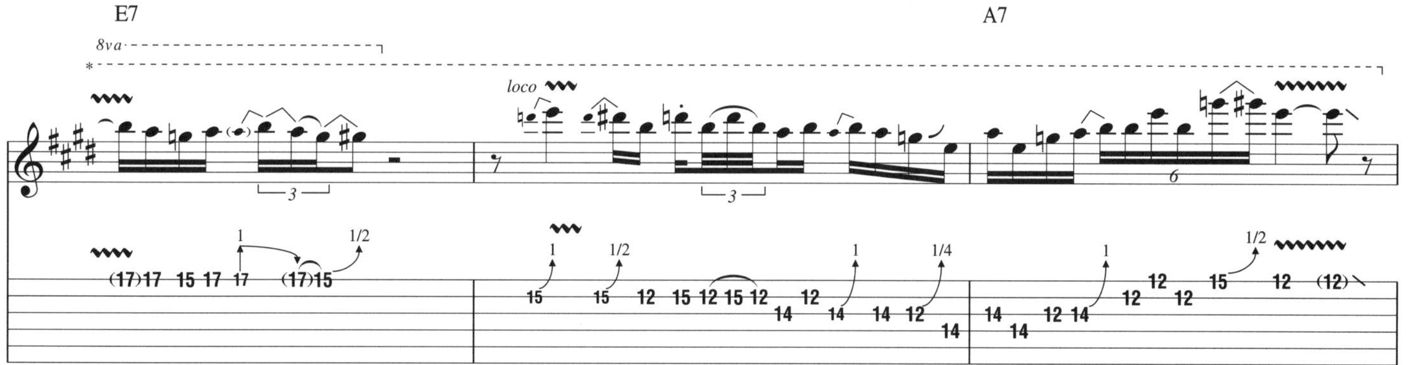

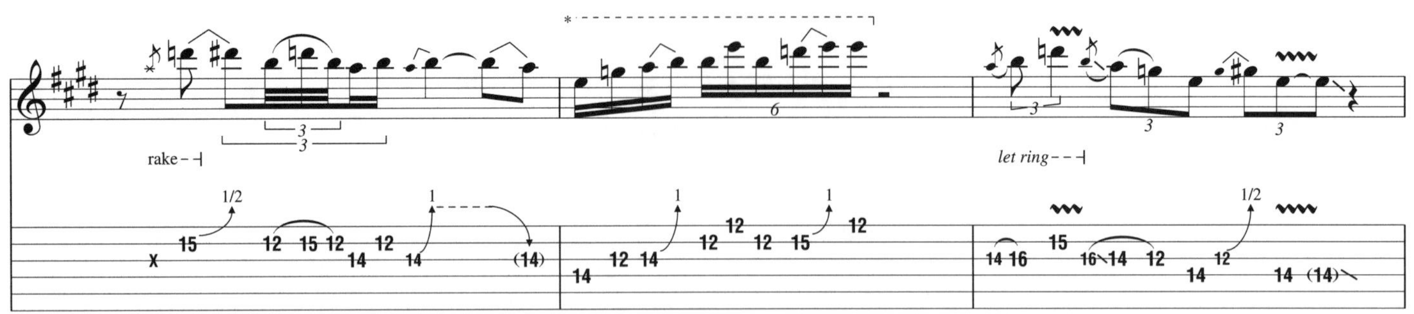
E7
rake
let ring
*Play as even eighths.

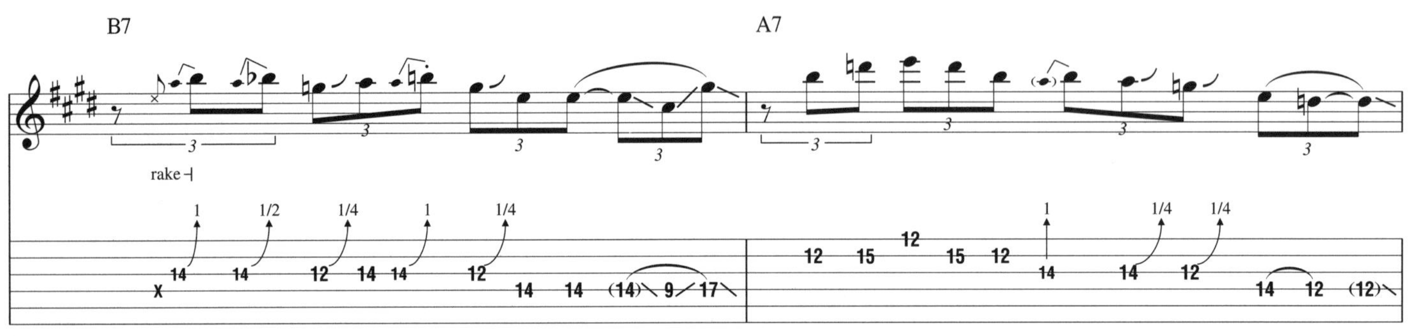
B7
A7
rake

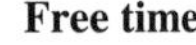
Free time

E7
N.C. E9
Gtr. 1
Gtr. 2
let ring

from Derek and the Dominos - *Layla and Other Assorted Love Songs*

Bell Bottom Blues

Words and Music by Eric Clapton

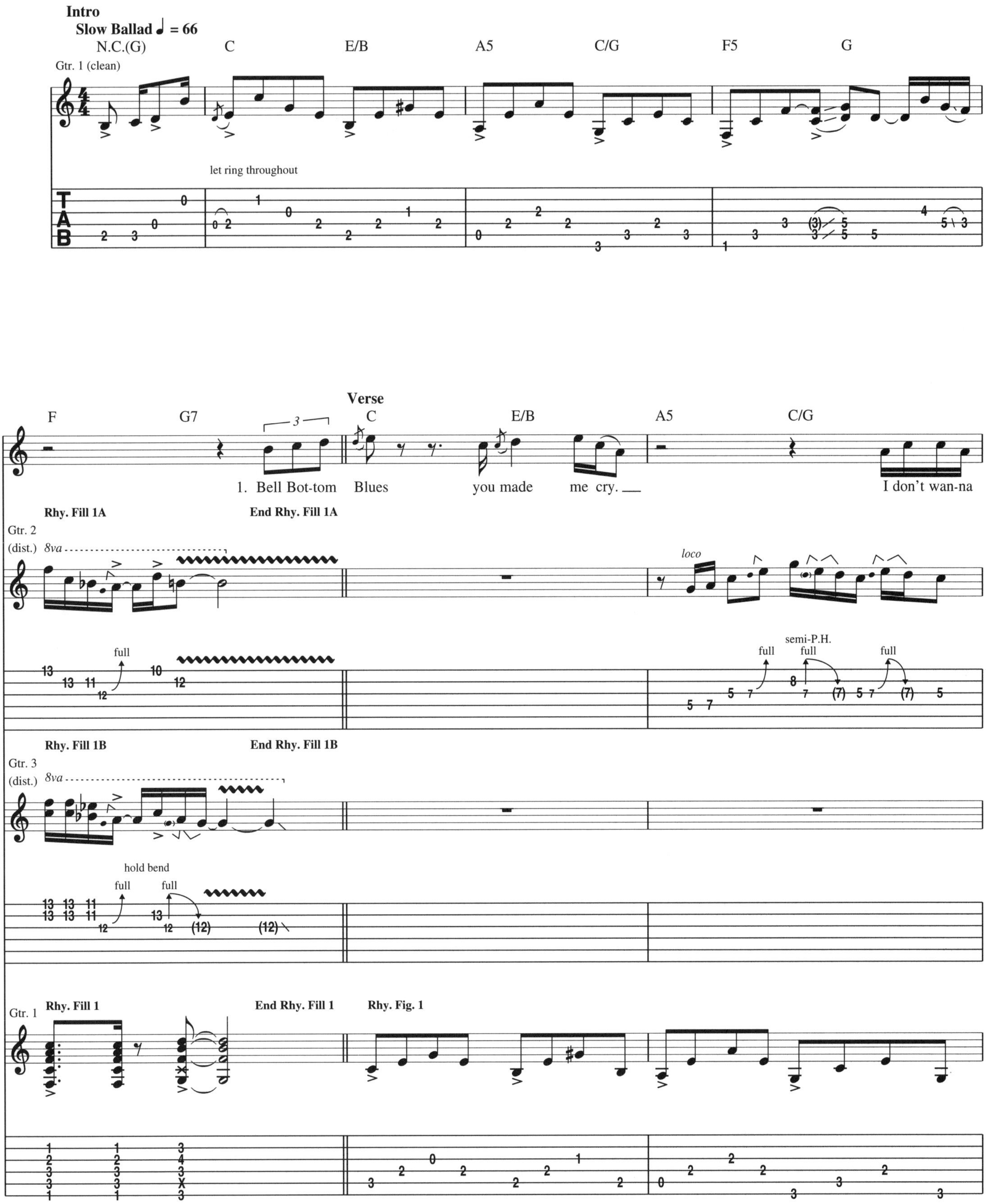

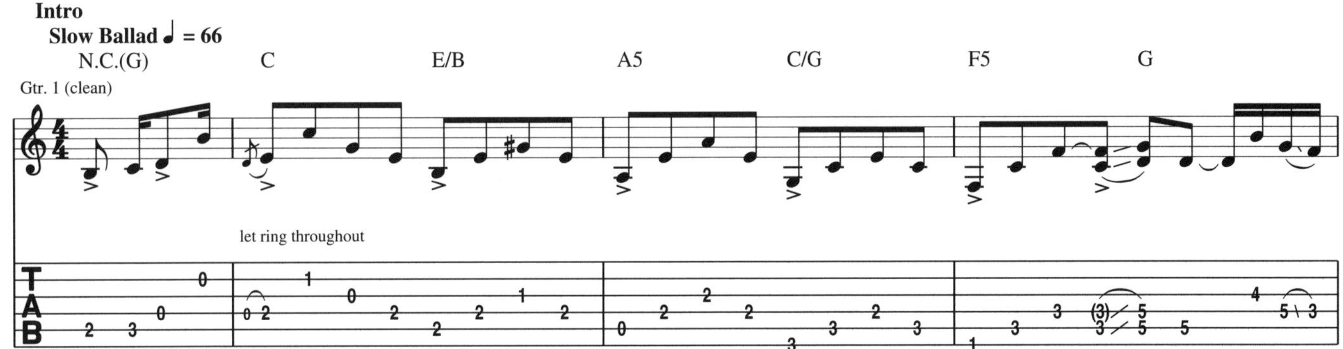

F
G7
Verse
C
E/B
A5
C/G

1. Bell Bot-tom Blues you made me cry. I don't wan-na

Rhy. Fill 1A
End Rhy. Fill 1A
Gtr. 2 (dist.) 8va
loco
full
semi-P.H.

Rhy. Fill 1B
End Rhy. Fill 1B
Gtr. 3 (dist.) 8va
hold bend
full

Gtr. 1
Rhy. Fill 1
End Rhy. Fill 1
Rhy. Fig. 1

F5
G5
F
G7
C
E/B
lose this feel - in'.
'N' if I could choose a place to
8va
full
hold bend
full
full
A5
C/G
F5
G
Pre-Chorus
A
E/G♯
die,
it would be in your arms.
Do you wan-na see me crawl a-cross the floor
8va
full
Harm.
full
semi-P.H.
full
loco
full
full
semi-P.H.
full
1/4
End Rhy. Fig. 1
Rhy. Fig. 2

F♯m
D
E
A7
E/G♯
F♯m
D5
E
to you?
Do you wan-na hear me beg you to take me back?
I'd glad - ly do it be-cause
8va
hold bend
full
1/2
End Rhy. Fig. 2
Chorus
A
Amaj7
A7
D5
E
I don't wan - na fade a - way.
Give me one more day, please.
Riff A
loco
Riff A1
Rhy. Fig. 3

To Coda 1
A
Amaj7
A7
D5
E
I don't want to fade a - way.
In your heart I want to stay.
End Riff A
End Riff A1
End Rhy. Fig. 3
To Coda 2
Verse
Gtr. 1: w/ Rhy. Fig. 1, simile
F
G7
C
E/B
A5
C/G
2. It's all wrong, but it's al - right.
3. Bell Bot-tom
The way that you
8va
full

F5 G5 F G7 C E/B

treat me ba - by. Mm. Once I was strong, but I lost the fight;

8va
Gtr. 2

full full

8va
Gtr. 3

hold bend
full full

Pre-Chorus

Gtr. 1: w/ Rhy. Fig. 2, simile

A5 C/G F5 G A E/G#

you won't find a bet-ter los - er. Do you wan-na see me crawl a - cross the floor

loco

loco

hold bend
full full

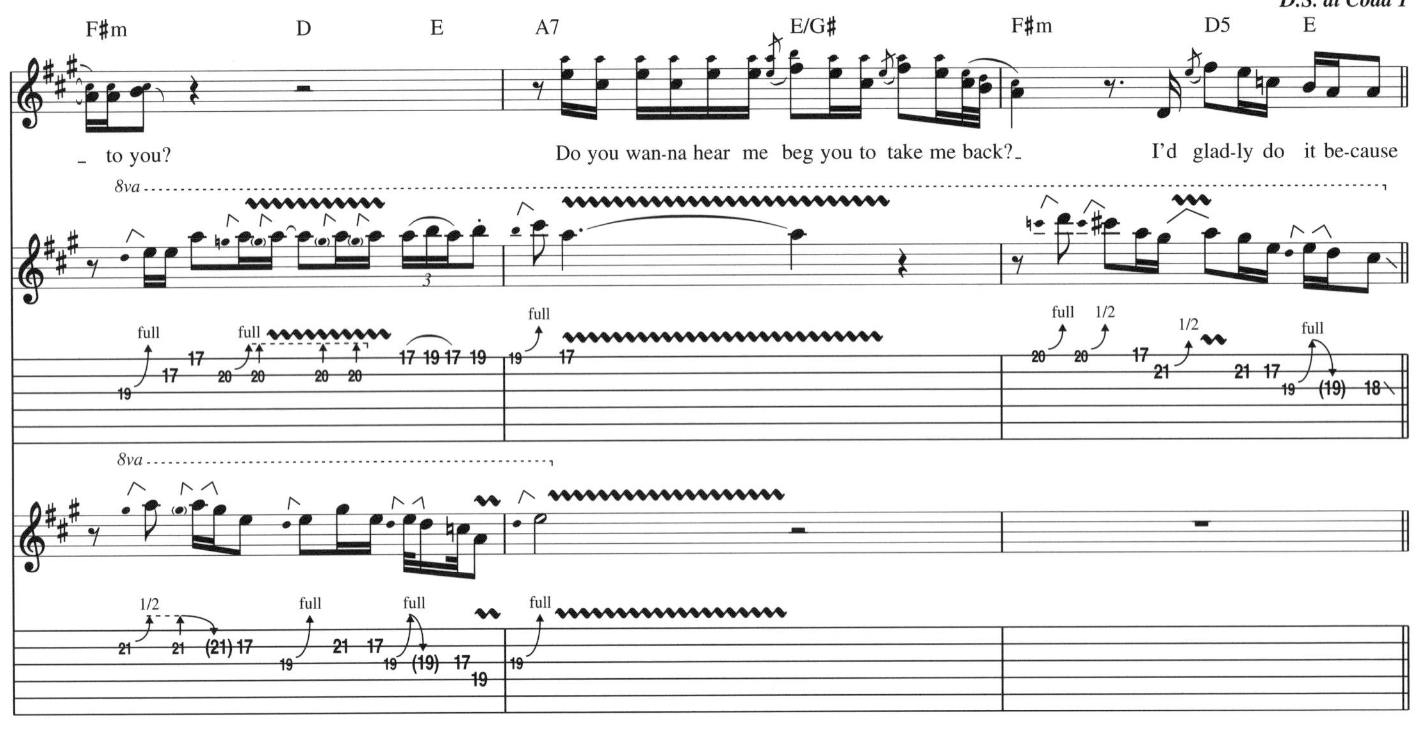
D.S. al Coda 1
F♯m D E A7 E/G♯ F♯m D5 E
to you? Do you wan-na hear me beg you to take me back? I'd glad-ly do it be-cause
8va
full
1/2

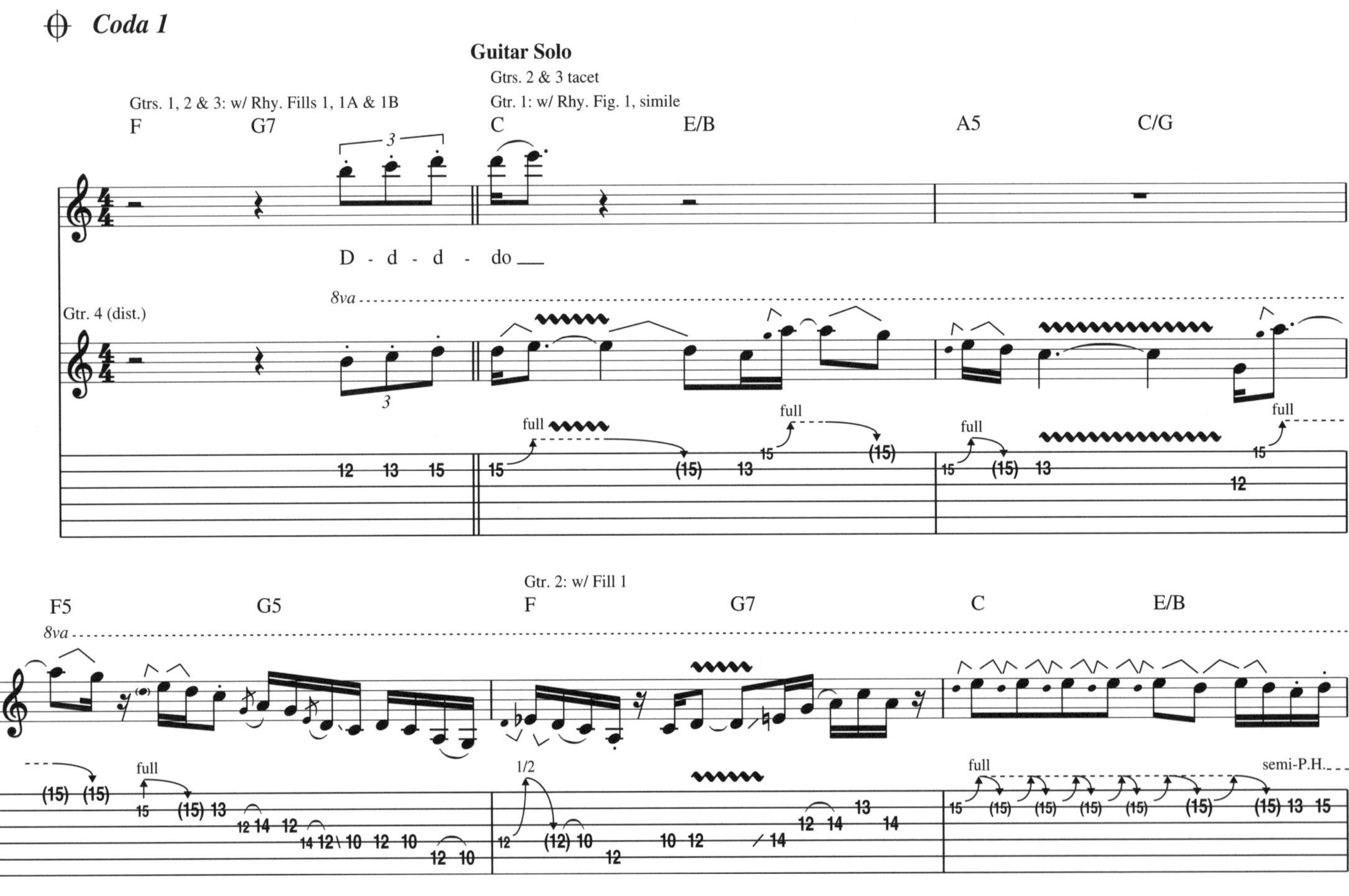
Coda 1
Guitar Solo
Gtrs. 2 & 3 tacet
Gtr. 1: w/ Rhy. Fig. 1, simile
Gtrs. 1, 2 & 3: w/ Rhy. Fills 1, 1A & 1B
F G7 C E/B A5 C/G
D - d - d - do
Gtr. 4 (dist.)
8va
full
Gtr. 2: w/ Fill 1
F5 G5 F G7 C E/B
1/2
semi-P.H.

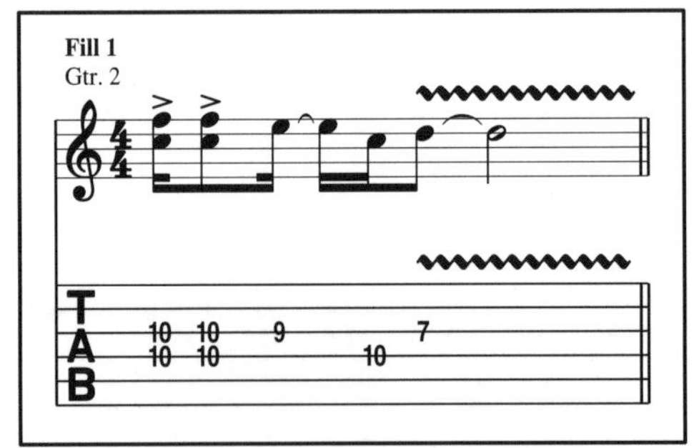
Fill 1
Gtr. 2
T
A
B

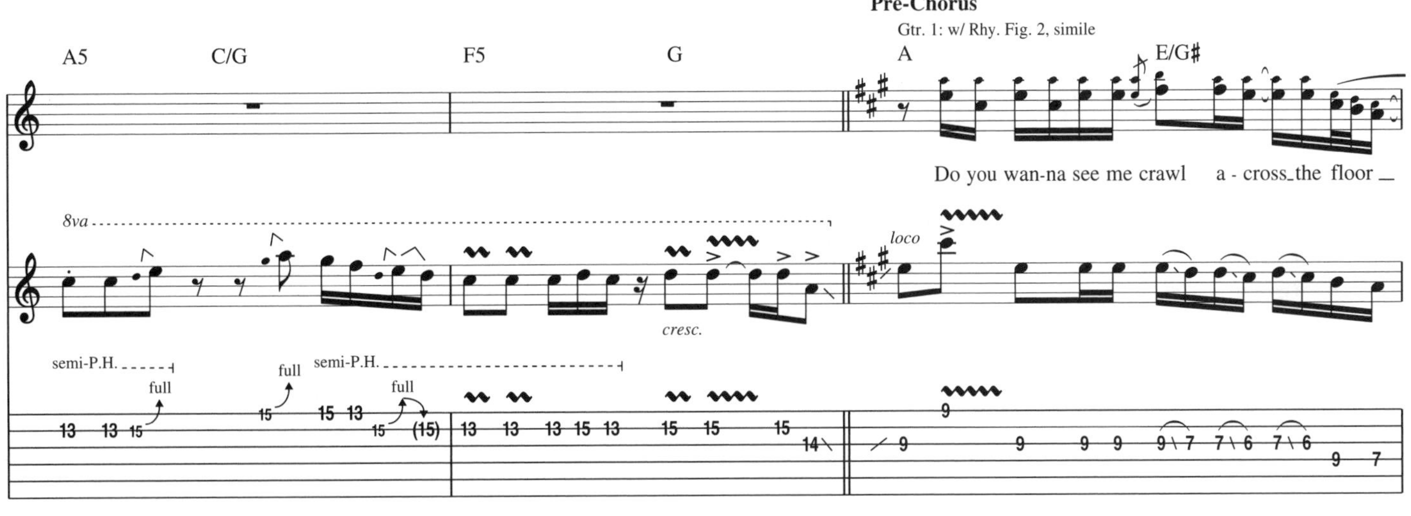
Pre-Chorus
Gtr. 1: w/ Rhy. Fig. 2, simile
A5
C/G
F5
G
A
E/G#
Do you wan-na see me crawl a - cross the floor
8va
loco
cresc.
semi-P.H.
full
semi-P.H.
full
full

D.S. al Coda 2
F#m
D
E
A7
E/G#
F#m
D5
E
to you?
Do you wan-na hear me beg you to take me back?
I'd glad - ly do it 'cause
full
full
1/2

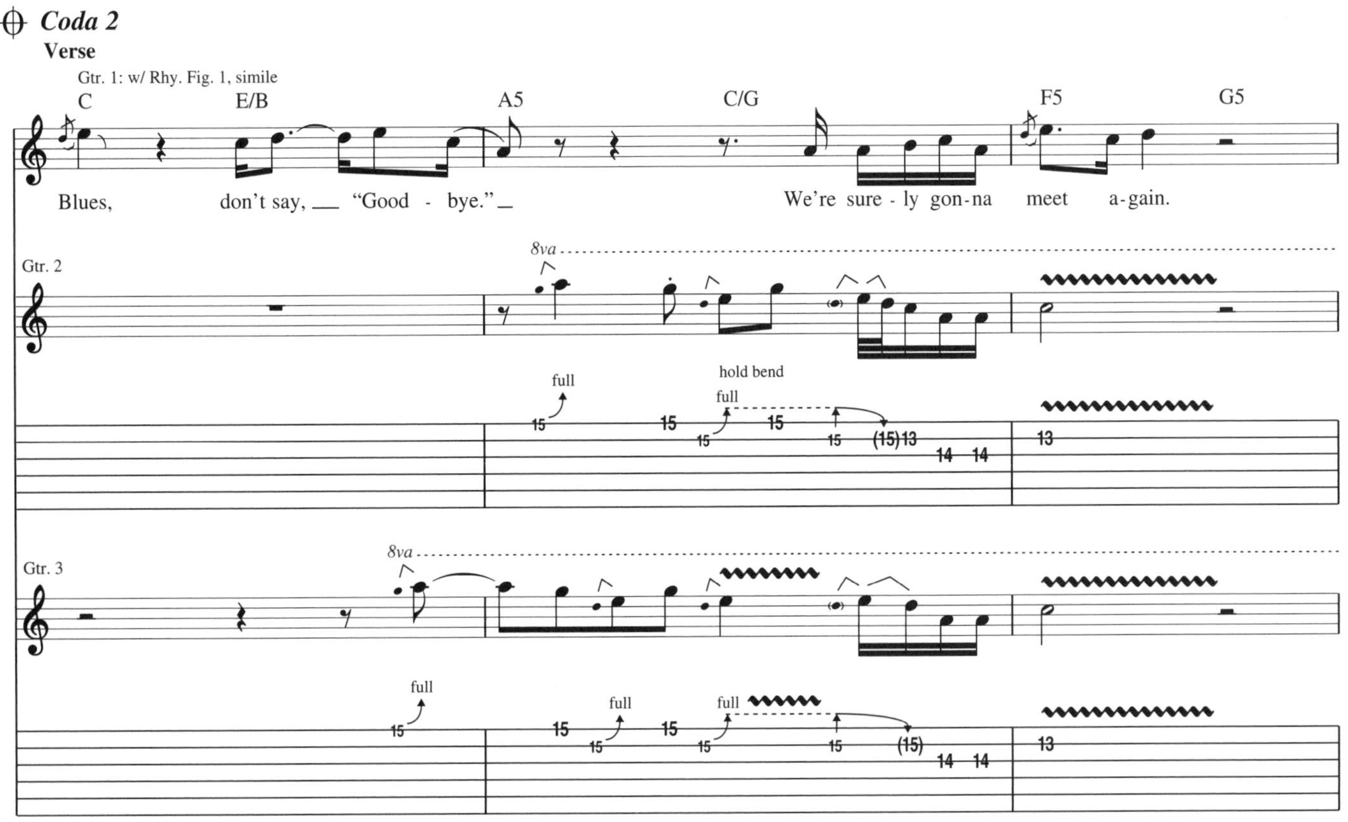
Coda 2
Verse
Gtr. 1: w/ Rhy. Fig. 1, simile
C
E/B
A5
C/G
F5
G5
Blues, don't say, "Good - bye."
We're sure - ly gon-na meet a-gain.
Gtr. 2
8va
full
hold bend
full
Gtr. 3
8va
full
full
full

F G7 C E/B A5 C/G

And if we do, __ don't you be sur-prised _ if you find me with an -

8va

full full full

8va

full full full

F5 G

oth-er lov-er. Oh. _

Pre-Chorus

Gtr. 1: w/ Rhy. Fig. 2, simile

A E/G♯ F♯m D E

Do you wan-na see me crawl a-cross the floor _____ to you?

8va

full full full full full full full full

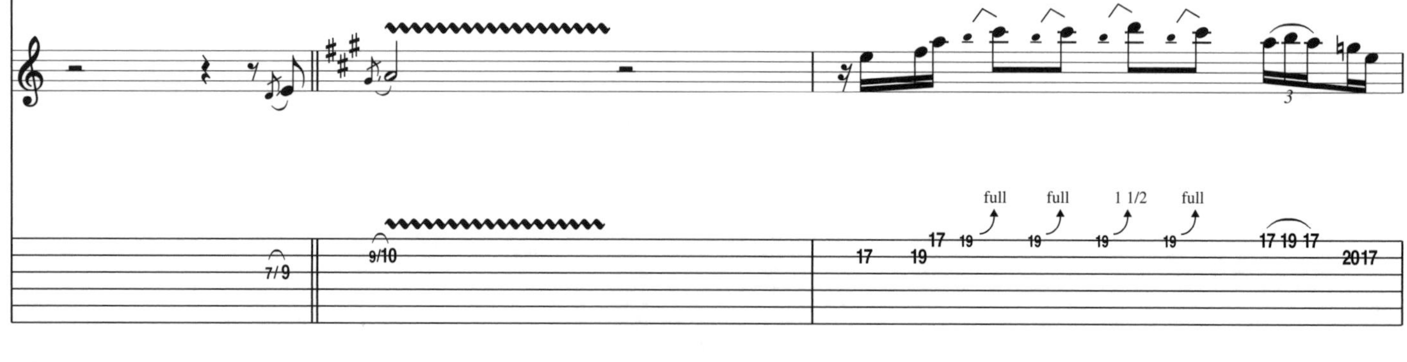

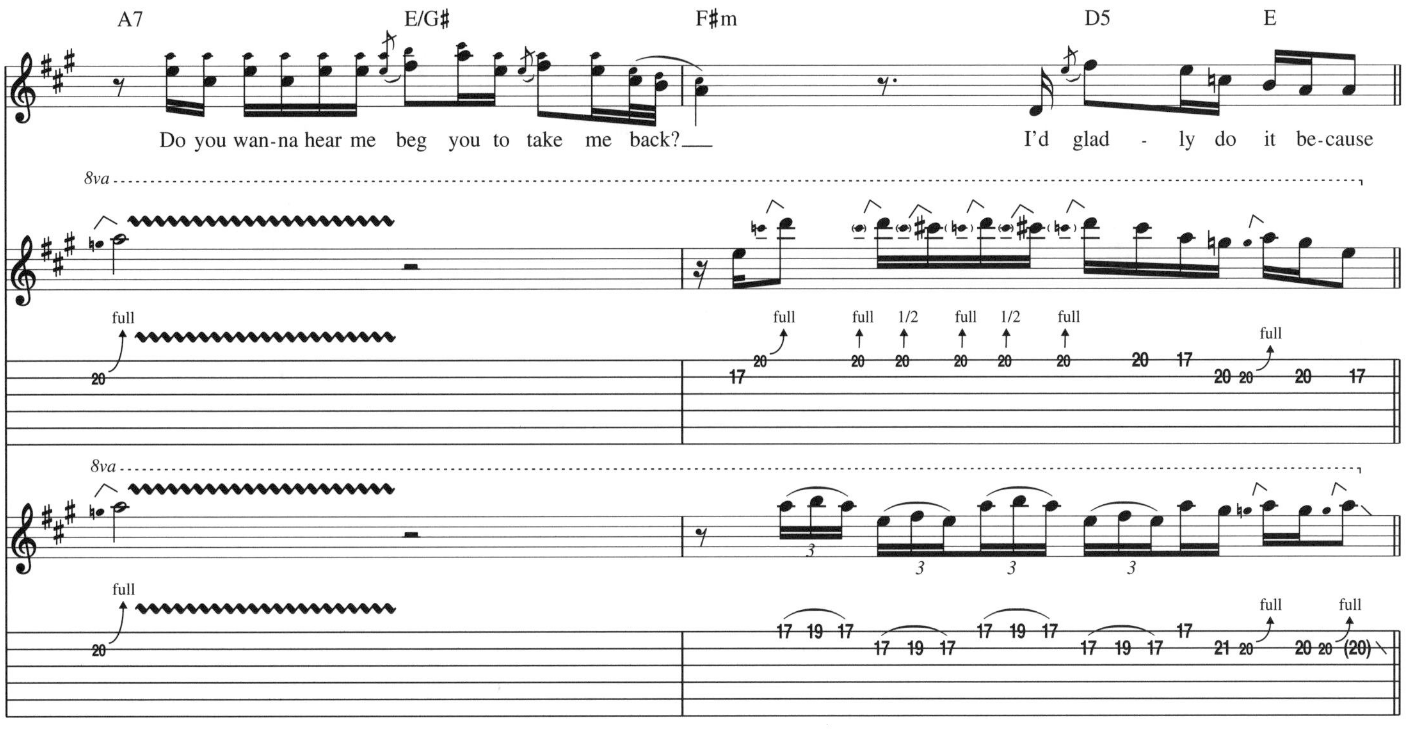

Outro-Chorus

Gtr. 1: w/ Rhy. Fig. 3, simile
Gtrs. 2 & 3: w/ Riffs A & A1

A Amaj7 A7 D5 E A Amaj7

I don't wan-na fade a - way.___ Give_me one_ more day,___ please._ I don't want to fade a - way._

A7 D5 E F G7

_ In your heart_ I want___ to stay.

play 3 times

Gtr. 2

loco

hold bend

full full

Gtr. 3

loco

full full

Gtr. 1

featured on the Motion Picture Soundtrack PHENOMENON

Change the World

Words and Music by Wayne Kirkpatrick, Gordon Kennedy and Tommy Sims

Verse
Gtr. 3 tacet
E
A/E
E7(no3rd)
1. If I could reach the stars,
A/E
E
pull one down for you.
Rhy. Fig. 2
A/E
E7(no3rd)
Shine it on my heart
A/E
E
so you could see the truth.
A
D/A
A7(no3rd)
Then this love I have in - side

D/A
A
E
A/E
E7(no3rd)
is ev - 'ry - thing it seems.
But for now I find
A/E
G#7
it's on - ly in my dreams.
And I can
End Rhy. Fig. 2
(cont. in slash)
Chorus
Gtr. 2 tacet
F#m7
Rhy. Fig. 3
G#7
C#m7
D#m7♭5
G#7
Gtr. 1
change the world.
(Change the world.
I will be the sun - light in your
I will be the sun - light in your
C#m7
D#m7♭5
G#7
u - ni - verse.
u - ni - verse.
You would think my love was real - ly
You would think my love,
Gtr. 2

C#m7
Cm7
Bm7
A
Eadd2/G#
End Rhy. Fig. 3
some - thing good, ba - by, if I could
some - thing good.)
E/G#
E°/G
F#m7type2
Gtr. 1
change the world.
Gtr. 2
Gtr. 3
Rhy. Fill 1
End Rhy. Fill 1
*vol. knob swell
Interlude
Gtr. 1: w/ Rhy Fig. 1, simile
Gtr. 3 tacet
E
F#m7
Gadd2
F#m7
E
Gtr. 2
Verse
Gtr. 1: w/ Rhy. Fig. 2, simile
E
A/E
E7(no3rd)
A/E
E
2. If I could be king, e - ven for a day,
1/2

A/E
E7(no3rd)
I'd take you as my queen,
I'd have it no oth - er way.
A
D/A
A7(no3rd)
And our love would rule in this king - dom we have made.
E
Till then I'd be a fool,
G♯7
wish - ing for the day.
And I can
Chorus
Gtr. 1: w/ Rhy. Fig. 3
Gtr. 2 tacet, 1st time; w/ Fill 1, 2nd time
F♯m7
C♯m7
change the world.
(Change the, change the world.
Fill 1
Gtr. 2

Gtr. 2: Fill 2, 2nd time
D♯m7♭5
G♯7
C♯m7
I will be the sun - light in your u - ni - verse.
I will be the sun - light in your u - ni - verse.
To Coda
D♯m7♭5
G♯7
C♯m7
Cm7
Bm7
You would think my love was real - ly some - thing good, ba - by,
You would think my love, some - thing good, oh,
A
Eadd2/G♯
E/G♯
E°/G
F♯m7
E
Gtr. 3
if I could change the world, ba - by,
if I could, yeah.)
Gtr. 2
Gtr. 1
Fill 2
Gtr. 2
T
A
B

Gtr. 2 & 3 tacet
A7
Eadd2/G♯
Gtr. 3: w/ Rhy. Fill 1
E/G♯
E°/G
F♯m7
if I could change the world.
Gtr. 1
Guitar Solo
Gtr. 1: w/ Rhy. Fig. 1 1½ times, simile
E
F♯m7
Gadd2
F♯m7
E
Gtr. 2
F♯m7
Gadd2
D.S. al Coda
F♯m7
G♯7
I can
Gtr. 2
Gtr. 1

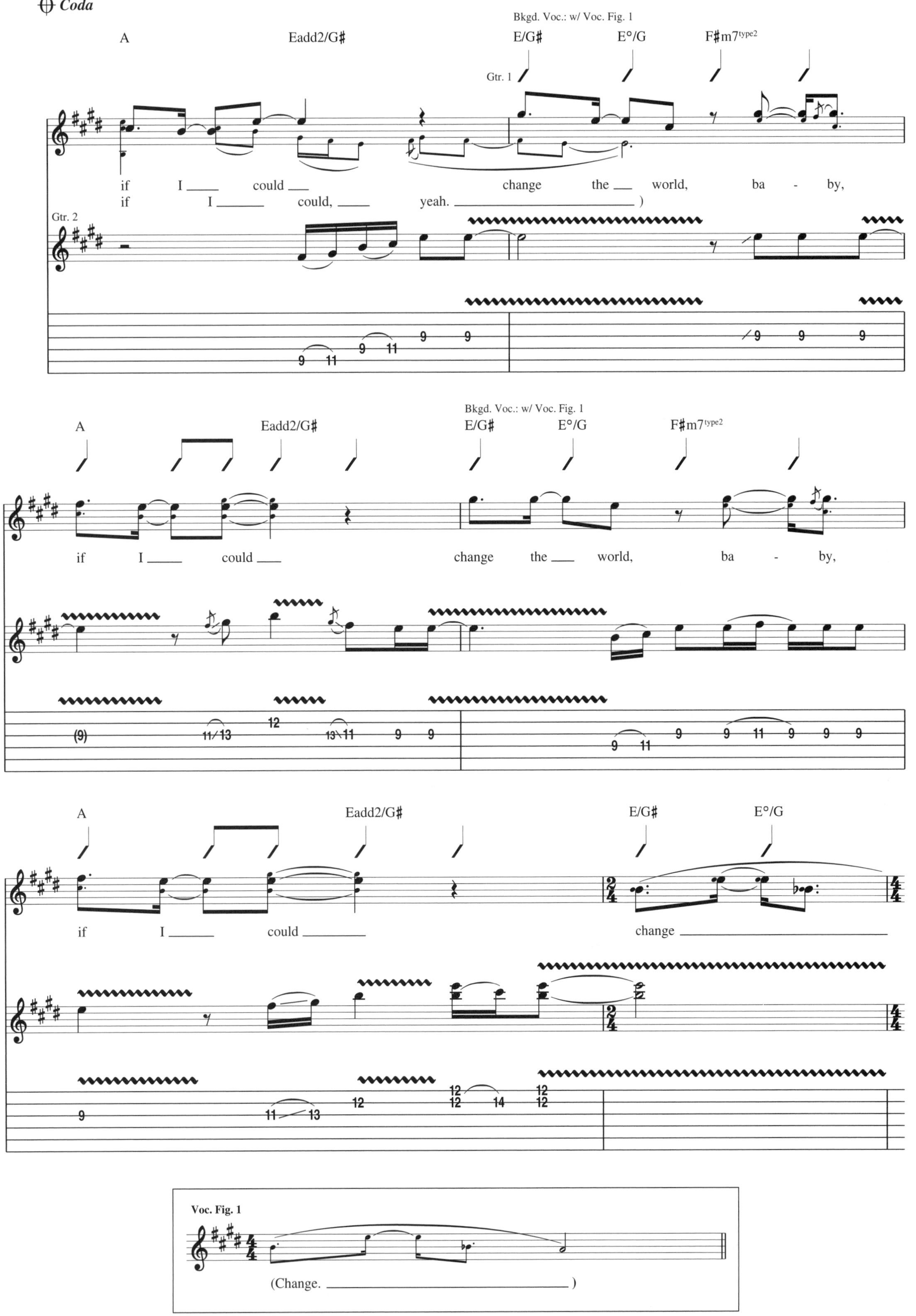
Coda
Bkgd. Voc.: w/ Voc. Fig. 1
A
Eadd2/G#
E/G#
E°/G
F#m7type2
Gtr. 1
if I could change the world, ba - by,
if I could, yeah.)
Gtr. 2
A
Eadd2/G#
E/G#
E°/G
F#m7type2
if I could change the world, ba - by,
A
Eadd2/G#
E/G#
E°/G
if I could change
Voc. Fig. 1
(Change.)

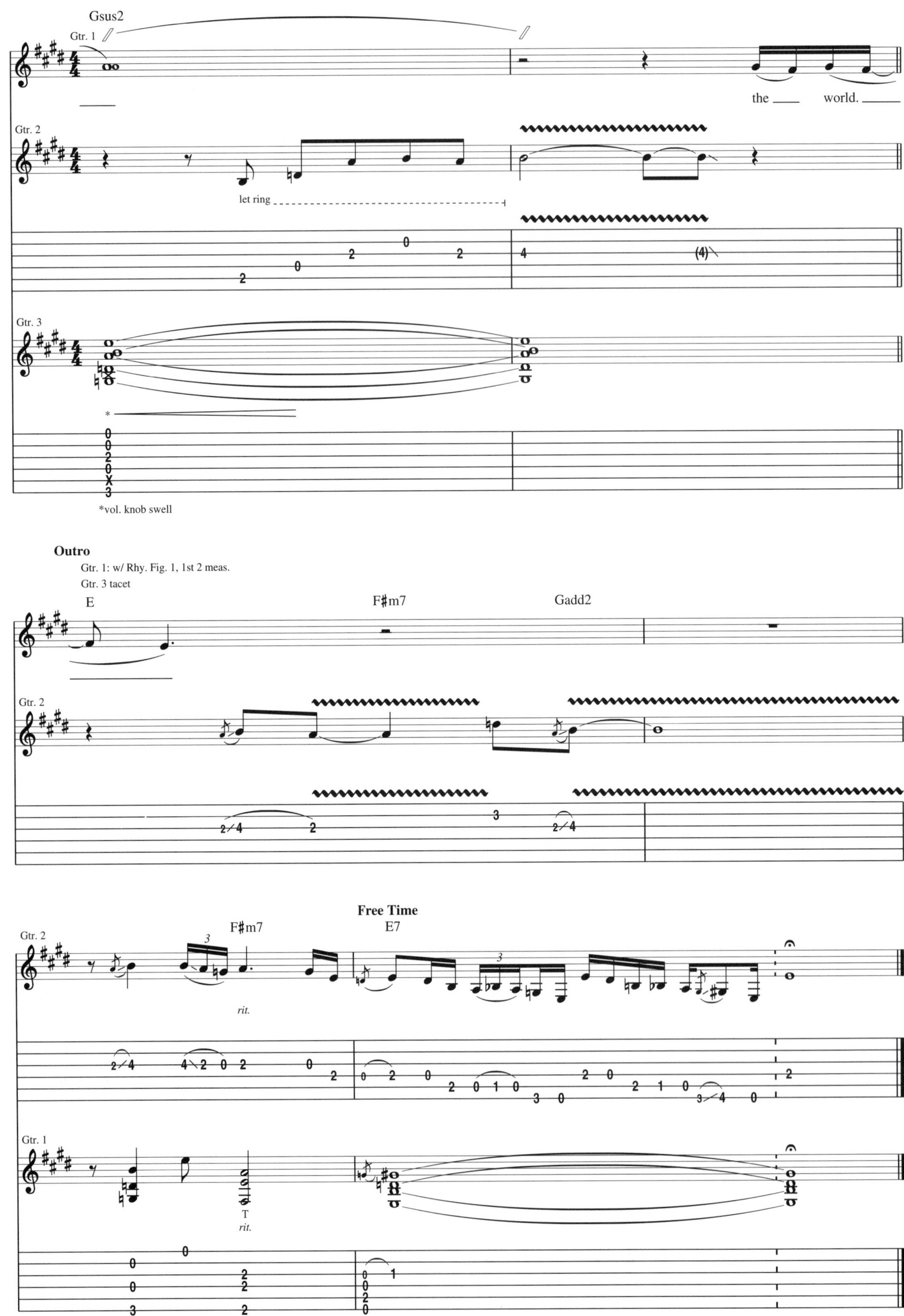
Gsus2
Gtr. 1
the world.
Gtr. 2
let ring
Gtr. 3
*vol. knob swell
Outro
Gtr. 1: w/ Rhy. Fig. 1, 1st 2 meas.
Gtr. 3 tacet
E
F♯m7
Gadd2
Gtr. 2
Free Time
E7
rit.
Gtr. 1
T
rit.

from Eric Clapton - *Slowhand*

Cocaine

Words and Music by J.J. Cale

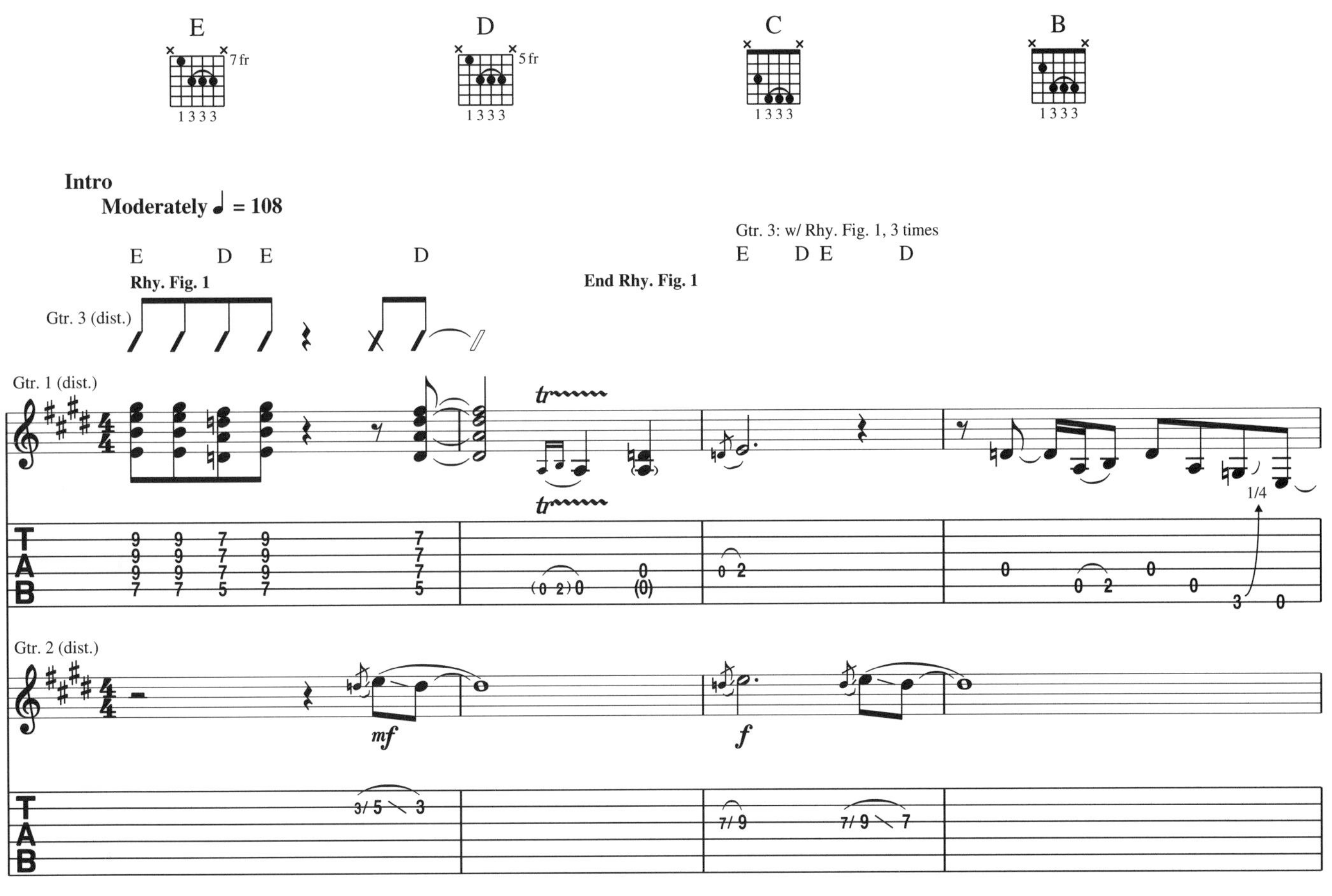

Verse
Gtr. 1 tacet
Gtr. 3: w/ Rhy. Fig. 1, 3 1/ 2 times
Gtr. 4: w/ Rhy. Fig. 3, simile
Gtr. 2: w/ Rhy. Fig. 2, 2nd time
E D E D
1. If you wan - na hang out, you've got - ta take her out, co - caine.
got bad news, you wan - na kick the blues, co - caine.
1/4
Rhy. Fig. 4
End Rhy. Fig. 4
End Rhy. Fig. 3
Gtr. 4 tacet
Gtr. 2: w/ Rhy. Fig. 2, 1st time
Gtr. 2: w/ Rhy. Fig. 4, 2nd time, simile
Gtr. 2: w/ Rhy. Fig. 4, 1 1/ 2 times, simile, 1st time
Gtr. 2: w/ Rhy. Fig. 2, 1 1/ 2 times, simile, 2nd time
Gtr. 4: w/ Rhy. Fig. 3
E D E D E D E D
If you wan - na get down, down on the ground, co - caine.
When your day is done an' you wan - na run, co - caine.
Gtr. 1
Riff A
End Riff A

Gtr. 4 tacet
E D E D E D C B
Rhy. Fig. 5
* Gtrs. 2 & 3
End Rhy. Fig. 5
(Gtr. 3 cont. in notation)
She don't lie, she don't lie, she don't lie, co - caine.
Riff B
End Riff B
3/5 3 3/5 3 4/5 4
* composite arr.

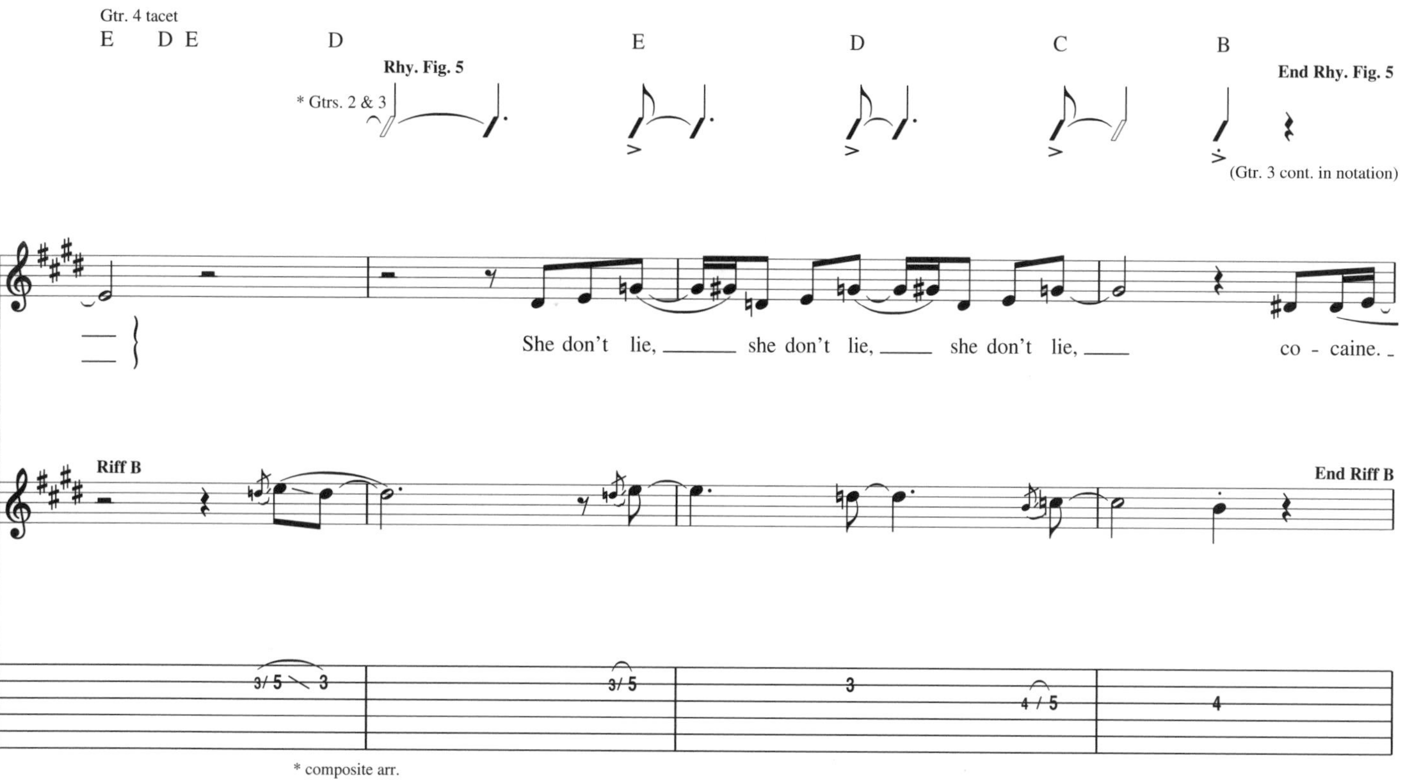

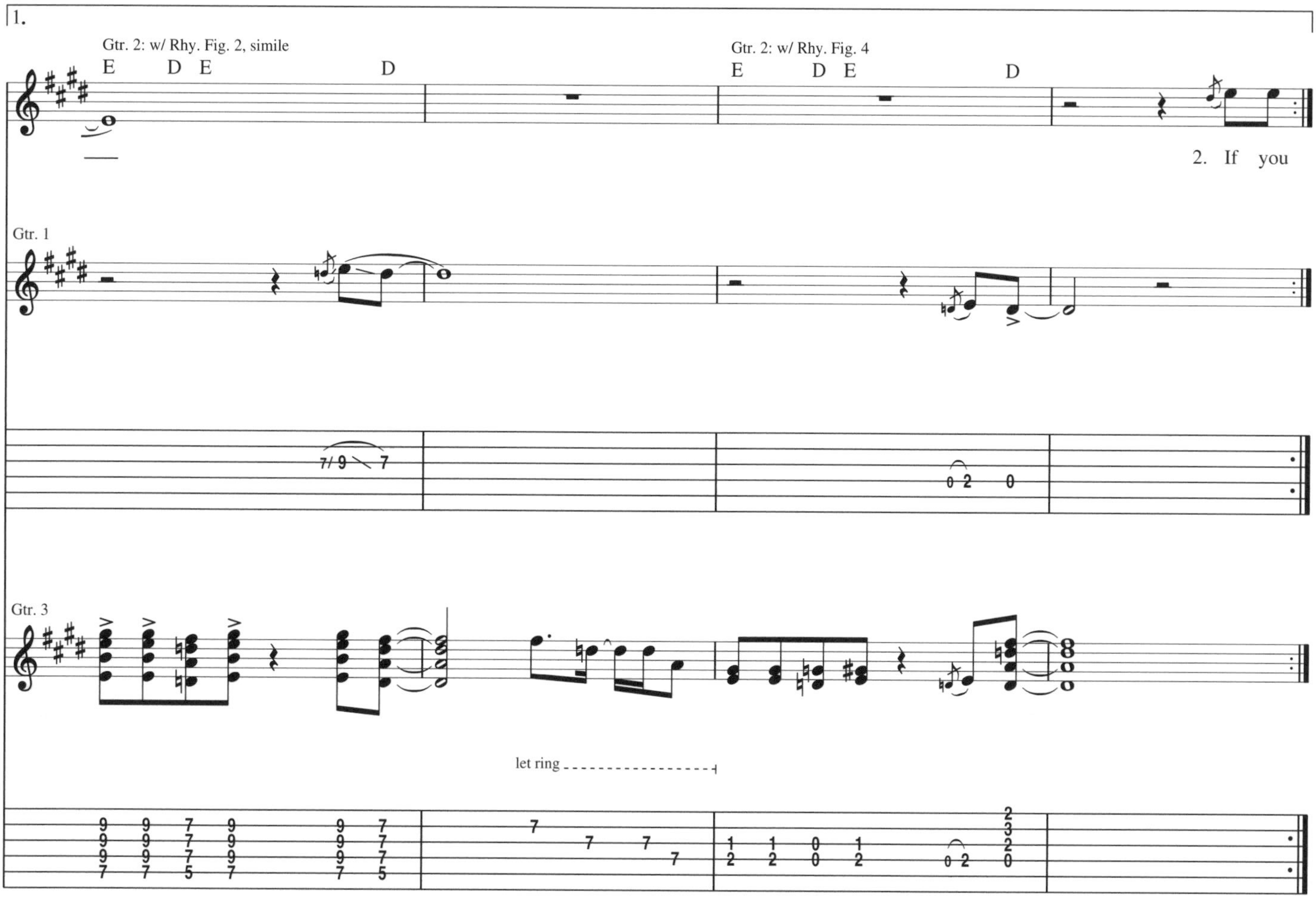

1.
Gtr. 2: w/ Rhy. Fig. 2, simile
E D E D
Gtr. 2: w/ Rhy. Fig. 4
E D E D
2. If you
Gtr. 1
7/9 7
0 2 0
Gtr. 3
let ring

2.
Gtrs. 2 & 3: w/ Rhy. Figs. 1 & 2, 2 times, simile
Gtr. 1
Rhy. Fig. 6
End Rhy. Fig. 6
vol. swell
Gtr. 4
Guitar Solo
Gtrs. 2 & 3: w/ Rhy. Figs. 1 & 2, 12 times, simile
Gtr. 4 tacet
let ring

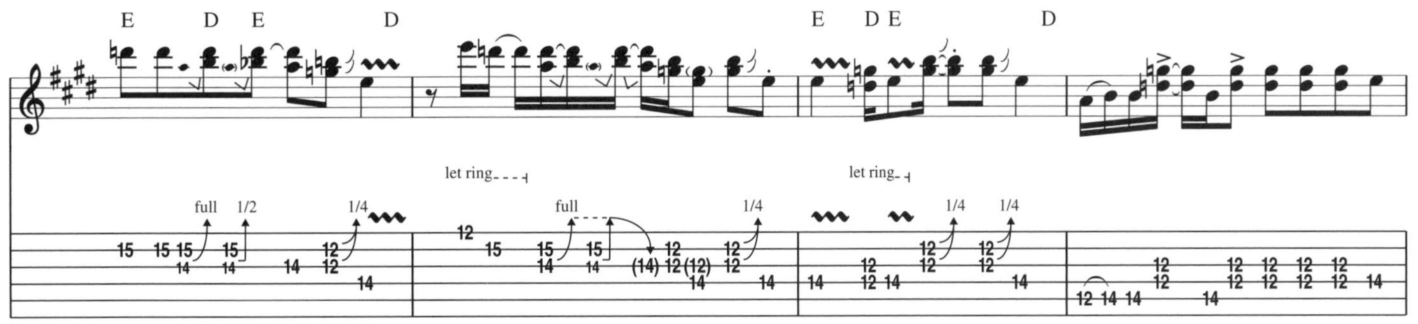

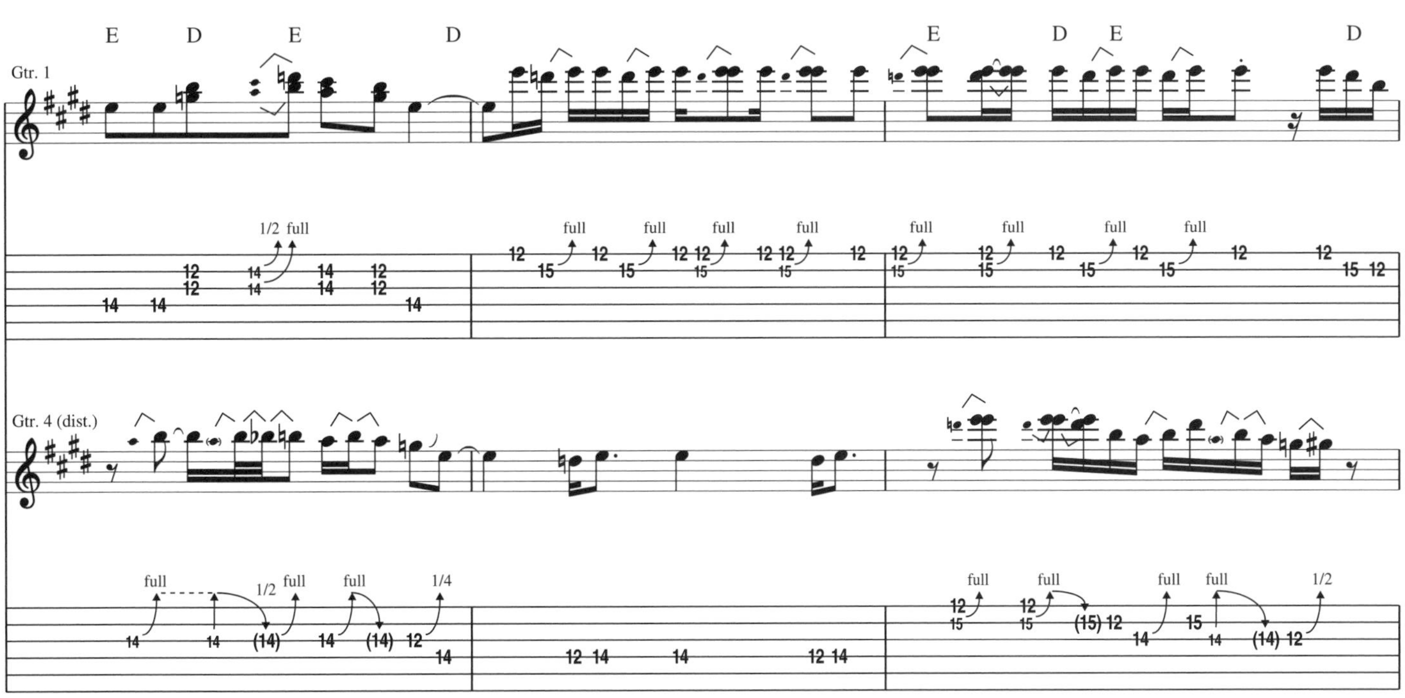

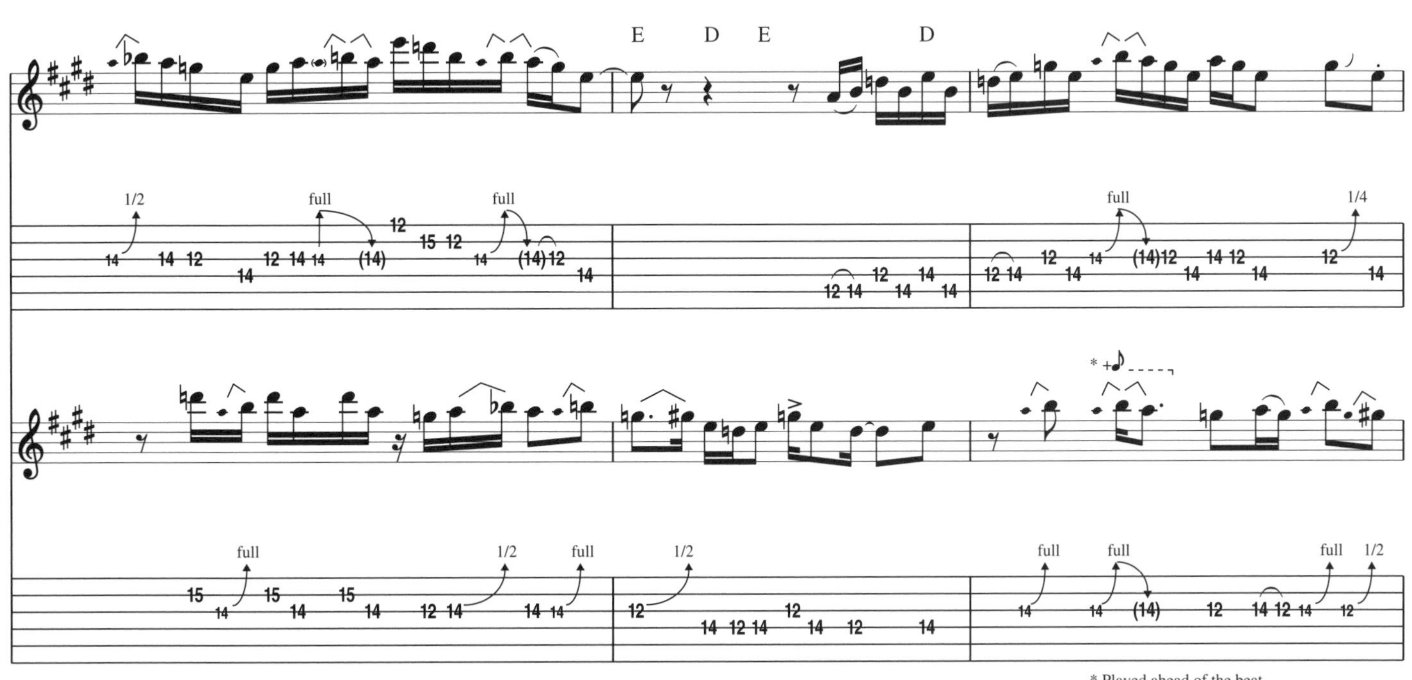

* Played ahead of the beat.

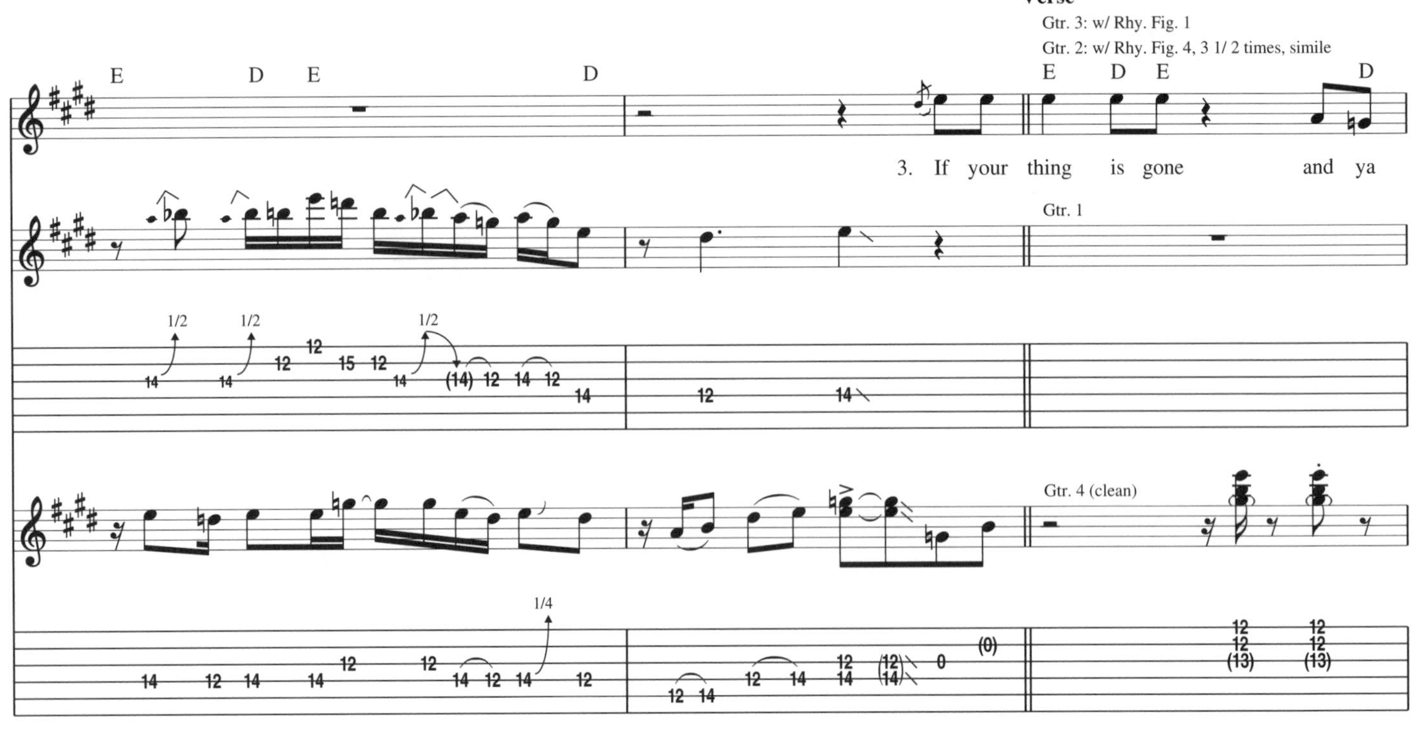
Verse
Gtr. 3: w/ Rhy. Fig. 1
Gtr. 2: w/ Rhy. Fig. 4, 3 1/ 2 times, simile
E D E D E D E D
3. If your thing is gone and ya
Gtr. 1
Gtr. 4 (clean)

Gtr. 1: w/ Riff A, 2 times
E D E D
wan - na ride on, co - caine. Don't for -
Gtr. 3

Gtr. 4: w/ Rhy. Fig. 3
Gtr. 4 tacet
Gtr. 1: w/ Riff B
Gtrs. 2 & 3: w/ Rhy. Fig. 5, simile
E D E D E D E D E
get this fact, can't get it back, co - caine. She don't lie, .
Gtr. 3

Gtr. 1: w/ Rhy. Fig. 6, simile
Gtr. 2: w/ Rhy. Fig. 2, 1 1/2 times
D C B E D E D
she don't lie, she don't lie, co - caine.
Gtr. 3
Gtr. 4
Gtr. 1: w/ Riff B
E D E D
Gtrs. 2 & 3: w/ Rhy. Fig. 5, simile
E D C B
She don't lie, she don't lie, she don't lie, co- caine.
Gtr. 1: w/ Riff A
Gtr. 2: w/ Rhy. Fig. 4, 2 times, simile
E D E D
Gtr. 1 tacet
E D E D
Gtr. 3
Rhy. Fig. 7
Gtr. 4
1/4 1/4

Outro
Gtrs. 2 & 3: w/ Rhy. Figs. 1 & 2, simile, till fade
Gtr. 4: w/ Rhy. Fig. 7, simile, till fade
E D E D E D E D
Gtr. 1
1/2
End Rhy. Fig. 7
1/2 1/2
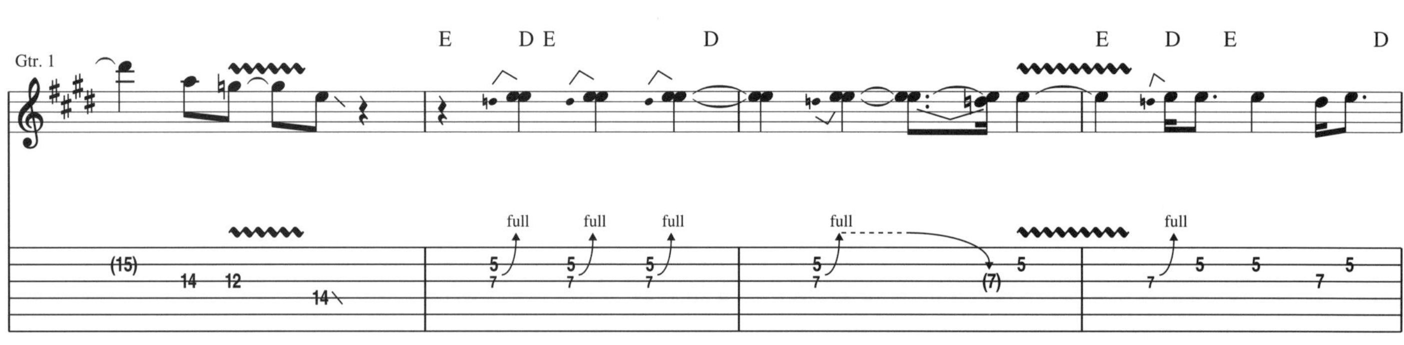
Gtr. 1
E D E D E D E D
full full full full full
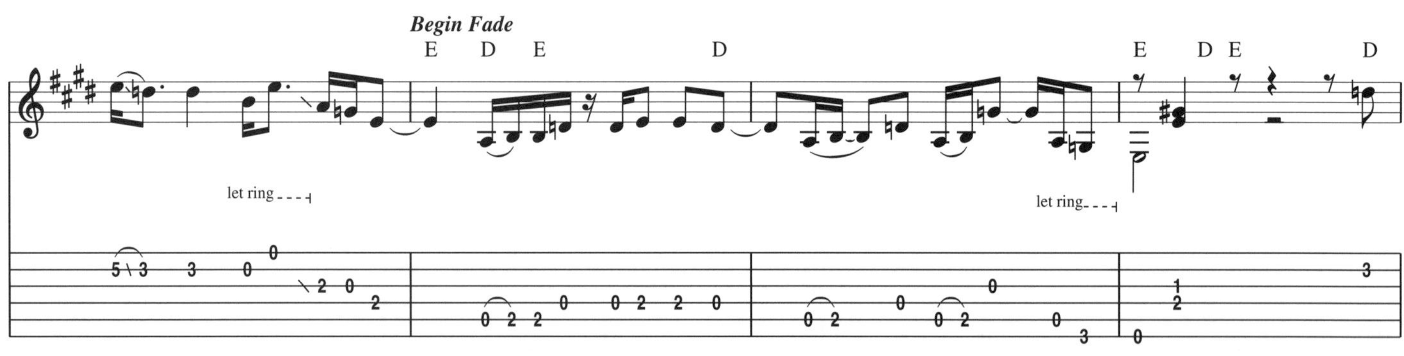
Begin Fade
E D E D E D E D
let ring
let ring
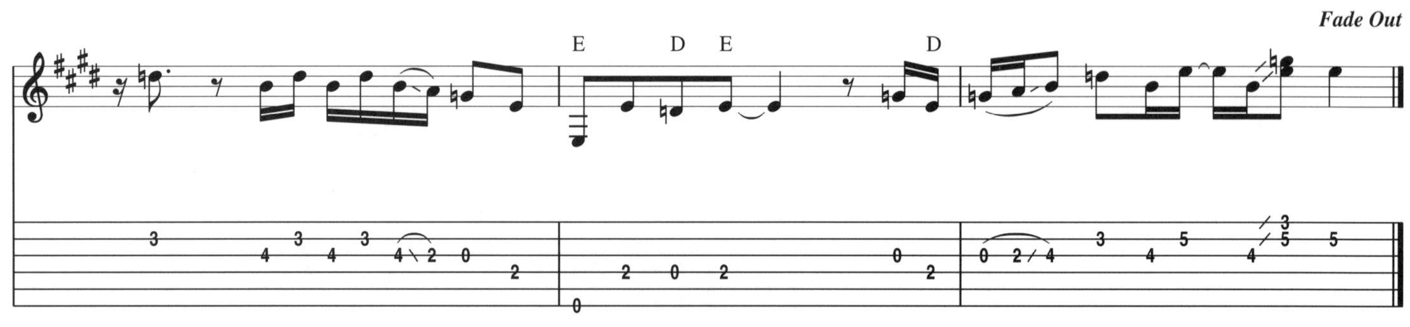
Fade Out
E D E D

from Delaney and Bonnie - "Comin' Home" single
from Eric Clapton - *Crossroads*

Comin' Home

Words and Music by Eric Clapton and Bonnie Bramlett

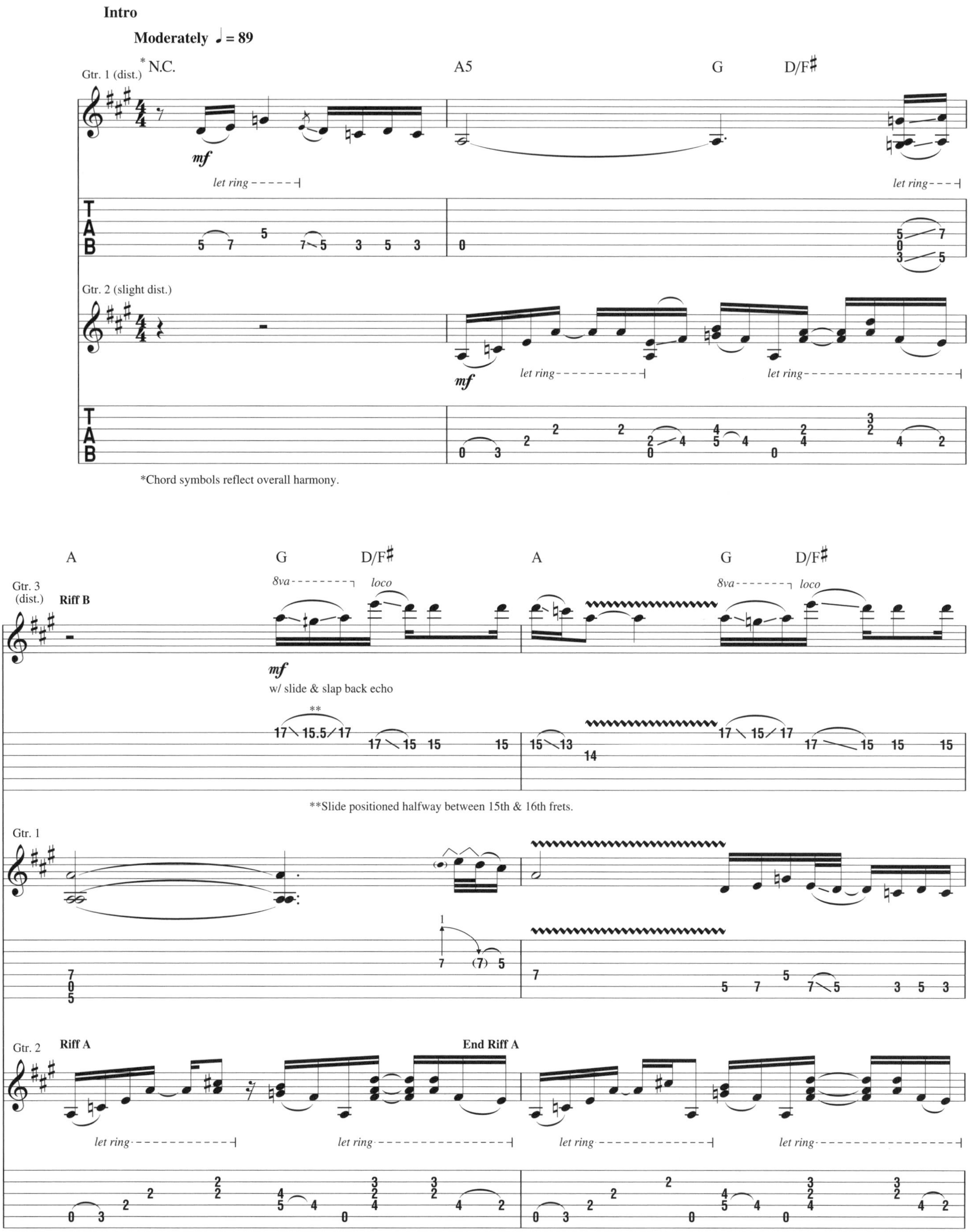

Intro

Moderately ♩ = 89

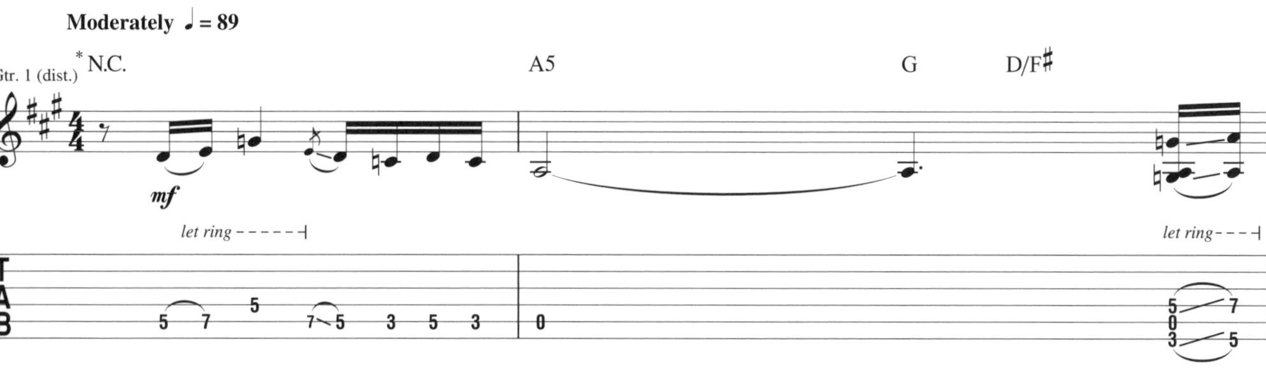

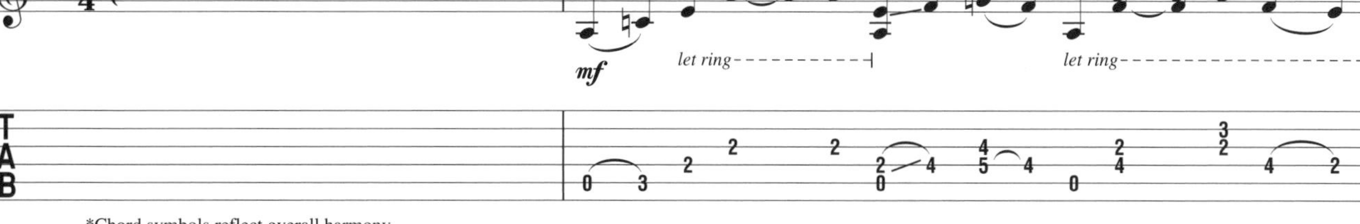

*Chord symbols reflect overall harmony.

A G D/F♯ A G D/F♯

Gtr. 3 (dist.) Riff B

8va loco 8va loco

mf

w/ slide & slap back echo

**Slide positioned halfway between 15th & 16th frets.

Gtr. 1

Gtr. 2 Riff A End Riff A

let ring

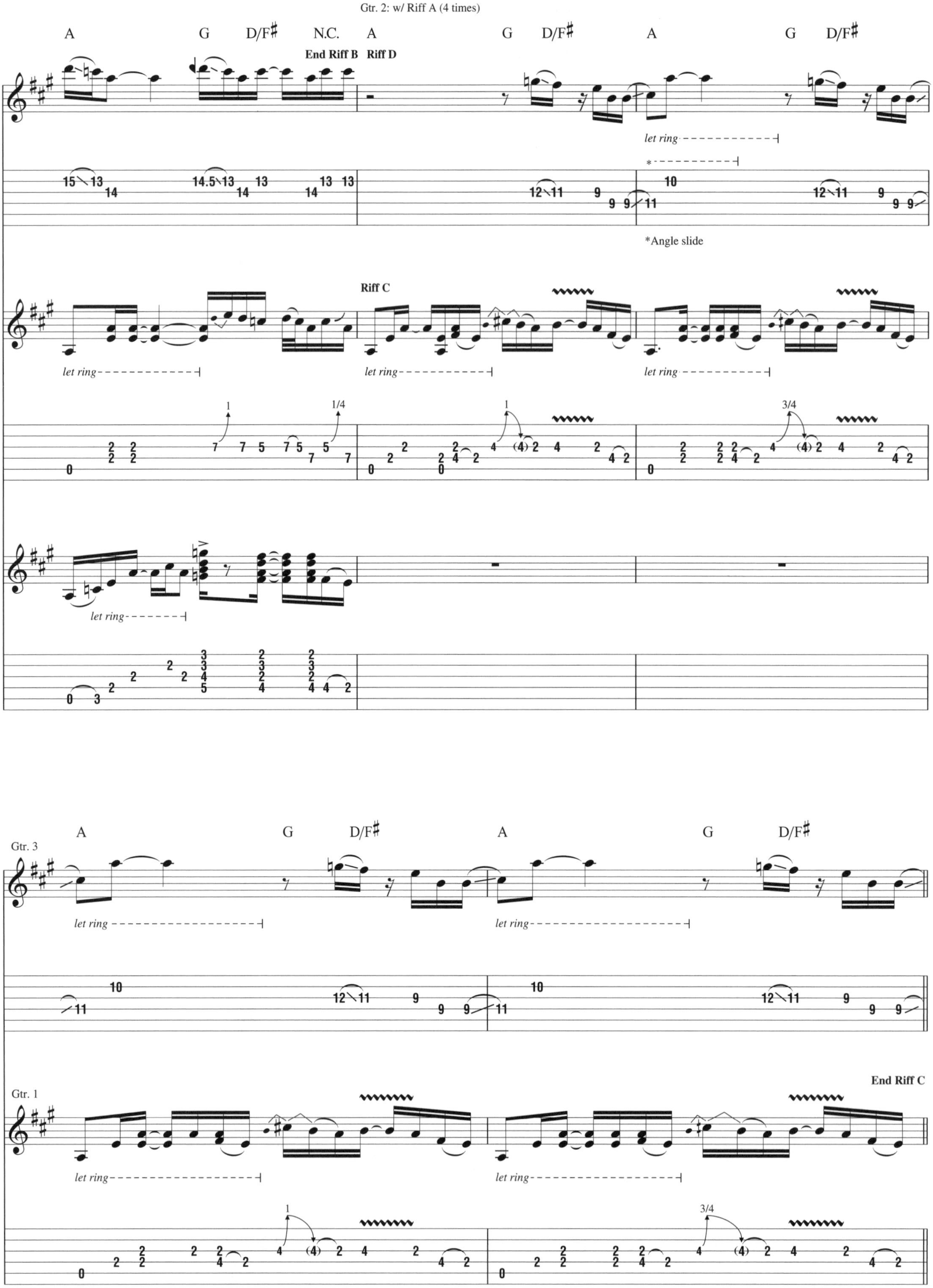

Gtr. 2: w/ Riff A (4 times)

A G D/F♯ N.C. A G D/F♯ A G D/F♯

End Riff B Riff D

let ring

*Angle slide

Riff C

let ring

let ring

let ring

let ring

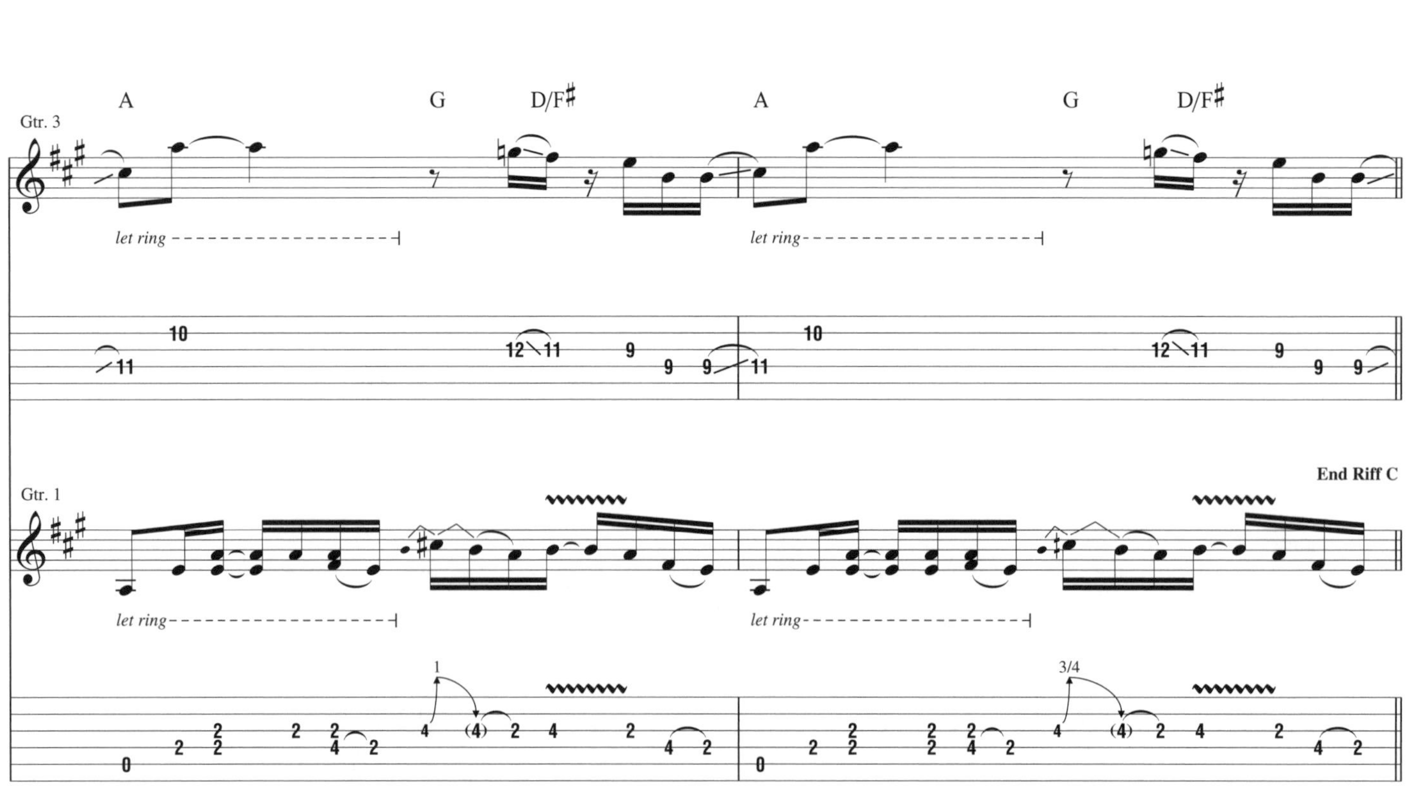

Verse
A5
Gtr. 3 tacet
1. Been out on the road 'bout six months
Gtr. 4 (dist.)
Riff E
End Riff E
mf
1 hold bend
Gtr. 3
End Riff D
let ring
Gtr. 1
Riff E1
End Riff E1
Gtr. 2
P.M.
Gtr. 1: w/ Riff E1 (3 times)
Gtr. 4: w/ Riff E (3 1/2 times)
too long. I want you so bad, I can hard - ly
let ring

stand it. I'm so tired and I'm all a - lone.
P.M.
let ring
1/4
1/4

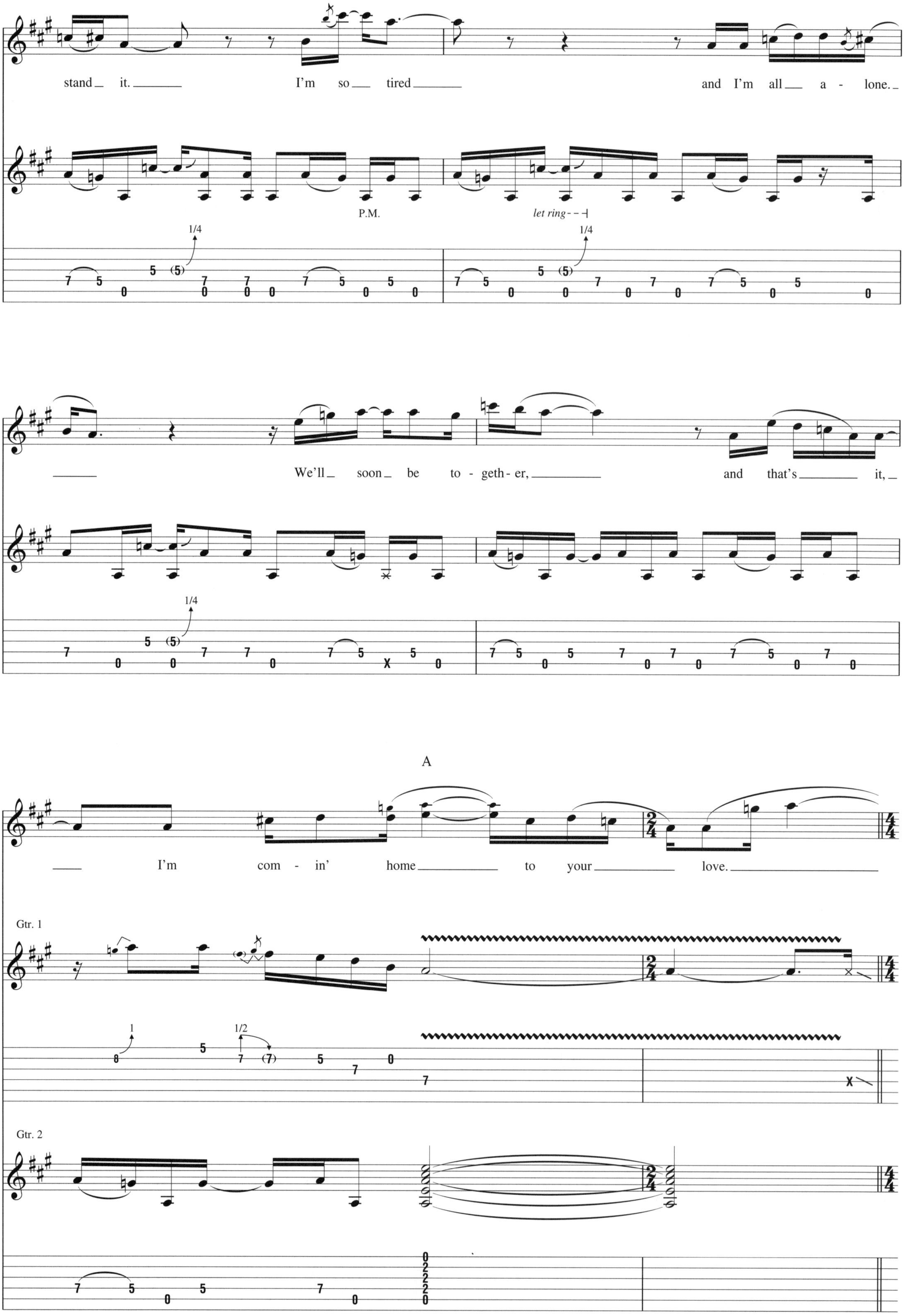

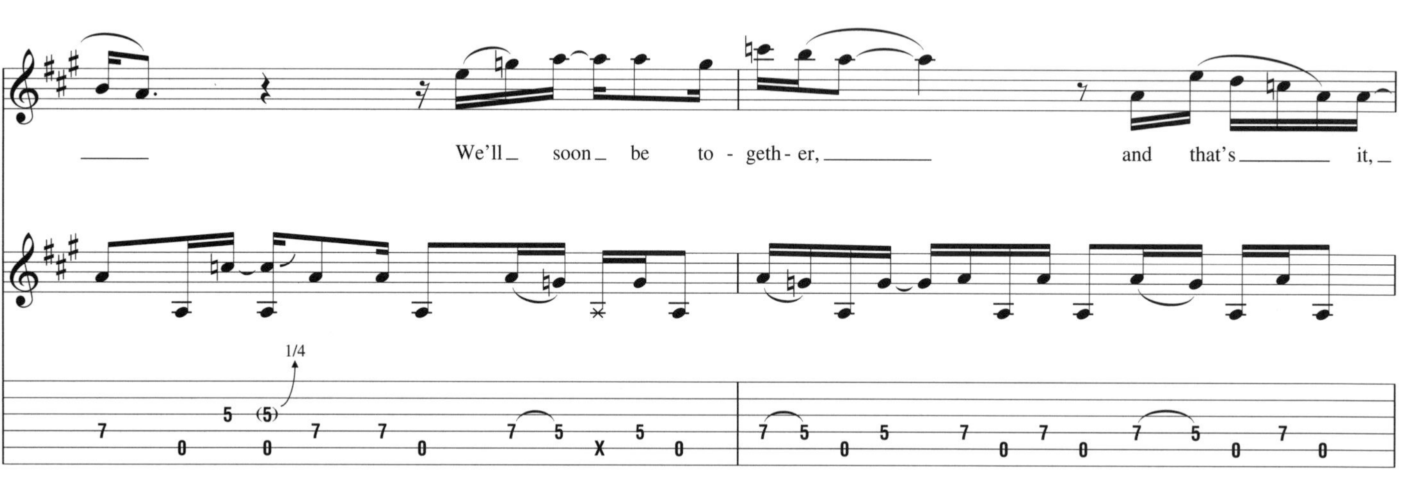
We'll soon be to - geth - er, and that's it,
1/4

A

I'm com - in' home to your love.

Gtr. 1

1
1/2

Gtr. 2

Interlude
Gtr. 2: w/ Riff A (8 times)
Gtr. 3: w/ Riff B
A G D/F♯ A G D/F♯
Gtr. 1
A G D/F♯ A G D/F♯
Gtr. 1: w/ Riff C
Gtr. 3: w/ Riff D
A G D/F♯ A G D/F♯ A G D/F♯ A G D/F♯
Verse
Gtr. 1: w/ Riff E1 (4 times)
Gtr. 4: w/ Riff E (4 1/2 times)
A
2. Hitch - hik - ing on the turn - pike all day long.
Gtr. 2
Riff F
End Riff F
Gtr. 5 (clean)
mf
P.M.

Gtr. 2: w/ Riff F (5 times)
No - bod - y seems to no - tice, they just pass me on
Gtr. 5
Riff G
End Riff G
Gtr. 5: w/ Riff G (2 times)
by. To keep from go-ing cra - zy, I got-ta sing my song. Got a whole lot of lov-
A5
- in', and ba - by that's why I'm com-in' home to your love.
Gtr. 4
Gtr. 2
Gtr. 1
Gtr. 5

Guitar Solo

Gtr. 5 tacet

E5 N.C. E5 E E5 N.C.

Gtr. 4

P.M. - -┤

*Note bumped accidentally.

Gtr. 2

Gtr. 1

Rhy. Fig. 1

End Rhy. Fig. 1

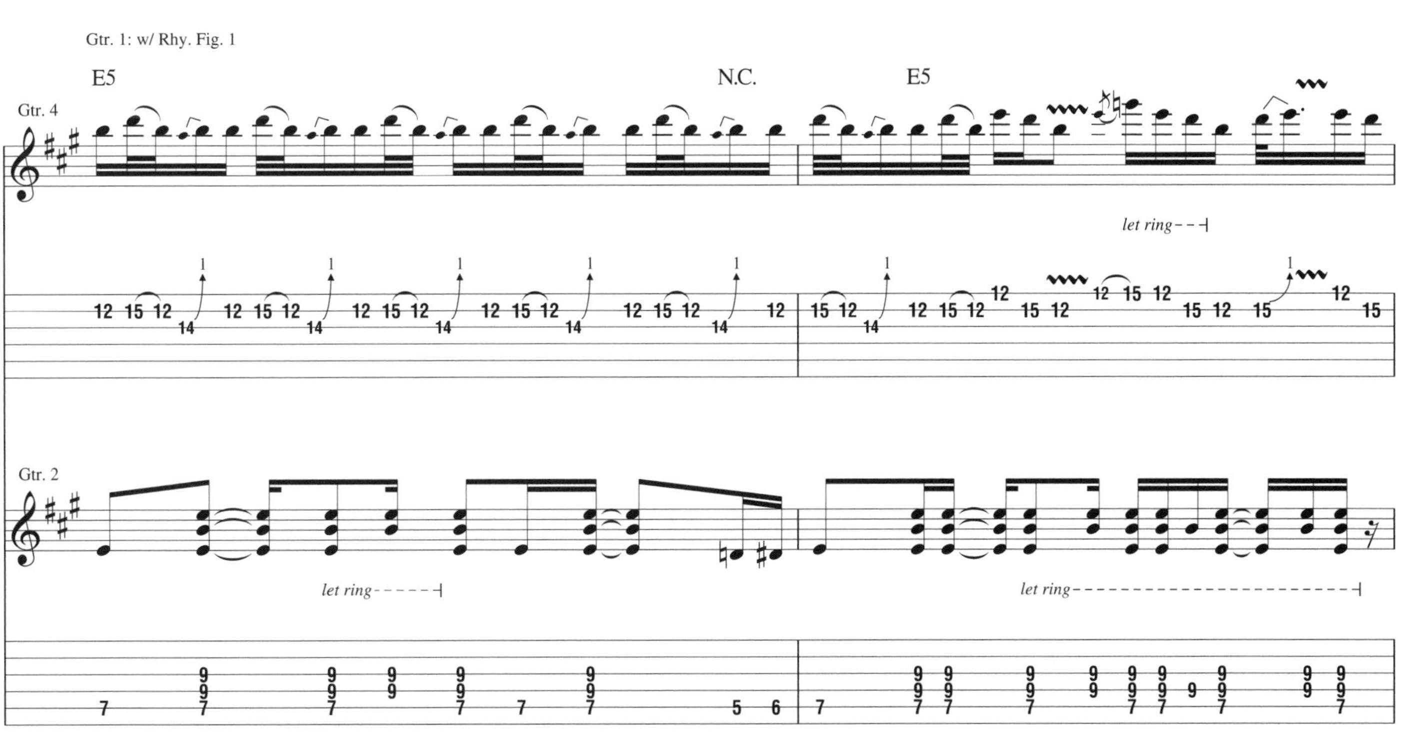

I'm com - in' home,
Gtr. 4
**Gtrs. 1 & 4
Gtr. 1
divisi
let ring
*Gtr. 1 to left of slash in tab.
**Composite arrangement
Gtr. 3
w/ slide
sim.
Gtr. 5
***Angle slide
Gtr. 2
divisi
oh.
A
Yeah.
let ring
P.M.
†Gtr. 2 notated to left of slash.

Interlude
Gtr. 2: w/ Riff A (4 times)
Gtr. 3 tacet
Gtr. 3: w/ Riff B
Gtrs. 4 & 5 tacet
A GD/F♯
A G D/F♯
A G D/F♯
A G D/F♯
Com - in' home,
(Home.)
Gtrs. 1 & 4
Gtr. 1
hold bend
Gtr. 5
Outro
Gtr. 2: w/ Riff A (till fade)
A G D/F♯
A G D/F♯
com - in' home.
(Home.)
Gtr. 3
Riff H
End Riff H
let ring
Gtr. 4
Riff I
End Riff I
Gtr. 1
hold bend

Gtr. 3: w/ Riff H (till fade)
Gtr. 4: w/ Riff I (till fade)
A
G
D/F♯
Com - in' home,
(Home.)
Gtr. 1
Riff J
End Riff J
let ring
1 hold bend
1 1/2
Gtr. 1: w/ Riff J (till fade)
com - in' home.
(Home.)
Home,
com - in'
home,
Gtr. 5
mp
home.
Com- in' home,
com- in' home.
(Here, I'm com - in',
real - ly, real - ly com - in',
sure I'm com - in',
mf

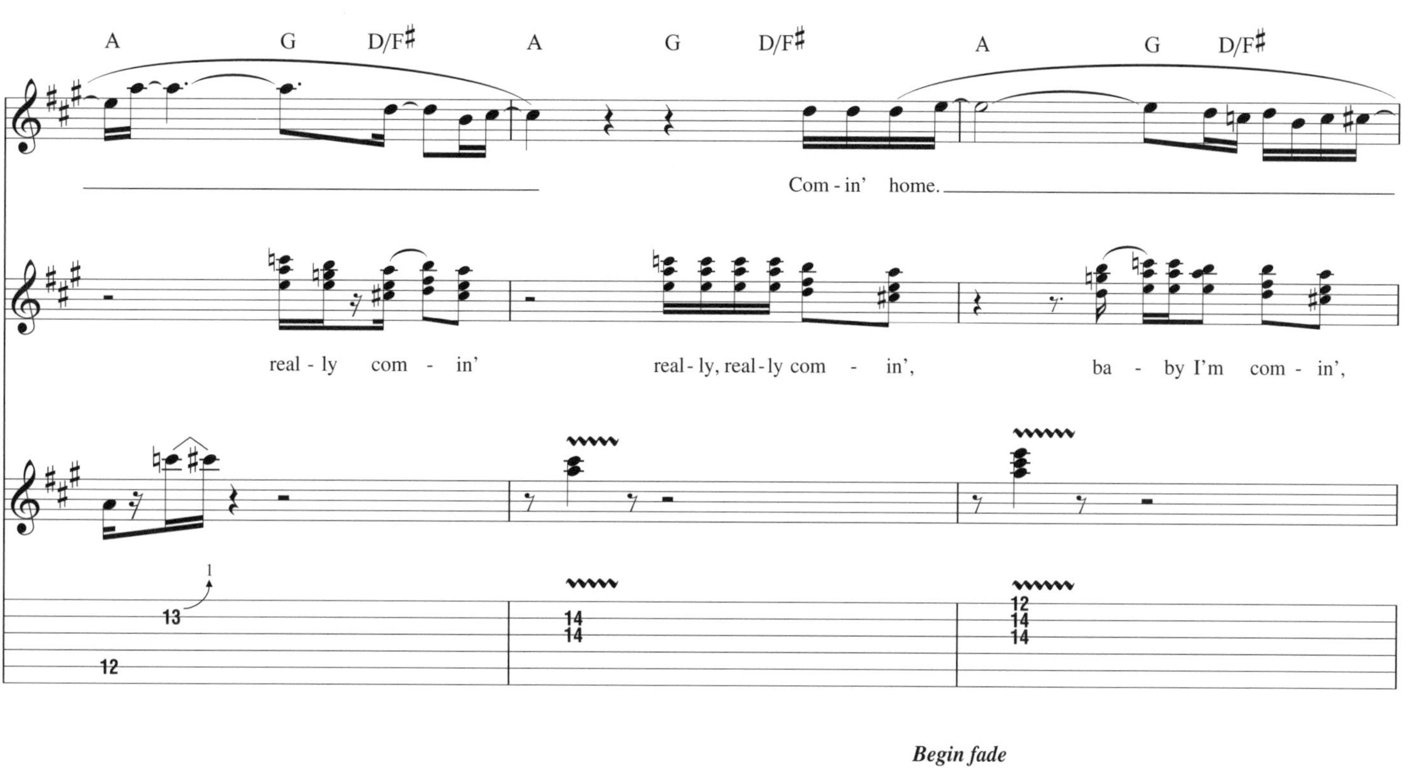
A G D/F♯ A G D/F♯ A G D/F♯
Com - in' home.
real - ly com - in' real - ly, real - ly com - in', ba - by I'm com - in',

Begin fade
A G D/F♯ A G D/F♯ A G D/F♯
Sure, I'm com - in', Sure, I'm com - in', where - ev - er I am, I'm com-
hon - ey I'm com - in', ba - by I'm com - in', real - ly com - in'.)

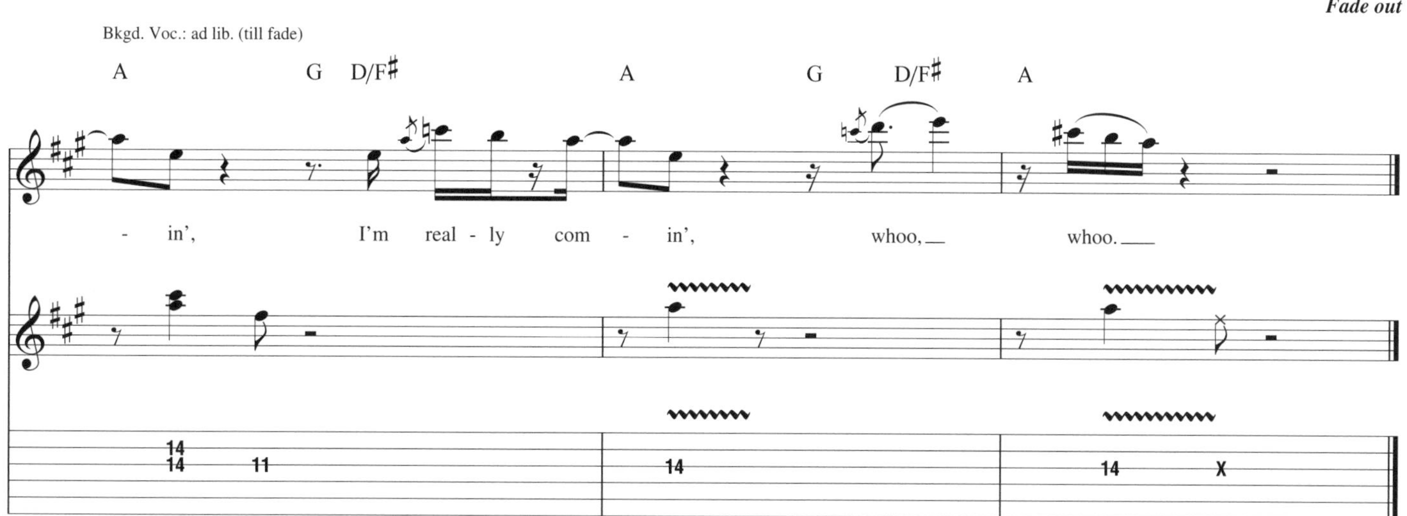
Fade out
Bkgd. Voc.: ad lib. (till fade)
A G D/F♯ A G D/F♯ A
- in', I'm real - ly com - in', whoo, whoo.

from Cream - *Wheels of Fire*

Cross Road Blues
(Crossroads)

Words and Music by Robert Johnson

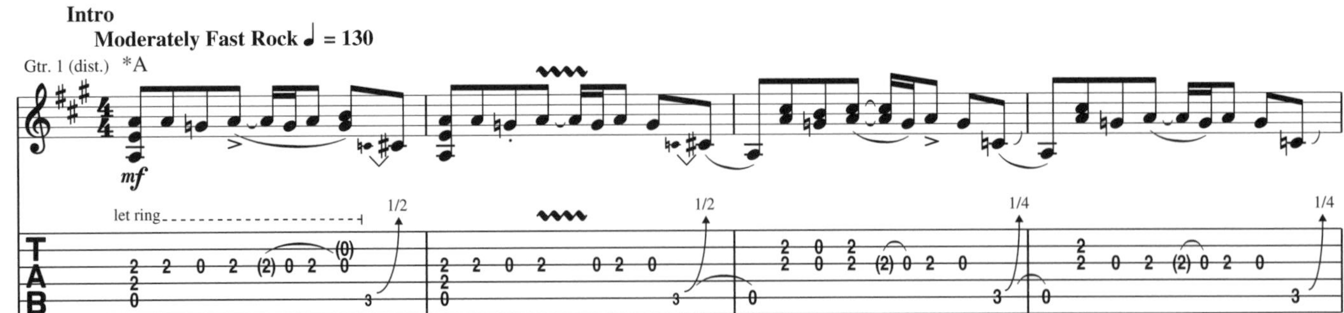

*Chord symbols reflect overall tonality throughout.

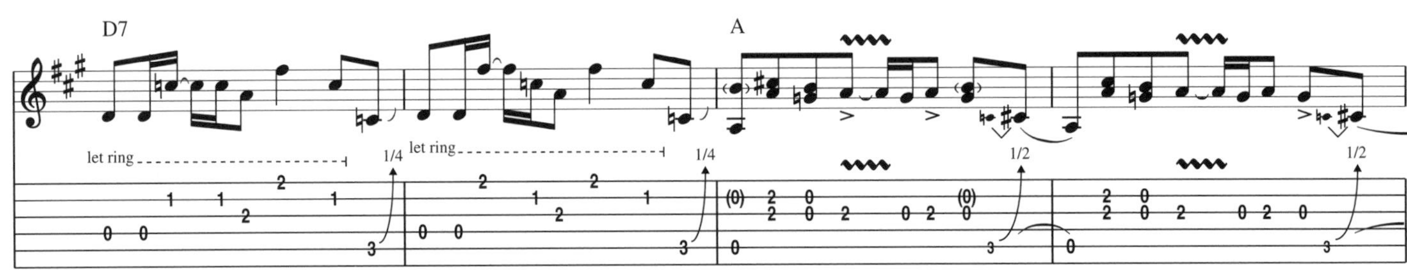

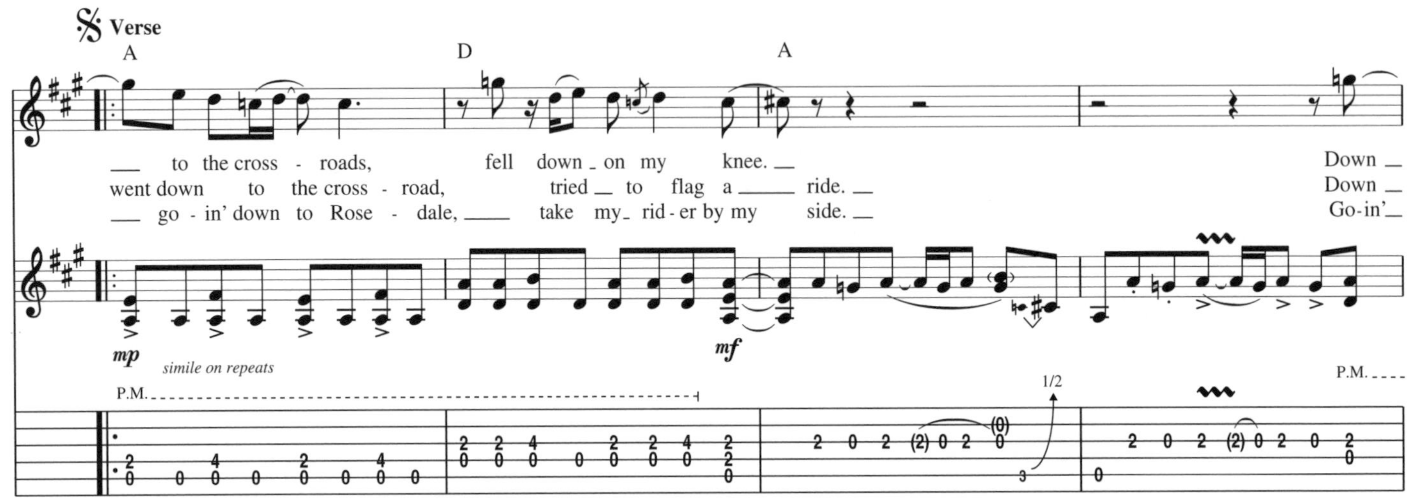

D
A
to the cross - roads fell down on my knee.
to the cross - road, tried to flag a ride.
down to Rose-dale take my rid - er by my side.
No -
We can
P.M.
1/4
E
1., 2.
D/F#
A
Asked the Lord a - bove for mer-cy, "Take me if you please."
bod-y seemed to know me, ev - 'ry-bod - y passed me by.
still bar - rel house ba - by,
2. I
3. Well I'm
P.M.
*T
*T
1/2
*T = Thumb
To Coda
Guitar Solo
3.
D
A
on the riv - er side.
mf
f
P.M.
1/2
full
D
A
D
let ring
full
full
A
E
1/2

D
A
E
A
D
A
E
D
A
D.S. al Coda
(3rd Verse, 3rd ending)
Coda
Guitar Solo
Gtr. 1
ff
let ring
P.M.
8va

8va
loco
E
D
let ring
1/2
full
A
E
A
rake
D
1/4
A
E
D
A
E
A

Outro-Verse

Free Time

from The Yardbirds - *Greatest Hits Volume 1: 1964-1966*

For Your Love

Words and Music by Graham Gouldman

To Coda
Em
G
A
Am
There'll be days I will ex - cite
to make you dream of me at night.
(For your love.
Chorus
Gtr. 1: w/ Rhy. Fig. 1, 3 times, simile
For your
love.
For your
love.
)
Slower ♩ = 132
N.C.
(drums)
Bridge
B
For your love,
for your love,
Gtr. 1
*w/ slight P.M.
*Vocals doubled throughout bridge.
*next 7 meas.
E
I would give the stars a - bove.
For your love,
for your love,

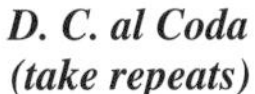
D. C. al Coda
(take repeats)

A
C♯
B
I would give you all I could.

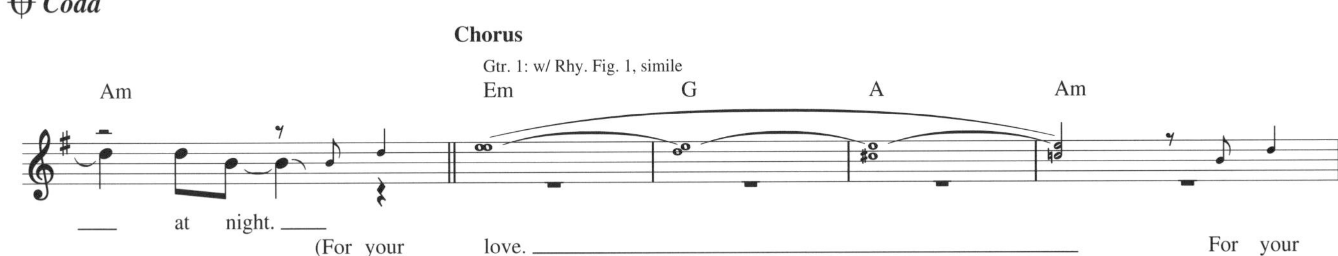
Coda
Chorus
Gtr. 1: w/ Rhy. Fig. 1, simile
Am
Em
G
A
Am
at night.
(For your love.
For your

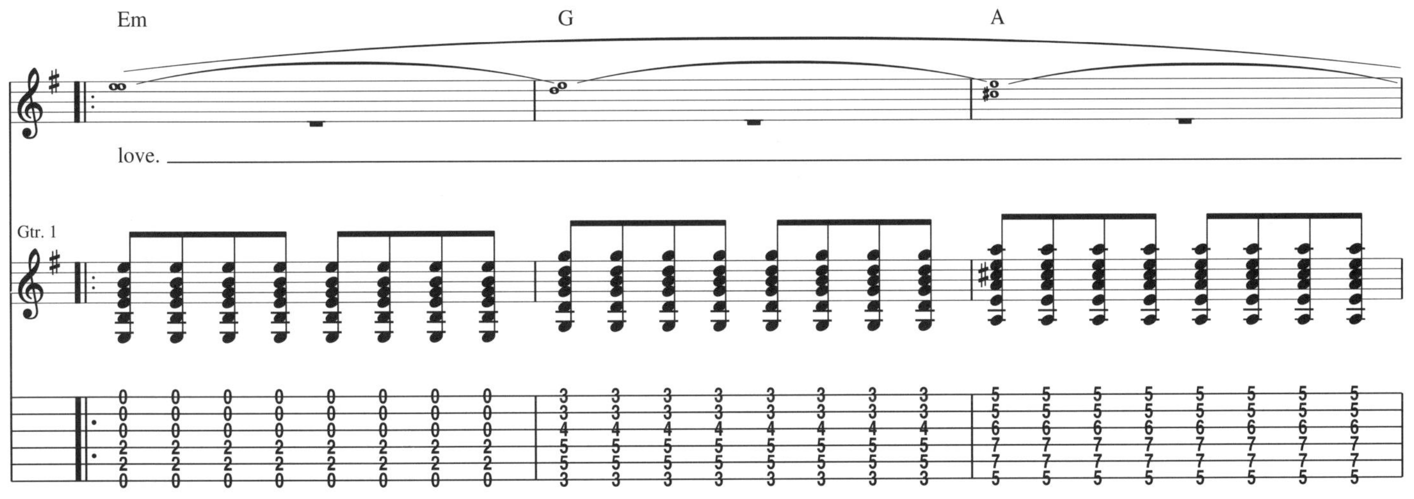
Em
G
A
love.
Gtr. 1

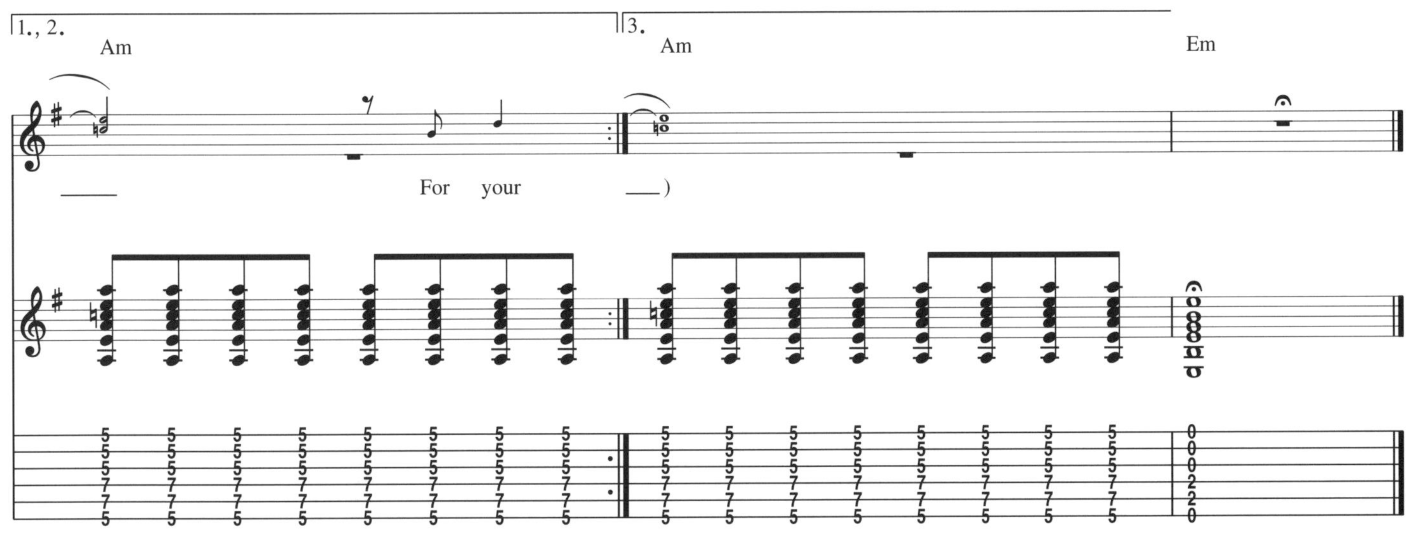
1., 2.
3.
Am
Am
Em
For your
)

from Eric Clapton - *E.C. Was Here*

Have You Ever Loved a Woman

Words and Music by Billy Myles

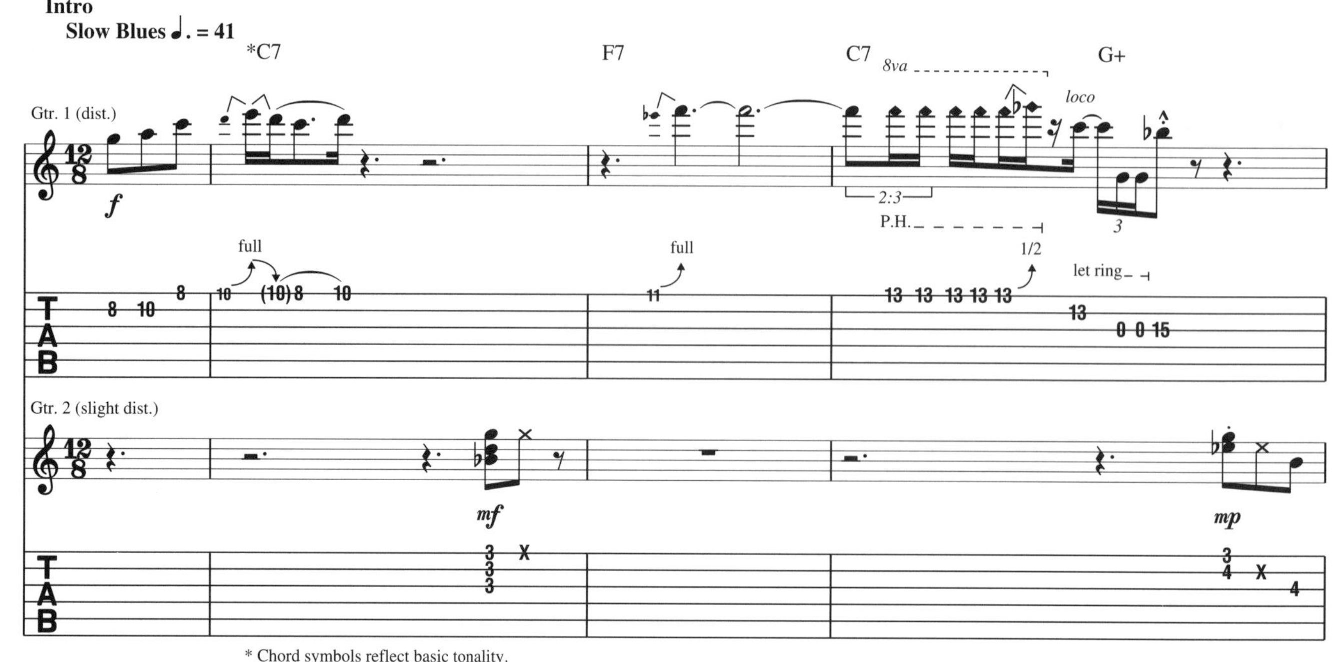

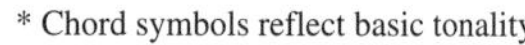

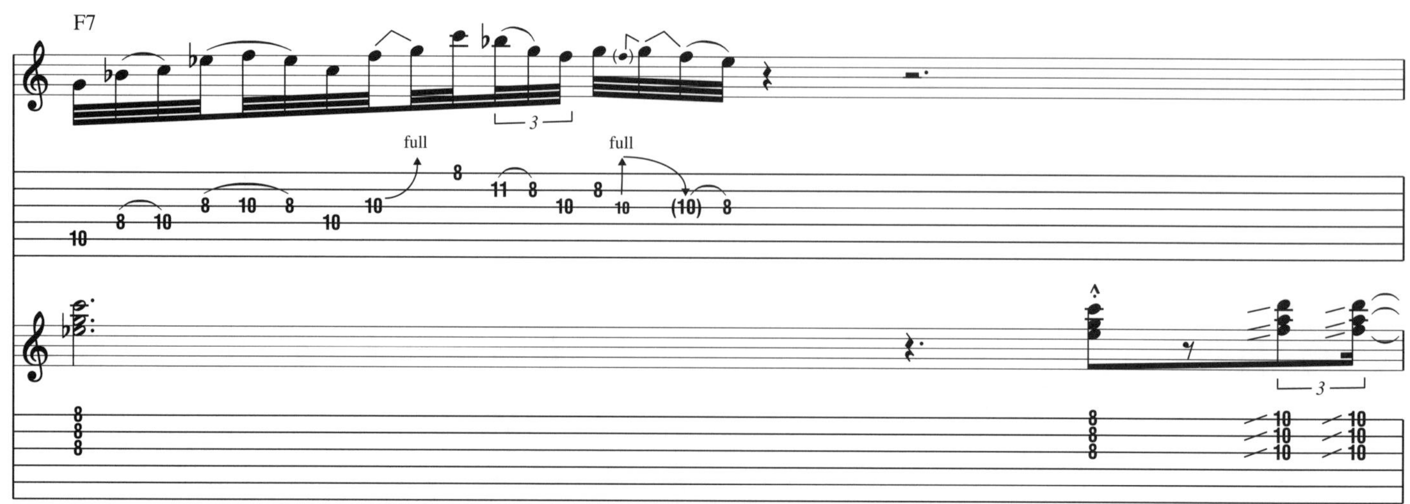

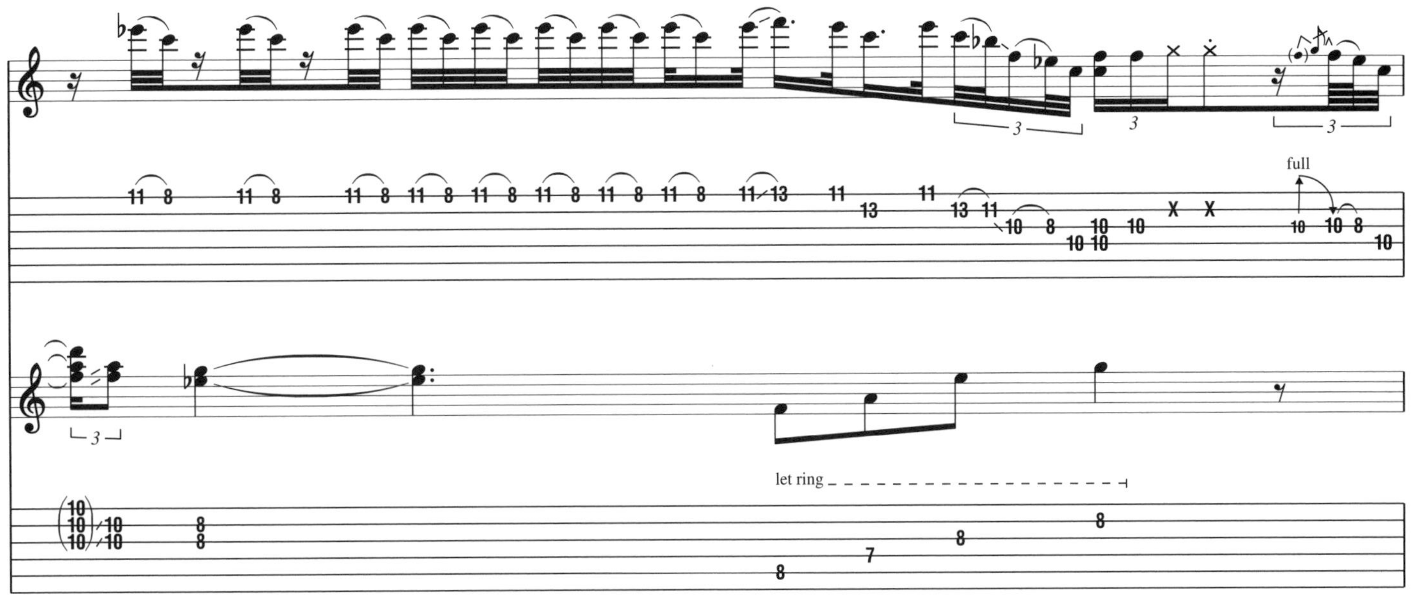
full
let ring

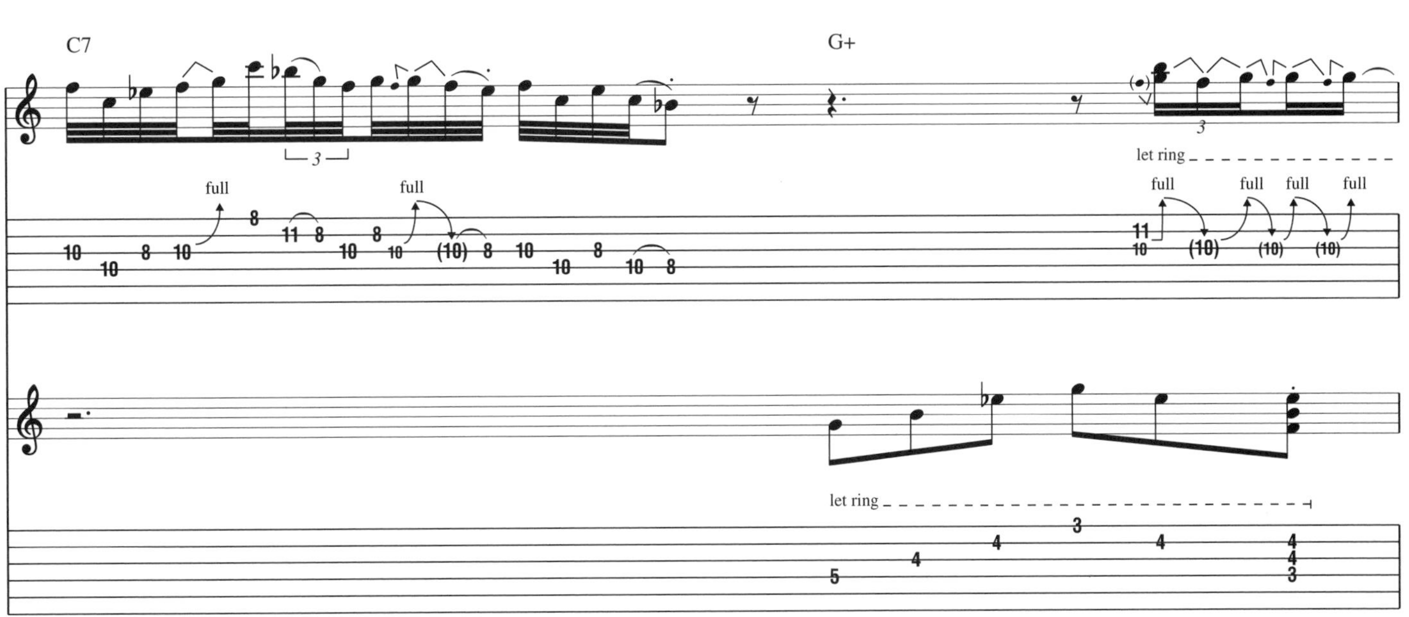
C7
G+
full
let ring

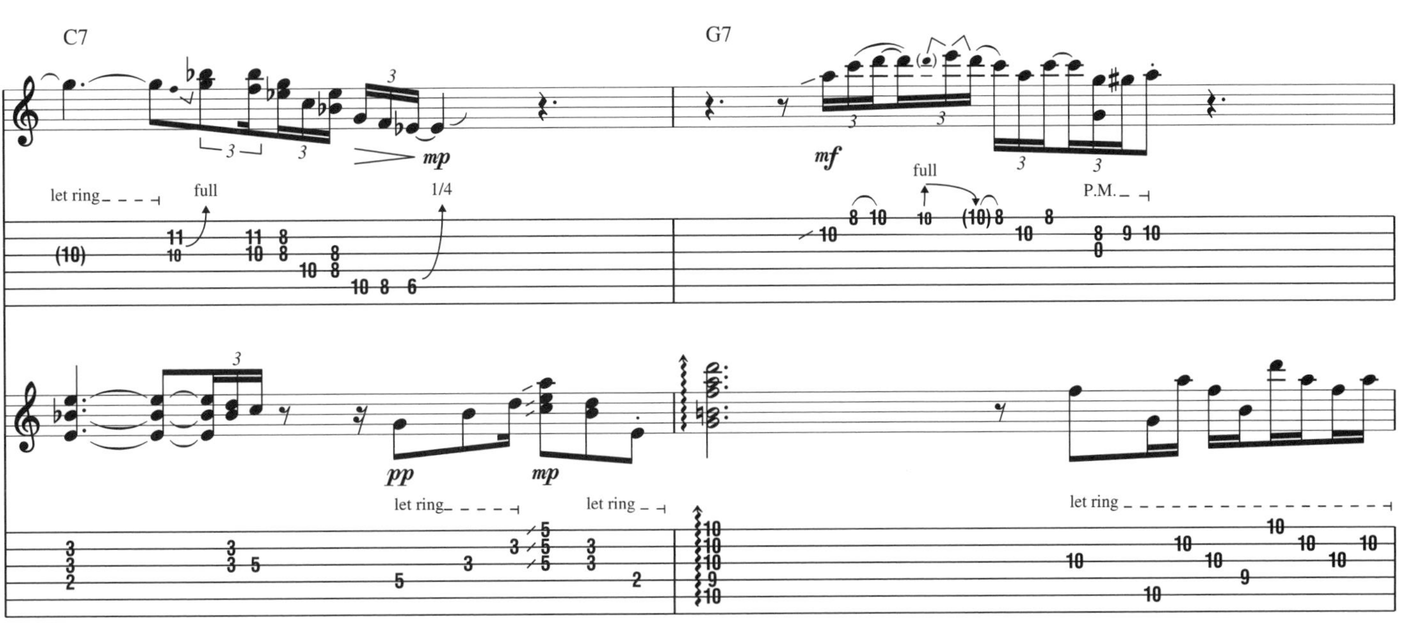
C7
G7
let ring
full
1/4
P.M.
mp
mf
pp

F7
15ma
8va
C7
F7
loco
P.H.
full
full
1 1/2
let ring
let ring
C7
G+
Verse
C7
1. Have you ev-er loved a wo-man
full
let ring
let ring
let ring
F7
C7
G+
so much, uh, that you trem-ble in pain?
full
let ring
let ring
let ring
let ring

C7
full
full
full
p
let ring
F7
Have you ev - er loved a
full
full
full
let ring
let ring
wo-man
C7
G+
so much
you trem-ble in pain?
mf
p
let ring
mf
p
mp
* vol. swell

C7 G7 F7

And all the time you know, uh,

ff *mf* *ff*

* vol. swell

C7 F7 C7 G7

oh, she still has an-oth-er man's name.

mp *ff* *f* *mf*

full full

Verse
C7
2. But you just,
wo-man,
ff
full
full
mp
F7
C7
G+
so much it's a shame
f
pp
p
C7
F7
and a sin.
You just...
p
mp
ff
f
mp
ff
full
full
full
full
full
mf
pp
p
let ring
P.M.

full
1/2
full
full
full
full
full
mf
P.M.
C7
G+
C7
so much
it's a shame _ and a sin.
mp
f
1/4
1/4
P.M.
P.M.
G7
F7
When all the time you know
she be-longs to...
mf
pp
p
P.M.
P.M.
P.M.
let ring
string noise

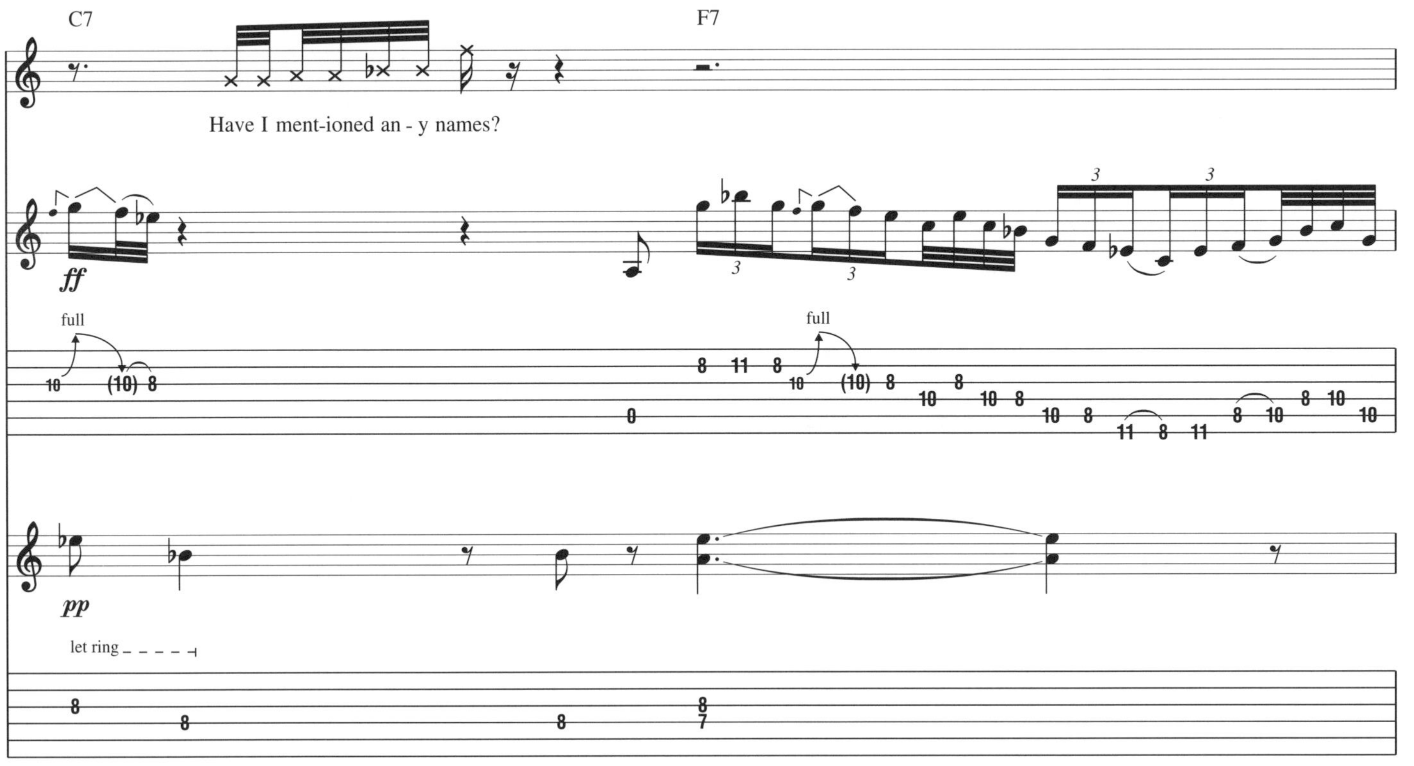
C7
F7
Have I ment-ioned an - y names?
ff
full
pp
let ring

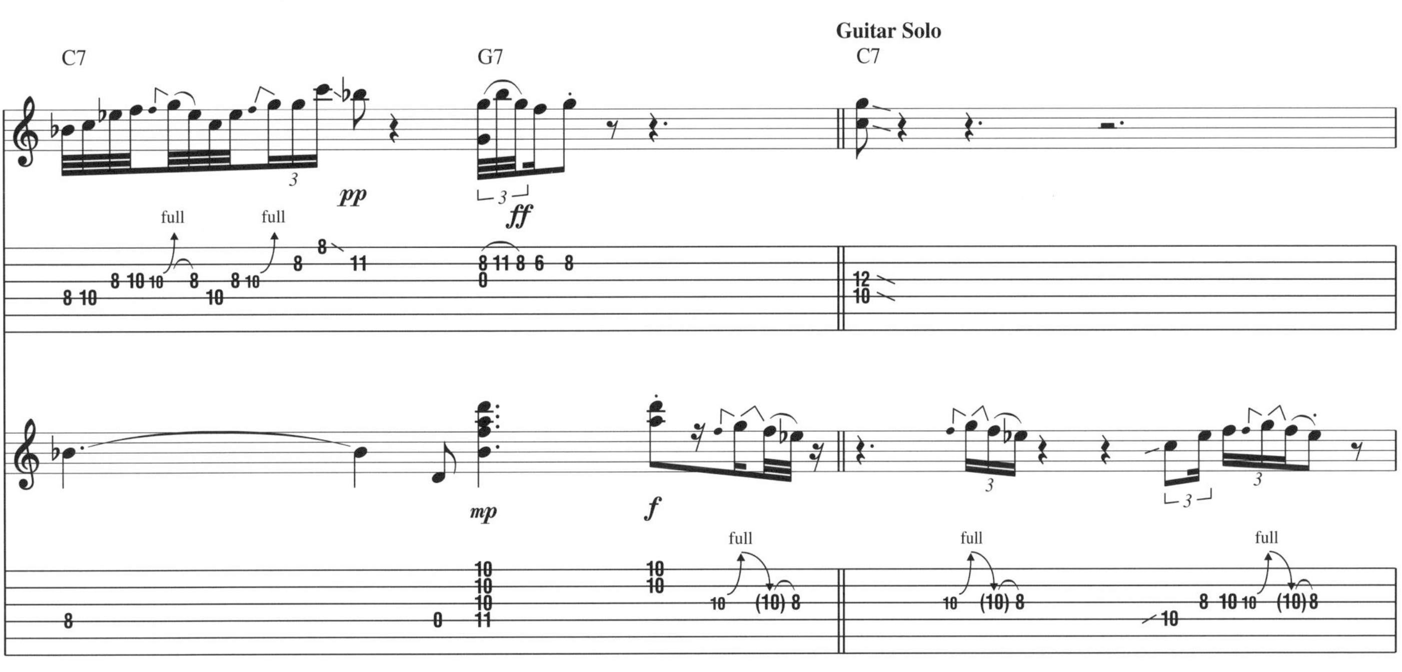
Guitar Solo
C7
G7
C7
pp
ff
full
mp
f

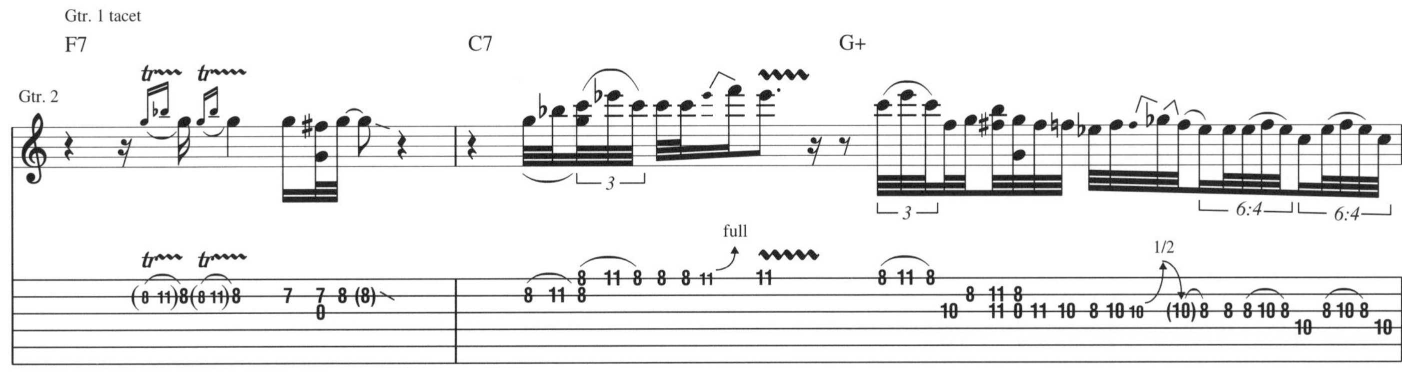
Gtr. 1 tacet
F7
C7
G+
Gtr. 2
full
1/2

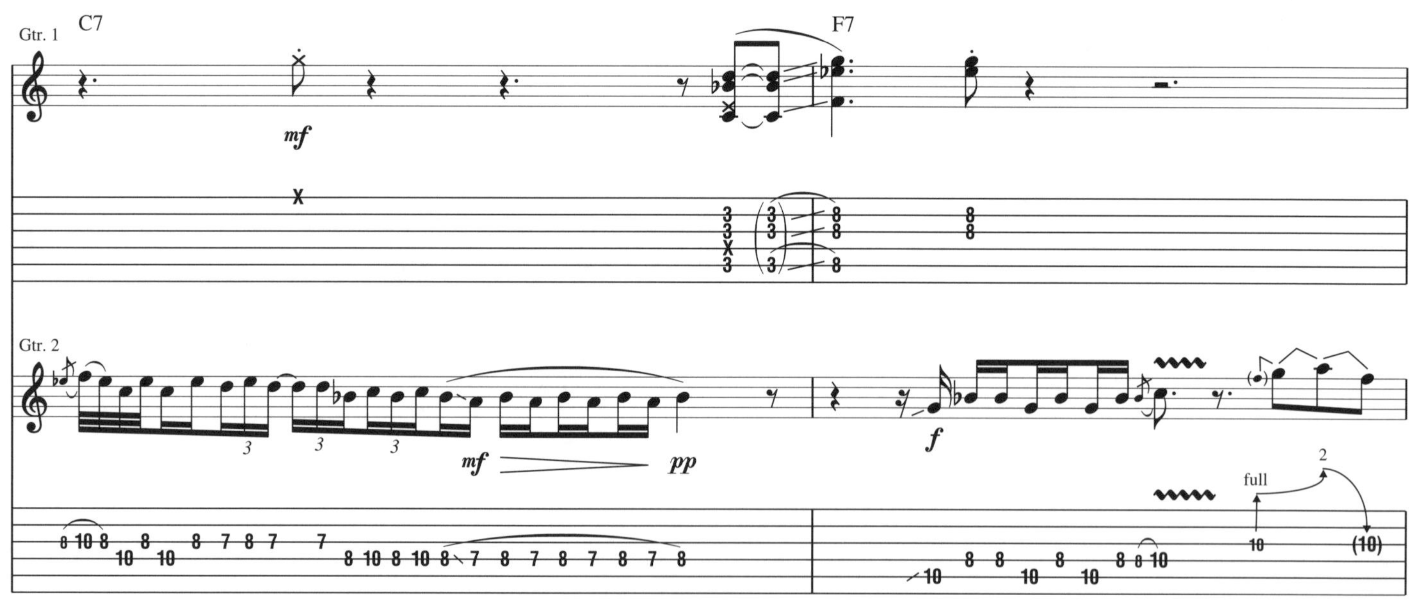
Gtr. 1
C7
F7
mf
Gtr. 2
mf
pp
f
full
2

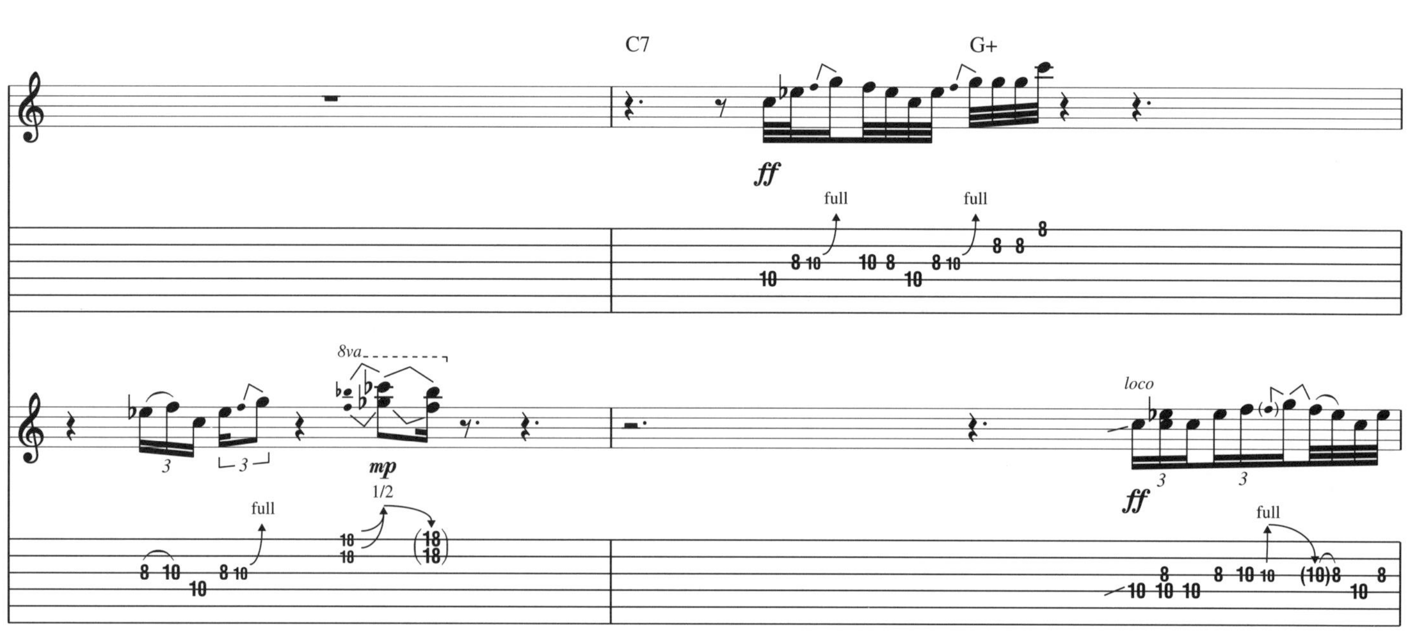
C7
G+
ff
full
full
8va
mp
1/2
loco
ff

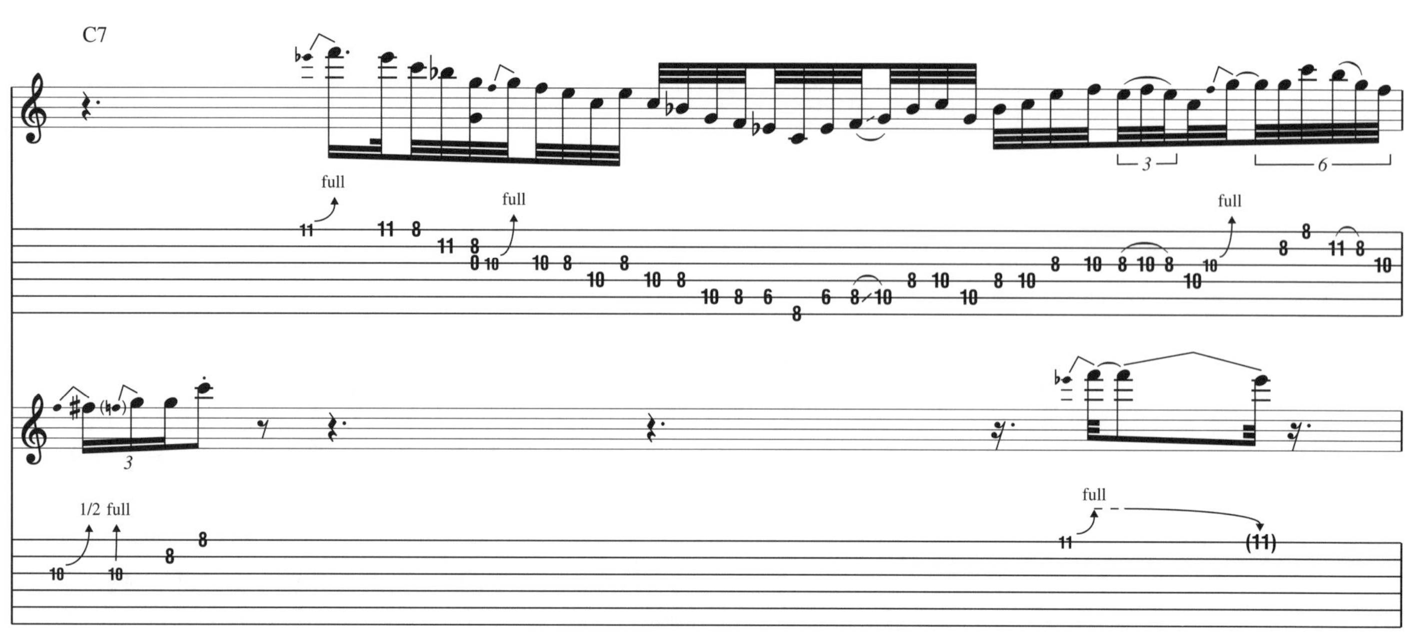
C7
full
full
full
1/2 full
full

G7
F7
8va
mp
mf
f
3:2
1/2
full
1 1/2
C7
F7
tr
C7
loco
G+
ff
let ring

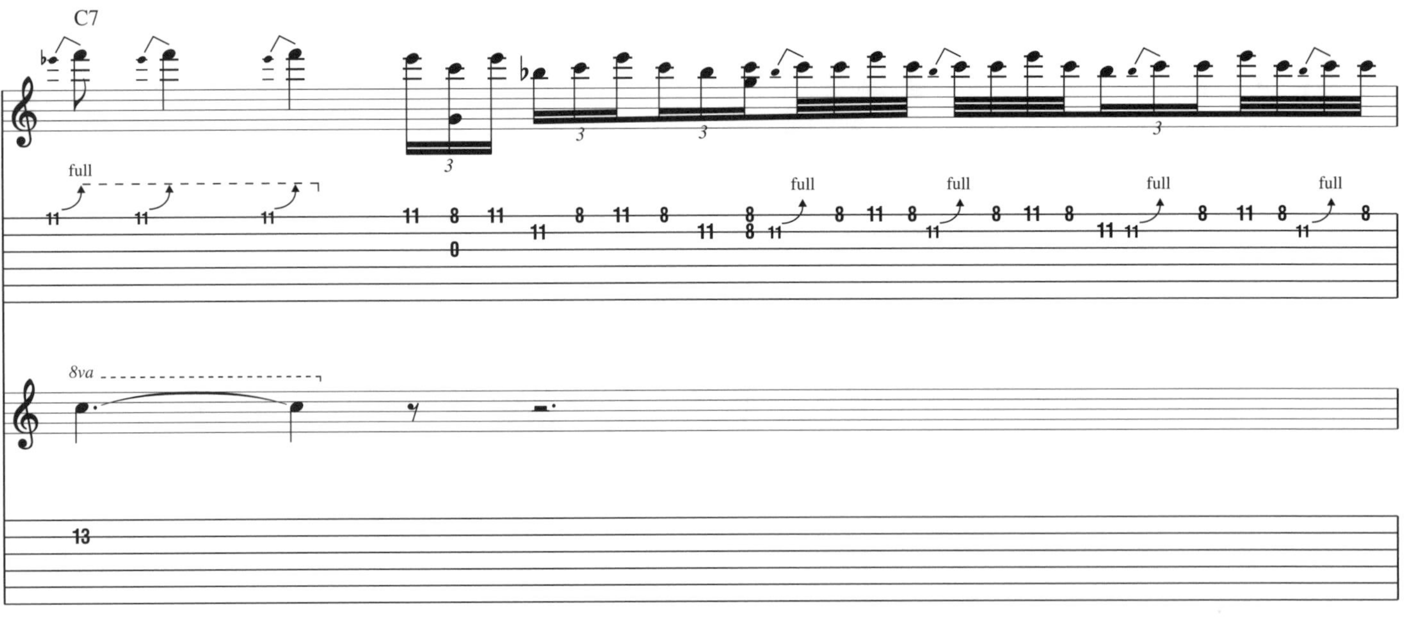
C7
full
full
full
full
full
8va

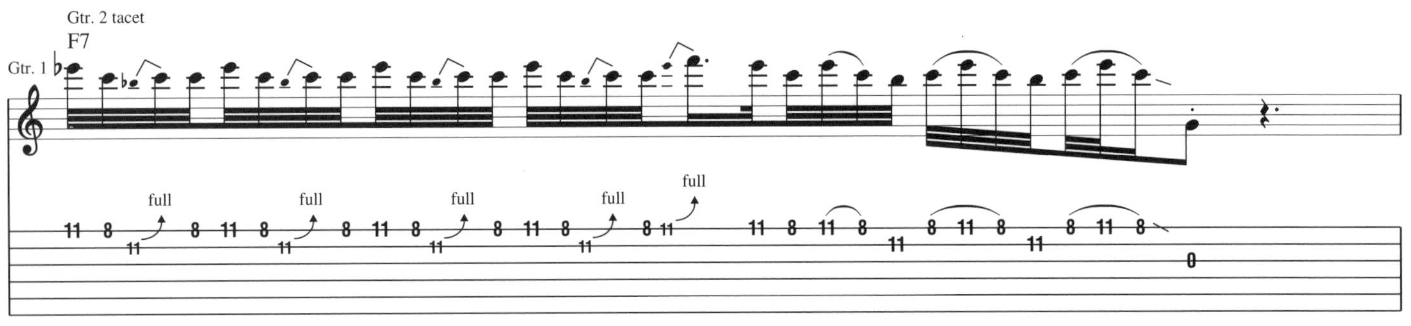
Gtr. 2 tacet
F7
Gtr. 1
full
full
full
full
full

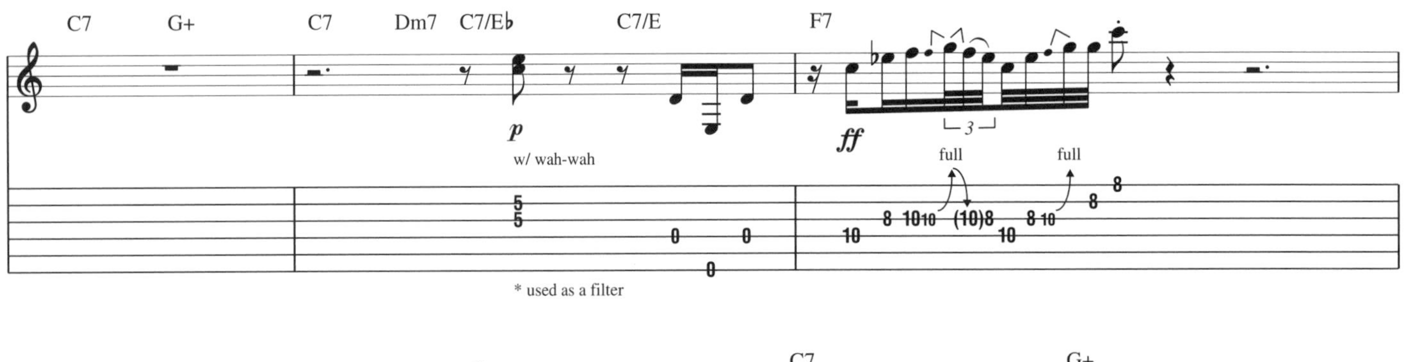
C7
G+
C7
Dm7
C7/E♭
C7/E
F7
p
w/ wah-wah
ff
full
full
* used as a filter

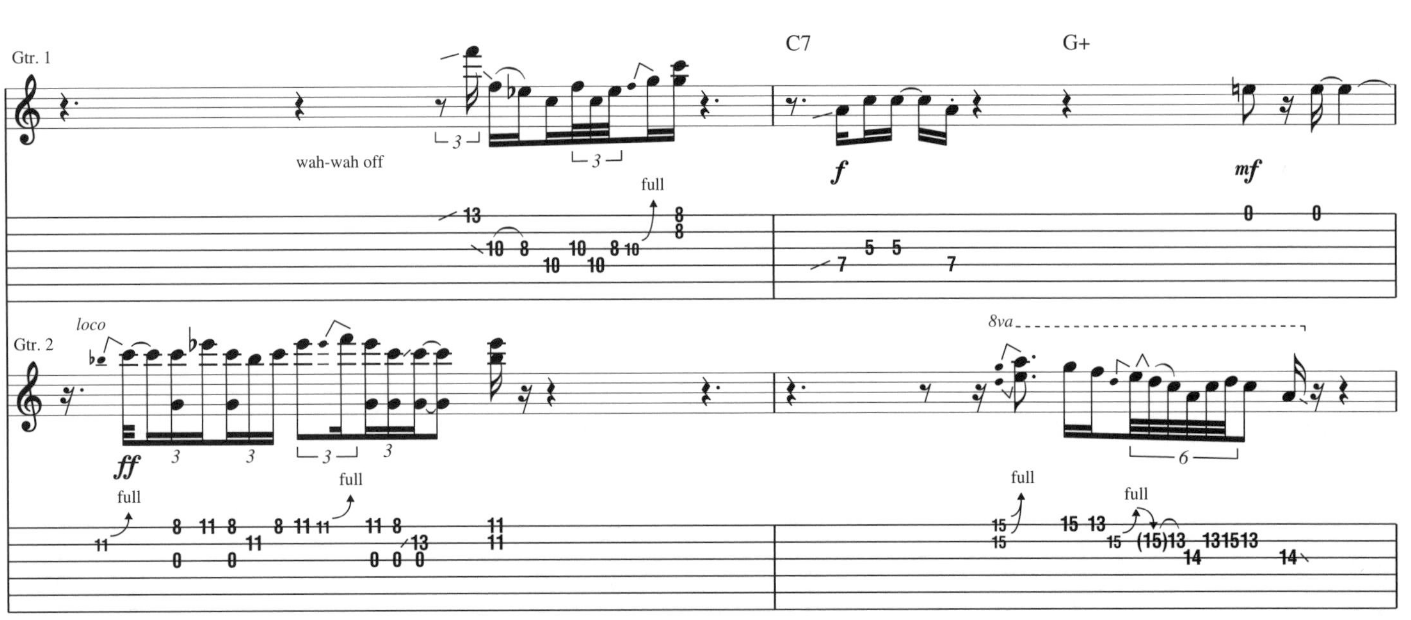
Gtr. 1
wah-wah off
full
C7
G+
f
mf
Gtr. 2
loco
ff
full
full
8va
full
full

C7
G7
F7
C7
F7
Fm
loco
8va
full

C7
G+
ff
full
full
Verse
C7
F7
C7
G+
George Ter-ry please.
So much,
and you know you can't leave her a-lone.
mf
ff
full
pp
mf
mp
C7
F7
'Cause you just _ love _ that wo-man
mf
ff
string noise
mf
mp
1/4
let ring
5:3
p
let ring

C7
G+
and you know you can't leave her a - lone.
mf
f
full
fdbk.
let ring
C7
let ring
let ring
G7
F7
N.C.
But some-thing deep in - side
won't let you wreck your best
string noise
pp
mp
p
let ring

Free Time
C7
G7
on cue:
C7
friends. Oh, oh, oh, oh.
pp
f
* Strings ring from releasing left hand.
13:12
let ring
mf
< ff
fdbk.
pitch: F
Gtr. 2 tacet
string noise
p
mf
rit.
mp
let ring
full

from Eric Clapton - *No Reason to Cry*

Hello Old Friend

Words and Music by Eric Clapton

Verse

Gtrs. 3 & 4: w/ Fill 1, 2nd time
Gtrs. 3 & 4: w/ Fill 5, 3rd time

G D C Em G

Rhy. Fig. 2 End Rhy. Fig. 2

Gtr. 1

I am stroll - ing down _ the gar - den path, _ I
saw you walk - ing un - der - neath _ the stars. _ I
old man passed _ me on ___ the street _ to - day. _ I

Gtr. 2
Riff C End Riff C

Gtr. 3

full full

Gtr. 4

full

Fill 1
Gtr. 3

8va

T
A
B

Gtr. 4

T
A
B

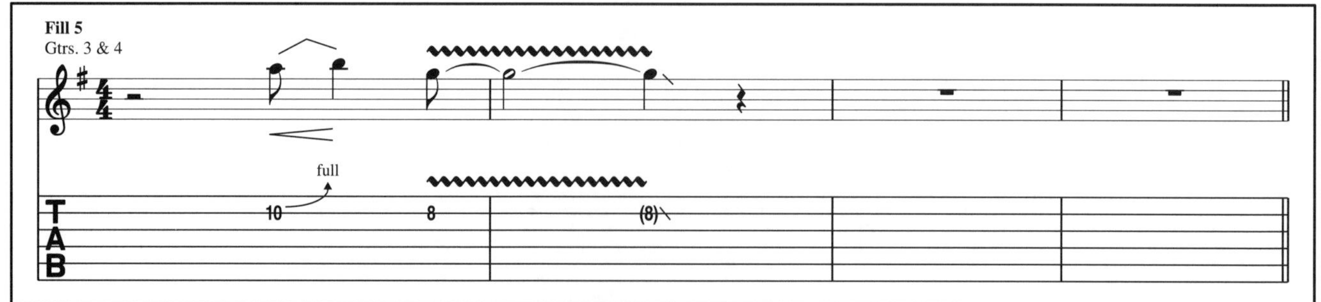

Gtr. 1: w/ Rhy. Fig. 2, 2 3/4 times, simile
Gtr. 2: w/ Riff C, 2 3/4 times, simile
Gtrs. 3 & 4: w/ Fill 2, 2nd time
Gtrs. 3 & 4: w/ Fill 6, 3rd time
G D C Em G
saw a flow - er glow - ing in the dark. It
could - n't stop 'cause I was in a car. I'm
thought I knew him, but I could - n't say. I
Gtr. 3
Gtr. 4
Fill 2
Gtr. 3
full
full
Gtr. 4
Fill 6
Gtr. 3
full
full
Gtr. 4
full
full
full

Gtr. 4 tacet, 2nd & 3rd times
Gtr. 3: w/ Fill 3, 2nd time
Gtr. 3: w/ Fill 7, 3rd time
G D C Em G
looked so pret - ty and it was u - nique. I
sure the dis - tance would - n't be too far if
stopped to think if I could place his frame, but
Gtr. 3
Gtr. 4
divisi
Gtrs. 3 & 4: w/ Fill 4, 2nd time (see next page)
Gtrs. 3 & 4: w/ Fill 8, 3rd time (see next page)
G D C Em G G
Gtrs. 1 & 2
(Gtr. 2 cont. in notation)
had to bend down just to have a peek.
I got out and walked to where you are.
when he tipped his hat I knew his name.
Hel - lo old friend,
Gtr. 3
Gtr. 4
Fill 3
Gtr. 3
Fill 7
Gtr. 3
8va
1 1/2
full

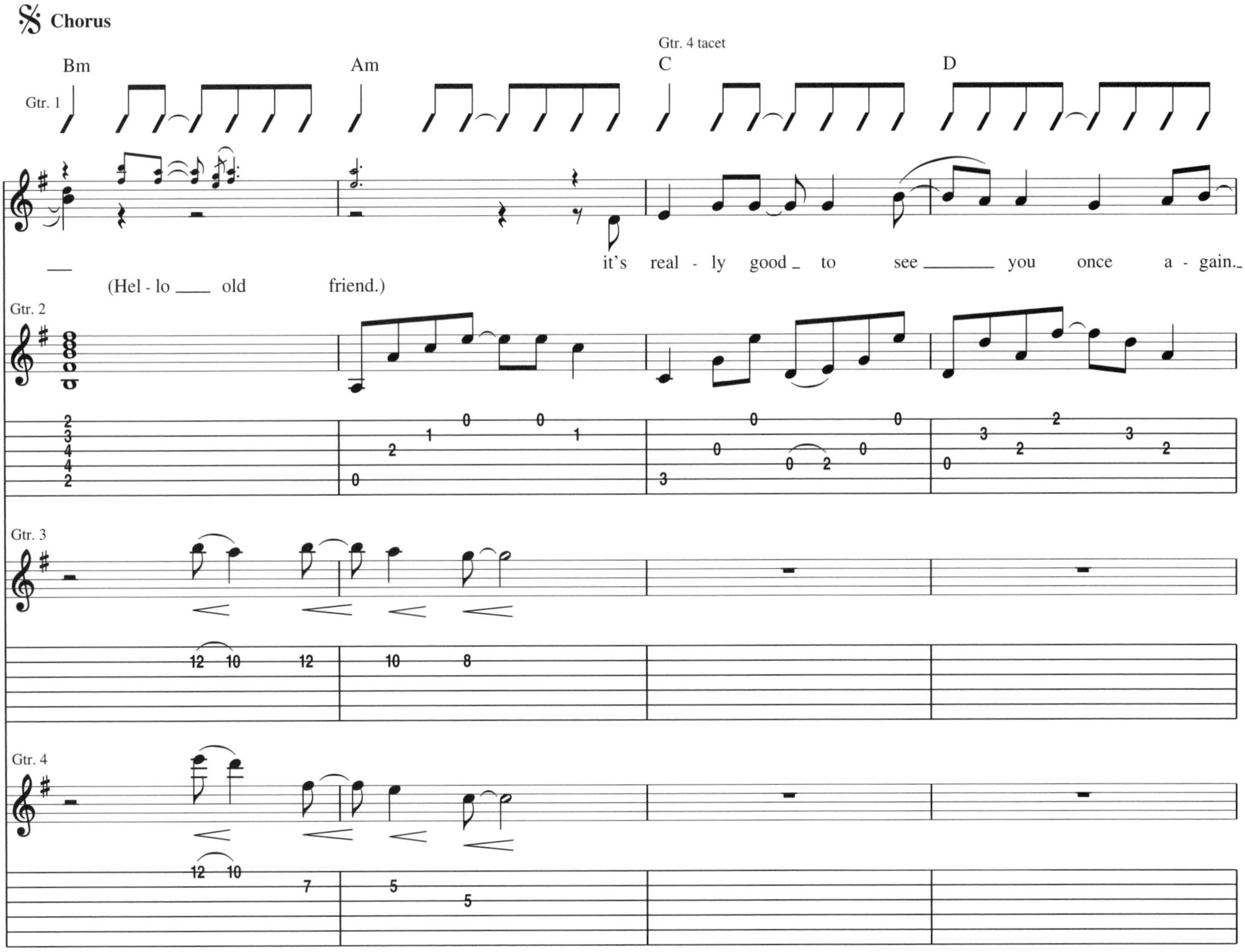

𝄋 Chorus

Gtr. 4 tacet

Bm Am C D

Gtr. 1

— it's real - ly good _ to see ______ you once a - gain._

(Hel - lo ____ old friend.)

Gtr. 2

Gtr. 3

Gtr. 4

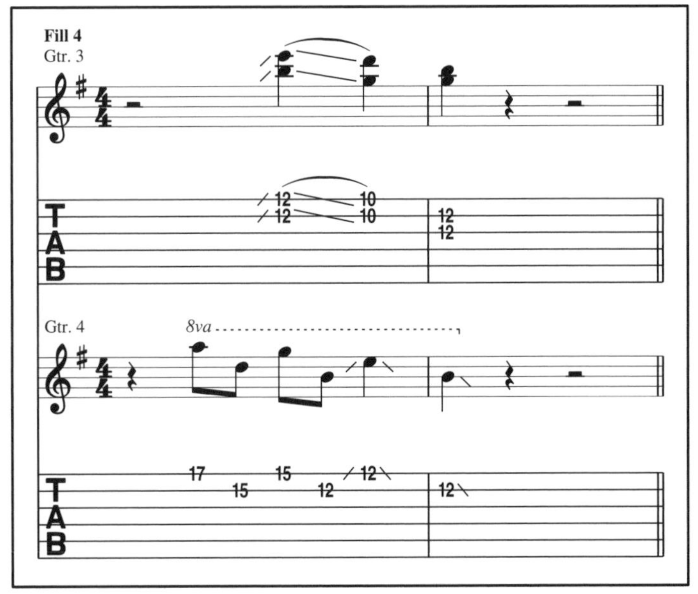

To Coda

Gtr. 3: w/ Fill 10, 4th time
Gtr. 3: w/ Fill 9, 3rd time
Gtr. 4: w/ Fill 9, 4th time
Em
Bm
Am
C
Hel-lo old friend, it's real - ly good to see you once a - gain.
(Hel - lo old friend, see you once a - gain.
Gtr. 2
Gtr. 3

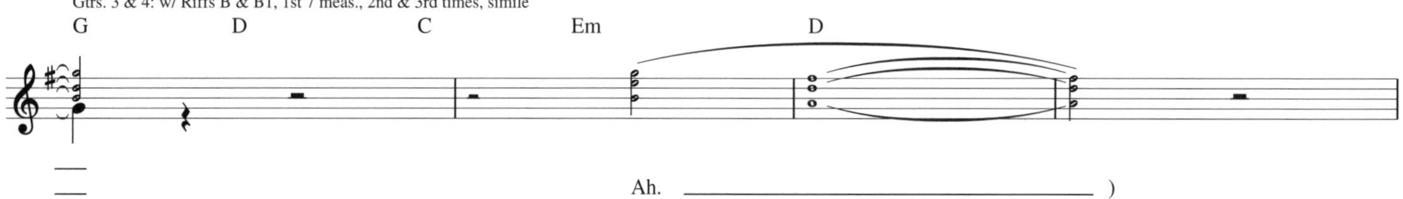
Gtr. 1: w/ Rhy. Fig. 1, 2 times, simile
Gtr. 2: w/ Riff A, 2 times, simile
Gtrs. 3 & 4: w/ Riffs B & B1, 1st time, simile
Gtrs. 3 & 4: w/ Riffs B & B1, 1st 7 meas., 2nd & 3rd times, simile
G
D
C
Em
D
Ah.)

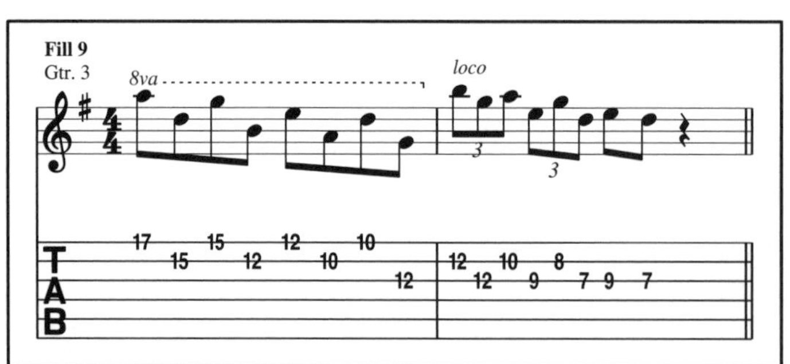
Fill 9
Gtr. 3
8va
loco

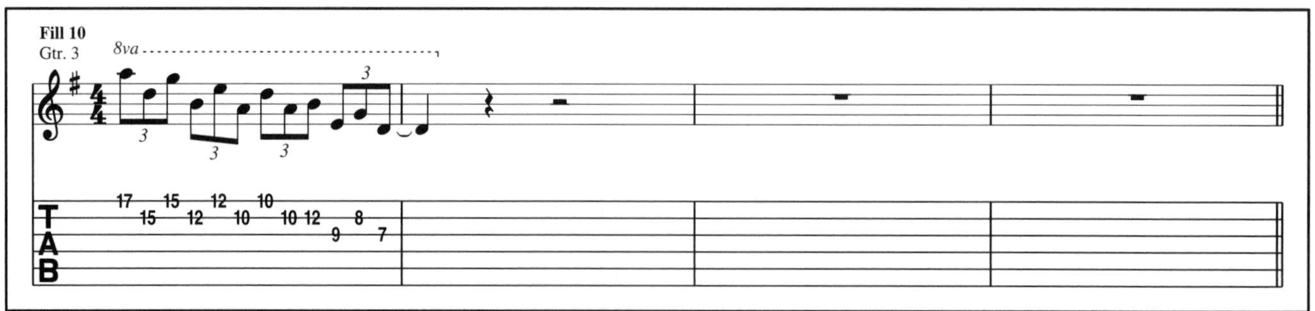
Fill 10
Gtr. 3
8va

G
D
C
Em
D
1.
2. I
2.
Guitar Solo
Gtr. 1: w/ Rhy. Fig. 1, 1 3/4 times, simile
Gtr. 2: w/ Riff A, 1 3/4 times, simile
Gtr. 3
Gtr. 4
8va
full
1 1/2
loco
Gtrs. 1 & 2
3. An

3.
Guitar Solo
Gtr. 1: w/ Rhy. Fig. 1, 2 times, simile
Gtr. 2: w/ Riff A, 2 times, simile
D G D C Em D
Gtr. 3
1 1/2
full
full
full
1/2
Gtr. 4
full
full
Gtr. 4 tacet
D.S. al Coda
G D C Em D
Hel-lo, old friend.
Gtr. 3
1 1/2
let ring
Coda
Outro
Gtr. 1: w/ Rhy. Fig. 1, 3 1/2 times, simile
Gtr. 2: w/ Riff A, 3 1/2 times, simile
Gtrs. 3 & 4: w/ Riffs B & B1, 1st 4 meas. only, simile
C G D C Em D
Gtr. 1
you
once a - gain.
Gtr. 2

G D C Em D
Gtr. 3
8va
1 1/2
Gtr. 4
loco
full
11/2
Gtrs. 1 & 2
rit.

from John Mayall's Bluesbreakers - *Bluesbreakers With Eric Clapton*

Hide Away

By Freddie King and Sonny Thompson

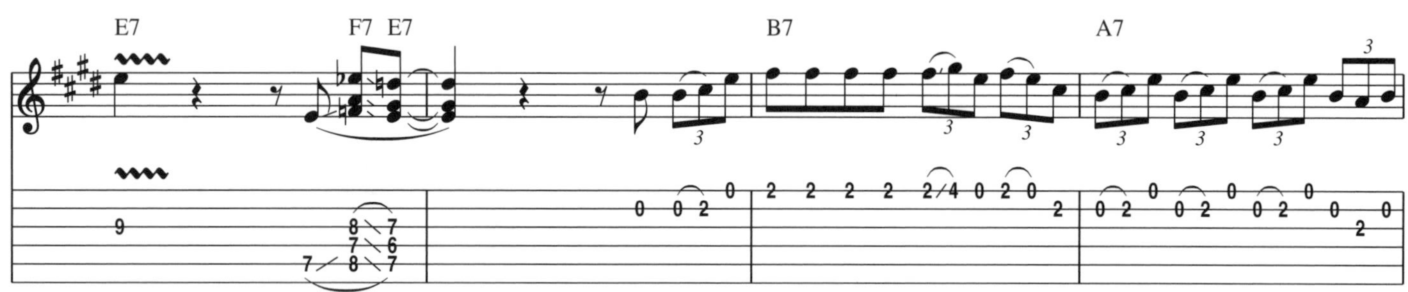

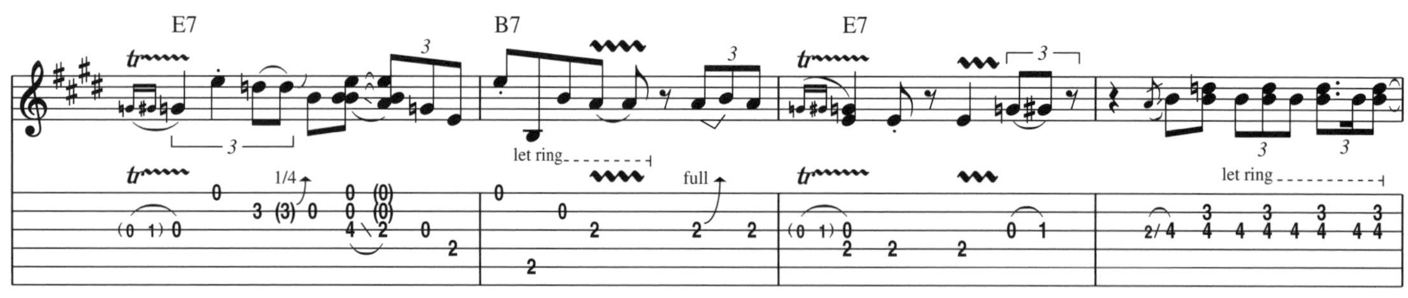

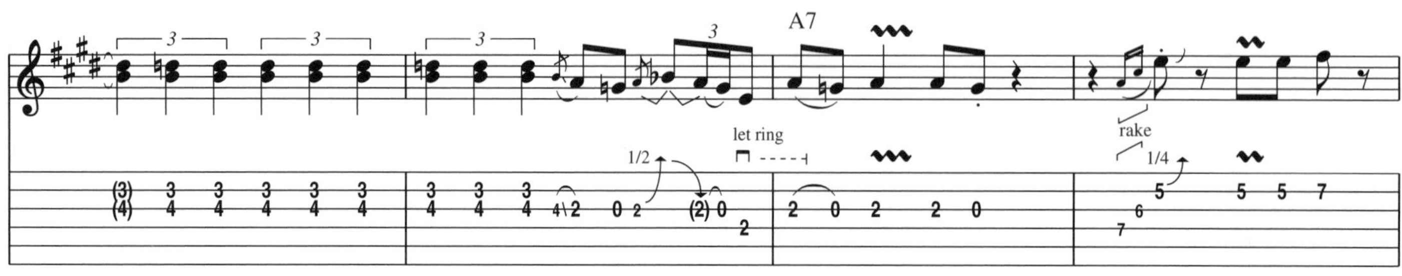

E7
B7
1/2
full
let ring
A7
E7
B7
let ring
even gliss.
B
E7
semi-P.M.
A7
E7
semi-P.M.
B7
E7
semi-P.M.
C
E7
even
full
1/2
1/4
even bends
1/2
full
1/2 full
1/4

A7
E7
even bend
1/2
full

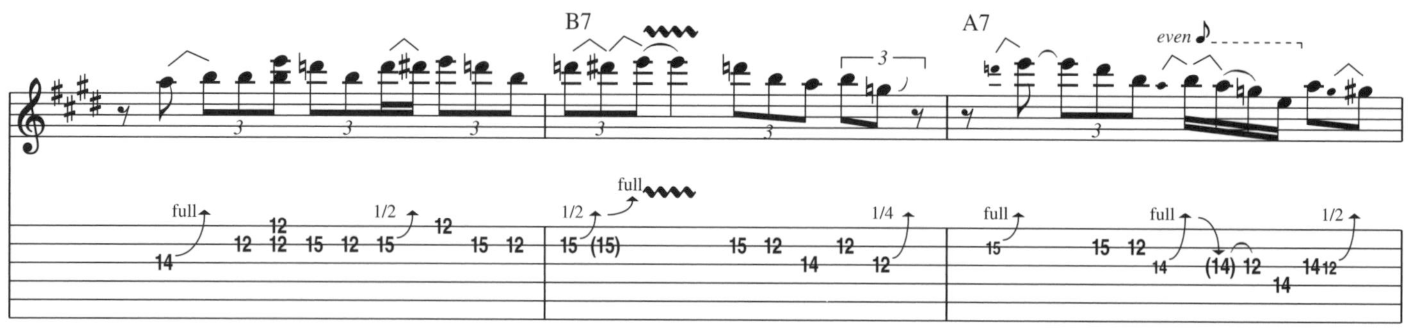
B7
A7
even
full
1/2
1/4

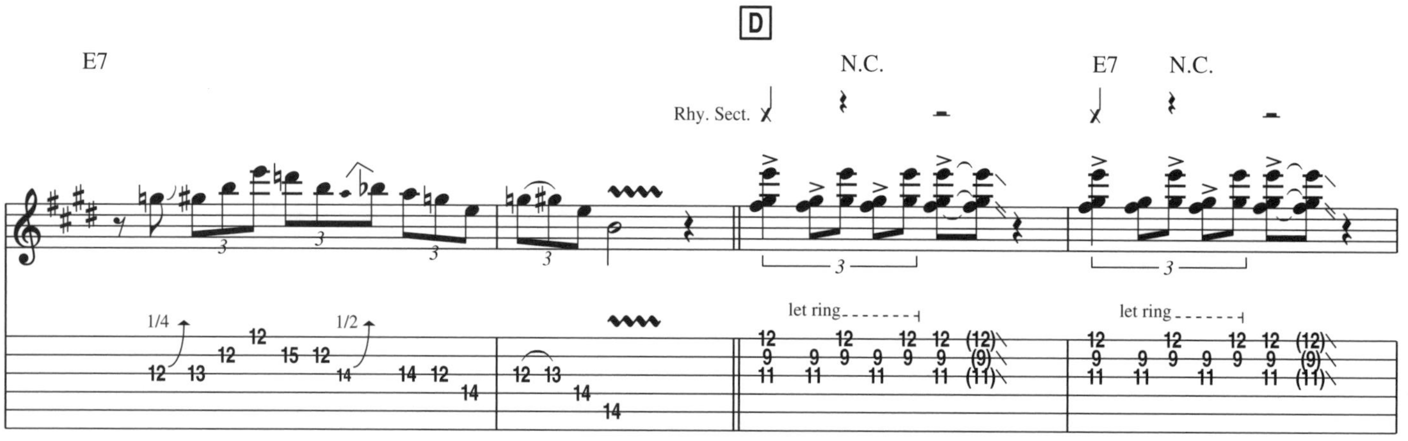
D
E7
N.C.
Rhy. Sect.
let ring
1/4
1/2

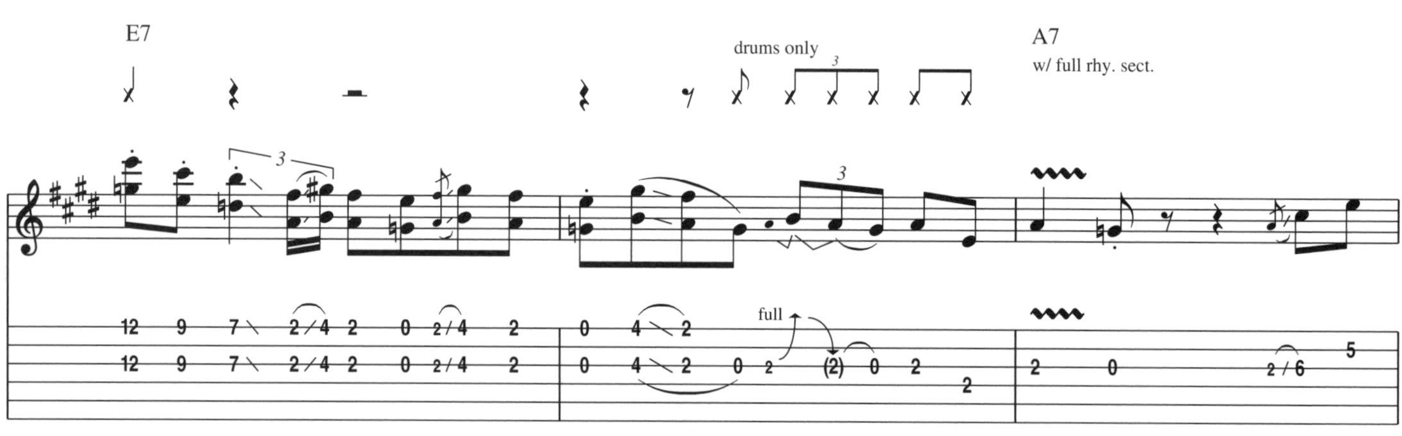
E7
drums only
A7
w/ full rhy. sect.
full

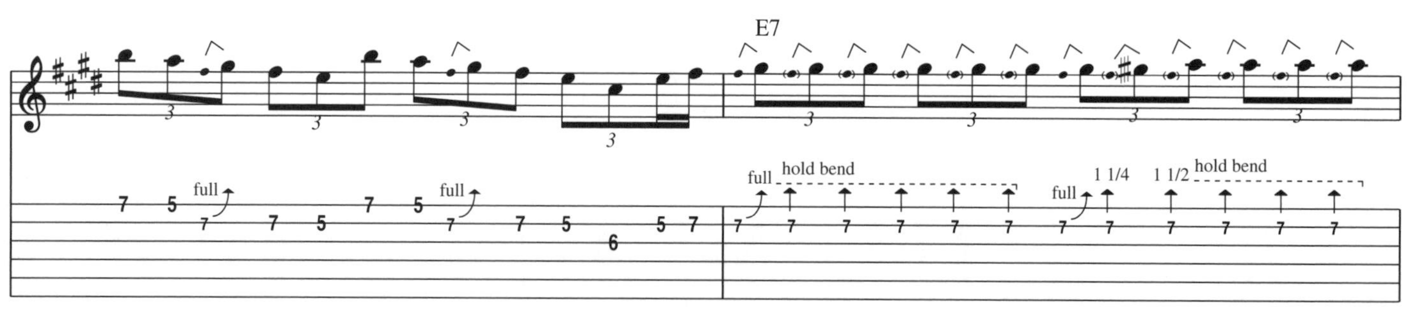
E7
full
hold bend
1 1/4
1 1/2

B7
A7
hold bend
full
1/2
1/4
even bend
E7
E
Even 8th's
even gliss.
semi-P.M.
resume swing feel
F
semi-Harm.
even bend
even

A7
E7
even
8va
B7
A7
8va
even
loco
A7
E7
B7
even bend
full
rake

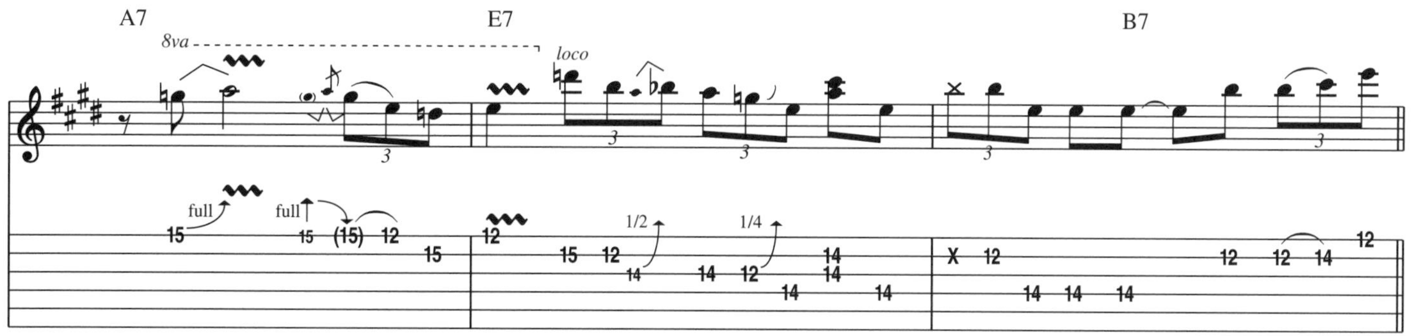
A7
8va
E7
loco
B7
full
full
1/2
1/4

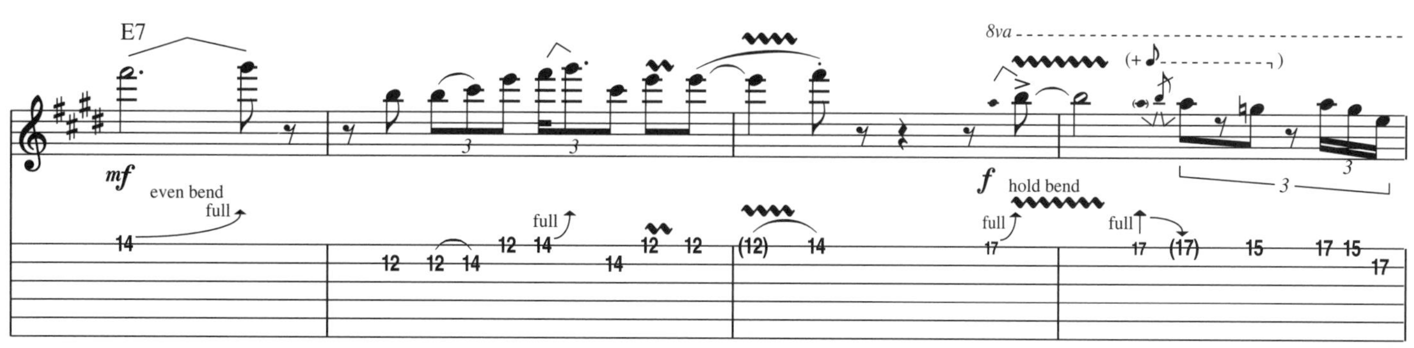
E7
mf
even bend
full
full
8va
f
hold bend
full
full

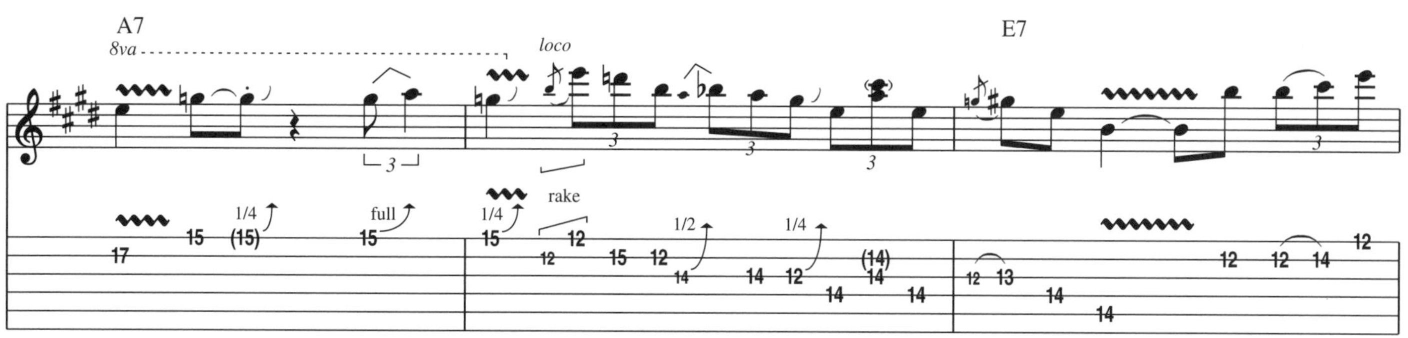
A7
8va
loco
E7
1/4
full
1/4
rake
1/2
1/4

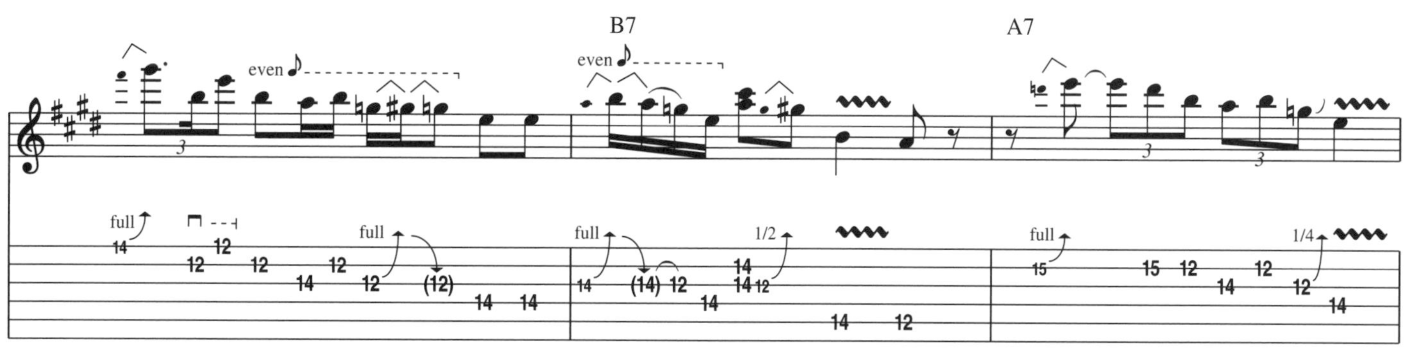
B7
A7
even
even
full
full
full
1/2
full
1/4

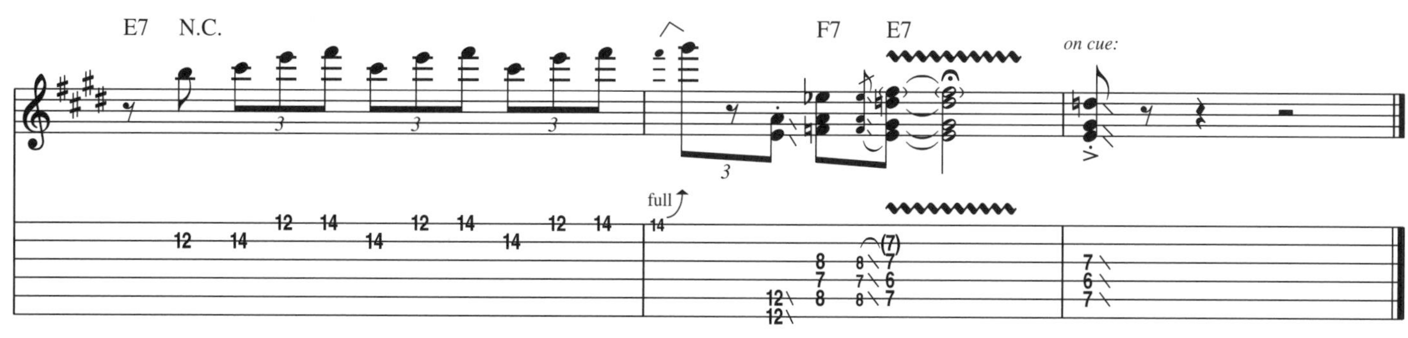
E7
N.C.
F7
E7
on cue:
full

from Eric Clapton - *Another Ticket*

I Can't Stand It

Words and Music by Eric Clapton

Gtr. 2 w/ Rhy. Fig. 1, 1st 3 meas.
Dm
Am
G
You've been sold
may - be it's time that you earned.

Chorus
G
E G A
5fr 8fr 5fr
Rhy. Fig 3A
F
G III
Am V
Gtr. 2
I can't stand it.
You're fool-in' a - round; I can't won't stand it.
You're
End Rhy. Fig. 2
Rhy. Fig. 3
P.M.

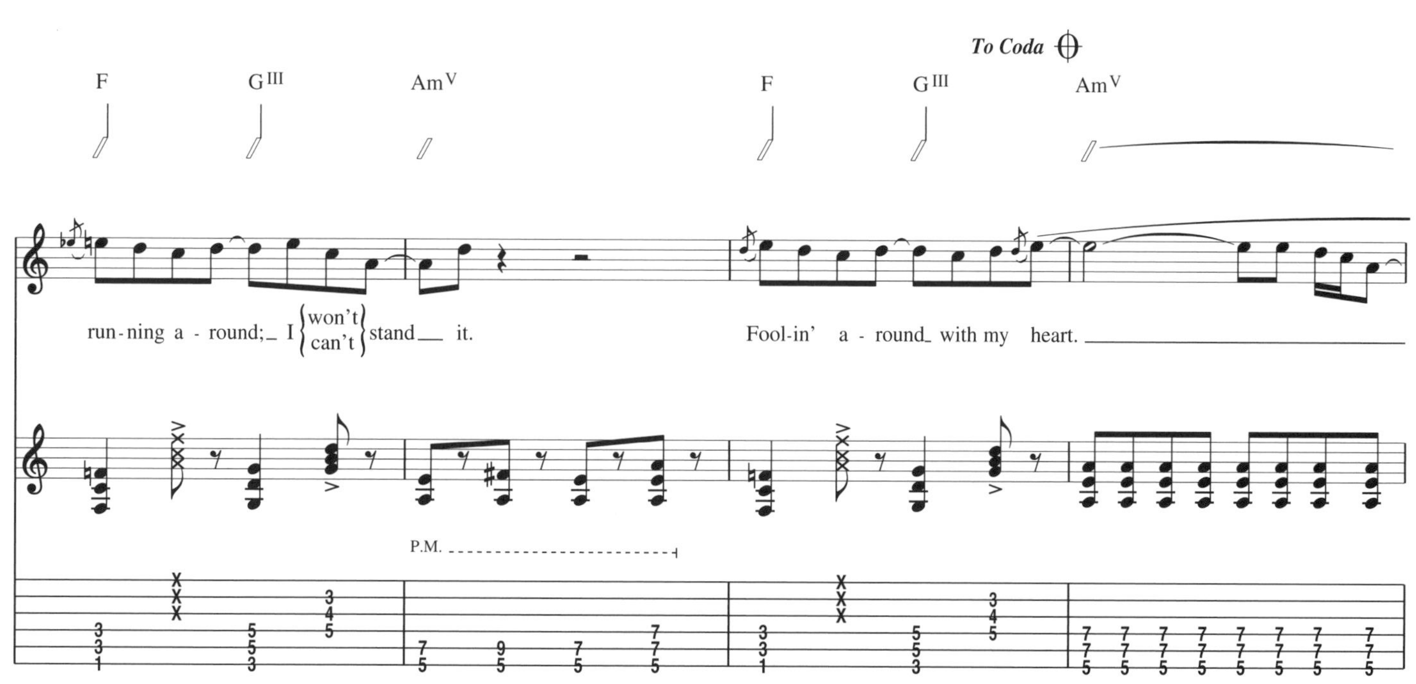
To Coda
F
G III
Am V
run-ning a - round; I won't can't stand it.
Fool-in' a - round with my heart.
P.M.

Verse
Gtr. 1: w/ Rhy. Fig. 2, simile
Dm
Am
G
End Rhy. Fig. 3A
Rhy. Fig. 4
2. I'll ex - plain
I feel like I'm be - in' used.
End Rhy. Fig. 3
D.S. al Coda
Gtr. 1: w/ Rhy. Fill 1
Make it plain,
so you don't get con - fused.
I can't stand
End Rhy. Fig. 4
Coda
Guitar Solo
Gtr. 2: w/ Rhy. Fig. 4, simile
Gtr. 2
Gtr. 3 (clean)
Gtr. 1
P.M.
let ring throughout
Rhy. Fill 1
Gtr. 1

G
Dm
Am
full
full
full
Chorus
Gtrs. 1 & 2: w/ Rhy. Figs. 3 & 3A
Gtr. 3 tacet
G
Am
F
G
Am
I can't stand it. You're run-ning a-round; I can't stand
full
F
G
Am
F
G
it. You're fool-in' a-round; I can't stand it. You're play-in' a-round with my heart.
Verse
Gtr. 3: w/ Fill 1 (see next page)
Gtr. 2: w/ Rhy. Fig. 4, simile
Gtr. 3 tacet
Am
Dm
Am
3. It's time time for me to let you know.
Gtr. 1

G
Dm
Am
Ain't no crime,
no crime to let your feel - ings show.

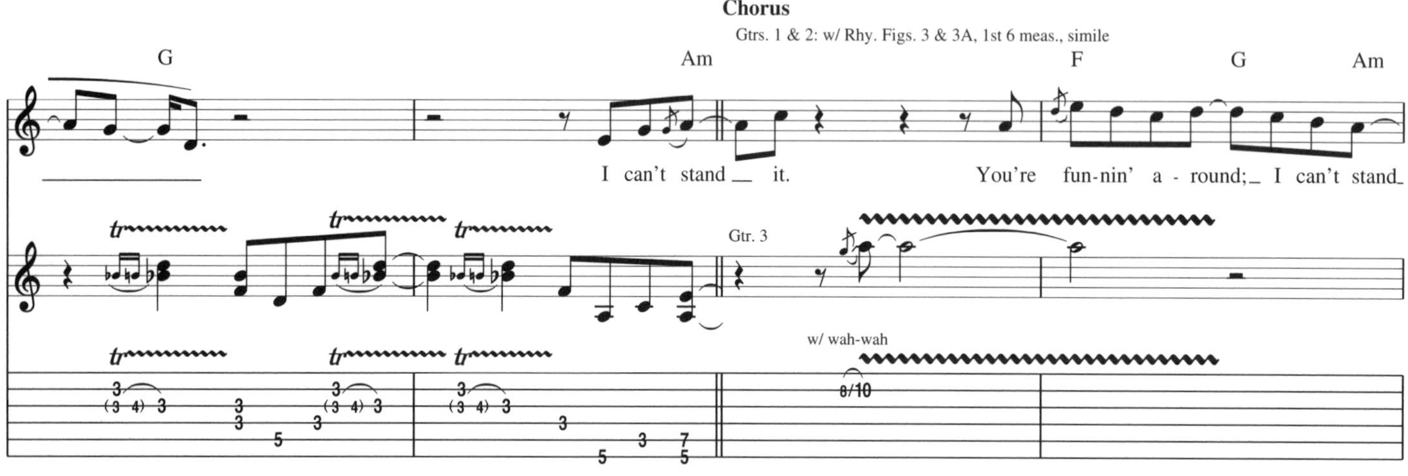
Chorus
Gtrs. 1 & 2: w/ Rhy. Figs. 3 & 3A, 1st 6 meas., simile
G
Am
F
G
Am
I can't stand it.
You're fun-nin' a - round; I can't stand
Gtr. 3
w/ wah-wah

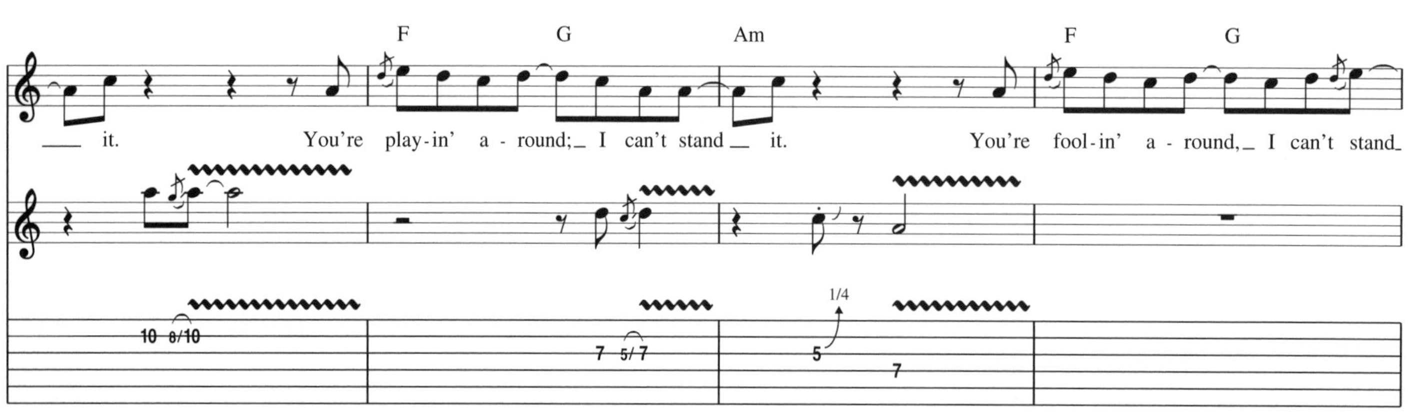
F
G
Am
F
G
it.
You're play-in' a - round; I can't stand it.
You're fool-in' a - round, I can't stand

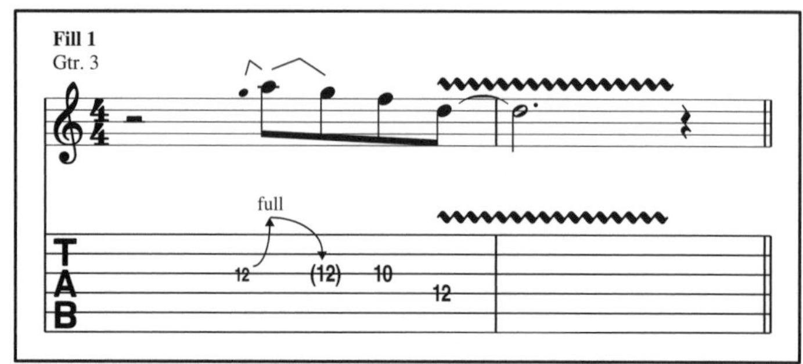
Fill 1
Gtr. 3
full

Gtrs. 1 & 2: w/ Rhy. Fill 2
Am
F
G
Gtrs. 1 & 2: w/ Rhy. Figs. 3 & 3A, 1st 6 meas., simile
it. You're run-nin' a - round, I can't stand it. You're play-ing a - round, I can't stand
full
1/4
it. Fool-in' a - round, I can't stand it. Run-nin' a - round, I can't stand
1/2
it. Run-nin' a - round, I won't stand it. Run-nin' a-round, I won't
Gtr. 2 tacet
Gtr. 3
Gtr. 1
P.M.
Rhy. Fill 2
Gtr. 2
TAB

Am F G Am F G
stand it. You're fool-in' a - round, I won't stand it. Play-in' a - round, I won't
P.M.
Am F G Am F G
stand it. You're fun-nin' a - round with my heart. You're fool-in' a - round with
full 1/4
P.M. P.M. P.M.
let ring
Am F G Am F G
my heart, my heart.
1/2 full
let ring

Am F G Am F G
Run-nin' a-round with, fool-in' a-round with my
8va
pp
let ring
Am F G Am F G
heart. Fool-in' a-round; I can't stand it. Run-nin' a-round; I won't
loco
f
full
Rhy. Fig. 5
let ring
Gtr. 1: w/ Rhy. Fig. 5, 4 1/4 times, simile
Am F G Am F G
stand it. Fool-in' a-round; I won't stand it. Fool-in' a-round; I won't
8va
1 1/2
full
End Rhy. Fig. 5

Am F G Am F G
stand it. Fool-in' a - round; I won't stand it. Run-nin' a - round; I can't
Gtr. 3
8va
full
Am F G Am F G
stand it. Fool-in' a - round; I can't stand it. Run-nin' a - round I...
full
hold bend
Am F G Am
Run - nin' a - round I...
loco
1/4
Begin Fade
Fade Out
F G Am F G Am
Run-nin' a - round I... Run-nin' a - round I...

from Eric Clapton - *461 Ocean Boulevard*

I Shot the Sheriff

Words and Music by Bob Marley

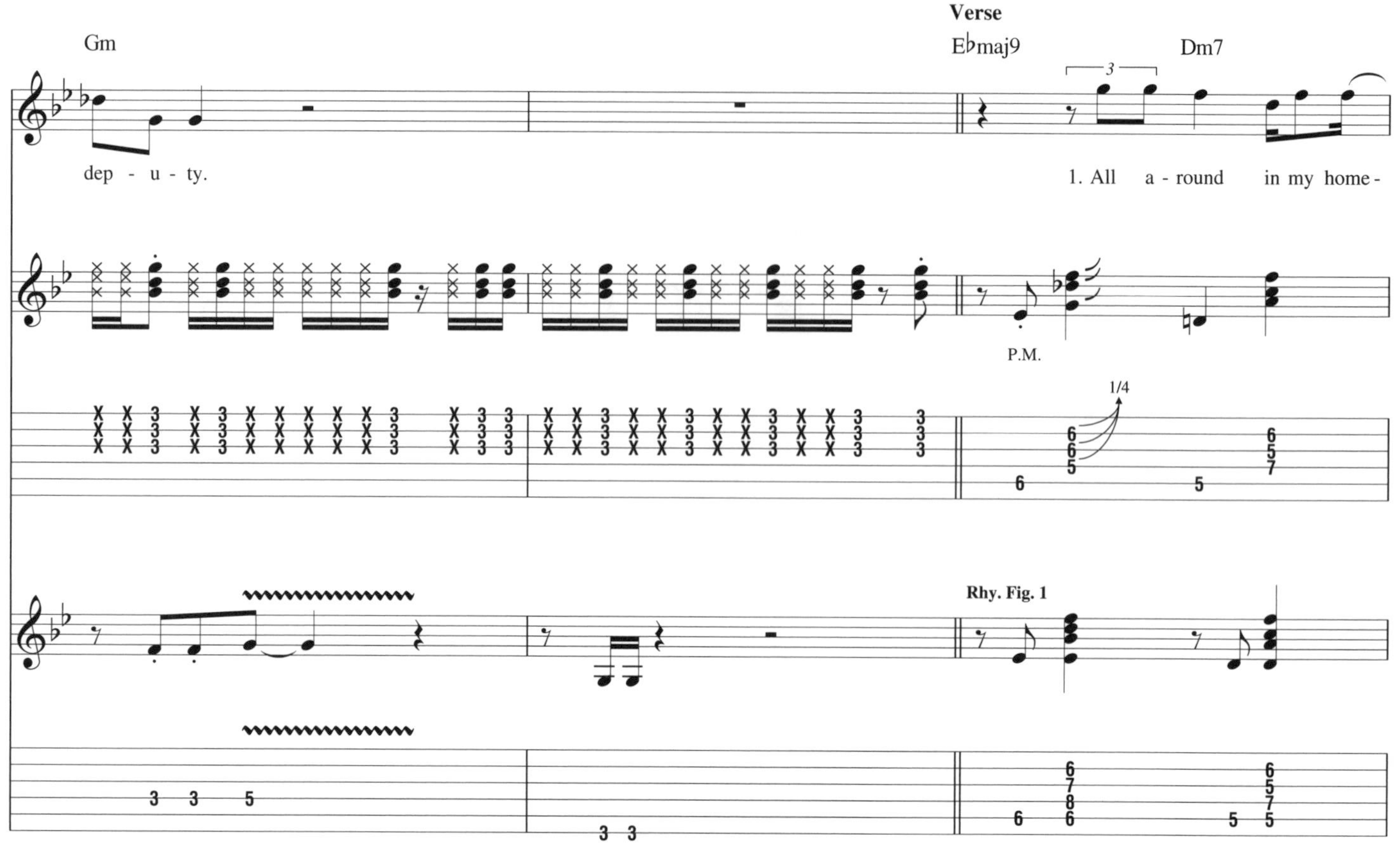
Verse
Gm
E♭maj9
Dm7
dep - u - ty.
1. All a - round in my home -
P.M.
1/4
Rhy. Fig. 1

Gm
E♭maj9
Dm7
Gm
- town,
they're try - ing to track me down.
They

E♭maj9
Dm7
Gm
E♭maj9
Dm7
say they want to bring me in guil - ty,
for the kil - lin' of the dep - u - ty,

Gm
E♭maj9
Dm7
Gm
for the life of the dep - u - ty.
But I say,

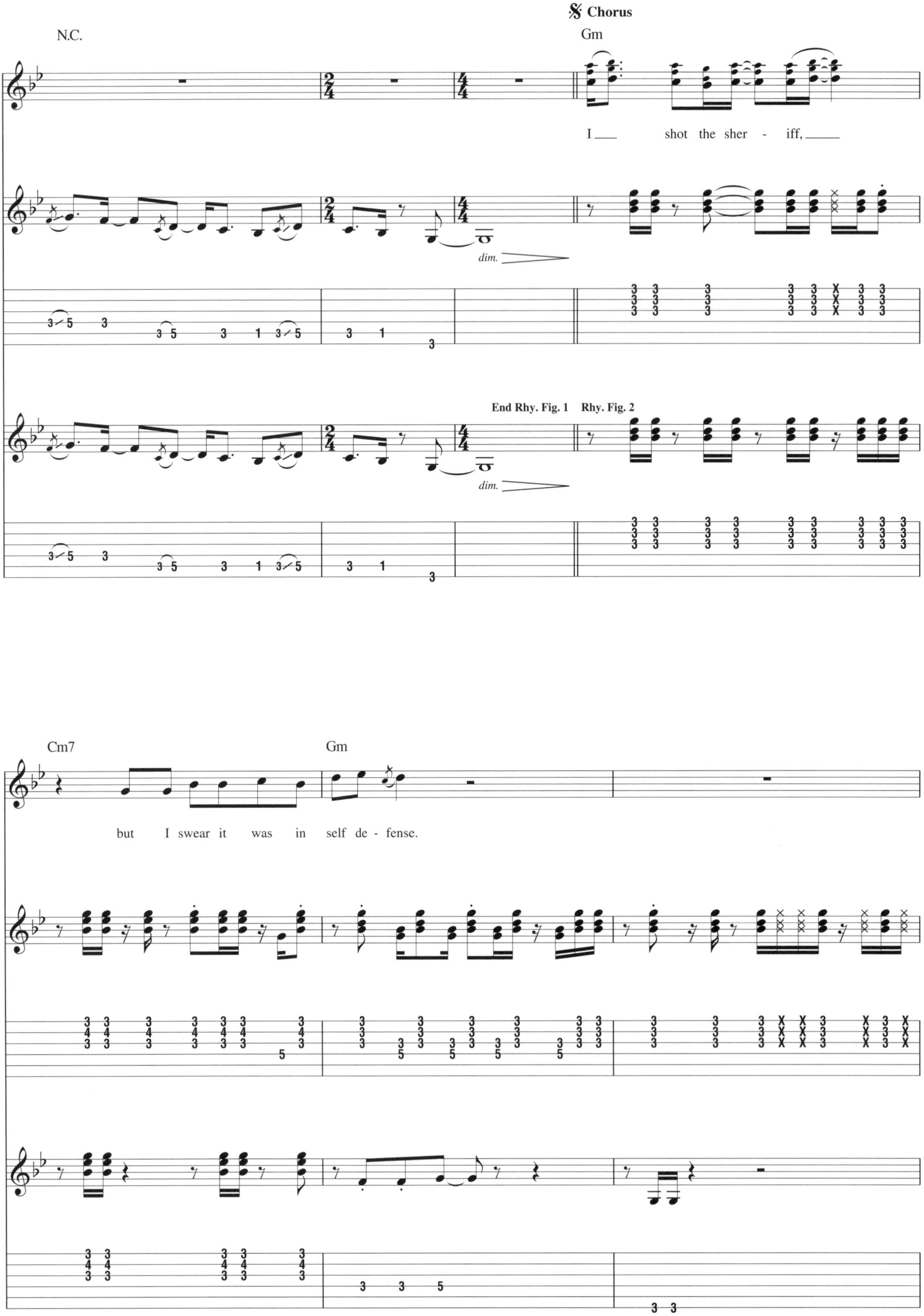

𝄋 **Chorus**

N.C.

Gm

I shot the sher - iff,

dim.

End Rhy. Fig. 1

Rhy. Fig. 2

dim.

Cm7
Gm
I shot the sher - iff,
and they say it is a cap - i - tal of - fense.
but I swear it was in self de - fense.

2nd time, Gtr. 1: w/ Rhy. Fill 1
To Coda 1
Verse
Gtr. 2: w/ Rhy. Fig. 1
E♭maj9
Dm7
Gm
2. Sher-iff John Brown al-ways hat - ed me.
End Rhy. Fig. 2

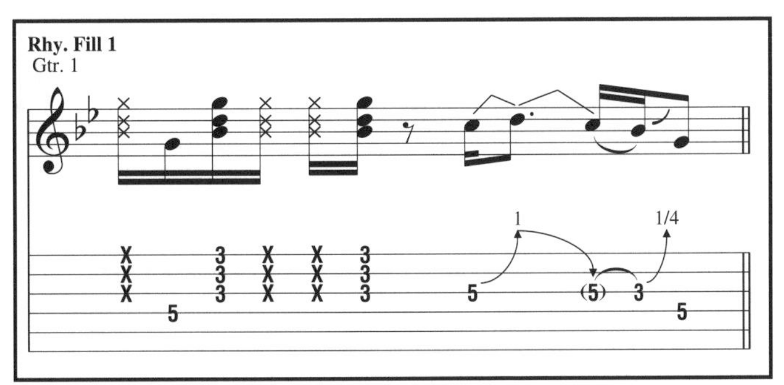
Rhy. Fill 1
Gtr. 1

Ebmaj9
Dm7
Gm
Ebmaj9
Dm7
For what, I don't know.
And ev - 'ry time that I
Gtr. 1

Gm
Ebmaj9
Dm7
Gm
plant a seed, he said, "Kill it be - fore it grows." He

D.S. al Coda 1

Ebmaj9
Dm7
Gm
N.C.
said, "Kill it be - fore it grows." I say,
let ring

Coda 1

Verse

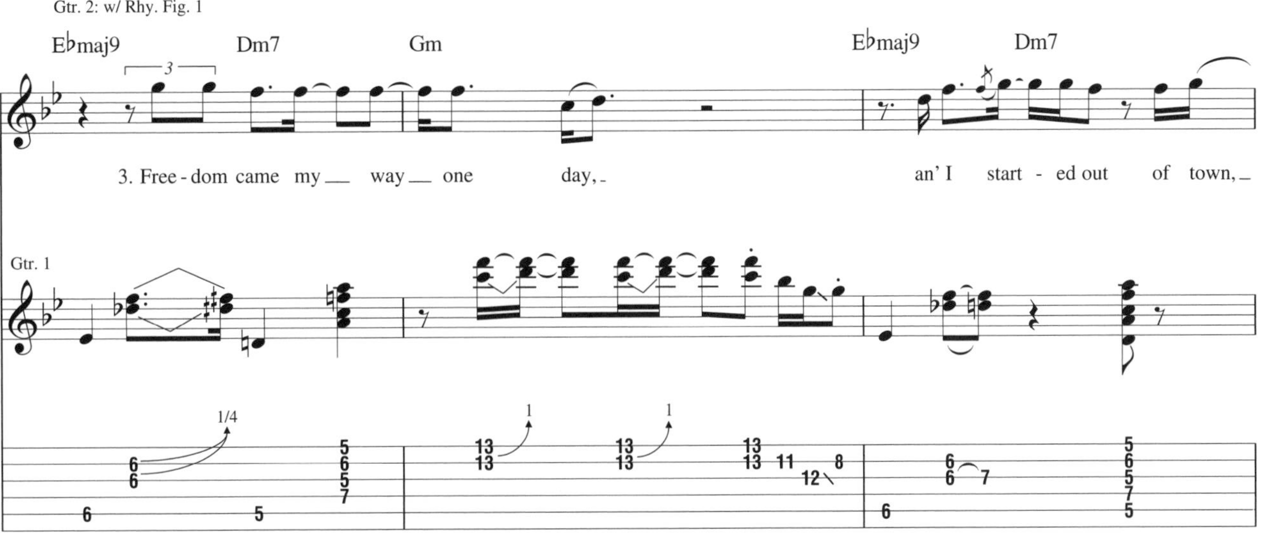
Gtr. 2: w/ Rhy. Fig. 1
E♭maj9
Dm7
Gm
E♭maj9
Dm7
3. Free - dom came my __ way __ one day, _ an' I start - ed out of town, _
Gtr. 1

Gm
E♭maj9
Dm7
Gm
__ yeah. All of a sud - den, I __ see sher - iff John _ Brown, _

E♭maj9
Dm7
Gm
E♭maj9
Dm7
aim - in' to shoot me __ down, _ so I shot, I shot him

Gm
N.C.
down.
An' I say,
1/4
Chorus
1st time, Gtr. 2: w/ Rhy. Fig. 2
2nd time, Gtr. 2: w/ Rhy. Fig. 2 (1st 6 meas.)
(Organ)
Gm
Cm7
I shot the sher - iff,
but I did not / did - n't shoot the
Gm
dep - u - ty.
I shot the sher - iff,
To Coda 2
Cm7
Gm7
but I did - n't shoot the / did not shoot no
dep - u - ty.

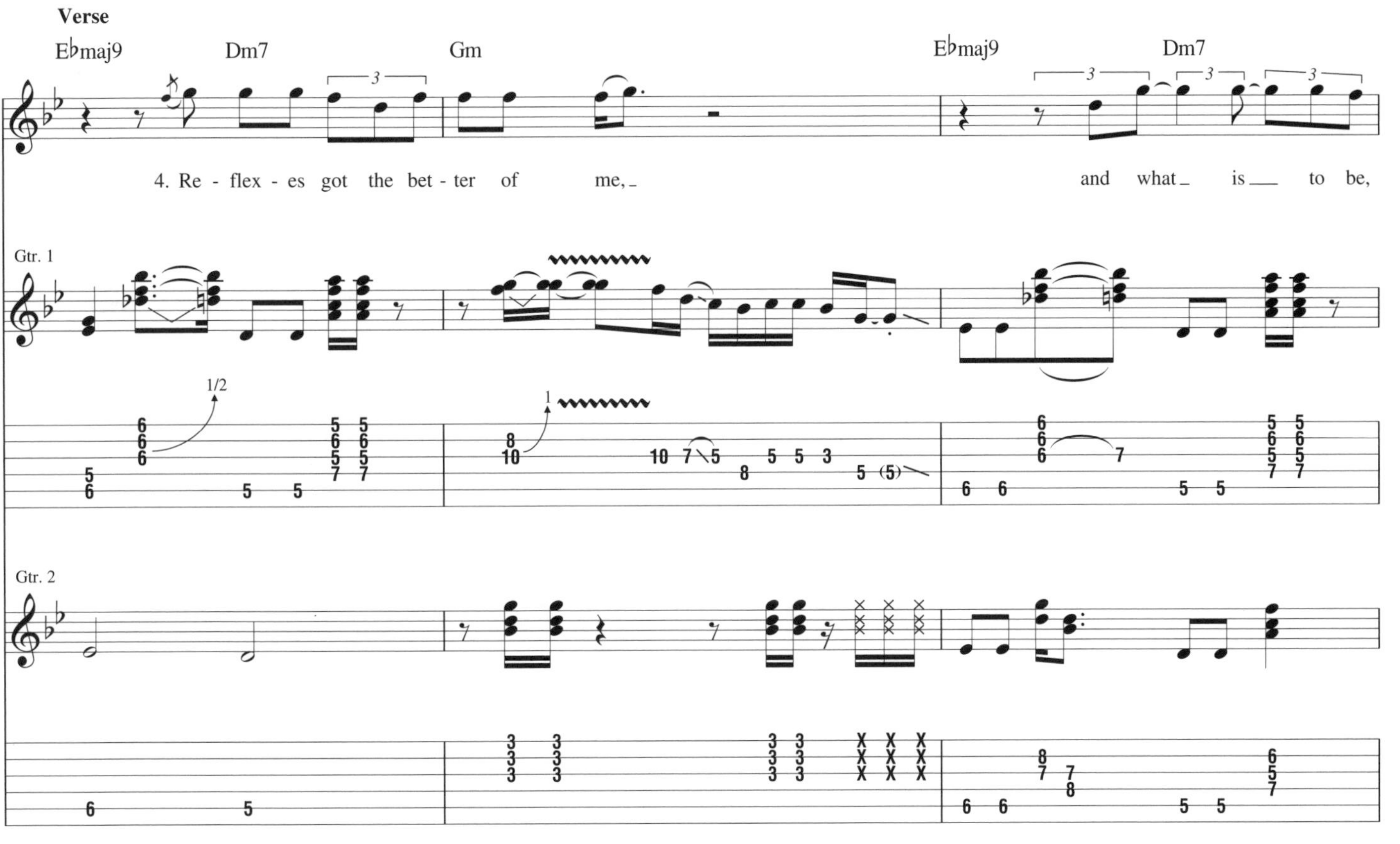
Verse
E♭maj9
Dm7
Gm
E♭maj9
Dm7
4. Re - flex - es got the bet - ter of me,
and what is to be,
Gtr. 1
Gtr. 2

Gm
E♭maj9
Dm7
Gm
must be.
Ev - 'ry day the buck - et goes to the well,

E♭maj9 Dm7 Gm E♭maj9 Dm7
but one day, the bot - tom will drop out.
Yes, one day the bot - tom will
*S S S
1/4
1/4
*S = Snap B string
let ring
let ring
let ring
let ring

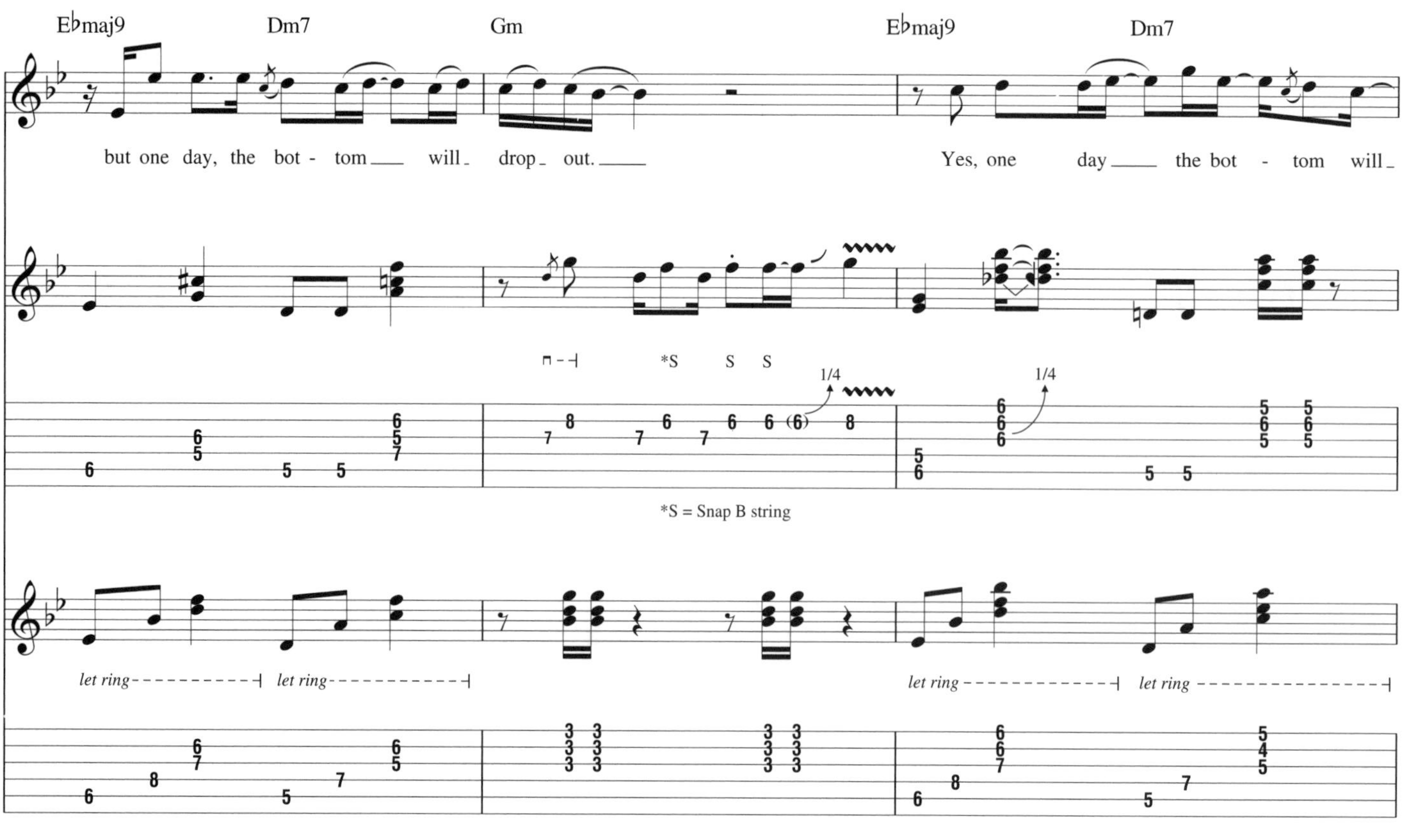

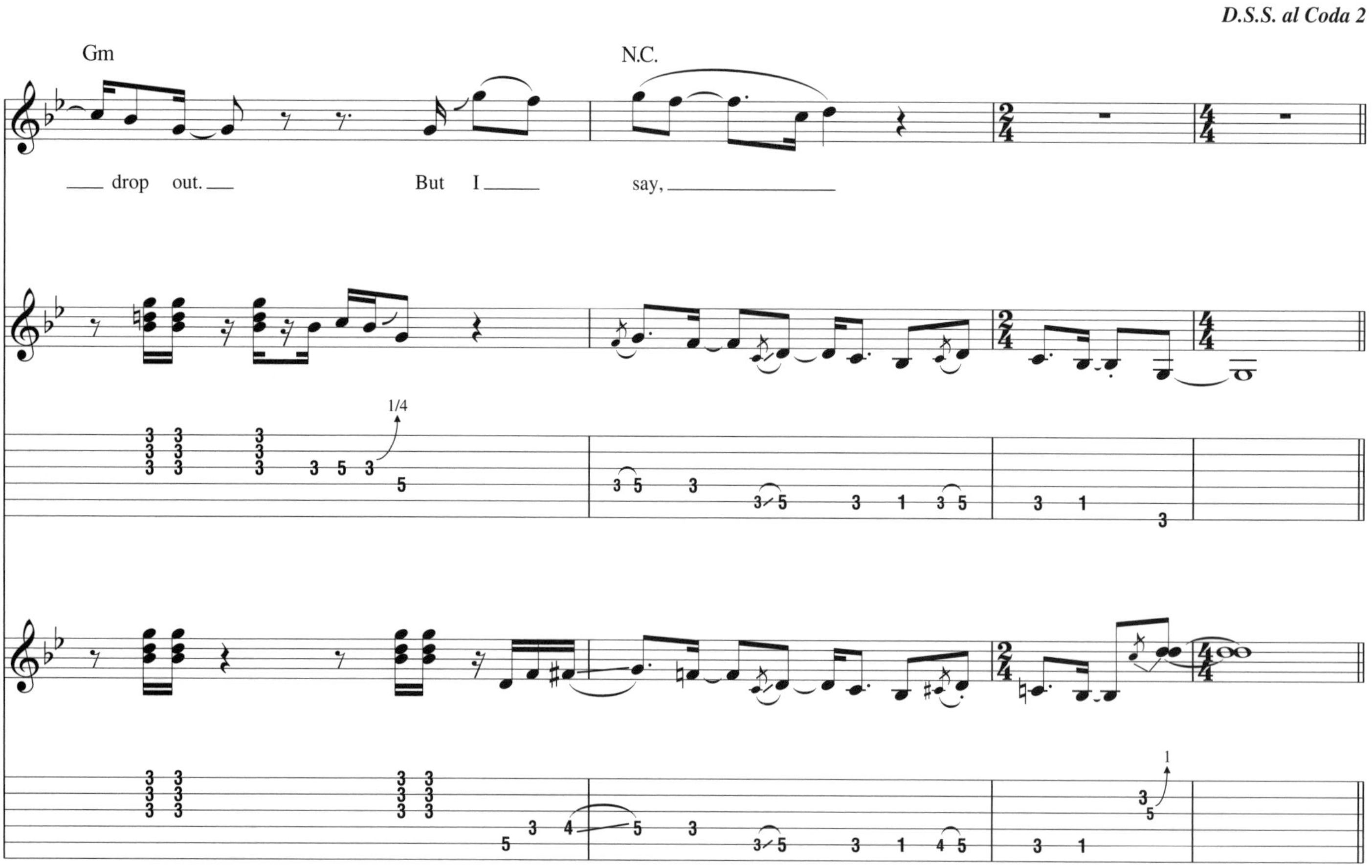

D.S.S. al Coda 2
Gm N.C.
drop out.
But I
say,
1/4
1

Coda 2

Outro
Gm
E♭maj9
Dm7
dep - u - ty,
oh no.
Gtr. 1
Gtr. 2
let ring
let ring

Gm
E♭maj9
Dm7
Gm
let ring
let ring

E♭maj9
Dm7
Gm
E♭maj9
Dm7
let ring
let ring
let ring
Begin fade
Gm
E♭maj9
Dm7
1/4
Gm
E♭maj9
Dm7
Gm
Fade out
1/4

from Eric Clapton - *From the Cradle*

I'm Tore Down

Words and Music by Sonny Thompson

Intro

* Chord symbols reflect suggested harmony.

F7
C7
tore down. I'm al - most lev - el with the ground. Why'd I
Rhy. Fig. 1

G7
F7
C7
feel like this when my ba - by can't be found?
End Rhy. Fig. 1

Verse
C7
N.C.
1. Went to the riv - er, to jump in. My ba - by showed up and said, "I will tell you when." Well, I'm
Gtrs. 1 & 2

Chorus

Verse

Gtr. 2: w/ Rhy. Fill 3, 2nd time only
To Coda
C7
C°7
C7
N.C.
Love you in the morn ing and in the eve - ning too. Ev-'ry time you leave me I get mad with you. Well, I'm
lie for you if you want me to. I real-ly don't be-lieve that your love is true. Well, I'm

Chorus

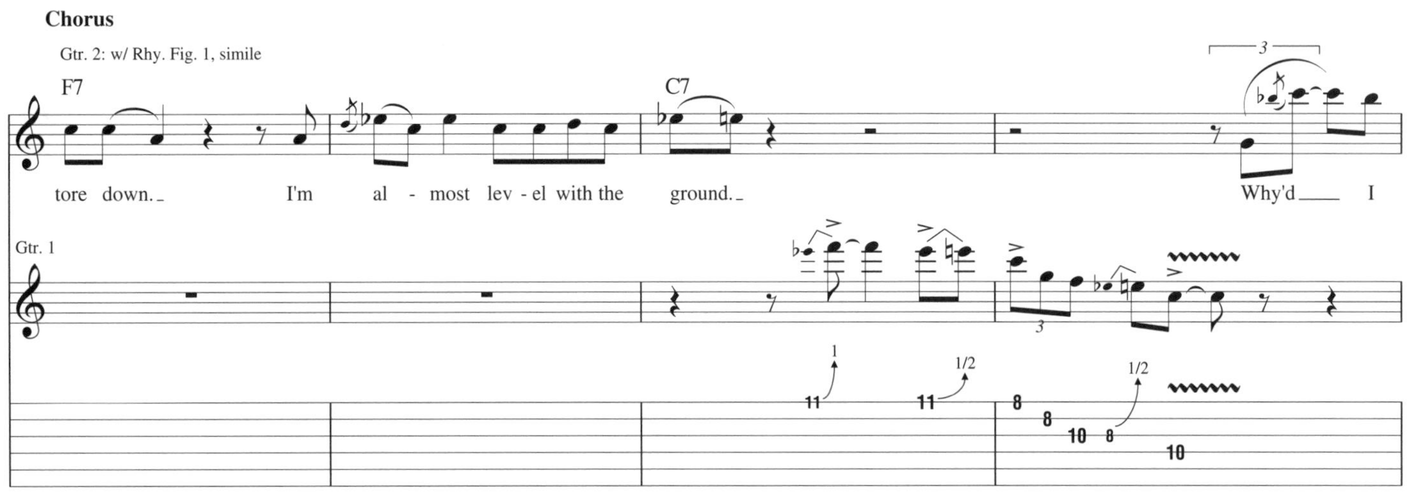
Gtr. 2: w/ Rhy. Fig. 1, simile
F7
C7
tore down. I'm al - most lev - el with the ground. Why'd I
Gtr. 1

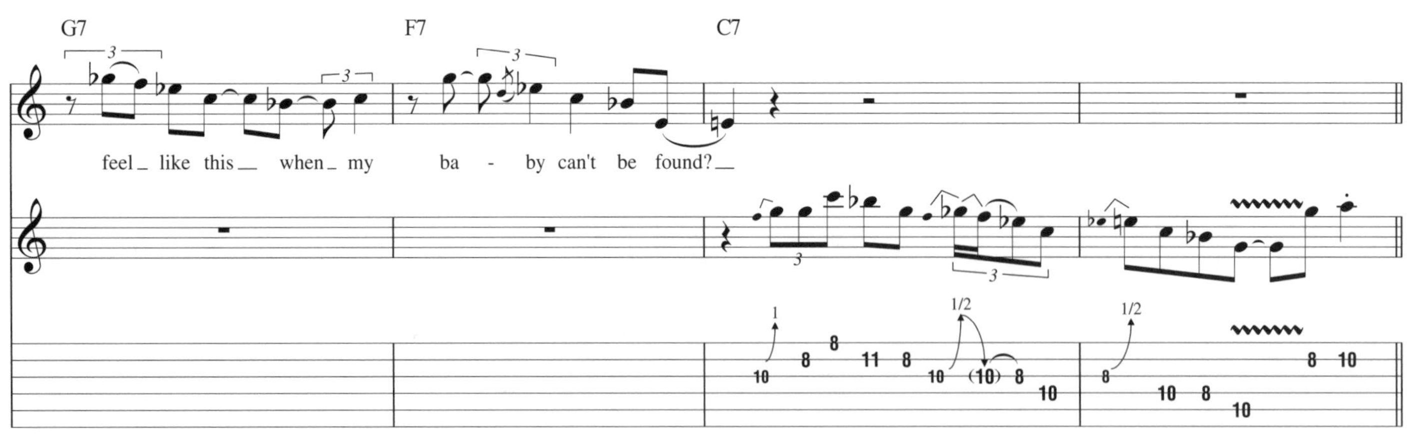
G7
F7
C7
feel like this when my ba - by can't be found?

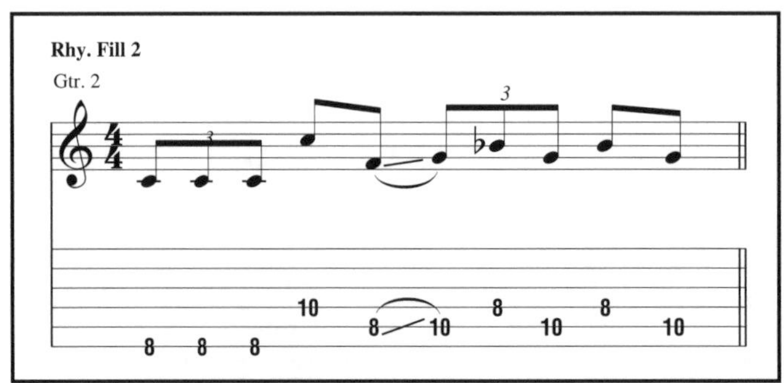
Rhy. Fill 2
Gtr. 2

Guitar Solo

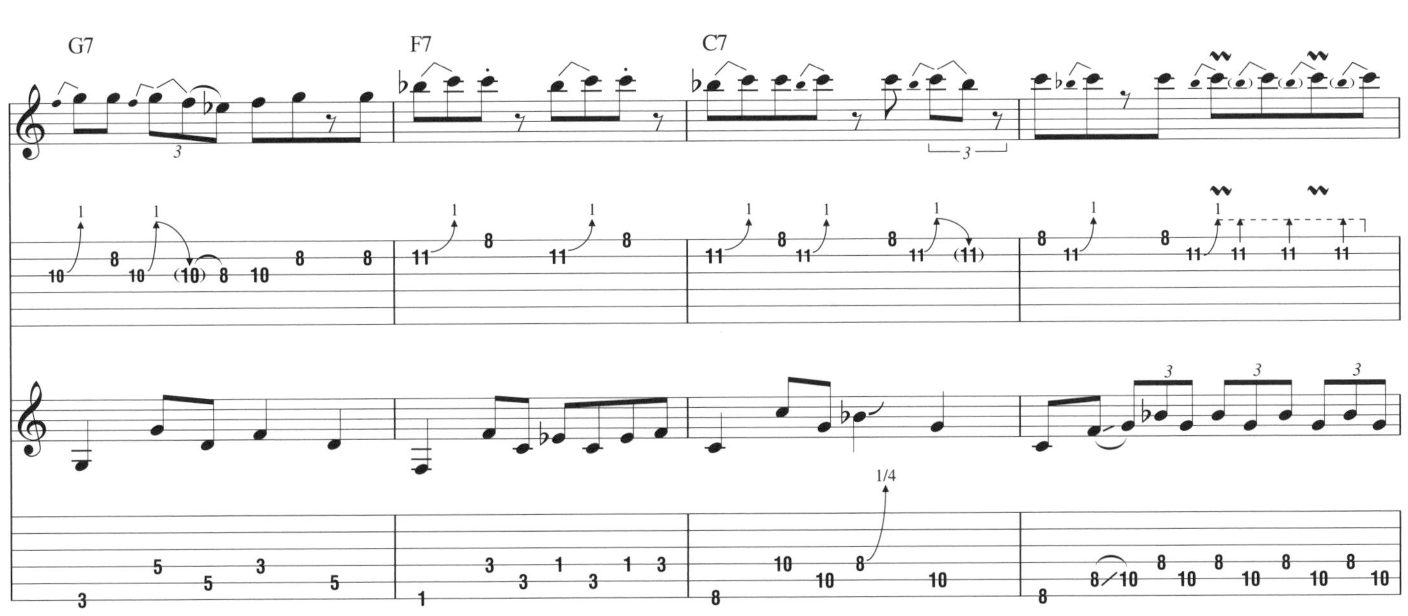

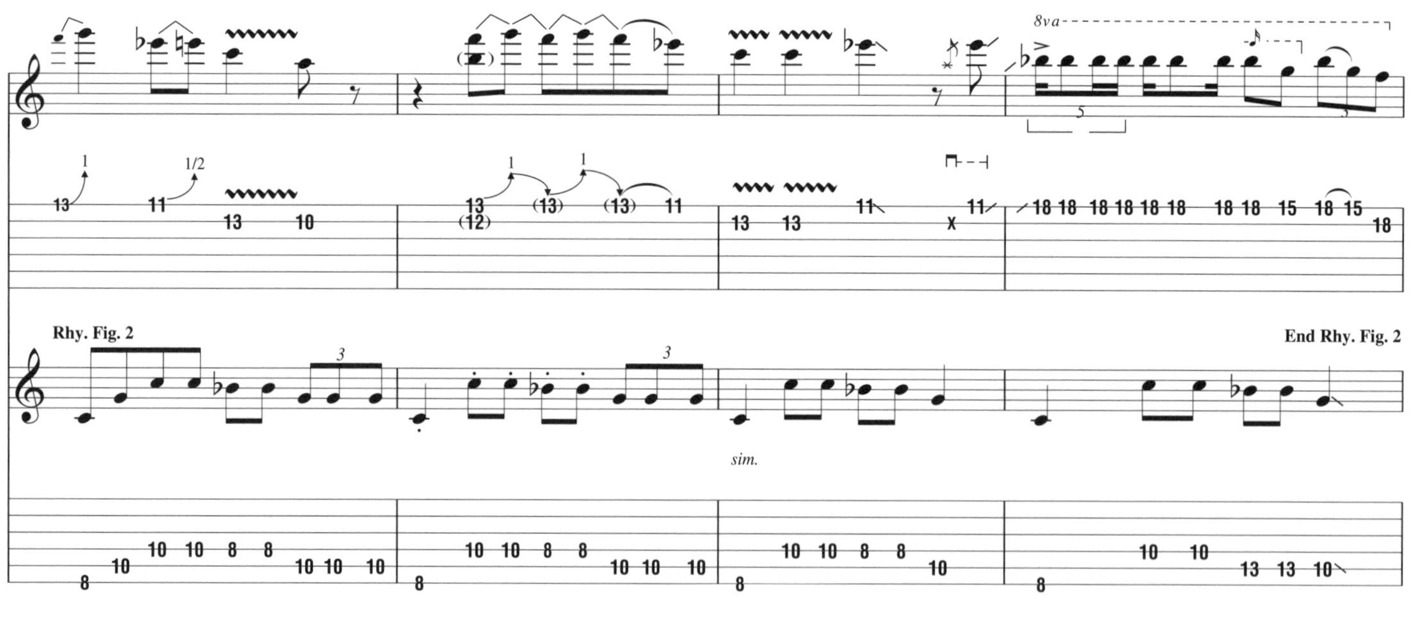

8va
Rhy. Fig. 2
End Rhy. Fig. 2
sim.

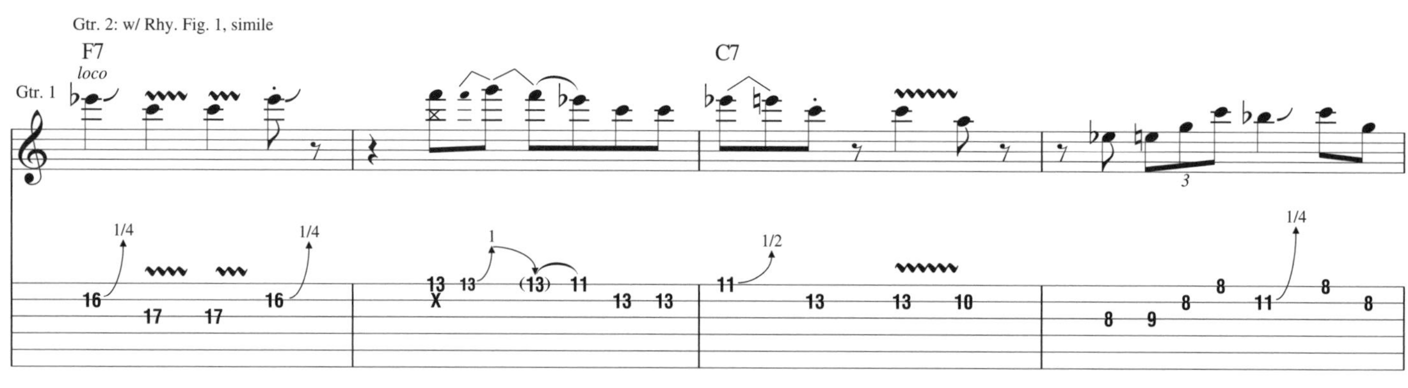

Gtr. 2: w/ Rhy. Fig. 1, simile
F7
loco
Gtr. 1
C7

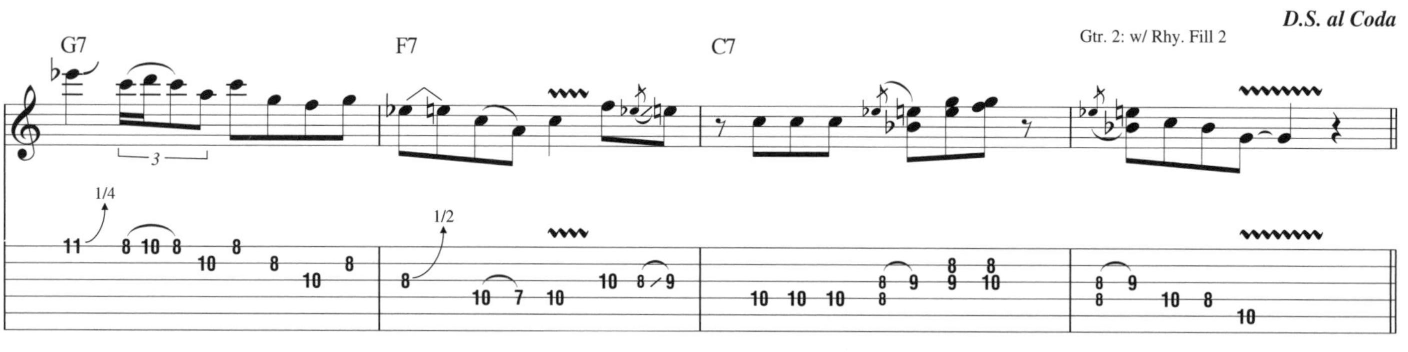

D.S. al Coda
Gtr. 2: w/ Rhy. Fill 2
G7
F7
C7

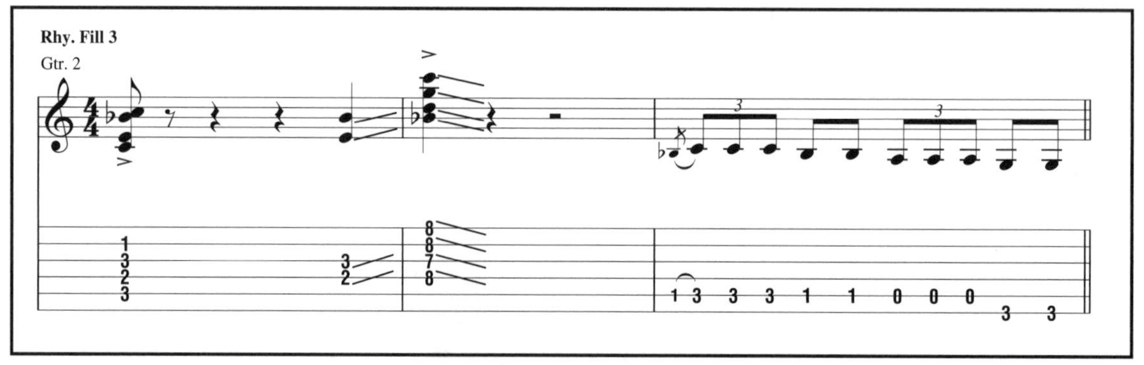

Rhy. Fill 3
Gtr. 2

Coda

Chorus

Gtr. 2: w/ Rhy. Fig. 1, simile

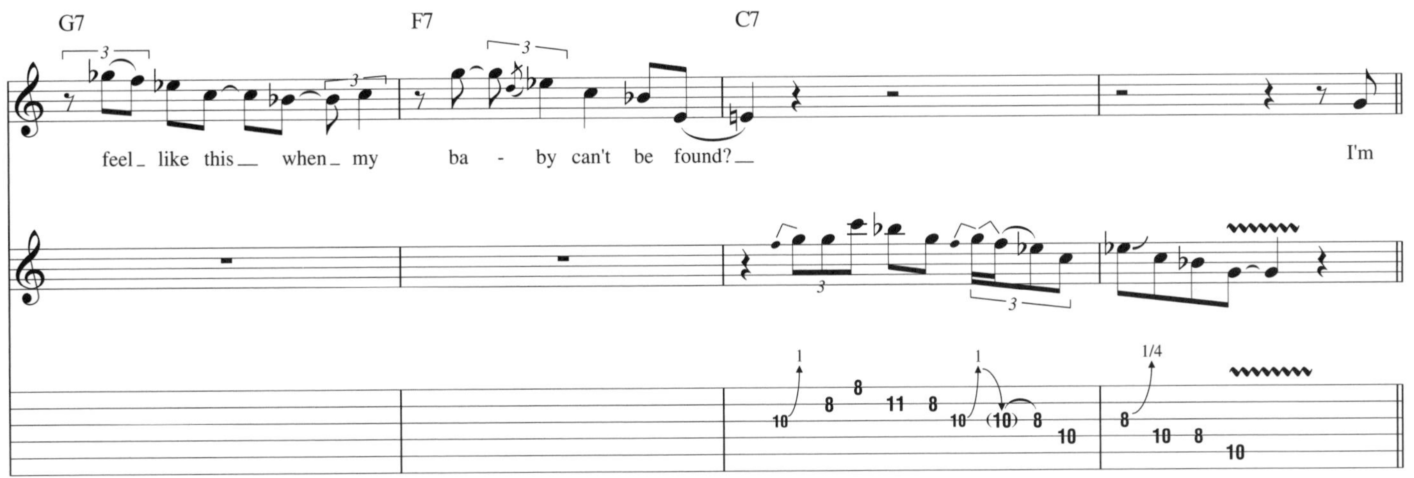

Outro-Chorus

Gtr. 2: w/ Rhy. Fig. 2, simile

C7

tore down al - most lev - el with the ground. Well, I'm

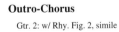

Gtr. 2: w/ Rhy. Fig. 1, simile, 1st 5 meas. only
F7
C7
tore down. I'm al - most lev - el with the ground. Why'd I

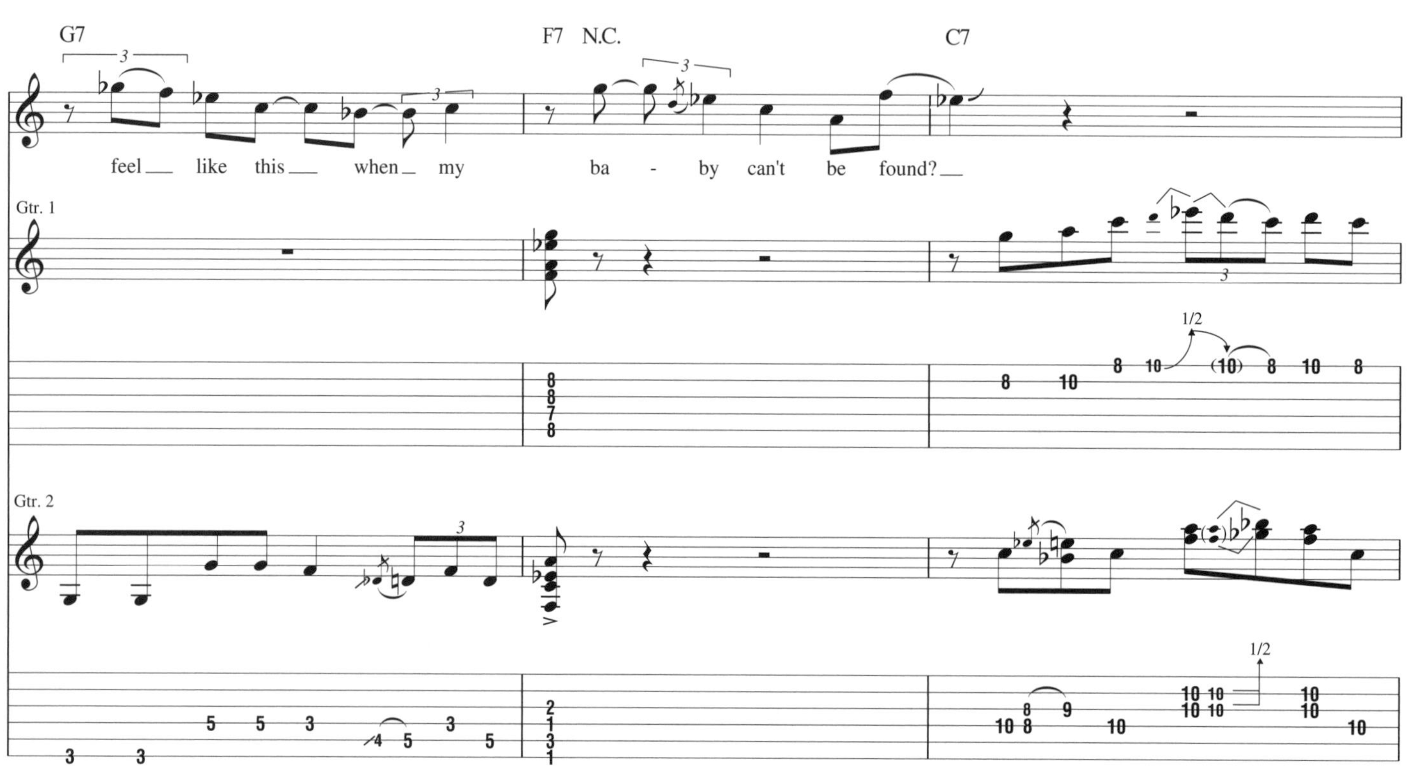
G7
F7 N.C.
C7
feel like this when my ba - by can't be found?
Gtr. 1
Gtr. 2

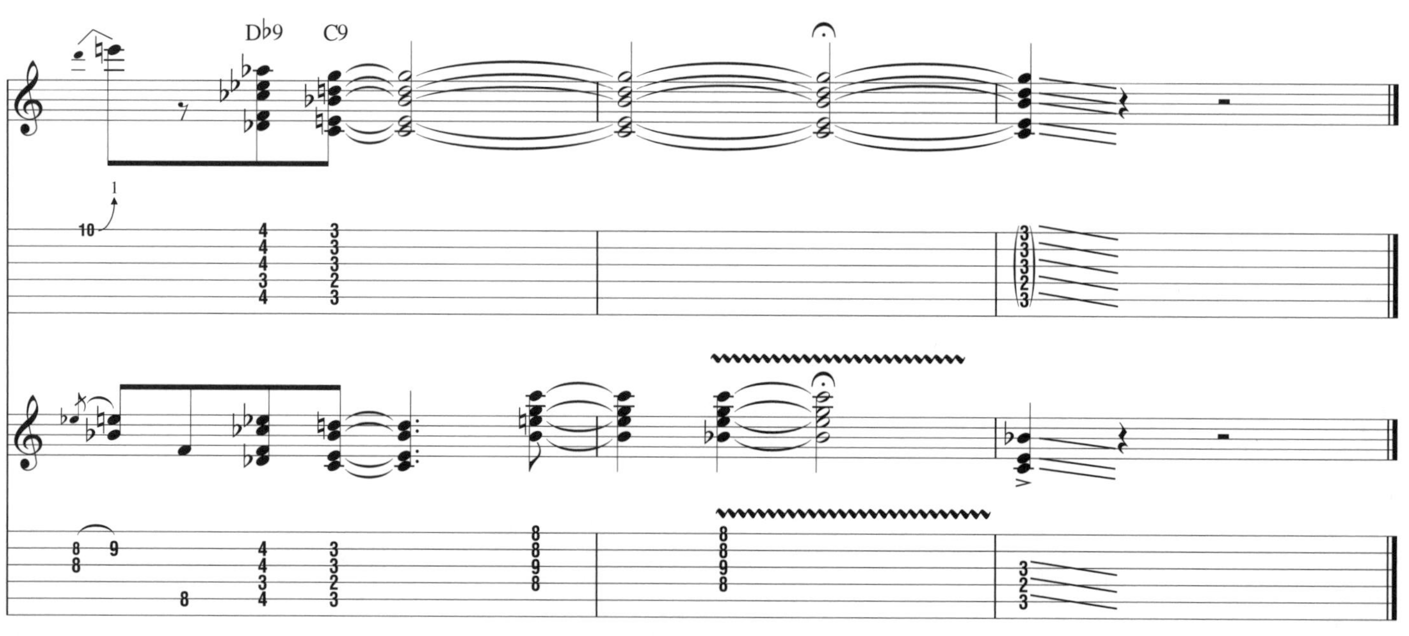
D♭9
C9

from Eric Clapton - *Slowhand*

Lay Down Sally

Words and Music by Eric Clapton, Marcy Levy and George Terry

Intro

Moderately fast ♩ = 190

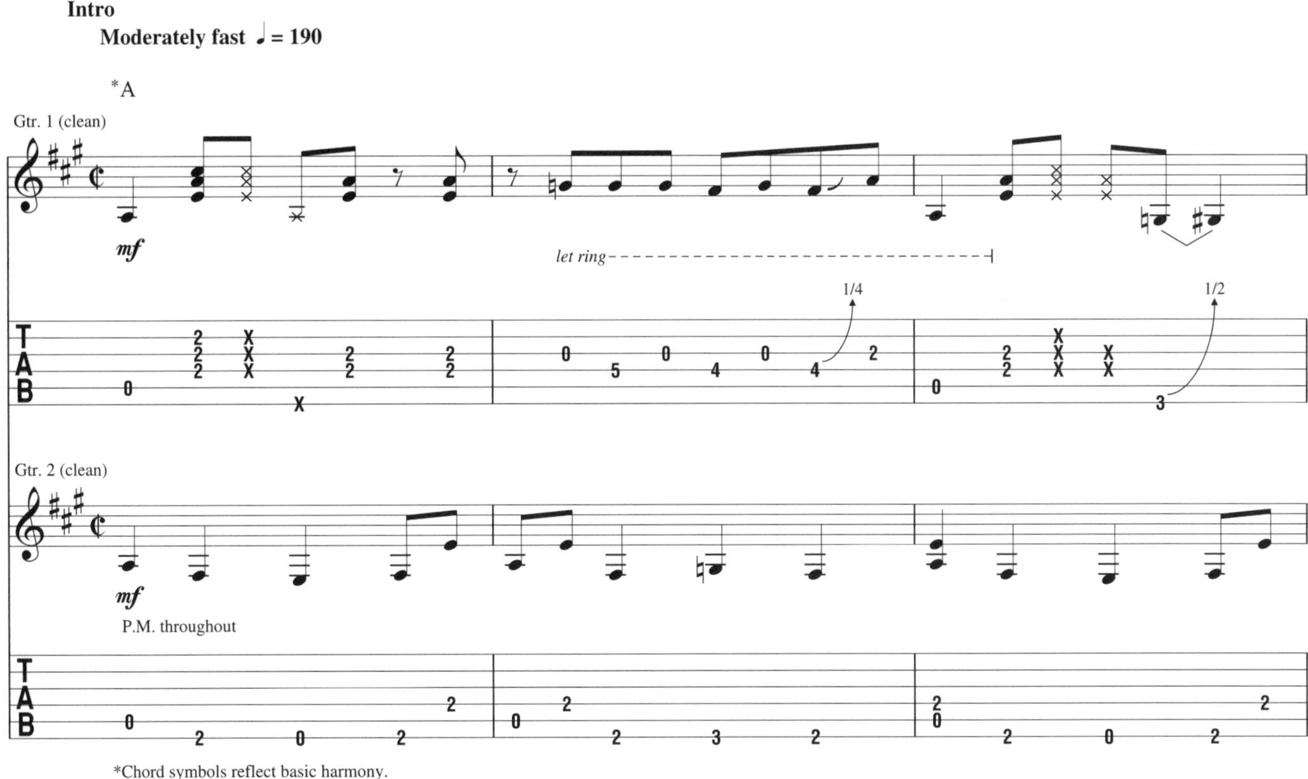

*Chord symbols reflect basic harmony.

let ring
1/4
let ring
1
1
*Played ahead of the beat.
let ring
1/2

Verse

A
1. There is noth - ing that is wrong in want - ing you to stay here with
Sun ain't near - ly on the rise, and we still got the moon and stars a -
long to see the morn - ing light col - or - ing your face so dream - i -
1/4

D
A
me. I know you've got some - where to go but
bove. Un - der - neath the vel - vet skies.
ly. So don't you go and say good - bye!
mp
mf

Chorus

E A

ev - er leave.
ev - er leave. Lay down Sal - ly, and
ev - er leave.

D
E
rest here in my arms.
Don't you think you want some - one to talk

A
to?
Lay down Sal - ly, no
let ring

To Coda
D
E
need to leave so soon.
I've been try - in' all night long just to
1.
A
talk to you.
let ring
let ring

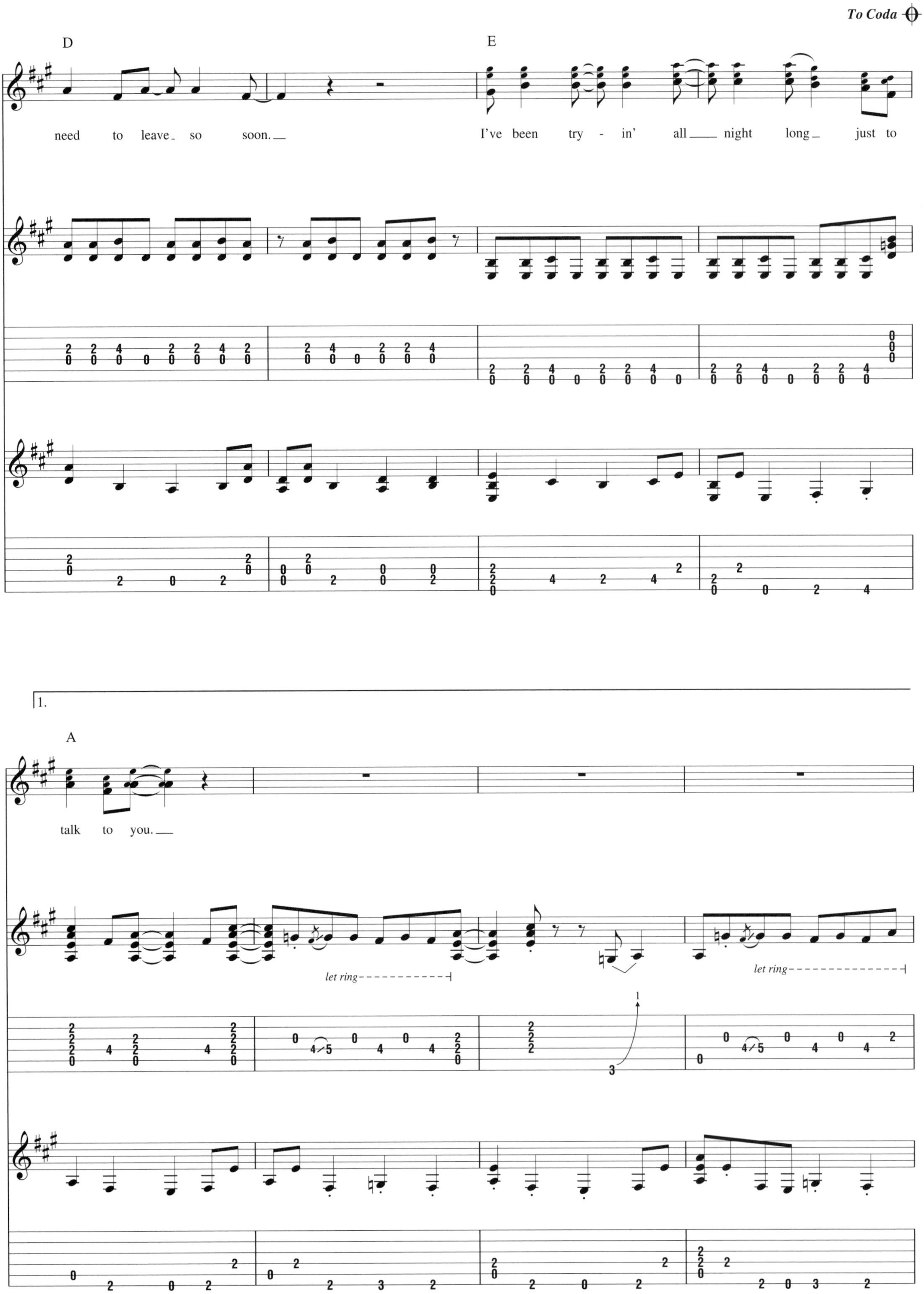

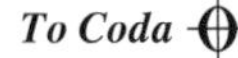

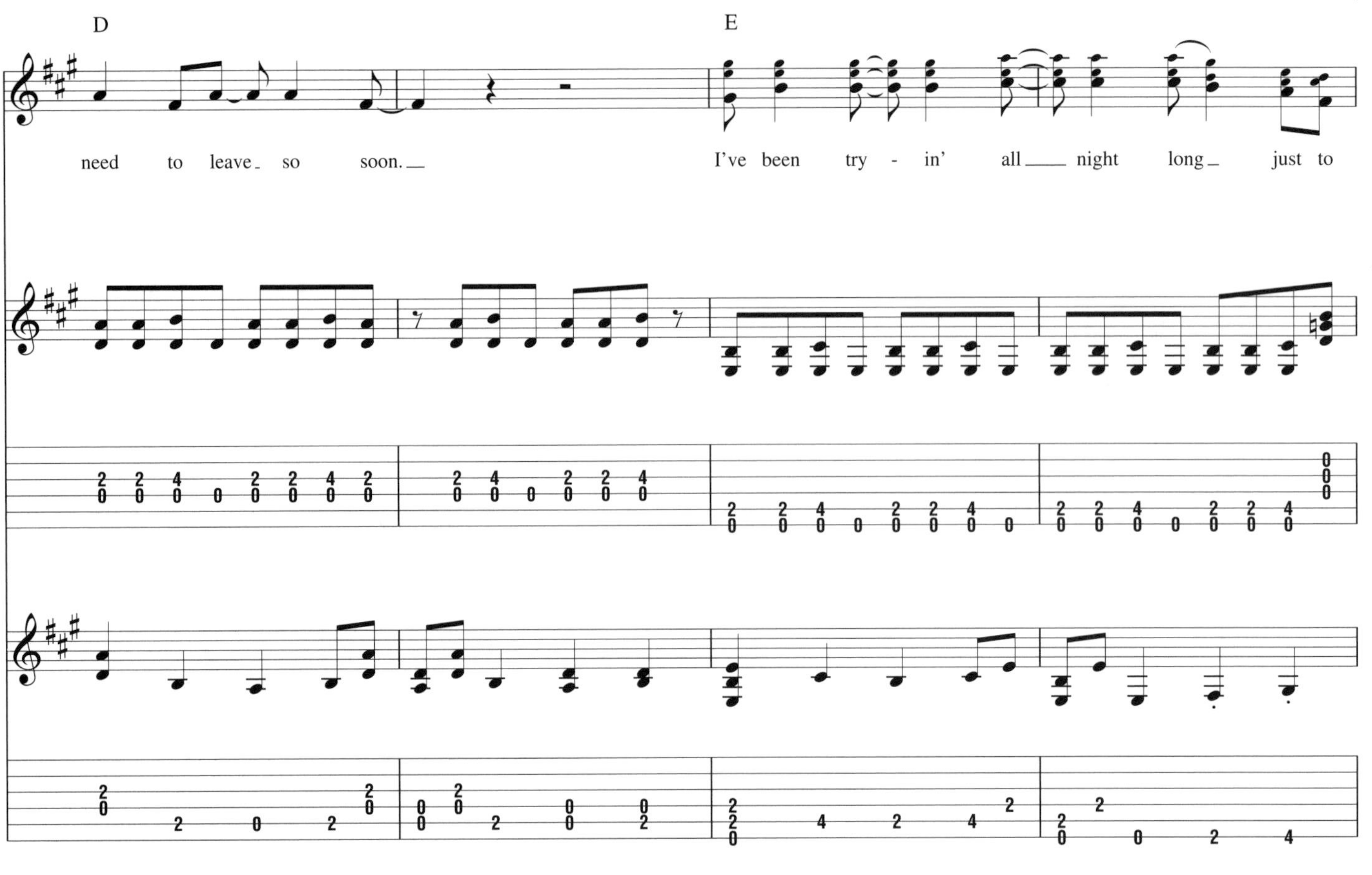

2.

A

talk to you.

let ring

let ring

Guitar Solo

A
let ring
don't pick
Riff A

End Riff A

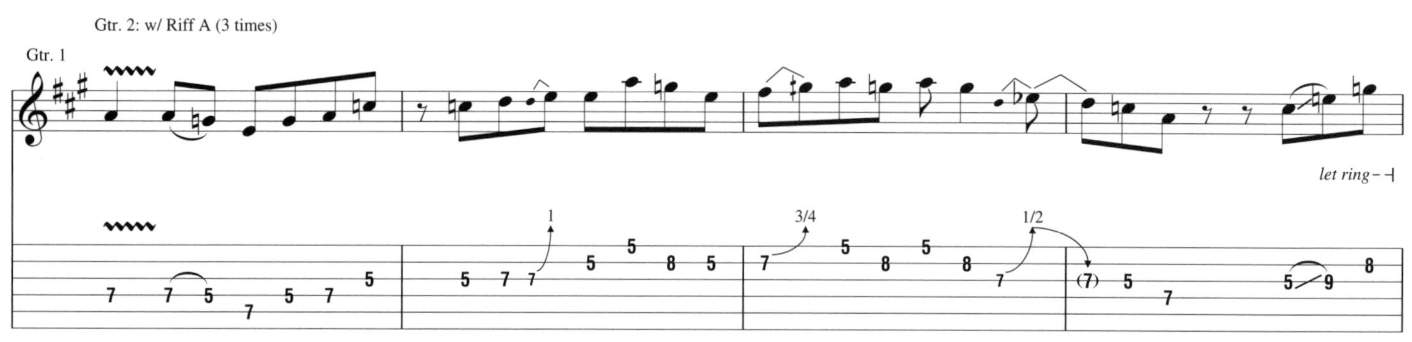
Gtr. 2: w/ Riff A (3 times)
Gtr. 1
let ring

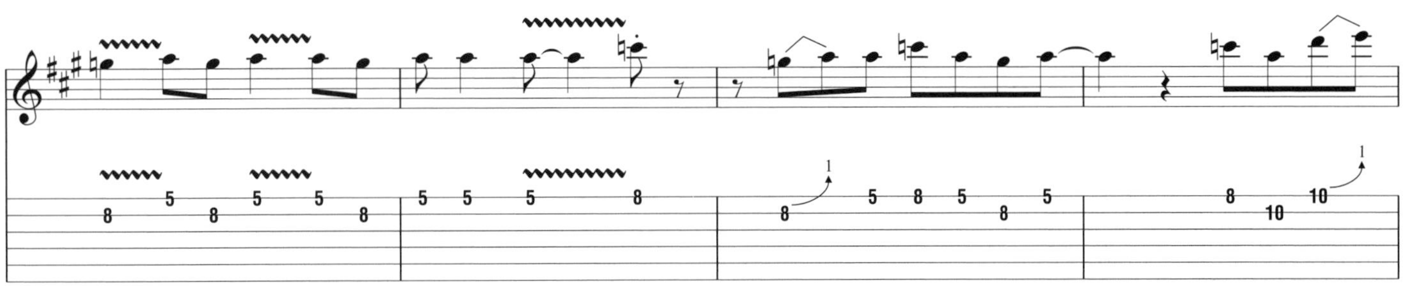

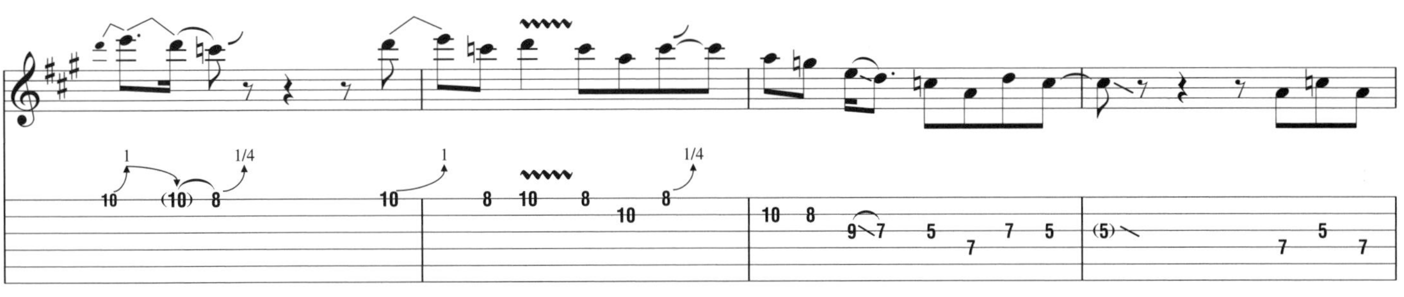

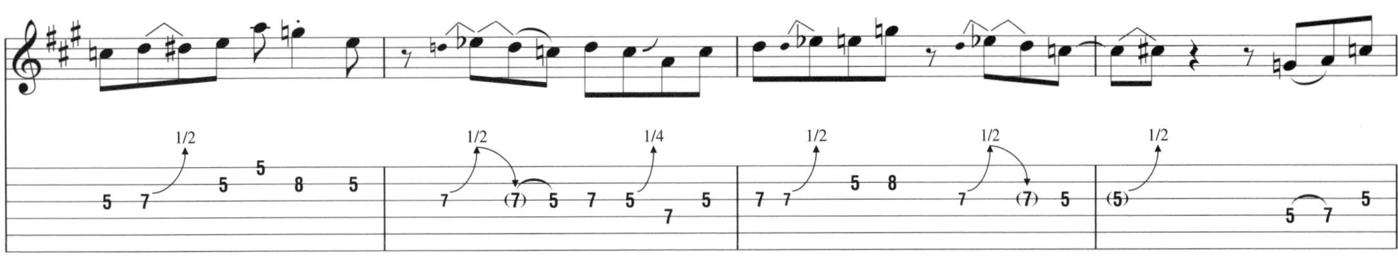

D.S. al Coda

Coda
Chorus
A
A
talk to you.
Lay down Sal - ly and

D
E
rest here in my arms.
Don't you think you want some - one to talk

A
to?
Lay down Sal - ly, there's no
let ring

D
E
need to leave so soon.
I've been try - ing all night long just to
P.M.

Outro
A
A
talk to you.
P.M.
let ring
X
X
X

P.M.
let ring

slight P.M.

let ring

Begin fade

let ring

Fade out

from Derek and the Dominos - *Layla and Other Assorted Love Songs*

Layla

Words and Music by Eric Clapton and Jim Gordon

* Composite arr. Gtr. 6 mixed down on this recording. It is easier to hear on previous releases.

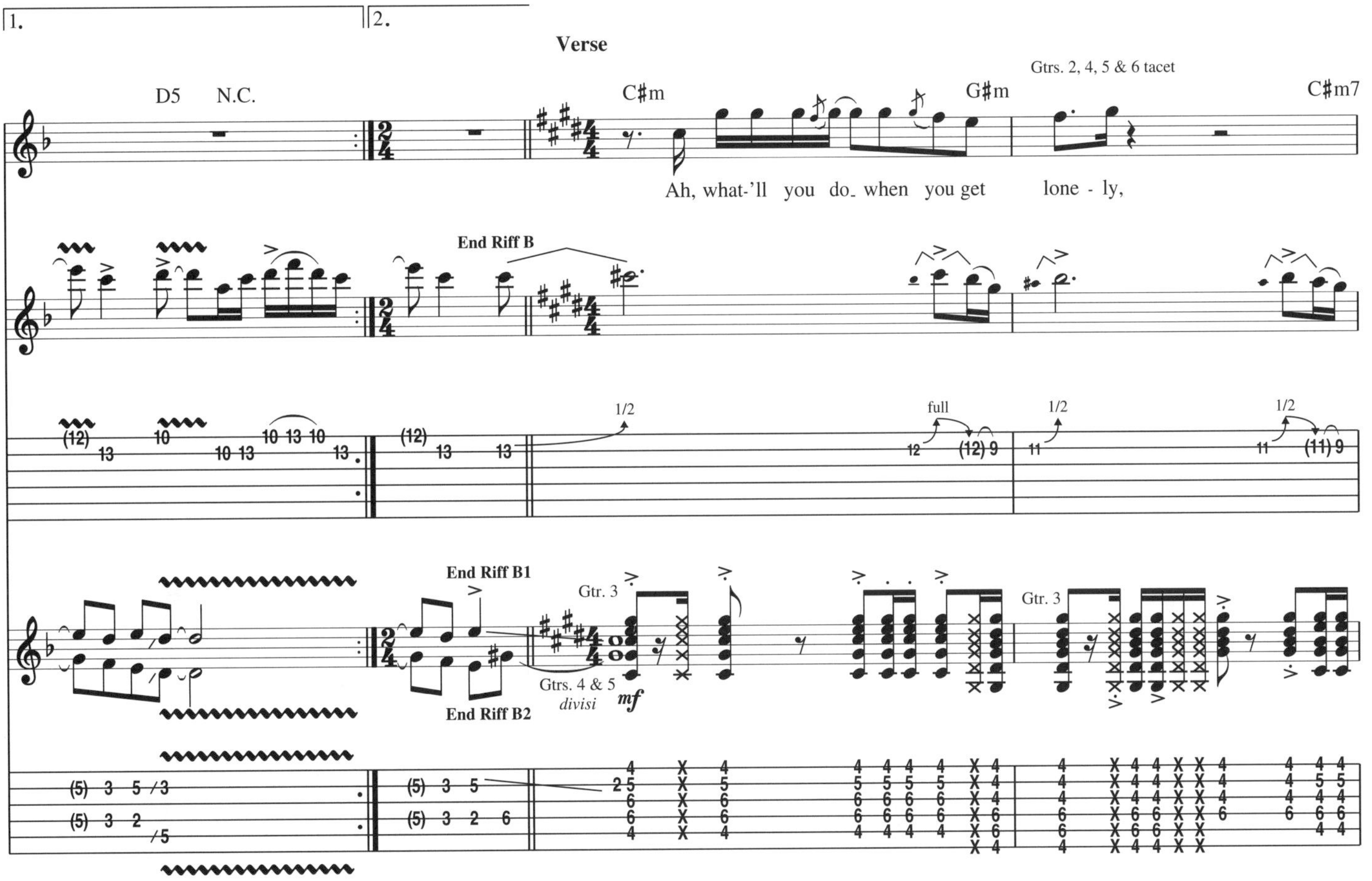

1.
2.
Verse
Gtrs. 2, 4, 5 & 6 tacet
D5 N.C.
C♯m
G♯m
C♯m7
Ah, what-'ll you do when you get lone - ly,
End Riff B
1/2
full
1/2
1/2
End Riff B1
Gtr. 3
Gtr. 3
End Riff B2
Gtrs. 4 & 5 divisi
mf

Fill 1
8va
Gtr. 6 (dist.)
f
w/ slide
w/o slide
1/4
w/o slide

Rhy. Fill 1
Gtr. 3

Rhy. Fill 2
Gtr. 2

Fill 2
Gtr. 6
8va
w/o slide
w/ slide

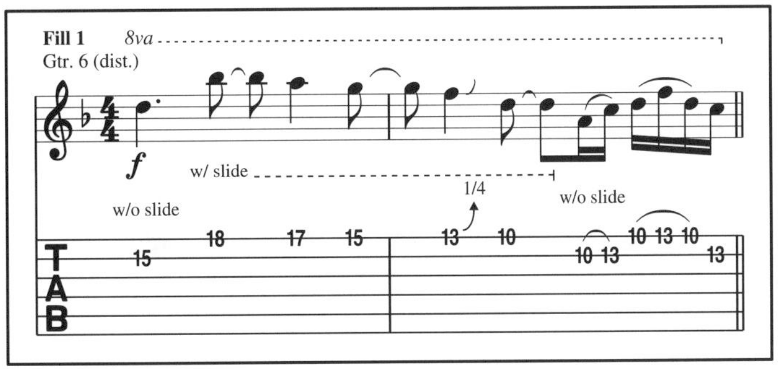

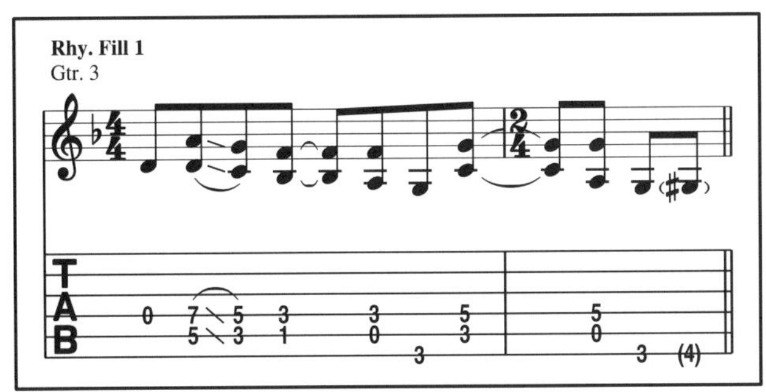

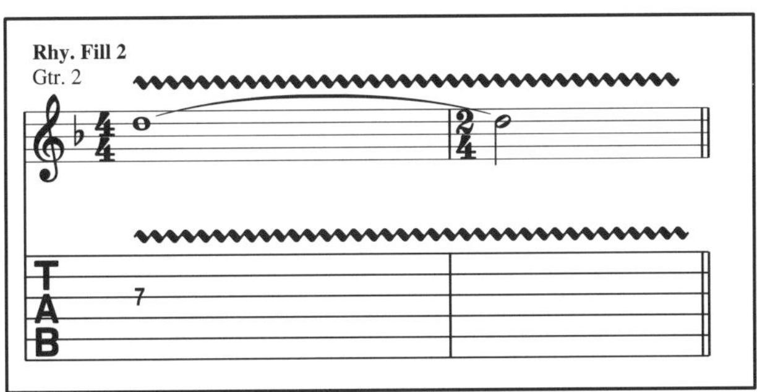

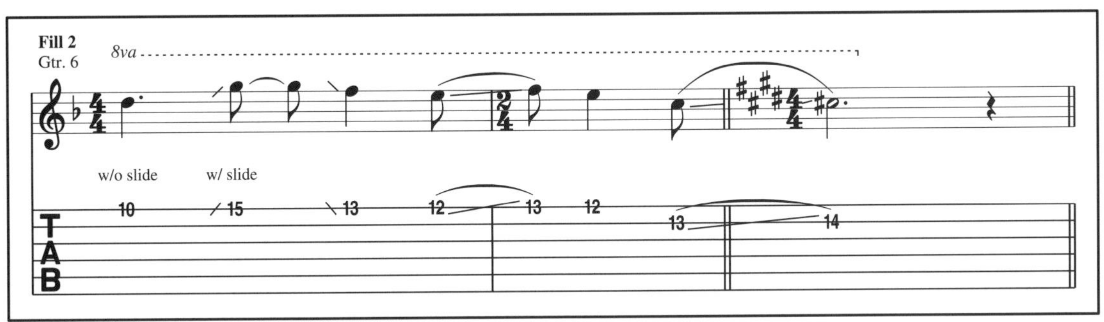

C7 D7 E7 F♯m(add9) B

and no-bod-y's wait - in' by your ___ side? You been run - nin' and

full full hold bend 1/2

E A F♯m B5 E N.C.

hid - in' much_too long, ___ you know it's just_your fool - ish pride.

(Lay -

Gtrs. 1 & 6

hold bend full hold bend full

let ring

Chorus

Gtrs. 1, 4 & 5: w/ Riffs B, B1 & B2, 1st & 2nd times; w/ Riffs B, B1 & B2, 1st 7 meas, 3rd time

Gtr. 2: w/ Riff A, 3 times

Gtr. 3: w/ Rhy. Fig. 1, 3 times

Gtr. 6: w/ Fill 3, 1st time; w/ Riff B, 1st 4 meas, 2nd time; w/ Riff B, 1st 2 meas., 3rd time

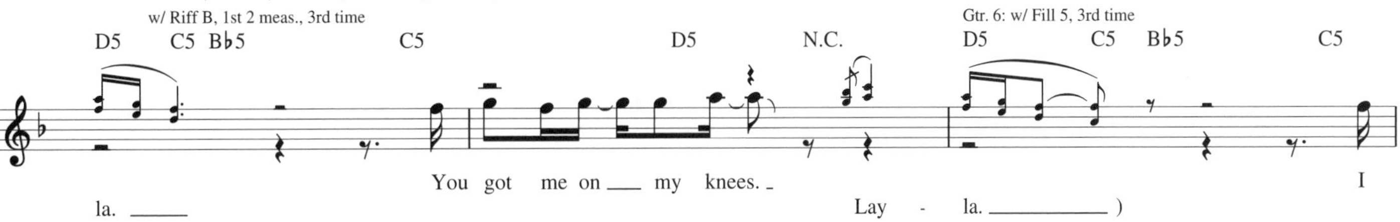

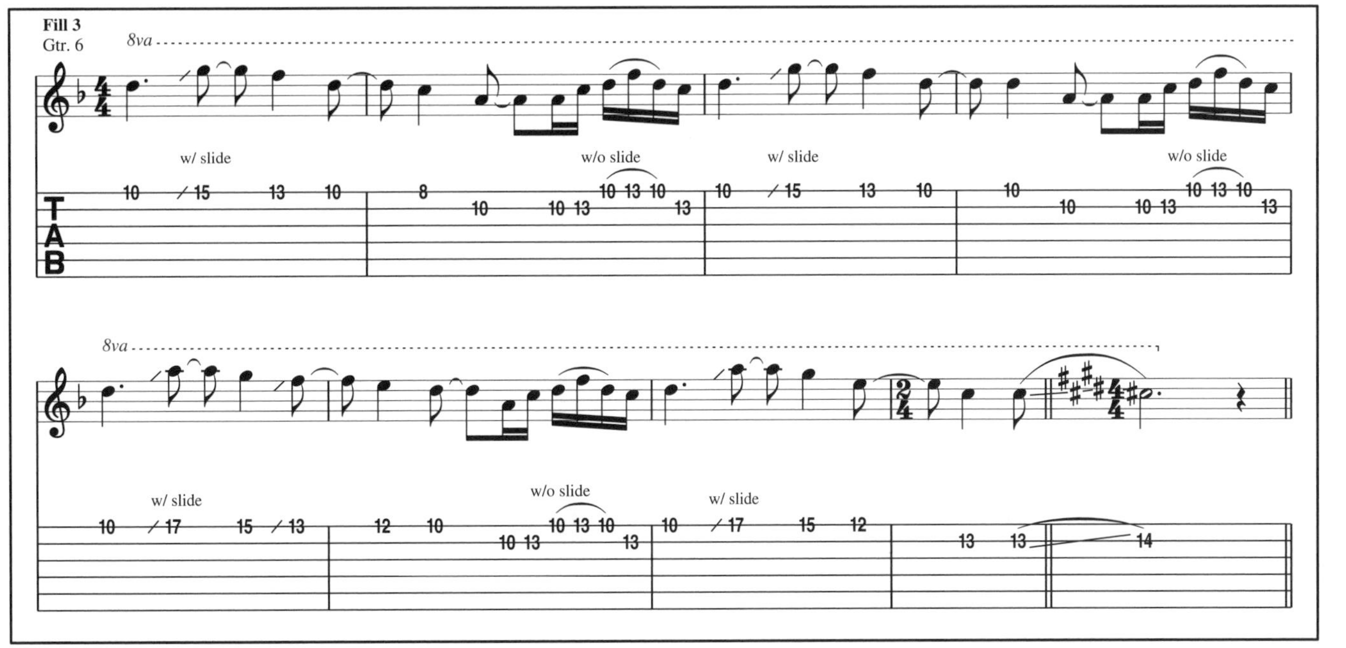

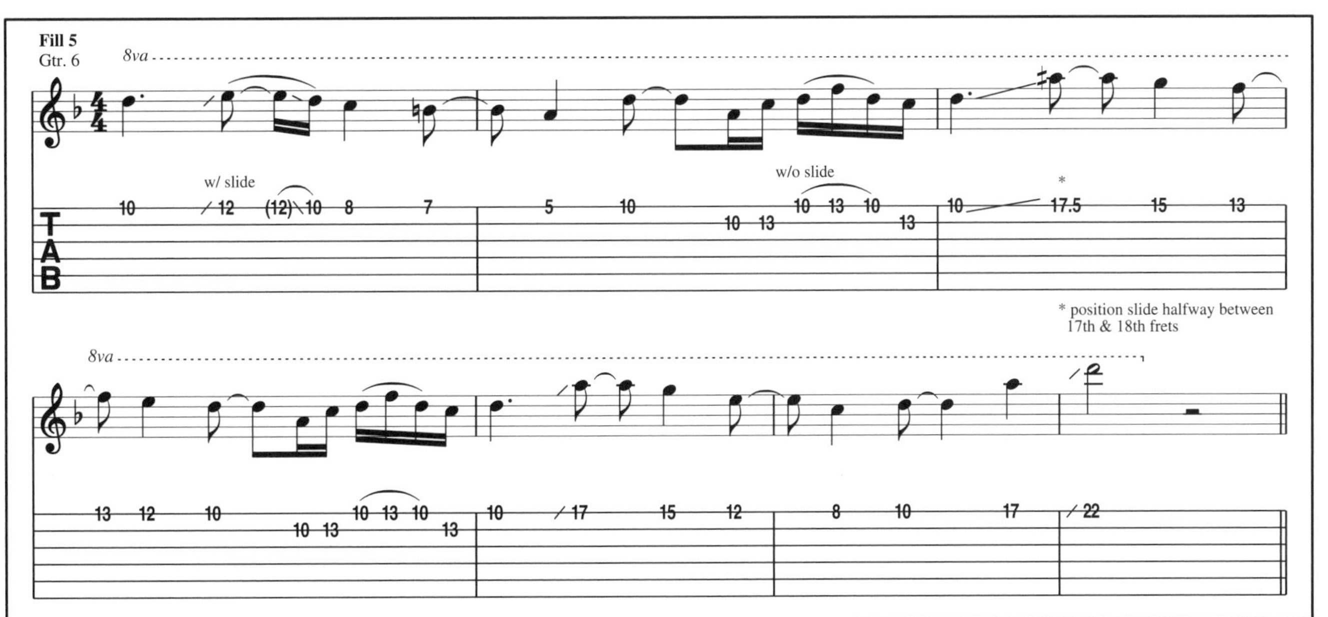

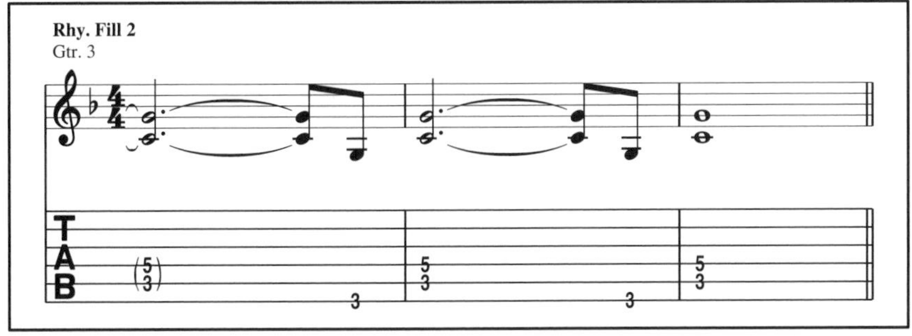

To Coda 2
To Coda 1
Gtr. 2: w/ Rhy. Fill 2, simile, 1st & 2nd times;
w/ Riff A, 1st meas., 3rd time
Gtr. 3: w/ Rhy. Fill 1, 1st & 2nd times;
w/ Rhy. Fig. 1, 3rd time
Gtr. 6: w/ Fill 1, simile, 2nd time
Gtr. 6: w/ Fill 4, 2nd time
D5 N.C. D5 C5 B♭5 C5 D5 N.C. D5 C5 B♭5 C5
beg you dar - lin' please, Lay - la, darlin' won't you ease my worried mind.
Verse
Gtrs. 2, 4, 5 & 6 tacet
C♯m G♯m7 C♯m7 C7 D7
2. I tried to give you con - so-la - tion when your old man, he let you
Gtr. 1
mf
1/2 full 1/2 full full
Gtr. 3
Gtrs. 4 & 5 divisi
dim.
E F♯m B E A
down. Like a fool, I fell in love with you,
full hold bend full
Fill 4
Gtr. 6
8va

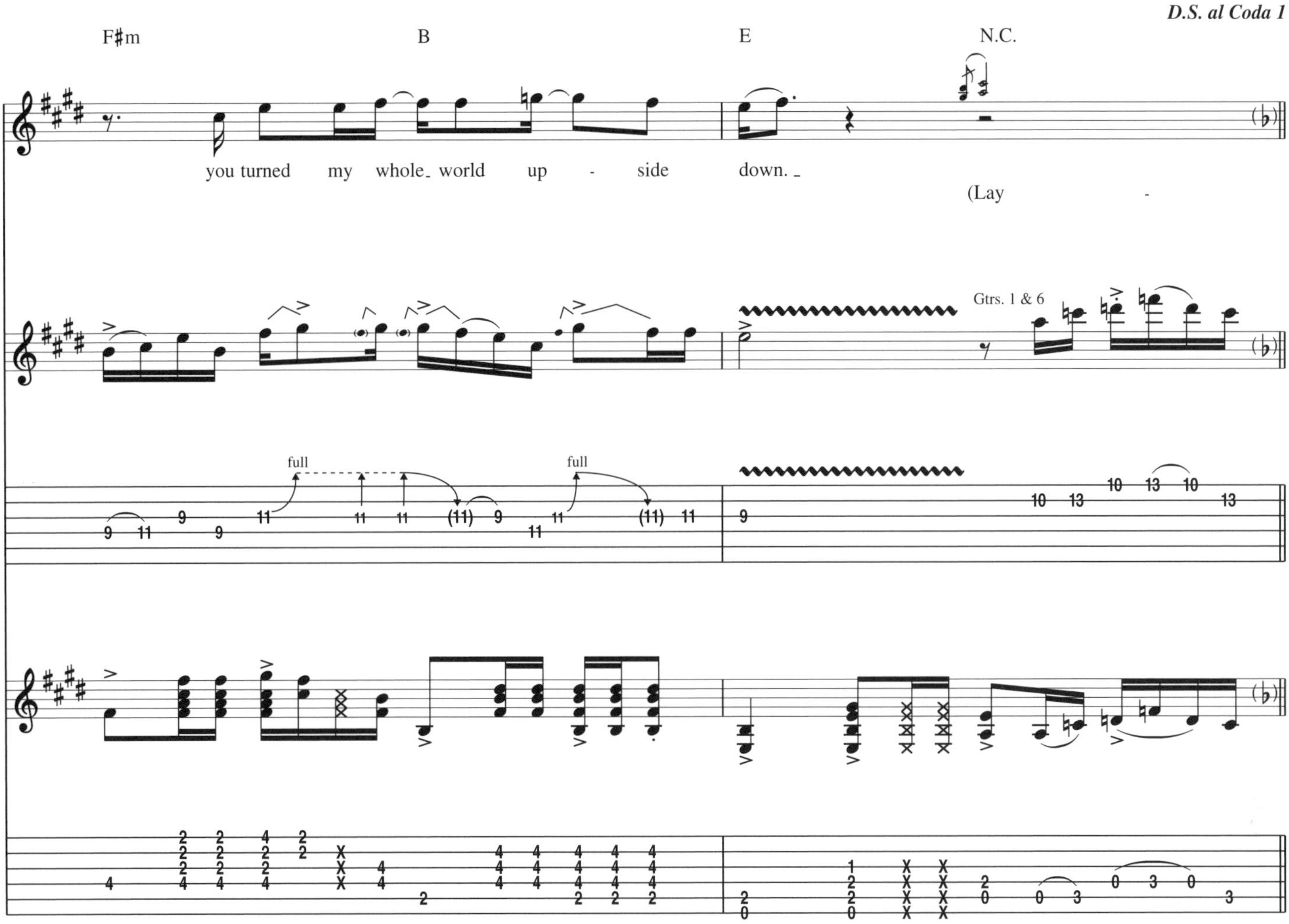

F♯m B E N.C.

you turned my whole world up - side down.

(Lay -

Gtrs. 1 & 6

full full

Coda 1

Verse

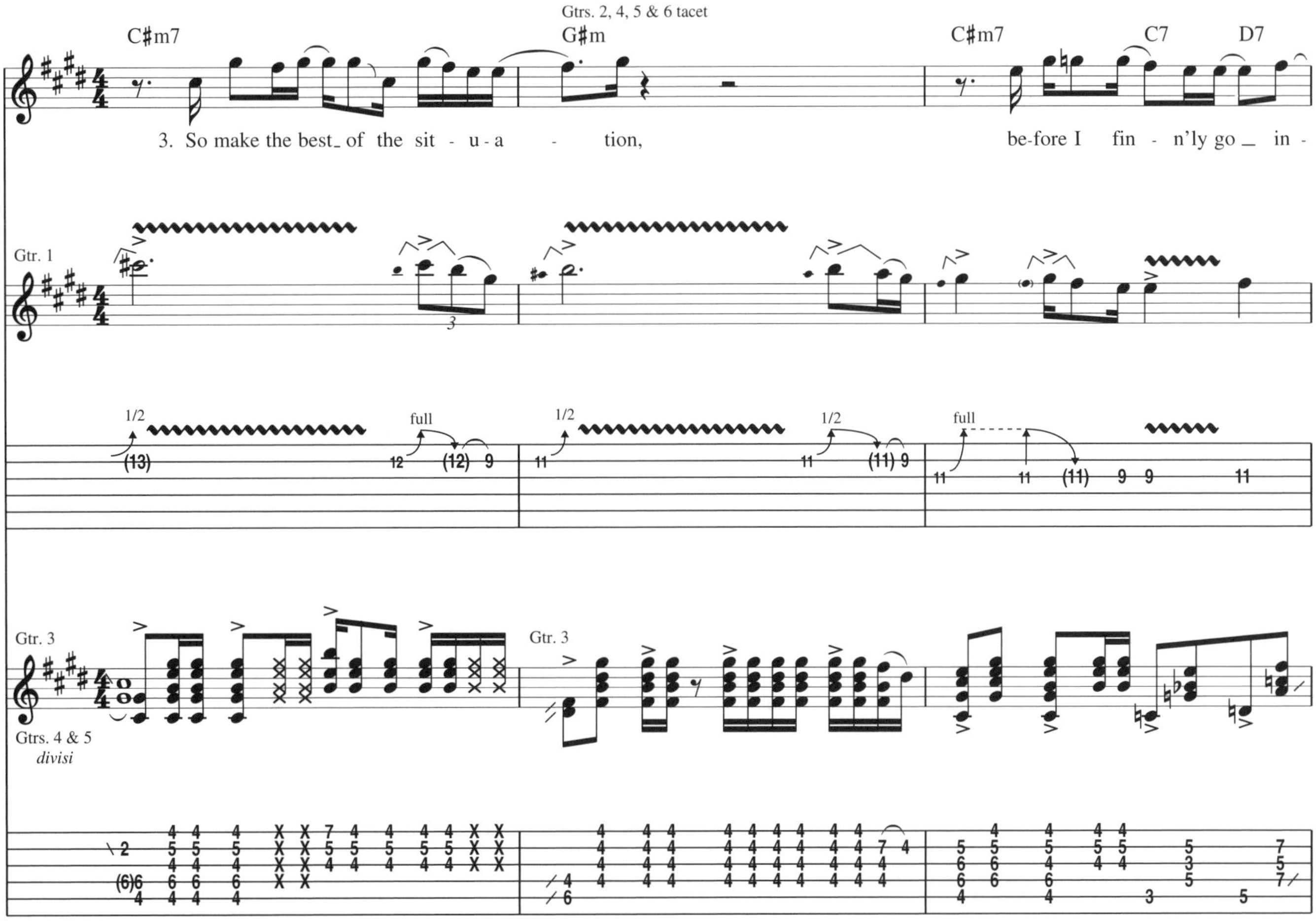

Gtrs. 2, 4, 5 & 6 tacet

C♯m7 G♯m C♯m7 C7 D7

3. So make the best of the sit - u - a - tion, be-fore I fin - n'ly go in -

Gtr. 1

1/2 full 1/2 1/2 full

Gtr. 3

Gtrs. 4 & 5 *divisi*

Gtr. 3

E
F#m
B
- sane.
Please don't say we'll
full
full
hold bend
E
A
F#m
B
nev - er find a way,
and tell me all my love's in
full
hold bend

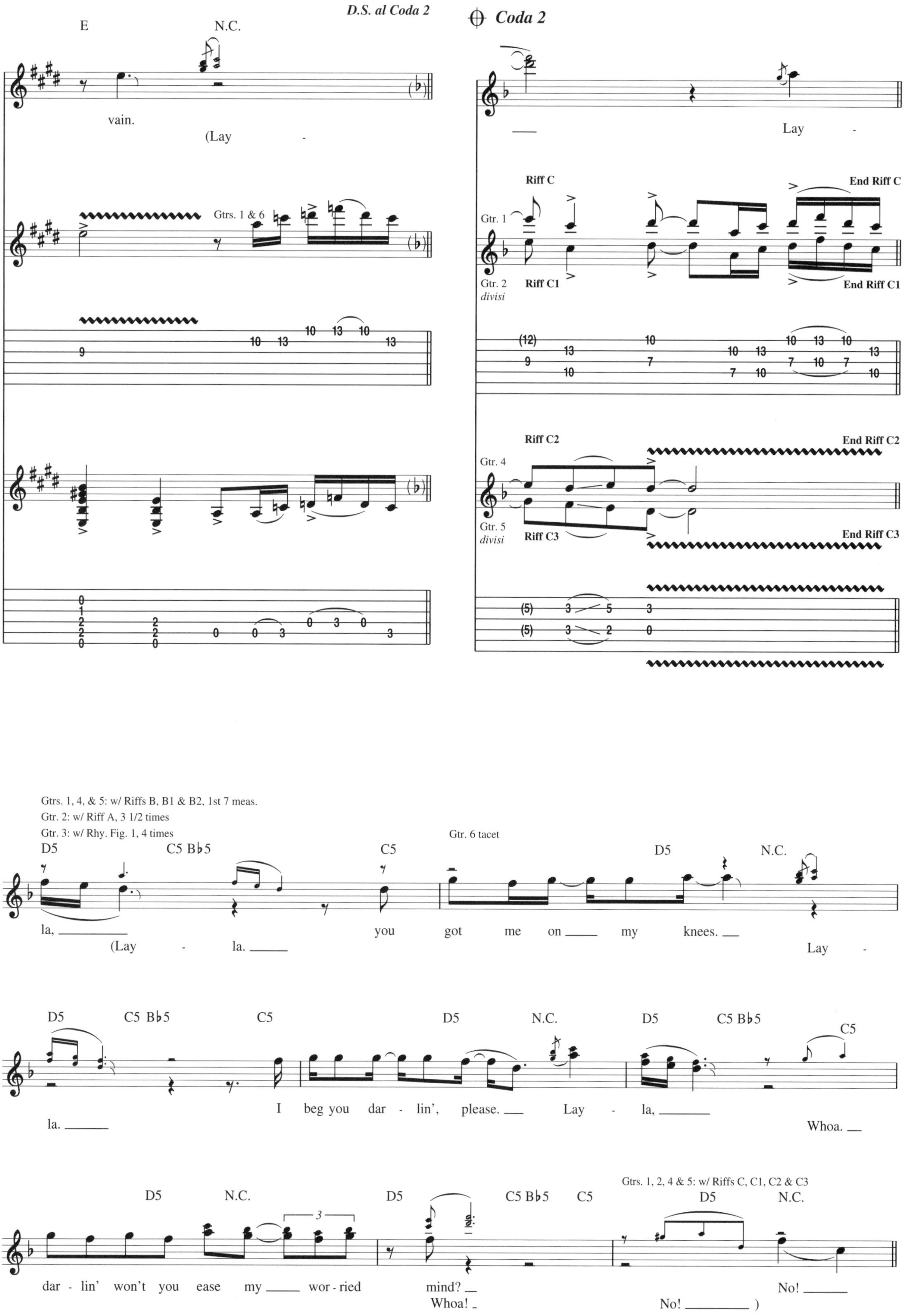

D.S. al Coda 2

Coda 2

E N.C.

vain.

(Lay -

Lay -

Riff C

End Riff C

Gtr. 1

Gtrs. 1 & 6

Gtr. 2 *divisi*

Riff C1

End Riff C1

Riff C2

End Riff C2

Gtr. 4

Gtr. 5 *divisi*

Riff C3

End Riff C3

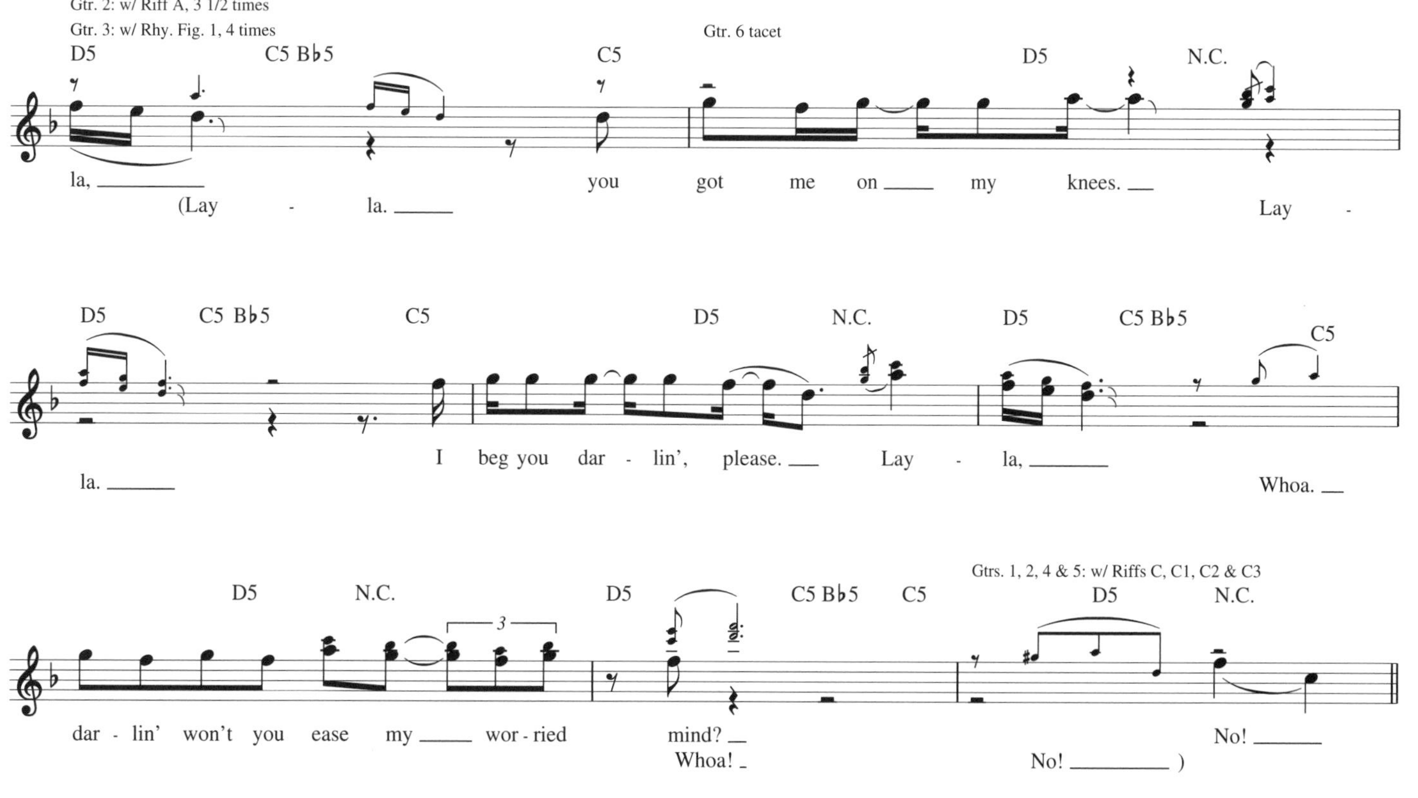

Gtrs. 1, 4, & 5: w/ Riffs B, B1 & B2, 1st 7 meas.
Gtr. 2: w/ Riff A, 3 1/2 times
Gtr. 3: w/ Rhy. Fig. 1, 11 1/2 times, simile

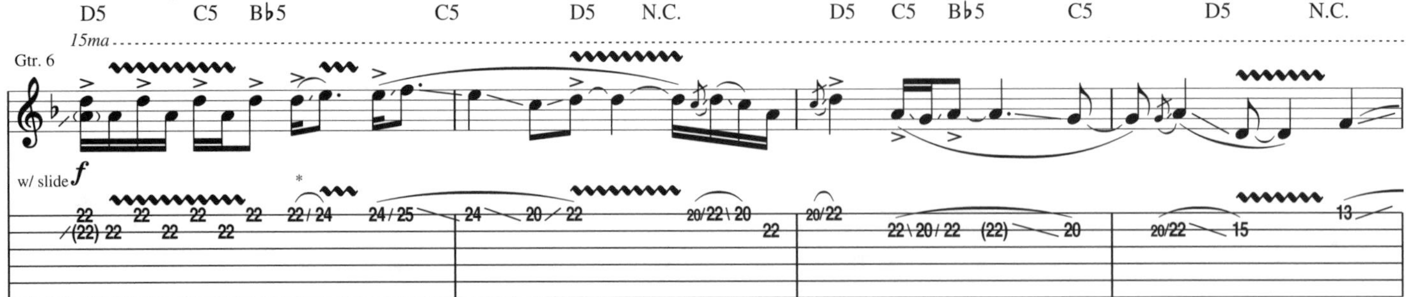

* TAB numbers based on location of notes beyond fretboard.

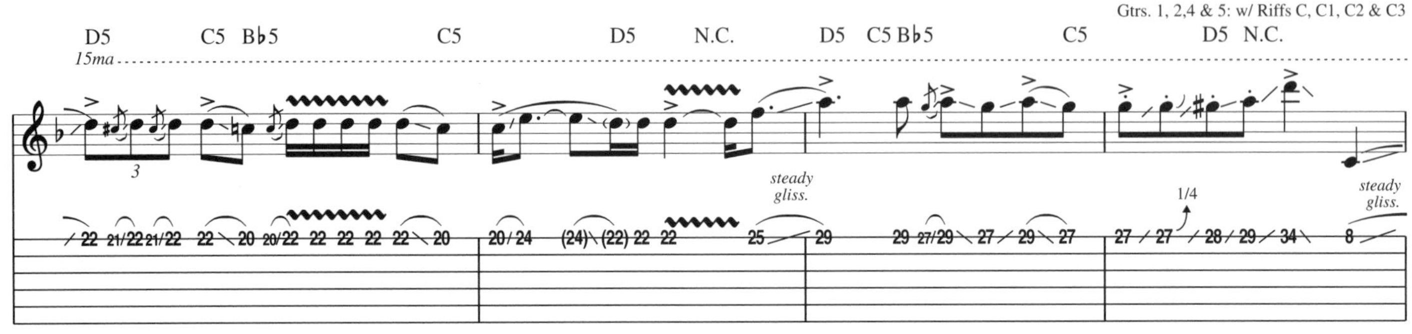

Gtrs. 1, 4 & 5: w/ Riffs B, B1 & B2, 1st 7 meas.
Gtr. 2: w/ Riff A, 3 1/2 times

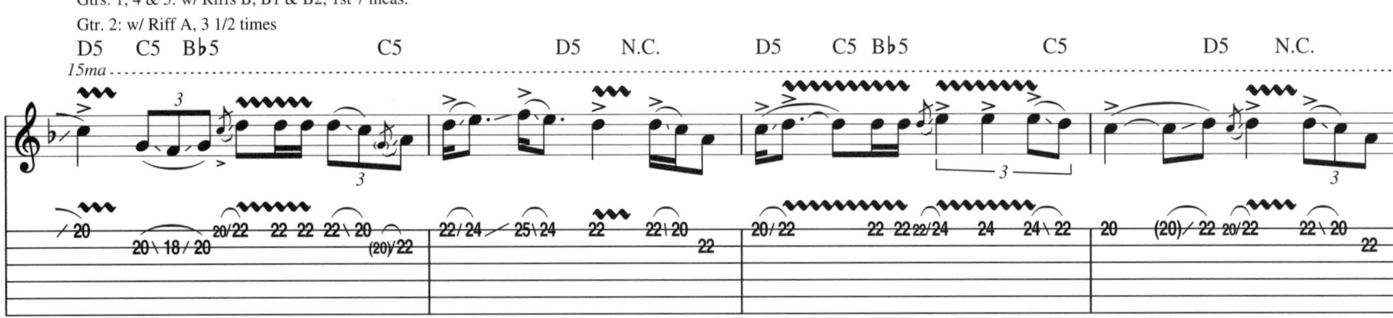

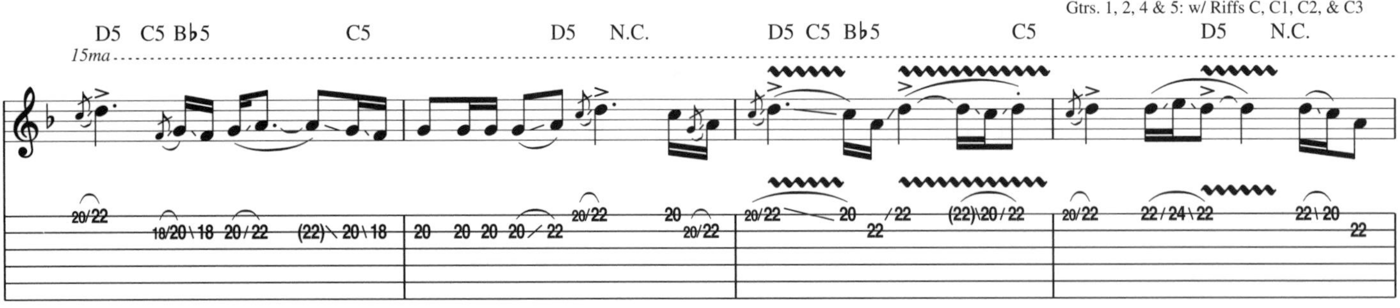

Gtrs. 1, 4 & 5: w/ Riffs B, B1 & B2, 1st 7 meas.
Gtr. 2: w/ Riff A, 3 1/2 times

D5 C5 B♭5 C5 D5 N.C. D5 C5 B♭5 C5 D5 N.C.

15ma

let ring

steady gliss.

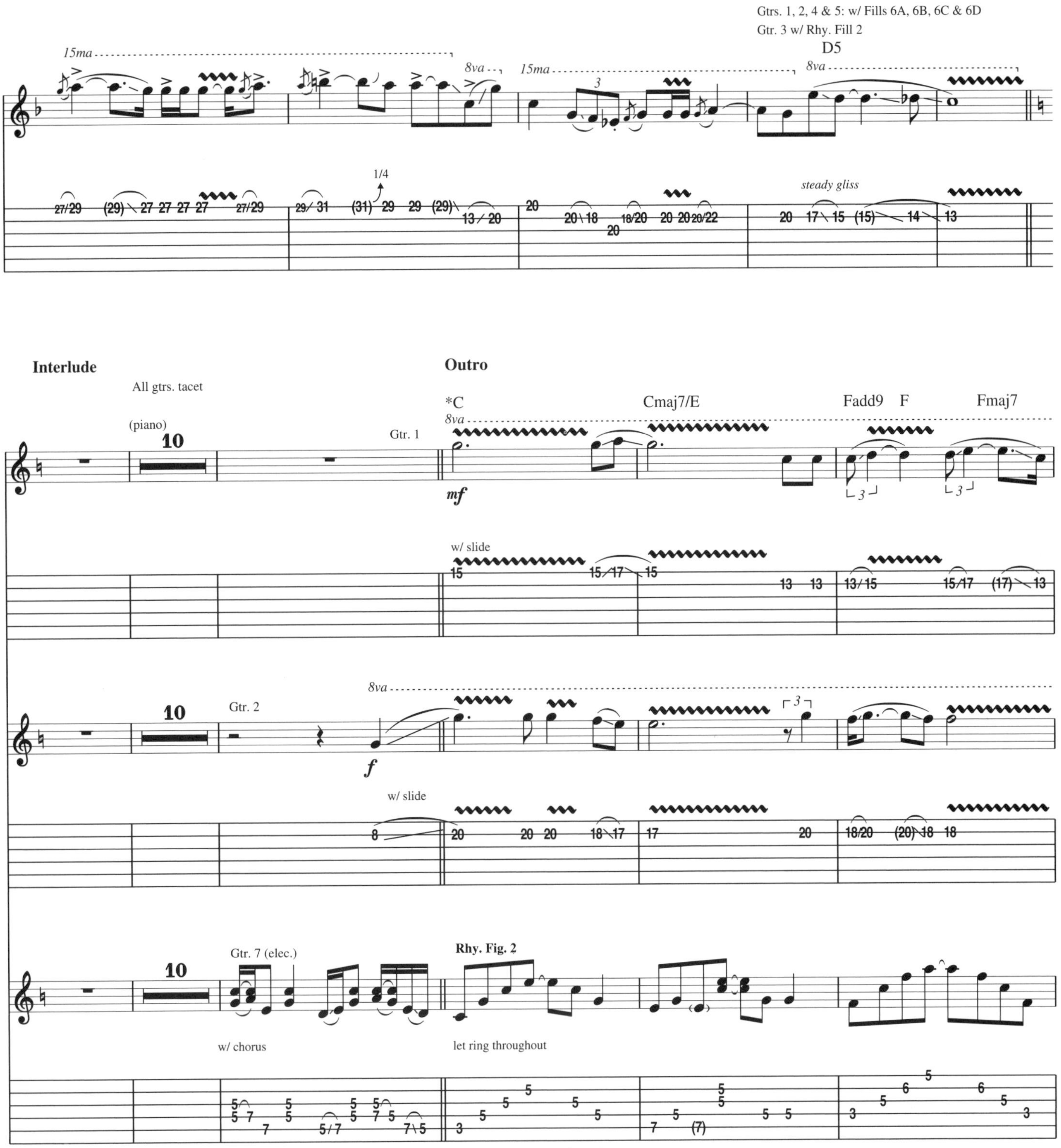

Gtrs. 1, 2, 4 & 5: w/ Fills 6A, 6B, 6C & 6D
Gtr. 3 w/ Rhy. Fill 2

D5

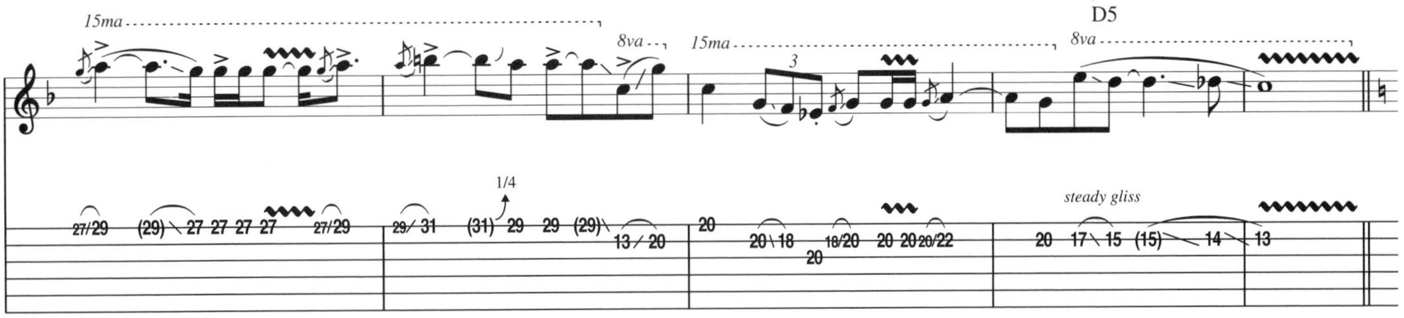

Interlude

All gtrs. tacet

(piano)

10

Gtr. 1

Outro

*C   Cmaj7/E   Fadd9   F   Fmaj7

8va

mf

w/ slide

Gtr. 2

8va

f

w/ slide

Gtr. 7 (elec.)

Rhy. Fig. 2

w/ chorus

let ring throughout

* Chord symbols come from piano.

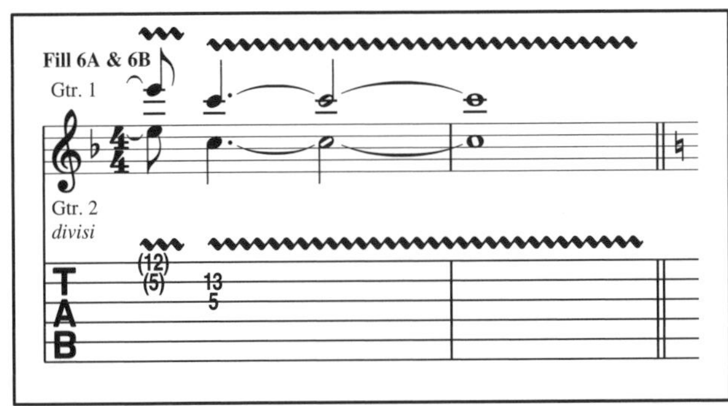

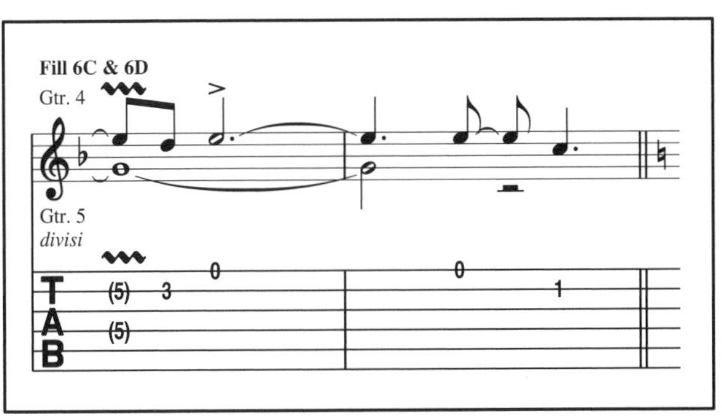

F6 F B♭7 B♭7(♭5) B♭7 C

8va loco

8va

P.M.

Gtr. 7: w/ Rhy. Fig. 2, 1st 5 meas., simile

C Cmaj7/E Fadd9 F Fmaj7

let ring

8va

End Rhy. Fig. 2

P.M. P.M.

F6 F B♭7 B♭7(♭5) B♭7 C C/B

8va

Gtr. 7

Rhy. Fig. 3

Am Dsus4 Dm G Gsus4 C E7

8va

f

8va

mf

Am
D
Gsus4
G
Gadd9
G5
8va
loco
w/ slide
End Rhy. Fig. 3
Gtr. 7: w/ Rhy. Fig. 2, 1st 4 meas., simile
C
C/E
Fadd9
F
Fmaj7
F6
F
Gtr. 7: w/ Rhy. Fig. 2, 3/4 time, simile
C
15ma
8va
f
w/ slide
C/E
Fadd9
F
Fmaj7
F6
F
B♭7
B♭7(♭5) B♭7
C
steady gliss.

Gtr. 7 w/ Rhy. Fig. 2, 1st meas.
Gtr. 7 w/ Rhy. Fill 3, simile
Gtr. 7 w/ Rhy. Fig. 2, 1st 7 meas., simile
C
Cmaj7/E
Fadd9
F
Fmaj7
8va
Gtr. 1
Gtr. 2
loco
Gtr. 8 (acous.)
Riff D
F6
F
B♭7
B♭7(♭5)
B♭7
C
Gtr. 7: w/ Rhy. Fill 4 (see next page)
End Riff D
Rhy. Fill 3
Gtr. 7
T
A
B

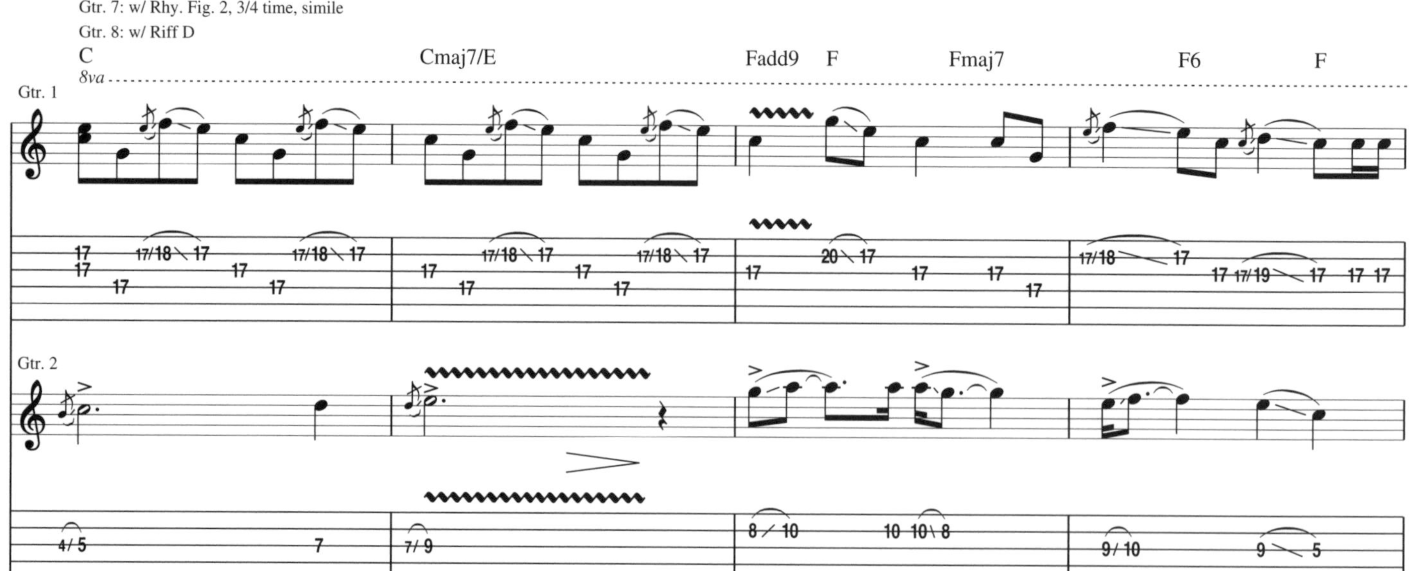
Gtr. 7: w/ Rhy. Fig. 2, 3/4 time, simile
Gtr. 8: w/ Riff D
C
Cmaj7/E
Fadd9
F
Fmaj7
F6
F
8va
Gtr. 1
Gtr. 2

B♭7
B♭7(♭5) B♭7
Gtr. 7: w/ Rhy. Fill 5
C
Gtr. 7: w/ Rhy. Fig. 3, simile
8va

Rhy. Fill 4
Gtr. 7

Rhy. Fill 5
Gtr. 7
P.M.

Am
Dsus4 Dm
G
Csus4
C
E7/B
8va
Gtr. 1
Gtr. 2
mp
semi-harm.
Gtr. 8
Gtr. 7: w/ Rhy. Fill 6 (see next page)
G
Gtr. 7: w/ Rhy. Fig. 2, 1st 4 meas., simile
C
C/E
Fadd9
F
Fmaj7
F6
F
steady gliss.
steady gliss.
Rhy. Fig. 4
End Rhy. Fig. 4

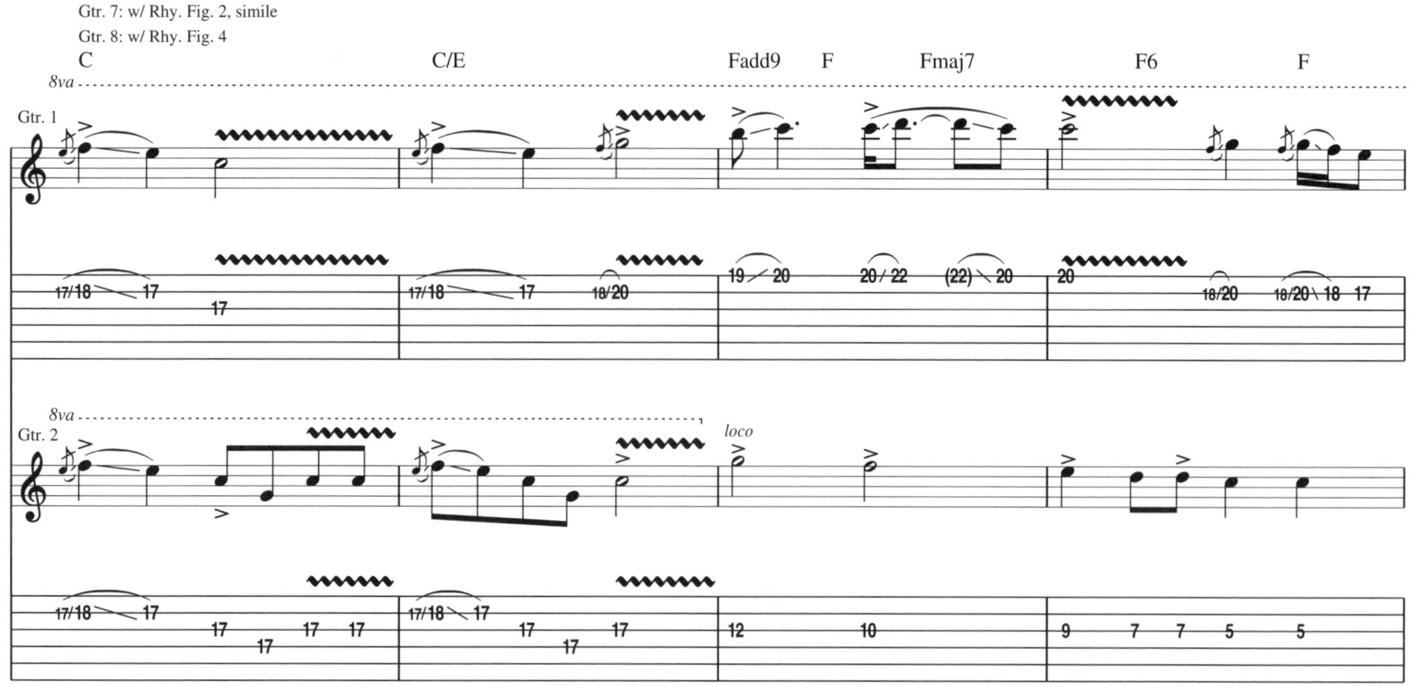

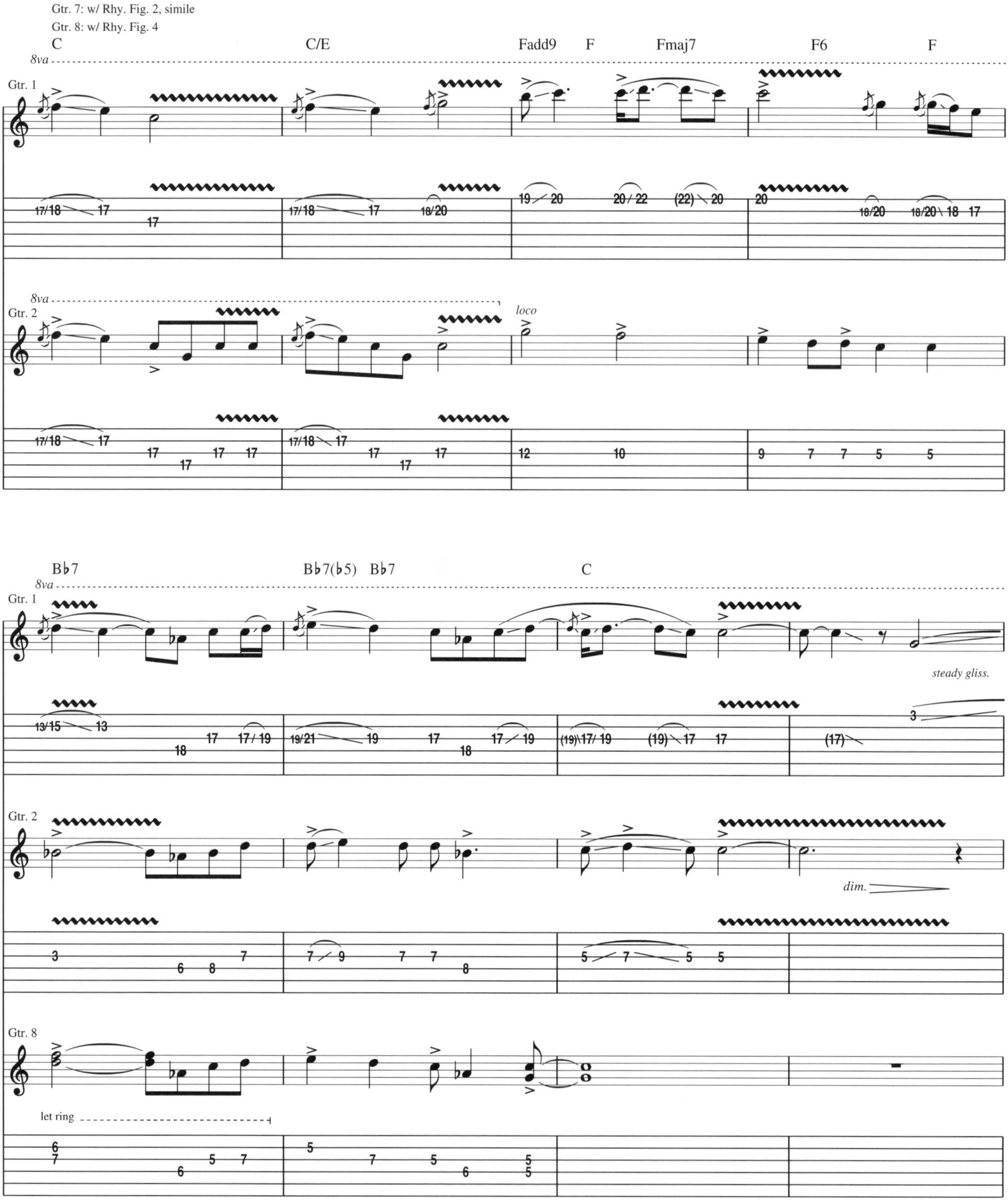

B♭7 B♭7(♭5) B♭7 C

8va

Gtr. 1

steady gliss.

Gtr. 2

dim.

Gtr. 8

let ring

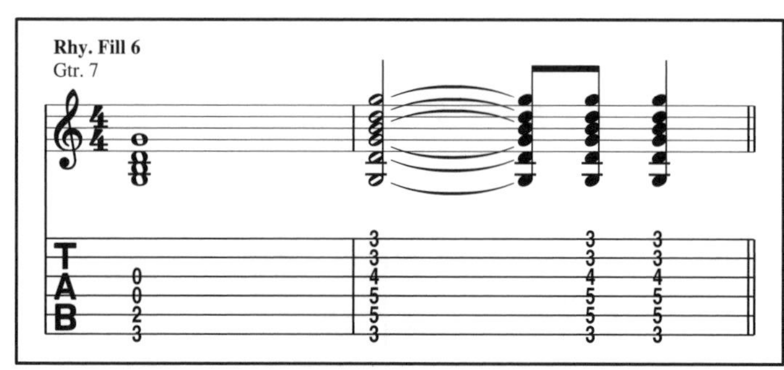

Gtr. 7: w/ Rhy. Fig. 2, 1st 4 meas., 5 times, simile
Gtr. 8: w/ Rhy. Fig. 4, 5 times
C
C/E
Fadd9 F
Fmaj7
F6
F
C
8va
mf
mf
C/E
Fadd9 F
Fmaj7
F6
F
C
C/E
Fadd9
F
Fmaj7
F6
F
C
C/E
Fadd9 F
Fmaj7

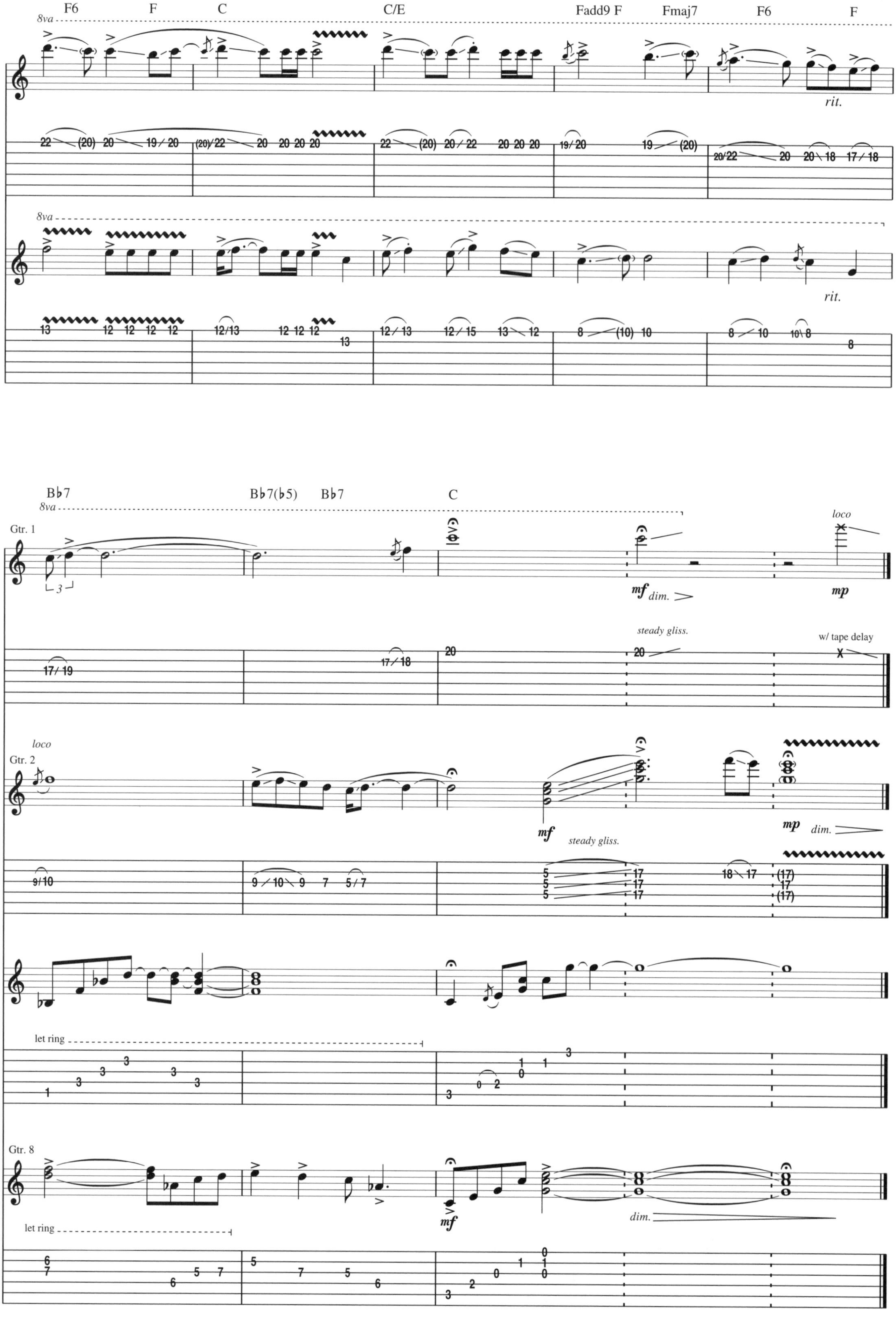

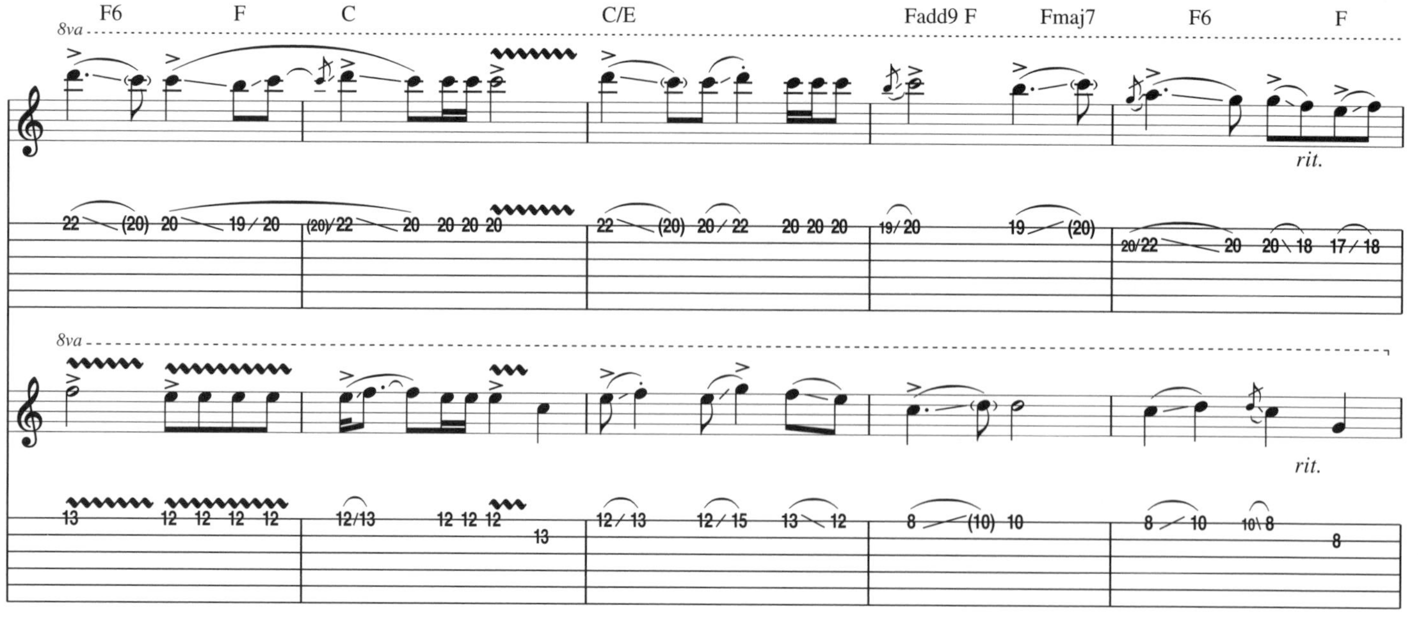

F6
F
C
C/E
Fadd9 F
Fmaj7
F6
F
8va
rit.
8va
rit.
B♭7
B♭7(♭5)
B♭7
C
8va
Gtr. 1
loco
mf dim.
mp
steady gliss.
w/ tape delay
loco
Gtr. 2
mf
steady gliss.
mp dim.
let ring
Gtr. 8
let ring
mf
dim.

from Eric Clapton - *Eric Clapton*

Let It Rain

Words and Music by Eric Clapton and Bonnie Bramlett

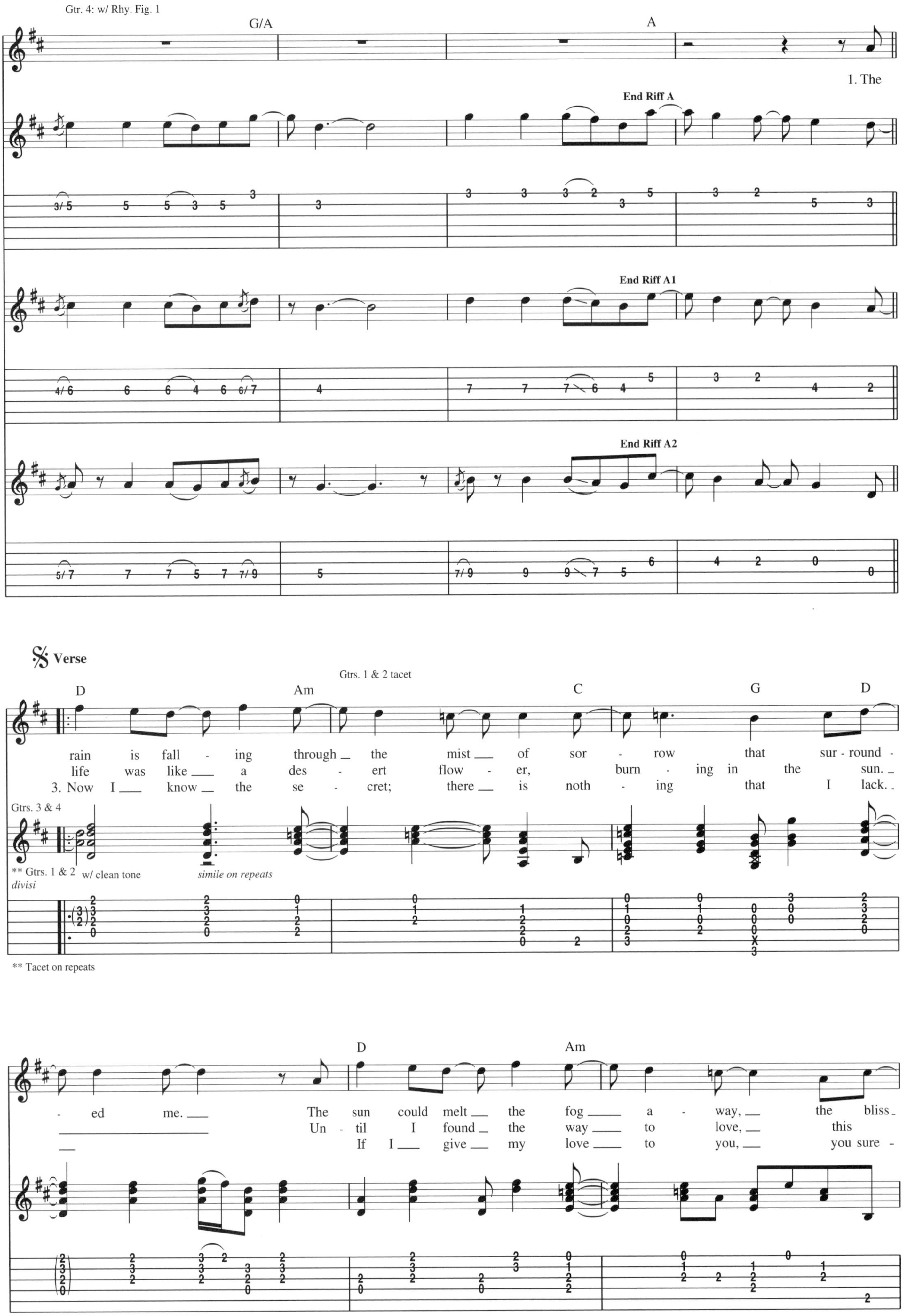

Gtr. 4: w/ Rhy. Fig. 1

G/A A

1. The

End Riff A

End Riff A1

End Riff A2

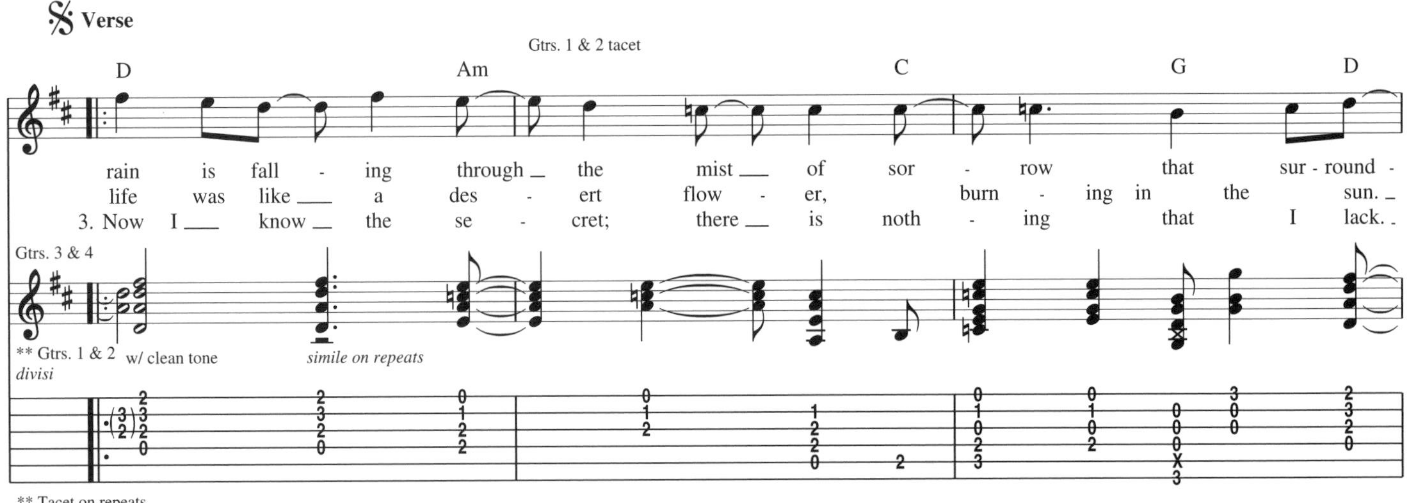

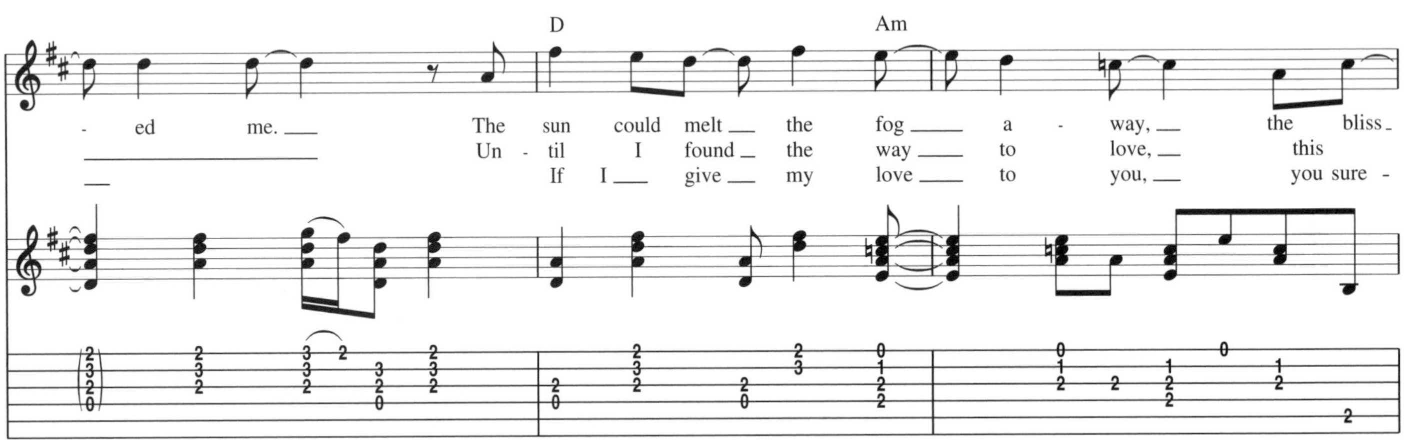

Chorus
C G D
D Am
Gtrs. 3 & 4
that lays a - round me.
heart was sad and done.
- ly give it back.
Let it rain; let it rain.
Rhy. Fig. 2
Gtr. 1
(cont. in slash)
let ring throughout
simile on repeats
Gtr. 2
Rhy. Fig. 2A
let ring throughout
D Am C G D
Let your love rain down on me. Let it rain;
End Rhy. Fig. 2
End Rhy. Fig. 2A
To Coda
1.
Gtrs. 1 & 2: w/ Rhy. Figs. 2 & 2A, 1st & 2nd times
Gtrs. 1 & 2: w/ Rhy. Figs. 2 & 2A, 2 3/4 times, 3rd time, simile
Am D Am C G D
let it rain. Let it rain, rain, rain.

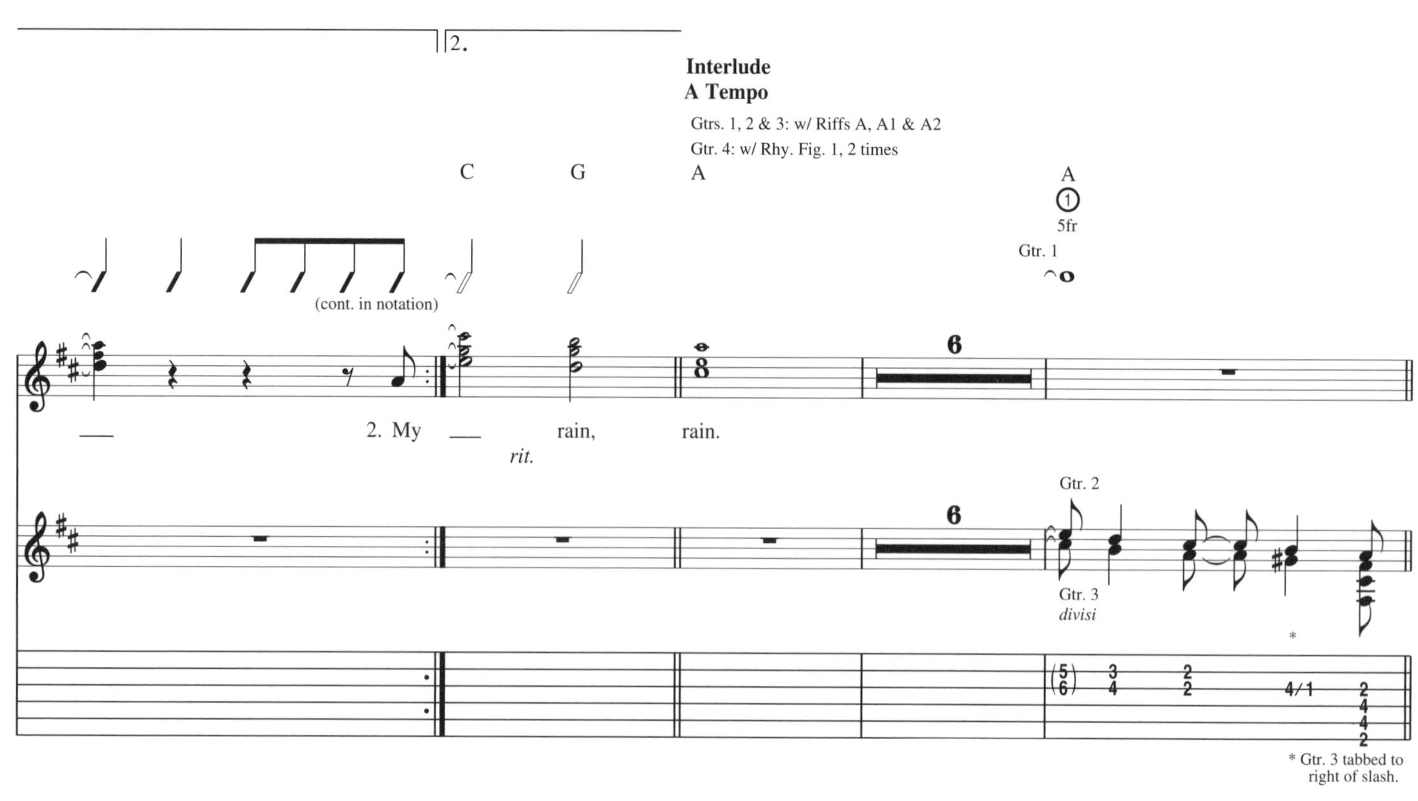

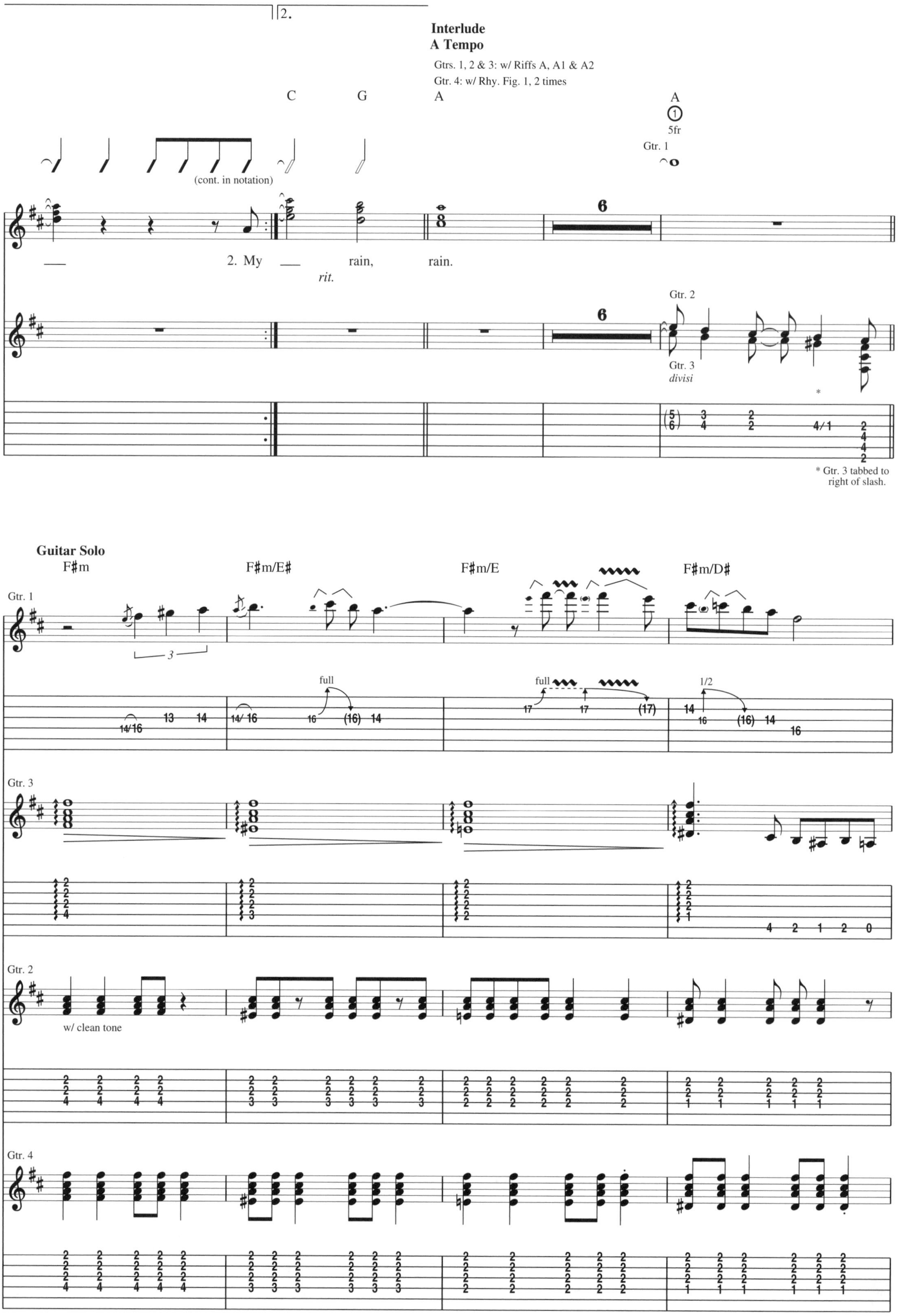

Guitar Solo

F♯m F♯m/E♯ F♯m/E F♯m/D♯

Gtr. 1

full full 1/2

Gtr. 3

Gtr. 2

w/ clean tone

Gtr. 4

Gtrs. 2, 3 & 4: w/ Rhy. Figs. 3 & 3A, 2 times, simile
Em7
A
Asus2
Asus4
Asus2
Em7
Gtr. 1
Gtr. 2
Rhy. Fig. 3
End Rhy. Fig. 3
let ring throughout
Gtrs. 3 & 4
Rhy. Fig. 3A
End Rhy. Fig. 3A
let ring throughout
D.S. al Coda
Asus2
Asus4
Asus2
Em7
A6
Asus2
Asus4
Asus2
Gtr. 1
Coda
C
G
D
Am
D
Am
Gtrs. 3 & 4
rain, rain. Let it rain; let it rain. Let your love
C
G
D
Am
D
Am
C
G
rain down on me. Let it rain; let it rain, let it rain rain.
Outro
Gtrs. 1, 2 & 3: w/ Riffs A, A1 & A2, 1st 4 meas., 16 3/4 times
Gtr. 4: w/ Rhy. Fig. 1, 2 times
G/A
Rhy. Fig. 3
Gtr. 4
rain.

G/A
A
End Rhy. Fig. 3
Gtr. 5
(elec.)
8va
w/ dist.
Gtr. 4: w/ Rhy. Fig. 3, 13 3/4 times, simile
G/A
A
Voc. Fig. 1
(Yeah.)
(Yeah.
loco
full
Bkgd. Voc.: w/ Voc. Fig. 1, 3 times, simile
G/A
End Voc. Fig. 1
)
full
8va
G/A
A
full
1/2
8va
G/A
full

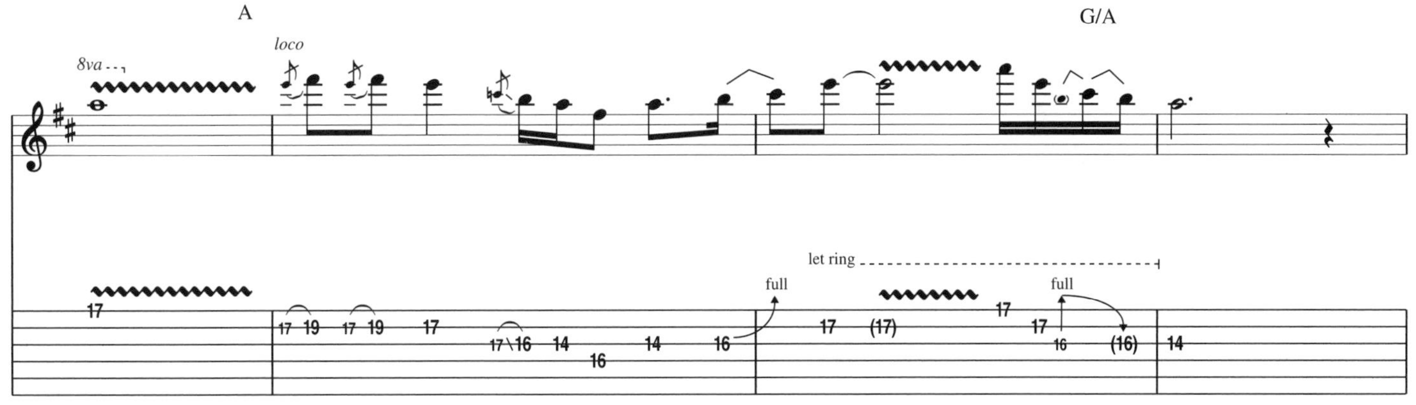
A
G/A
8va
loco
let ring
full
full
17
17 19 17 19 17 17 16 14 16 14 16
17 (17) 17 17 16 (16) 14

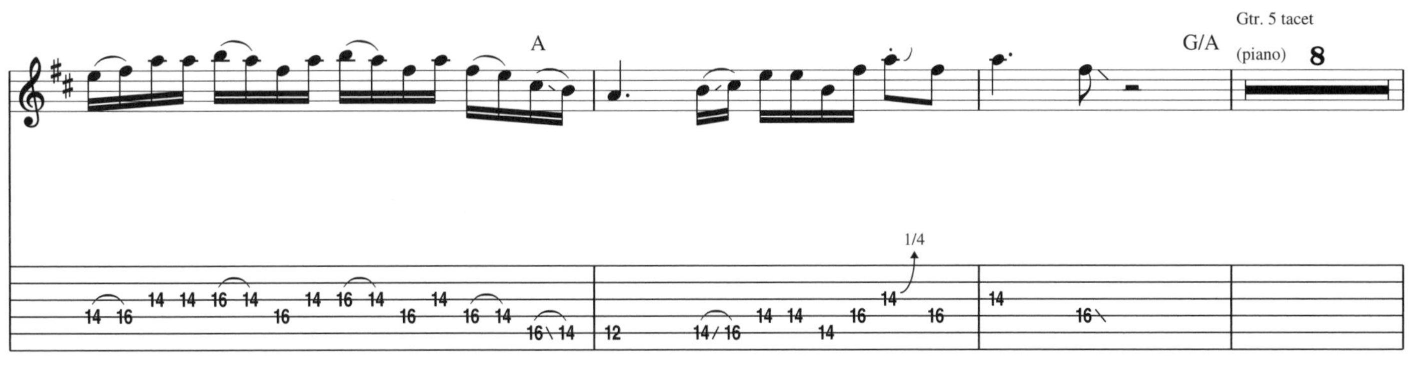
A
G/A
Gtr. 5 tacet
(piano)
8
1/4
14 16 14 14 16 14 16 14 16 14 16 14 16 16 14 16 14
12 14 16 14 14 14 16 14 16
14 16

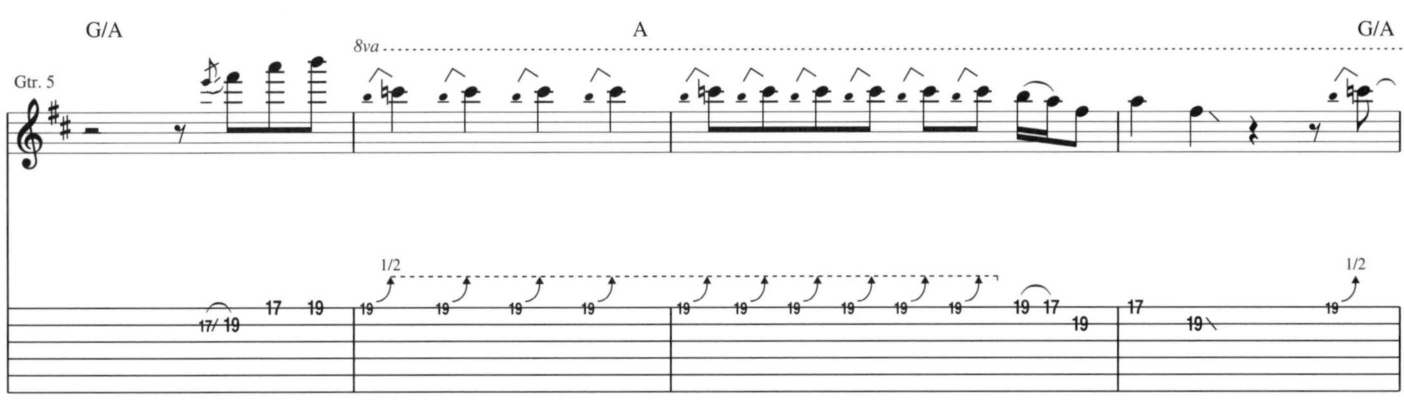
G/A
A
G/A
Gtr. 5
8va
1/2
1/2
17 19 17 19
19 19 19 19
19 19 19 19 19 19 19 17 19
17 19 19

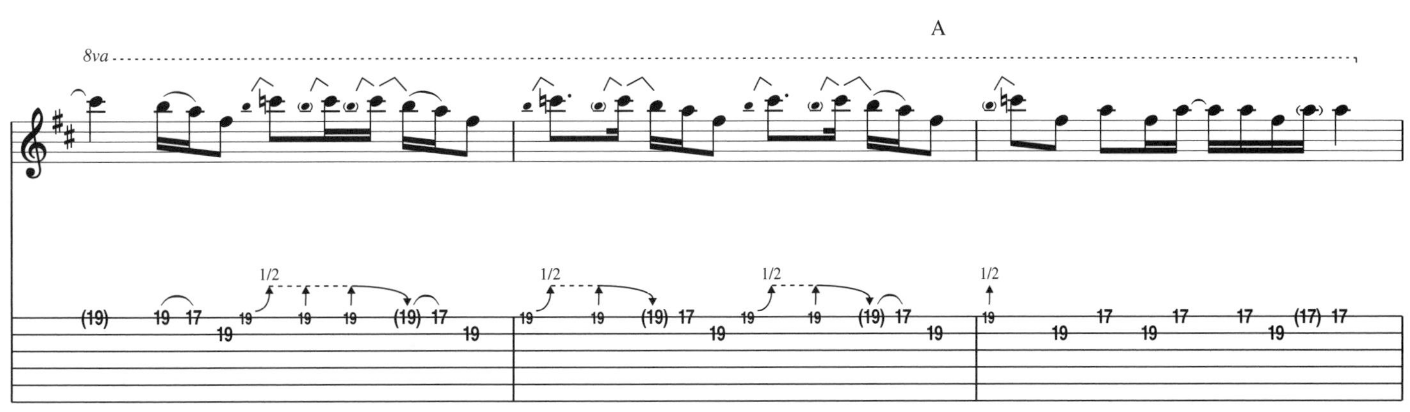
A
8va
1/2
1/2
1/2
1/2
(19) 19 17 19 19 19 19 (19) 17 19
19 19 (19) 17 19 19 19 (19) 17 19
19 19 17 19 17 17 19 (17) 17

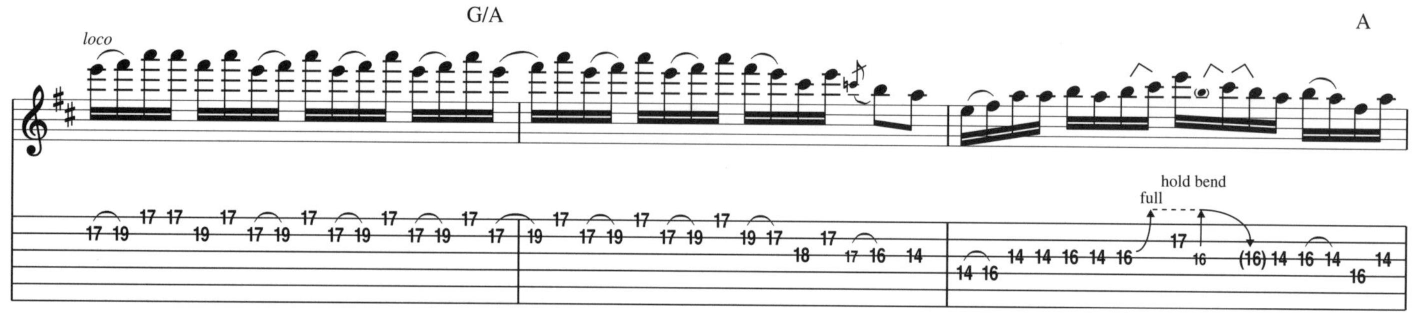
G/A
A
loco
hold bend
full

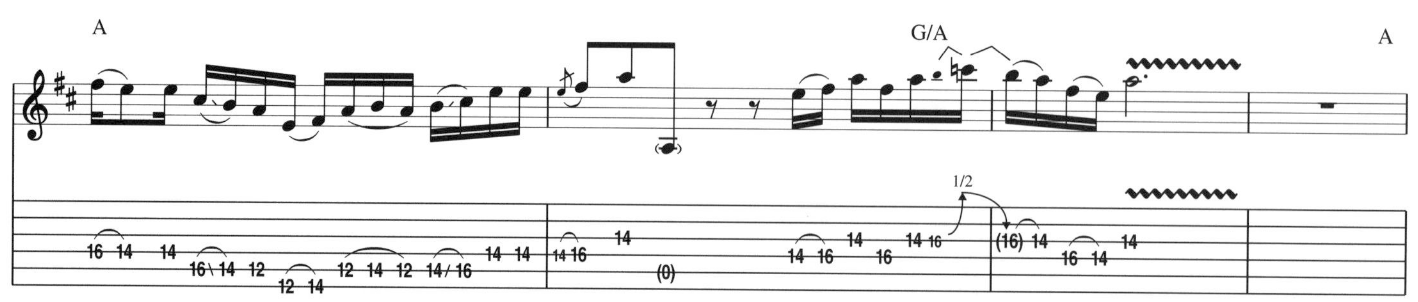
A
G/A
A
1/2

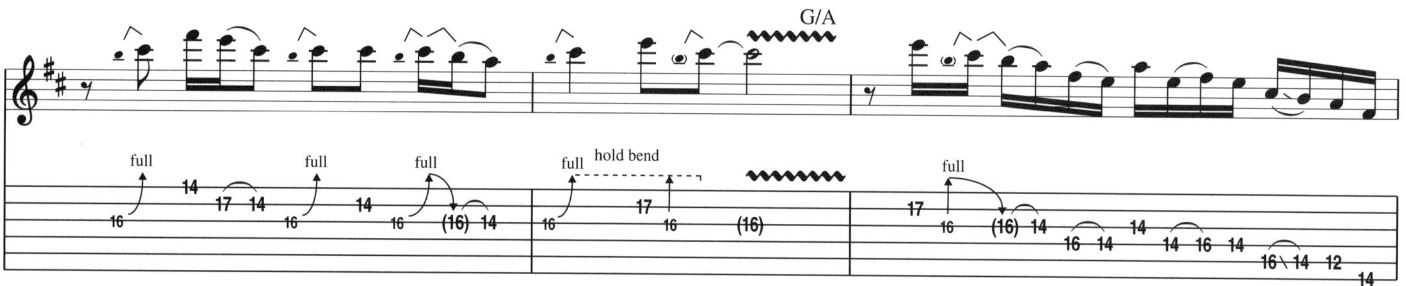
G/A
full
hold bend

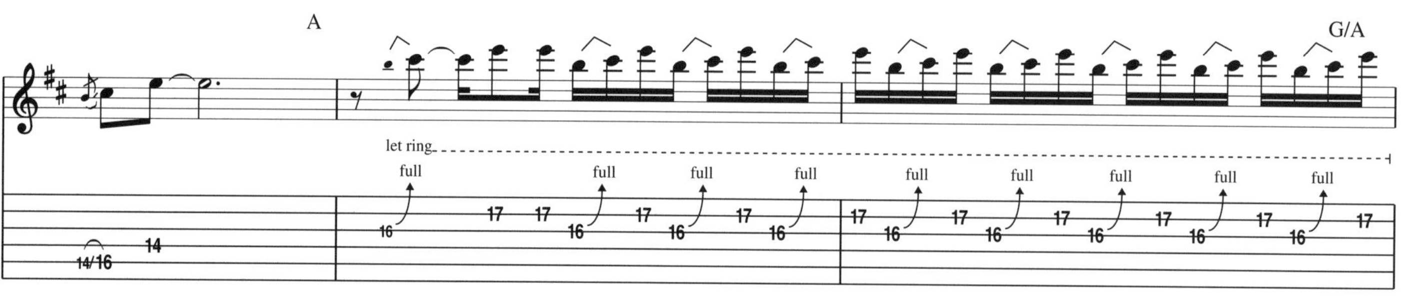
A
G/A
let ring
full

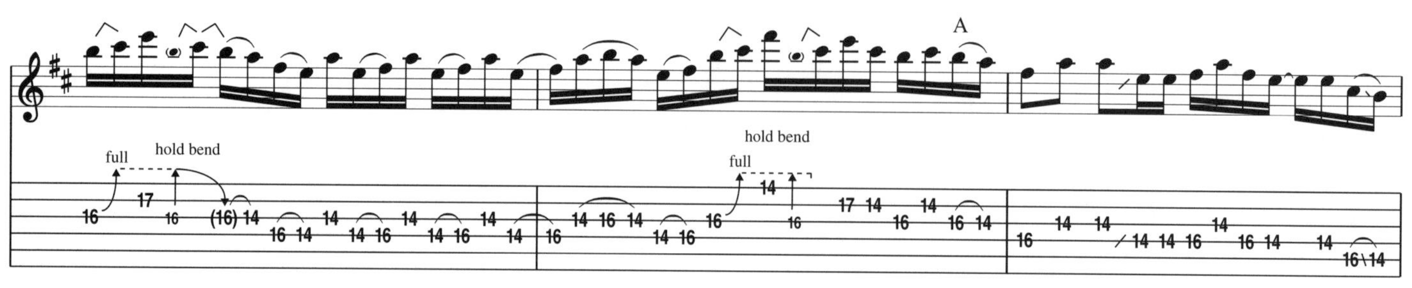
A
full
hold bend

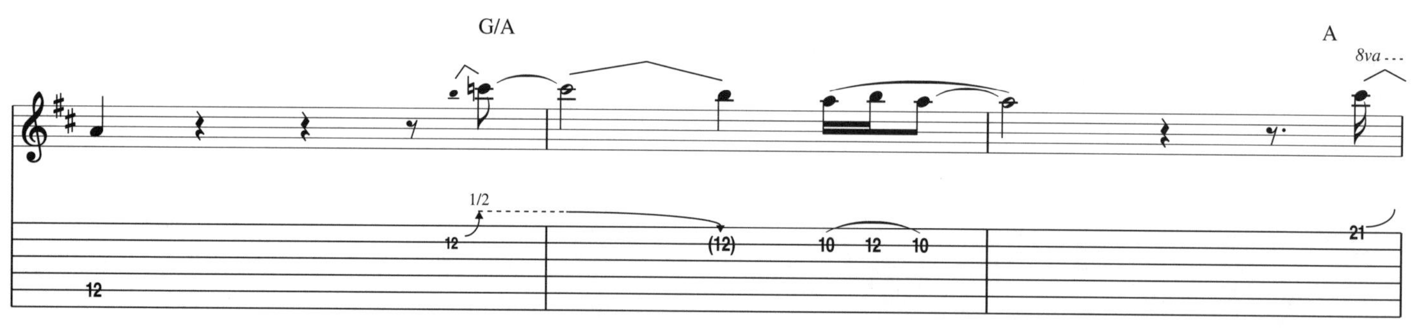
G/A
A
8va
1/2

A
G♯
2
9fr
Gtr. 4
(cont. in notation)
8va
Gtr. 5
loco
decresc.
1/2
Gtr. 1
decresc.
Gtr. 2
decresc.
Gtr. 3
decresc.

Freely
A7
P.M.
Gtr. 5
1/2
1/2

from Eric Clapton - *Pilgrim*

My Father's Eyes

Words and Music by Eric Clapton

E A D/F♯ A/E E F♯

Verse

B Emaj7

1. Sail-in' down be-

Gtr. 4

Gtr. 2

Rhy. Fig. 2

End Rhy. Fig. 2

Rhy. Fig. 3

* T

T

Gtr. 3

* T

T

* T = Thumb on ⑥

Gtr. 3 tacet

F♯ B

Gtr. 4 tacet

C♯/E♯ C♯m/E F♯ B Emaj7

hind the sun, wait-in' for the prince to come. Pray-in' for the

Gtr. 4

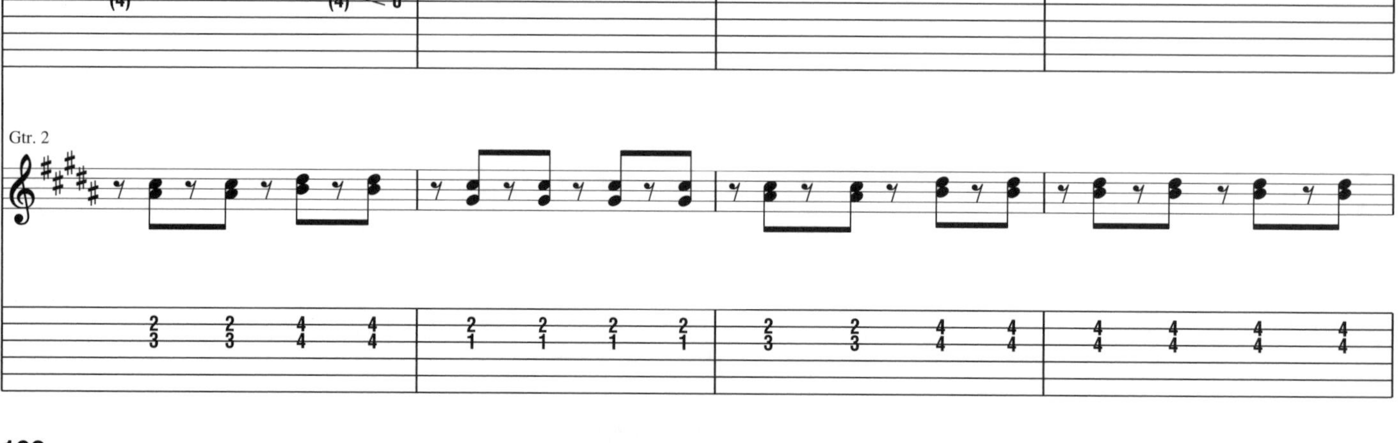

F#
G#m
C#/E#
D/F#
A/E
E
heal - in' rain
to re - store
my soul
a - gain.
Gtr. 2
End Rhy. Fig. 3
Gtr. 3

Pre-Chorus

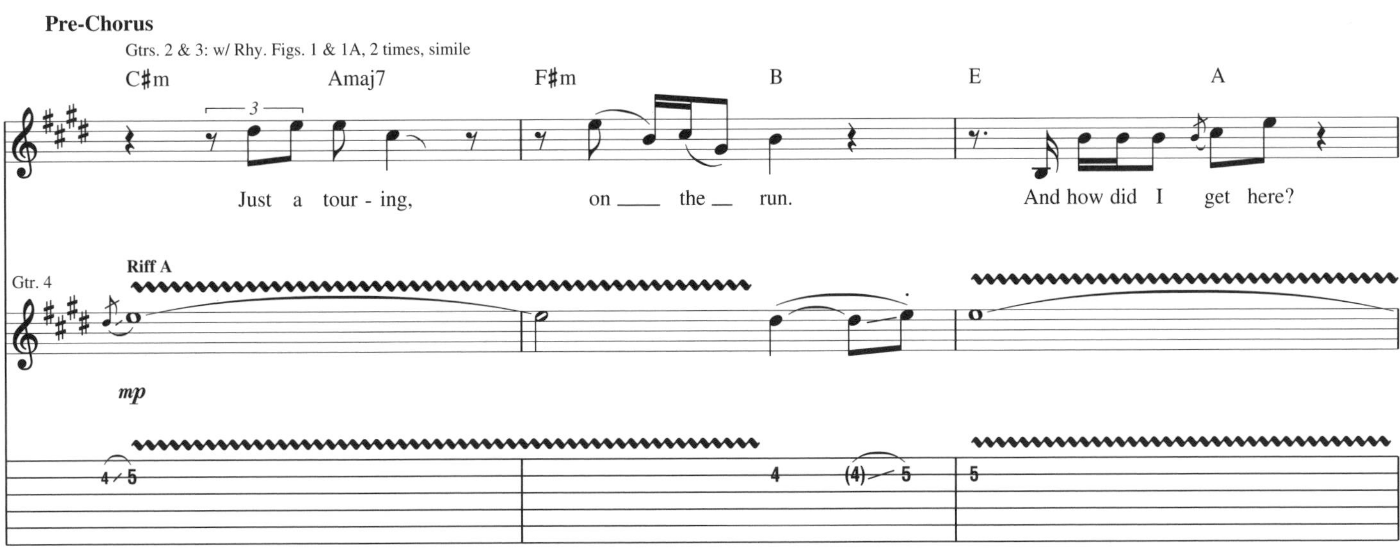
Gtrs. 2 & 3: w/ Rhy. Figs. 1 & 1A, 2 times, simile
C#m
Amaj7
F#m
B
E
A
Just a tour - ing,
on the run.
And how did I get here?
Riff A
Gtr. 4
mp

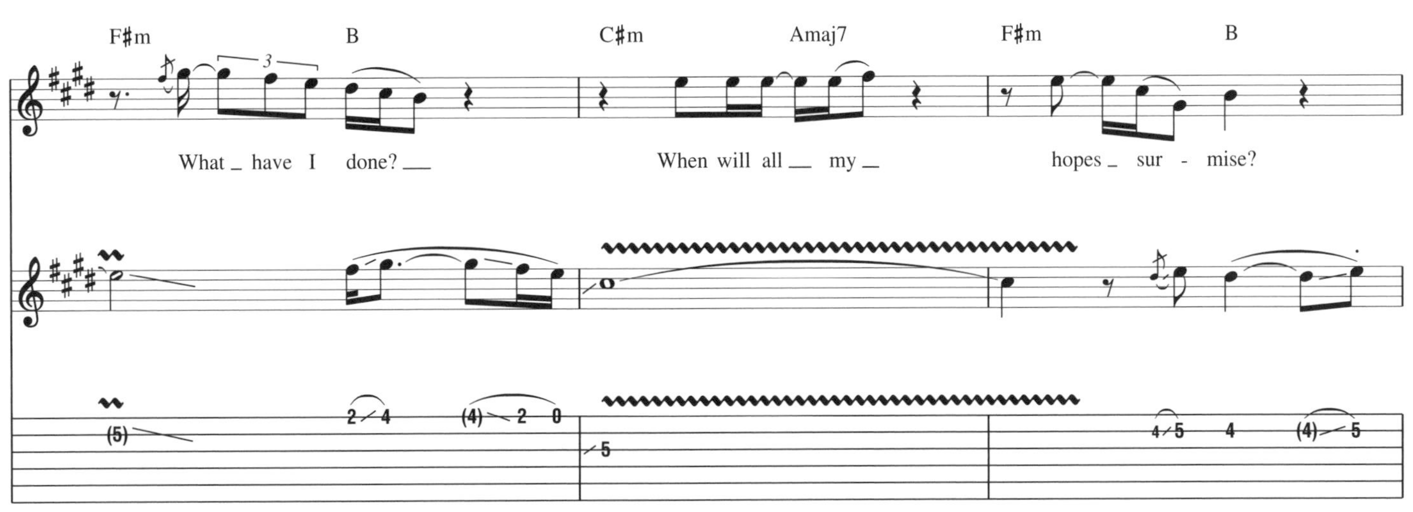
F#m
B
C#m
Amaj7
F#m
B
What have I done?
When will all my
hopes sur - mise?

Chorus
Gtrs. 2 & 3: w/ Rhy. Figs. 1 & 1A, 1 3/4 times, simile
E
A
F♯m
B
C♯m
Amaj7
Voc. Fig. 1
And how will I know him
when I look in my fa - ther's eyes?
(Look in - to my fa -
End Riff A
Riff A1
F♯m
B
End Voc. Fig. 1
E
A
F♯m
B
C♯m
Amaj7
Voc. Fig. 2
My fa-ther's eyes.
When I look in my fa - ther's eyes.
- ther's eyes.)
(Look in - to my fa -
Gtrs. 2 & 3: w/ Rhy. Fig. 2
F♯m
B
End Voc. Fig. 2
E
A
D/F♯
A/E
E
F♯
My fa-ther's eyes.
- ther's eyes.
End Riff A1
Verse
Gtr. 2: w/ Rhy. Fig. 3
B
Emaj7
F♯
B
C♯/E♯
C♯m/E
F♯
B
2. Then the light be - gins to shine.
I hear those an - cient lul - la - bys.
Gtr. 4
Gtr. 3
Rhy. Fig. 3A

Emaj7 F# G#m C#/E# D/F# A/E E
And as I watch the seed-ling grow, feel my heart start to o-ver-flow.
End Rhy. Fig. 3A
Pre-Chorus
Gtrs. 2 & 3: w/ Rhy. Figs. 1 & 1A, 2 times
C#m Amaj7 F#m B E A F#m B
Where do I find the words to say? How do I teach him? What do we play?
Gtr. 4
C#m Amaj7 F#m B E A F#m B
Bit by bit, I've real-ized that's when I need them. That's when I need my fa-
Chorus
Bkgd. Voc.: w/ Voc. Fig. 1
Gtrs. 2 & 3: w/ Rhy. Figs. 1 & 1A, 1 3/4 times
Gtr. 4: w/ Riff A1
C#m Amaj7 F#m B E A F#m B
-ther's eyes. My fa-ther's eyes. That's when I need my fa-

Bkgd. Voc.: w/ Voc. Fig. 2
C♯m
Amaj7
F♯m
B
E
A
Voc. Fig. 3
- ther's eyes. My fa - ther's eyes.
(Yeah.)
F♯
G♯
Guitar Solo
Gtr. 3 tacet
E Aadd9
Rhy. Fig. 4
Gtrs. 2 & 6 (acous.)
Badd4 E
End Rhy. Fig. 4
End Voc. Fig. 3
Gtr. 2
Gtr. 7 (Dobro)
w/ slide
(cont. in slash)
Gtr. 3
Rhy. Fig. 4A
Gtr. 5 (elec.)
End Rhy. Fig. 4A
w/ slide & dist.
Gtrs. 2 & 6: w/ Rhy. Fig. 4
Gtr. 5: w/ Rhy. Fig. 4A, simile
E Aadd9
Badd4 E
Gtrs. 2 & 3: w/ Rhy. Figs. 1 & 1A, 1 3/4 times
C♯m Amaj7 F♯m B
Gtr. 4
Gtr. 7
Gtr. 3
* Played behind the beat.

E A F♯m B C♯m Amaj7 F♯m B E A F♯m A5 E
Gtrs. 2 & 3
Gtr. 4
8va
loco
Gtr. 7
Verse
Gtr. 7 tacet
Gtrs. 2 & 3: w/ Rhy. Figs. 3 & 3A
B Emaj7 F♯ B C♯/E♯ C♯m/E F♯ B
3. Then the jag - ged edge ap - pears through the dis - tant clouds of tears.
Emaj7 F♯ G♯m C♯/E♯ D/F♯ A/E E
I'm like a bridge that was washed a - way. My foun - da - tion's one made of clay.
mp

Pre-Chorus

Gtrs. 2 & 3: w/ Rhy. Figs. 1 & 1A, 2 times
Gtr. 4: w/ Riff A
C♯m Amaj7 F♯m B E A F♯m B
And as my soul slides down to die, how could I lose him? What did I try?
Gtr. 7
C♯m Amaj7 F♯m B E A F♯m B
Bit by bit, I've real - ized that he was here with me and I looked in - to my fa -
Outro-Chorus
Bkgd. Voc.: w/ Voc. Fig. 1
Gtrs. 2 & 3: w/ Rhy. Figs. 1 & 1A, till fade
C♯m Amaj7 F♯m B E A
- ther's eyes. My fa - ther's eyes.
Gtr. 7
Gtr. 4

Bkgd. Voc.: w/ Voc. Fig. 2
F♯m
B
C♯m
Amaj7
F♯m
B
I looked in - to my _ fa - ther's eyes. _
My fa - ther's eyes. _
Riff B
E
A
F♯m
B
C♯m
Amaj7
My fa - ther's eyes. ___
(Look in - to my fa -
F♯m
B
E
A
F♯m
B
My fa - ther's eyes. ___
- ther's eyes. _)
I looked in - to my _ fa -
End Riff B

Gtr. 4: w/ Riff B, simile, till fade
C♯m
Amaj7
F♯m
B
E
A
- ther's eyes.
(Look in - to my fa - ther's eyes.)
My fa - ther's eyes.
Gtr. 7
Bkgd. Voc.: w/ Voc. Fig. 1
Begin Fade
Bkgd. Voc.: w/ Voc. Fig. 2
Bkgd. Voc.: w/ Voc. Fig. 3
let ring
Fade Out

from Eric Clapton - *Journeyman*

Pretending

Words and Music by Jerry Williams

A7 A7sus2 A7 A7sus4 A7

Verse

E

1. How man-y times must we tell the tale?

fdbk.

Rhy. Fig. 1

G/E

How man-y times must we fall?

A7/E

Liv-in' in lost

*T

T

*T=Thumb on ⑥

A7sus4/E
A7/E
E
mem-o-ry you just re-called.
let ring
fdbk.
End Rhy. Fig. 1
Verse
Gtr. 2: w/ Rhy. Fig. 1, 1st 7 meas.
E
G/E
2. Work-in' on the sound of the band, try'n' to get the mu-sic right.
Gtr. 1
full
A7/E
A7sus4/E
A7/E
E
Gtr. 2: w/ Fill 1
N.C.
Two go out working, three stay home at night.
full
1/4
*vol. swell
Fill 1
Gtr. 2

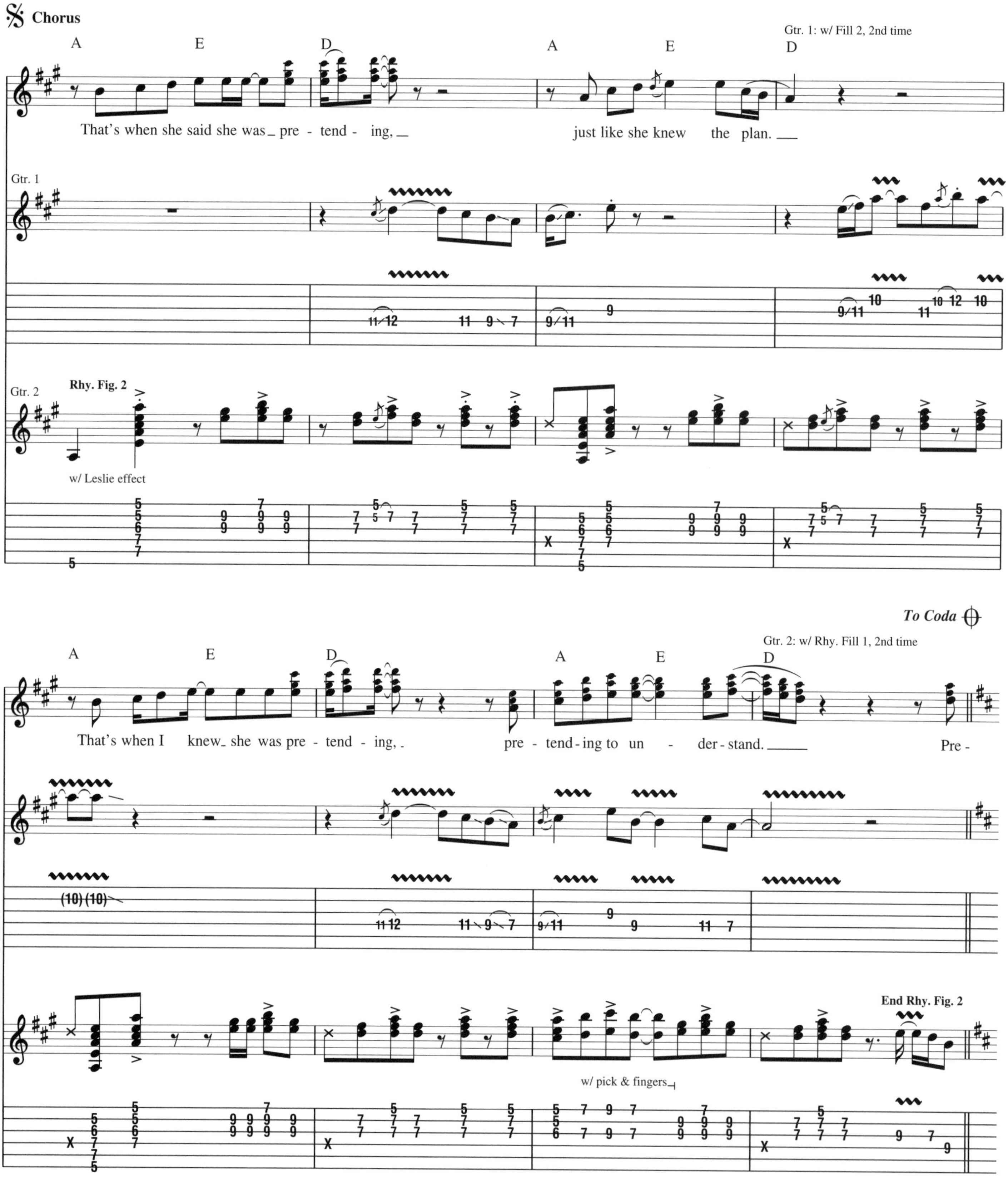

𝄋 **Chorus**

Gtr. 1: w/ Fill 2, 2nd time

A E D A E D

That's when she said she was _ pre - tend - ing, _ just like she knew the plan. _

Gtr. 1

Gtr. 2 **Rhy. Fig. 2**

w/ Leslie effect

To Coda ⊕

Gtr. 2: w/ Rhy. Fill 1, 2nd time

A E D A E D

That's when I knew _ she was pre - tend - ing, _ pre - tend - ing to un - der - stand. _ Pre -

w/ pick & fingers

End Rhy. Fig. 2

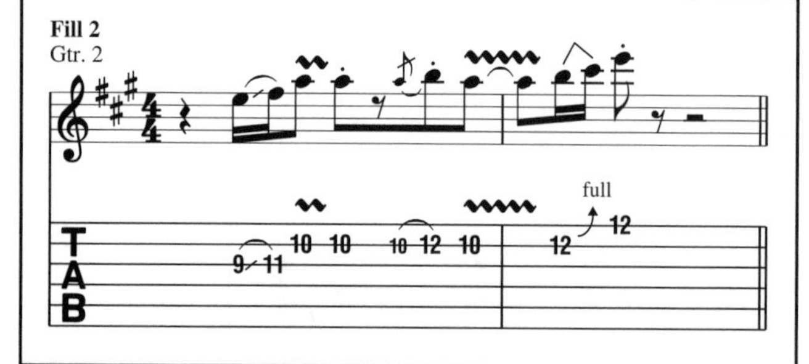

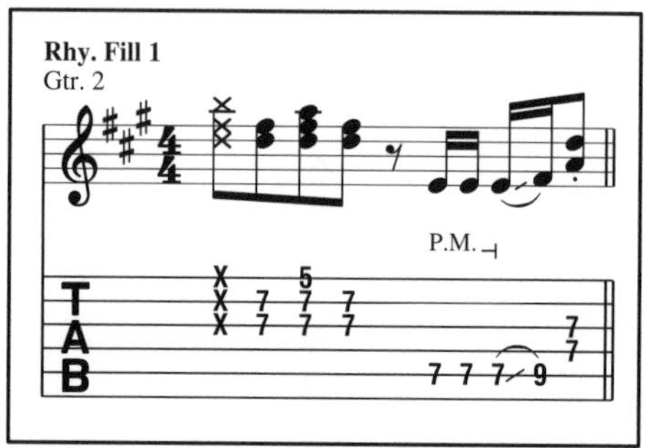

Gtr. 2: w/ Riff A, 2 times
E7
tend - ing,
pre - tend - ing,
pre -
Gtr. 1
full
full
A7
E7
tend - ing,
pre - tend - ing.
full
full
Verse
Gtr. 2: w/ Rhy. Fig. 1
E
G/E
3. Sa-tis - fied,
but lost in love,
sit - u - a - tions change.
Harm.
A7
A7sus4
A7
E
N.C.
D.S. al Coda
Gtr. 2: w/ Fill 1
You're nev-er who you used to think you are,
how strange.

Coda
Gtr. 2: w/ Riff A, 2 times
E7
tend - ing, pre - tend - ing,
Gtr. 1
full
A7
pre - tend - ing,
pre -
1/4
E7
tend - ing.
(Pre - tend - ing, pre - tend - ing.)
Guitar Solo
Gtr. 2: w/ Rhy. Fig. 1
E
G/E
A7
hold bend
even release
A7sus4
A7
E
Verse
Gtr. 2: w/ Rhy. Fig. 1, 1st 7 meas.
E
4. I get lost in
full
1/2
1 1/2

G/E
A7
al - i - bis,
sad - ness can't
pre - vail.
Ev-'ry-bod-y
fdbk.
A7sus4
A7
E
Gtr. 2: w/ Fill 1
N.C.
Chorus
Gtr. 2: w/ Rhy. Fig. 2, simile
A
E
knows strong love can't
fail.
Don't be pre - tend - ing
1/4
D
A
E
D
A
E
a-bout how you feel.
Don't be pre - tend - ing
D
A
E
1.
D
2.
D
your love is real.
Don't be pre -
Pre -

Gtr. 2: w/ Riff A, 2 times
E7
tend - ing, pre - tend - ing, pre -
let ring
1/2

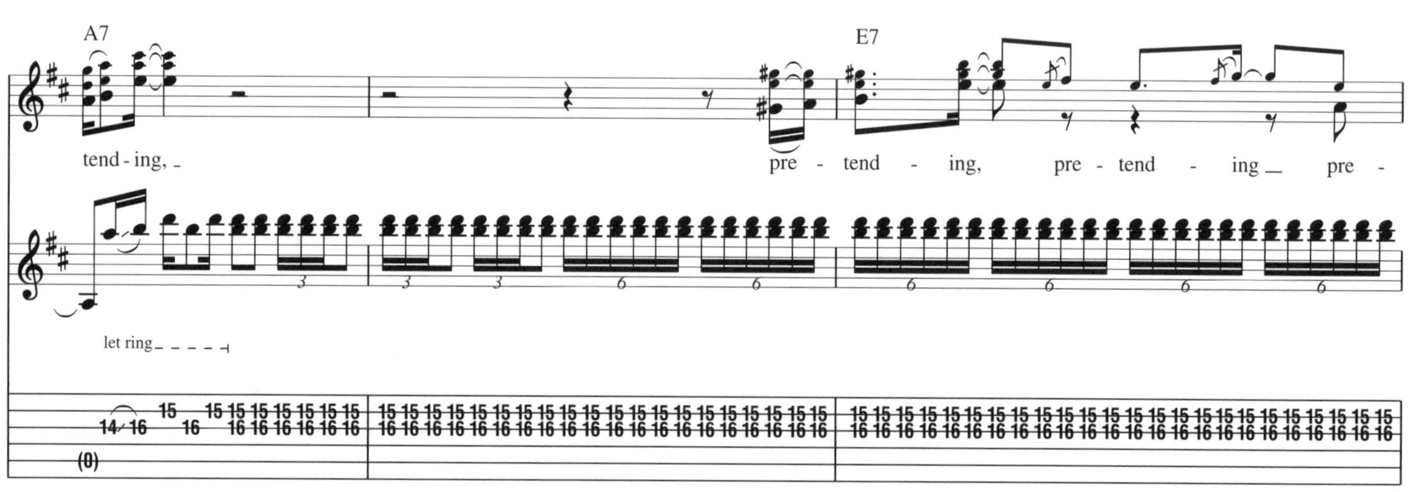
A7
E7
tend - ing, pre - tend - ing, pre - tend - ing pre -
let ring

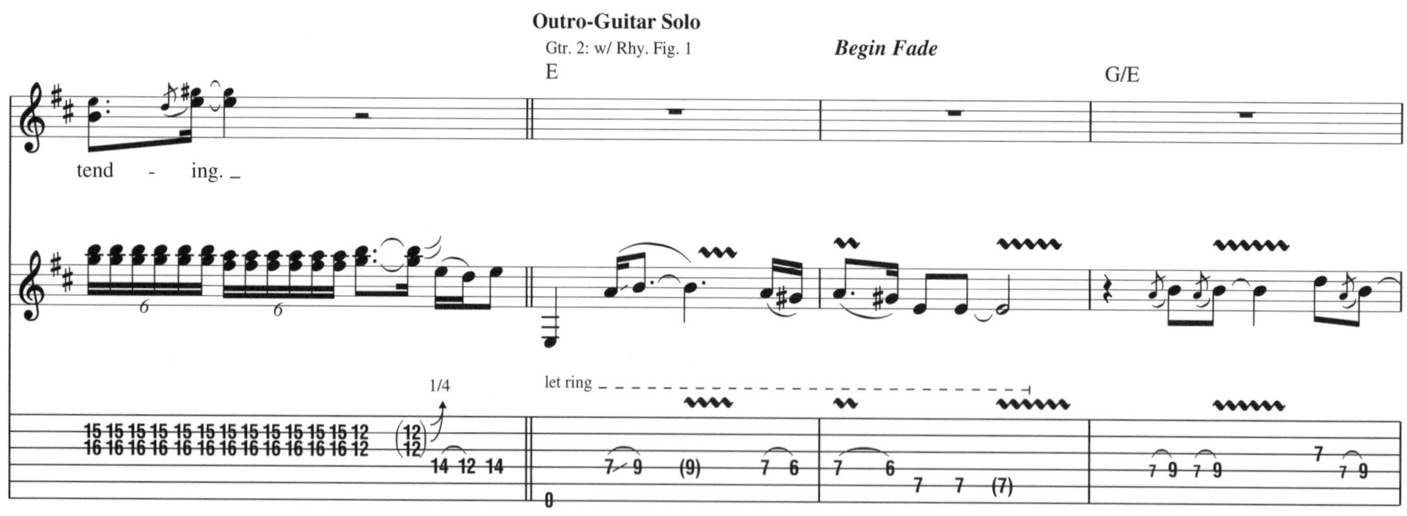
Outro-Guitar Solo
Gtr. 2: w/ Rhy. Fig. 1
Begin Fade
E
G/E
tend - ing.
1/4
let ring

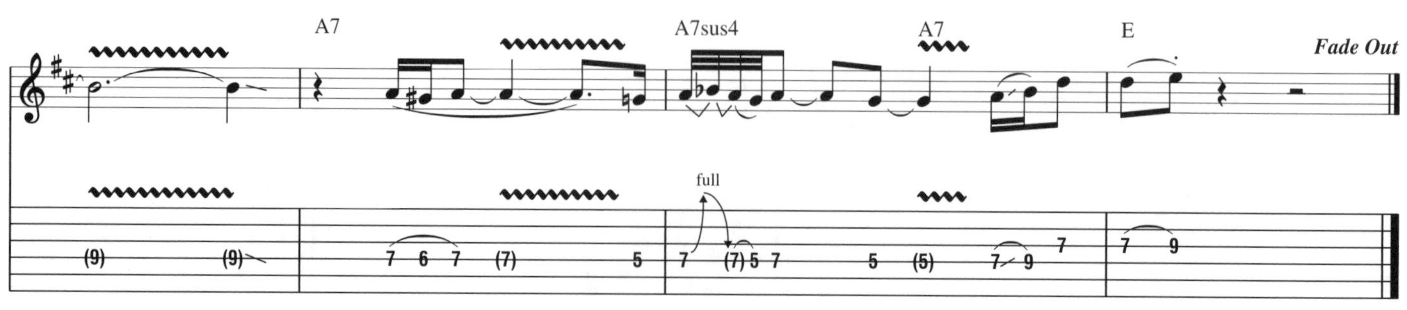
A7
A7sus4
A7
E
Fade Out
full

from Eric Clapton - *Backless*

Promises

Words and Music by Richard Feldman and Roger Linn

2.
G5
Chorus
G ⑥ 3fr
A ⑤ open
B ⑤ 2fr
C ⑤ 3fr
B ⑤ 2fr
End Rhy. Fig. 1
Rhy. Fig. 2
Gtr. 2
mine.
La, la,
la, la, la, la,
Gtr. 1
Gtr. 3 (clean elec.)
Riff A
mf
steady gliss.
w/ slide
steady gliss.

D5 C ⑤ 3fr C5 B ⑤ 2fr

la. La, la, la, la, la, la,

dim. steady gliss.

D5 F♯ ⑥ 2fr G5 Gtr. 3 tacet G ⑥ 3fr

End Rhy. Fig. 2

la. 3. I

End Riff A

dim.

Verse
Gtr. 2: w/ Rhy. Fig. 1, simile
G5
C5
don't care what you do at night. Oh, and I don't care how you get
4. I tried to love you for years up - on years. You re - fused to take me for real.
Gtr. 1
simile on 2nd time
Gtr. 4
(dobro)
tacet 1st time
w/ slide
G5
your de - lights. I'll leave you a - lone; I'll just let it be. I
It's time you saw what I want you to see, and I'd
steady gliss.
D5
G5
don't love you and you don't love me.
still love you if you'd just love me.

Bridge

C5 G C5 G/B

Rhy. Fig. 3

Gtr. 2

I've got a prob - lem. Can you re - late?
I've got a prob - lem. Can you re - late?

Gtr. 1

Gtr. 4

G B A7(no3rd) G A

I got a wom - an
I got a wom - an cal - lin' love

steady gliss.

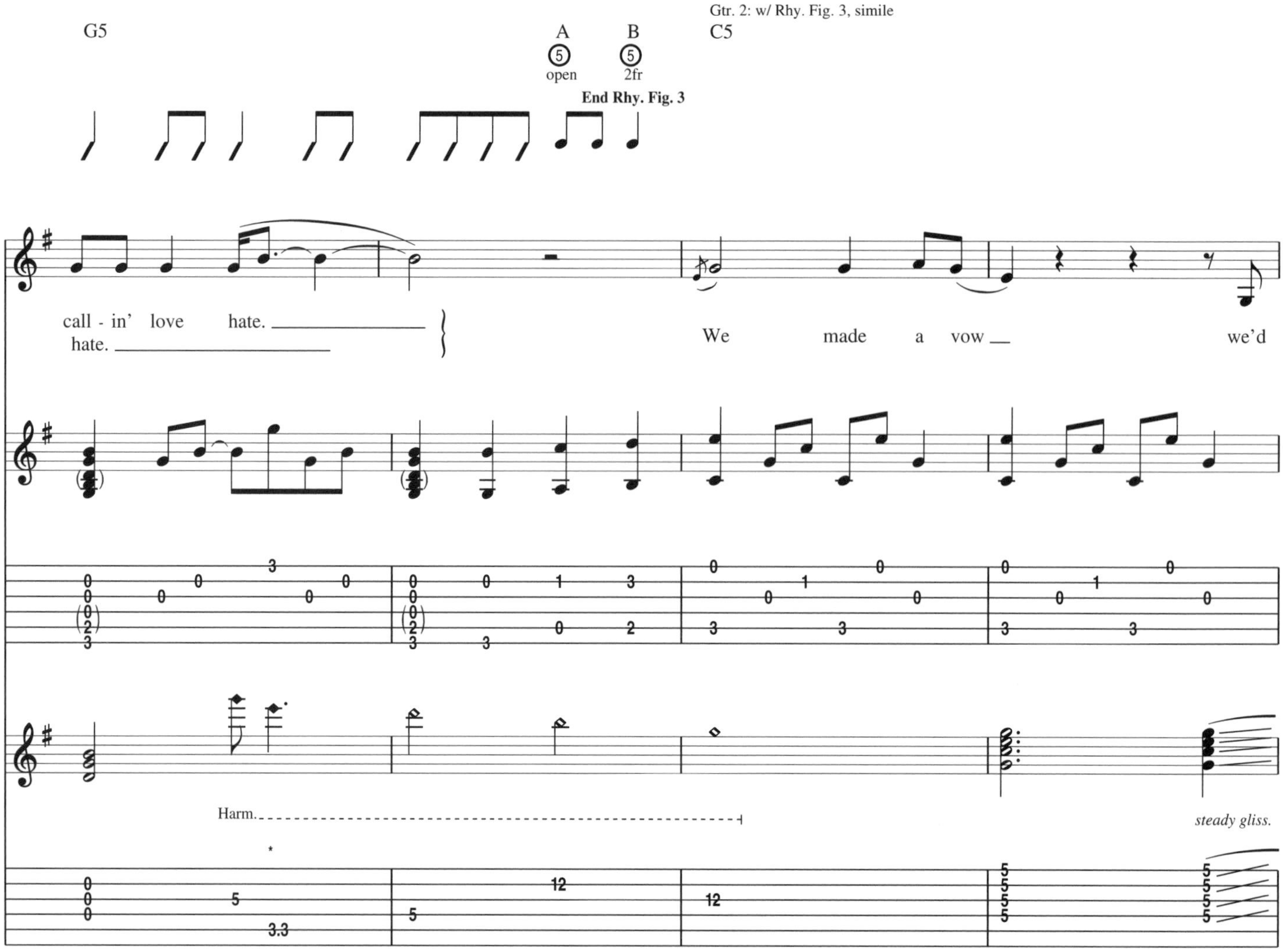

Gtr. 2: w/ Rhy. Fig. 3, simile

G5 A B C5

⑤ open ⑤ 2fr

End Rhy. Fig. 3

call - in' love hate.
hate.

We made a vow we'd

Harm.

steady gliss.

* position halfway between 3rd & 4th fret

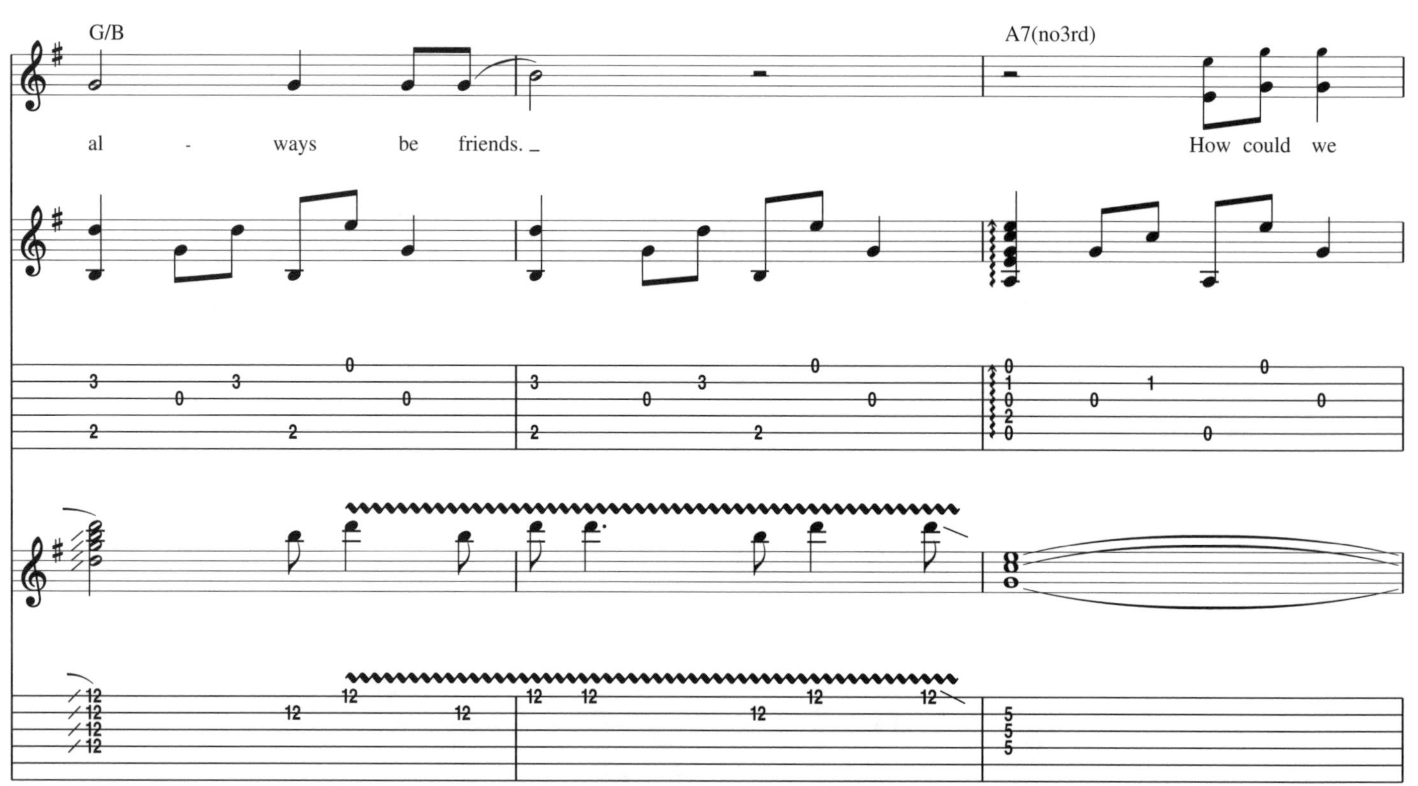

Gtr. 4: w/ Fill 1, 2nd time
G5
C
D
13fr
15fr
Gtr. 3
know that prom - i - ses end?
La
* play 1st time

Chorus

Gtr. 2: w/ Rhy Fig. 2, simile, 1st time
Gtr. 2: w/ Rhy Fig. 2, 1st 7 meas., simile, 2nd time
Gtr. 3: w/ Riff A, 1st time
Gtr. 3: w/ Riff A, 1st 7 meas., 2nd time
Gtr. 4: w/ Fill 2, 2nd time
C5
G/B
D5
la, la, la, la, la, la, la.
dim.

Fill 1
Gtr. 4
1/2

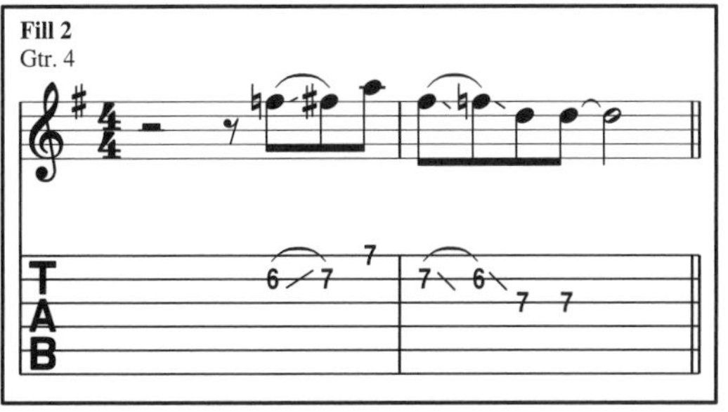
Fill 2
Gtr. 4

C5 G/B

La, la, la, la, la, la,

To Coda

D.S. al Coda

Gtr. 4: w/ Fill 3, 2nd time (see next page)

D5 D/F# G5

la.

steady gliss.

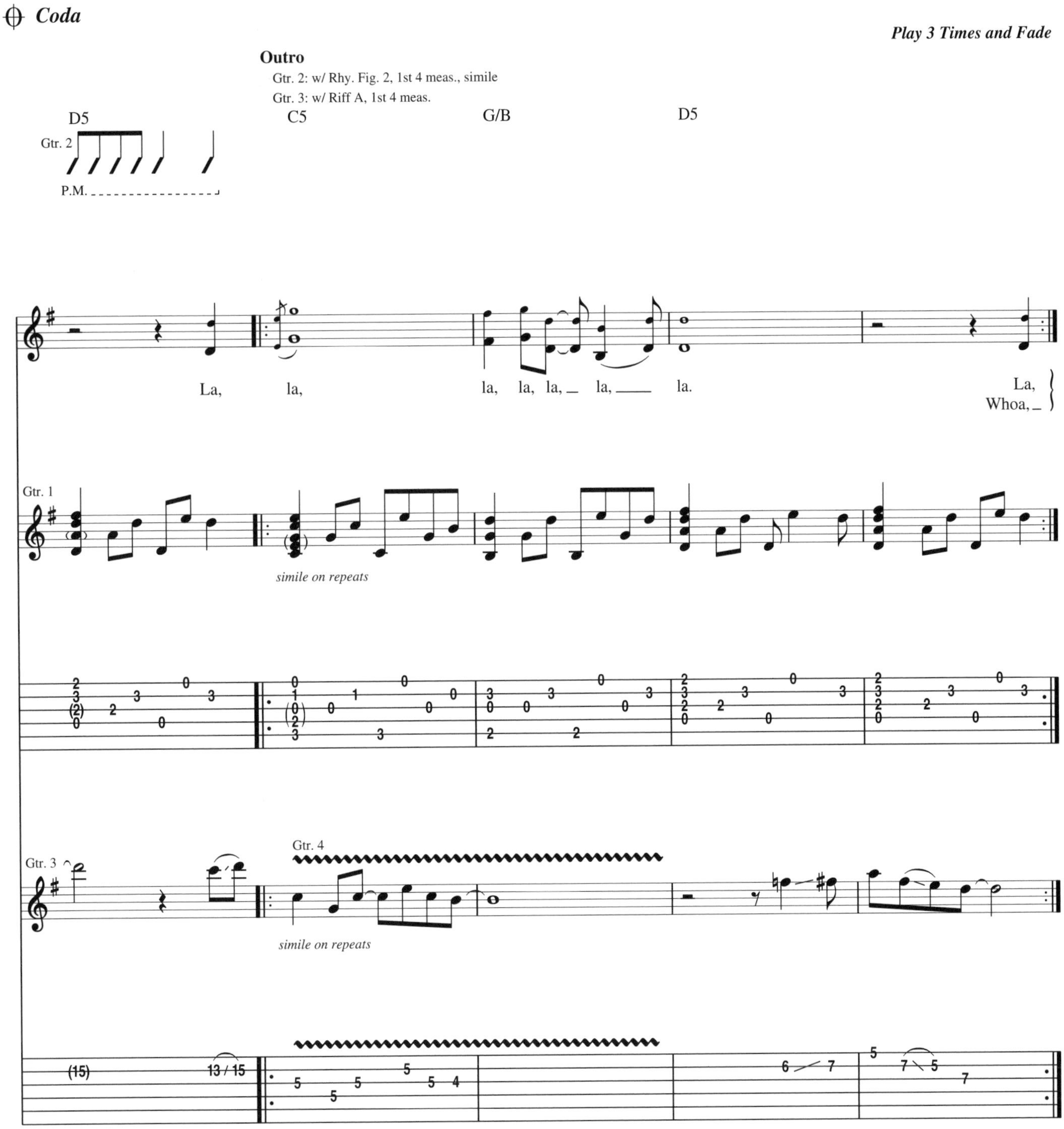

Coda

Play 3 Times and Fade

Outro

Gtr. 2: w/ Rhy. Fig. 2, 1st 4 meas., simile

Gtr. 3: w/ Riff A, 1st 4 meas.

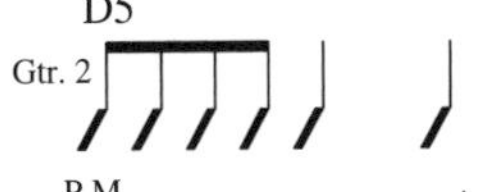

C5 G/B D5

La, la, la, la, la, la, la.

La, Whoa,

Gtr. 1

simile on repeats

Gtr. 3

Gtr. 4

simile on repeats

from B.B. King & Eric Clapton - *Riding With the King*

Riding With the King

Words and Music by John Hiatt

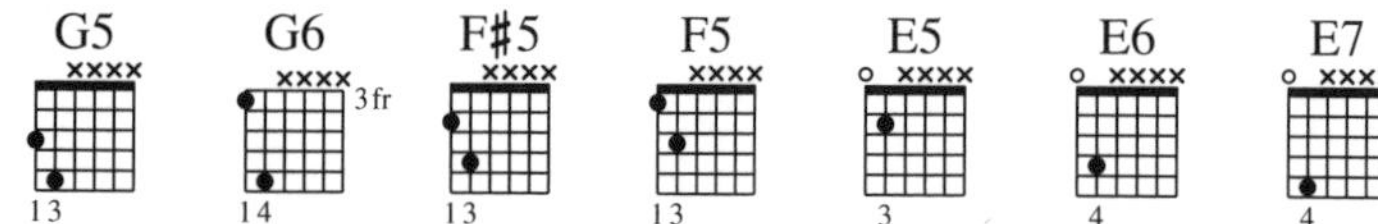

Intro

Moderate Blues ♩ = 102

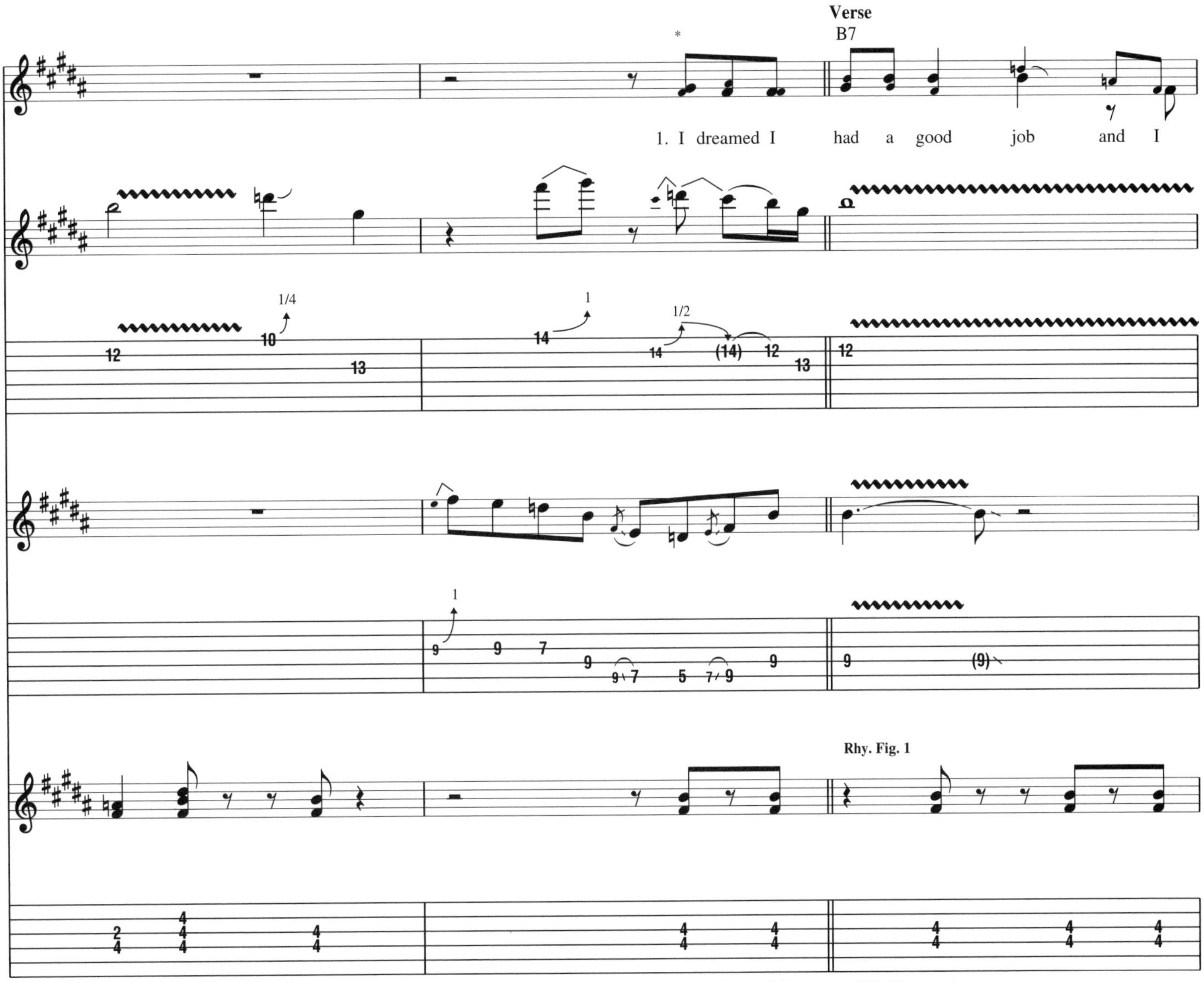

Verse
B7
1. I dreamed I had a good job and I
Rhy. Fig. 1

* Eric Clapton-full size notes, B.B. King-cue size notes.

Gtr. 2 tacet
E7
got well - paid. _ I blew it all at the pen-ny ar - cade.
Gtr. 3
Gtr. 1

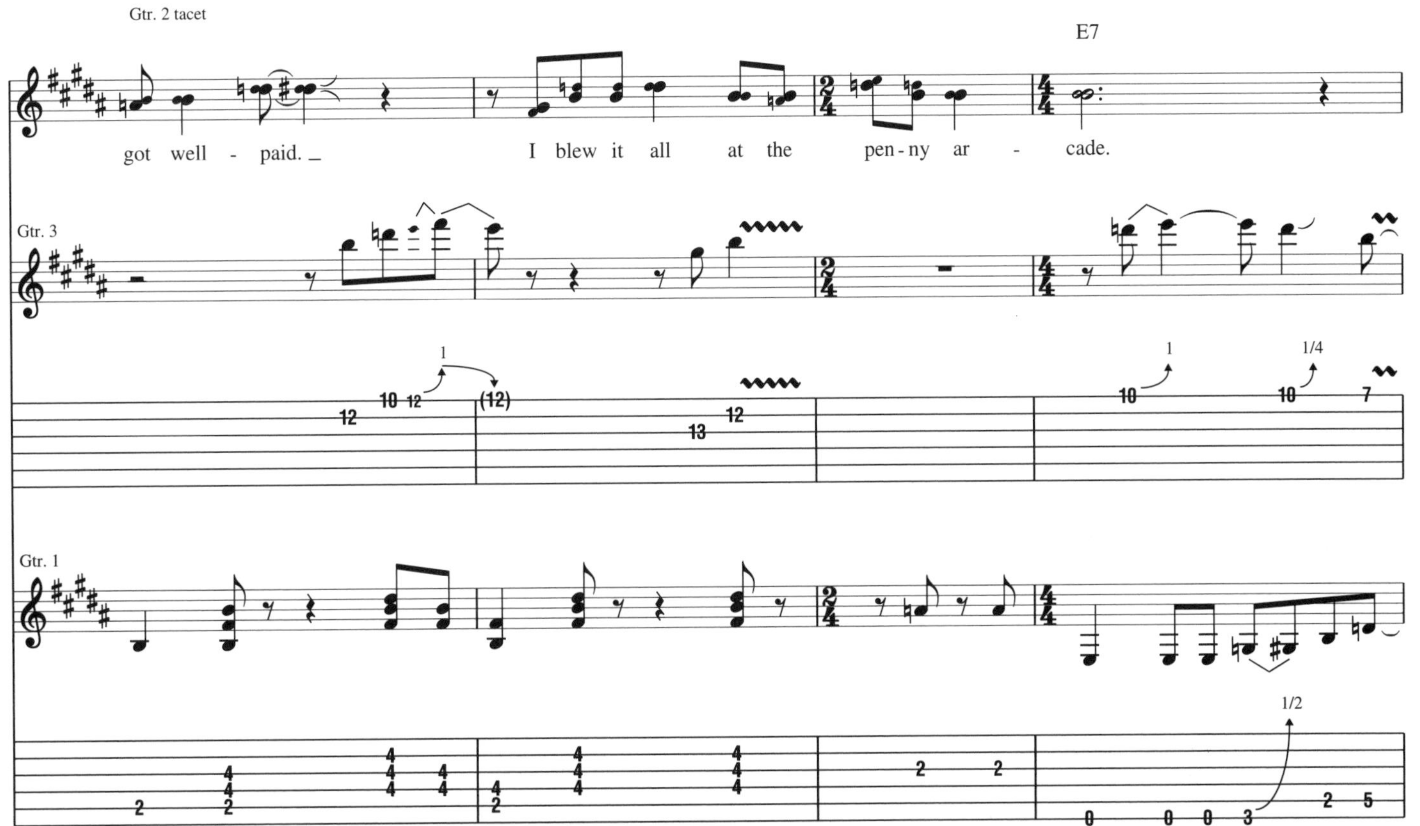

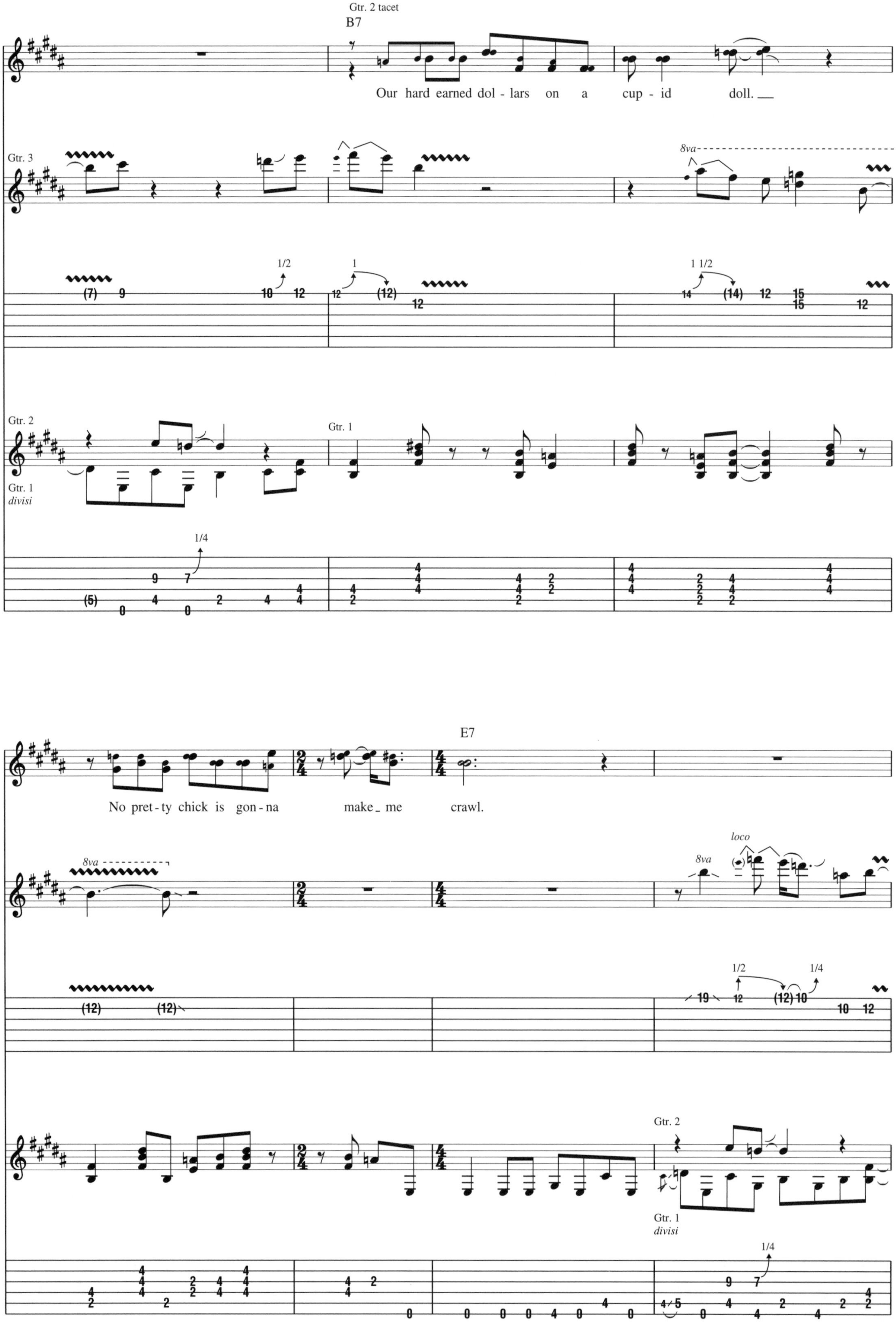

Gtr. 2 tacet

B7

Our hard earned dol - lars on a cup - id doll.

Gtr. 3

8va

1/2 1 1 1/2

(7) 9 10 12 12 (12) 12 14 (14) 12 15 15 12

Gtr. 2

Gtr. 1

Gtr. 1 *divisi*

1/4

E7

No pret - ty chick is gon - na make me crawl.

8va

loco

8va

1/2 1/4

(12) (12) 19 12 (12) 10 10 12

Gtr. 2

Gtr. 1 *divisi*

1/4

B7
Chorus
G5 G6 G5 G6
Rhy. Fig. 2
Gtr. 1
Get on a T. W. A. to the
(To the
Gtr. 3
1/4
(12)
10
Riff B
Gtr. 2
12
(12)
End Rhy. Fig. 1
(cont. in slash)
G5 G6 G5 F♯5 F5 E5 E6 E5 E6 E5 E7 E5 E6 G5
Prom-ised Land. Ev - 'ry wo-man, child, and man gets a
Prom-ised Land. Child and man.
w/ pick & fingers

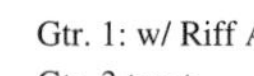

G6 G5 G6 G5 G6 G5 A

End Rhy. Fig. 2

open

Cad - il - lac and a great big dia - mond ring.

Great big dia - mond ring.

End Riff B

* Cue notes are female harmony (next 2 meas.).
Eric Clapton upstem notes,
B.B. King downstem notes.

**Eric Clapton-full size notes,
B.B. King-cue size notes,

Verse
Gtr. 1: w/ Rhy. Fig. 1
B7
mis-sion of mer-cy to a new fron - tier.
He's gon-na check us all out, out of here.
Gtr. 3
Gtr. 2
E7
B7
Up to that man-sion on the hill, on the hill,
Gtr. 3 tacet
where you can get your pre - scrip - tion filled
E7
B.B. King, Spoken: Any kind of pill, folks,
Gtr. 2

B7
ha, ha, ha, ha.
Get on a
Gtr. 3
8va
1 1/2
1/2
Gtr. 2
let ring
1
1/2
Chorus
Gtr. 1: w/ Rhy. Fig. 2
Gtr. 2: w/ Riff B
* G7
F#7 F7 E7
T. W. A. to the Prom - ised Land.
(Ev - 'ry - bod -
Gtr. 3
loco
1/2 1/4
* Chord symbols reflect overall harmony.
Gtr. 3 tacet
G7
Ev - 'ry - bod - y, clap your hands.
- y. Clap your hands.)
And don't you girls love the
Gtr. 1: w/ Riff A
A7
way that it seems.
Don't you know we're rid - in' with The
(Rid - in' with The
* Cue notes are female harmony (next 2 meas.)
Eric Clapton - upstem notes
B.B. King - downstem notes

B7
E7
A7
King?
King.
Spoken: Yeah, you're ridin' with The King.
We're rid-in' with The King.
Don't you know you're rid-in' with The
You're rid-in' with The
Gtr. 3
Gtr. 2
Gtr. 1
* as before
B7
E7
A7
King?
King.)

Bridge
Gtr. 3 tacet
D7
B7
A tux - e - do and a shin - y Three - thir - ty - five.
B.B. King, Spoken: That's me.
Gtr. 2
Gtr. 1

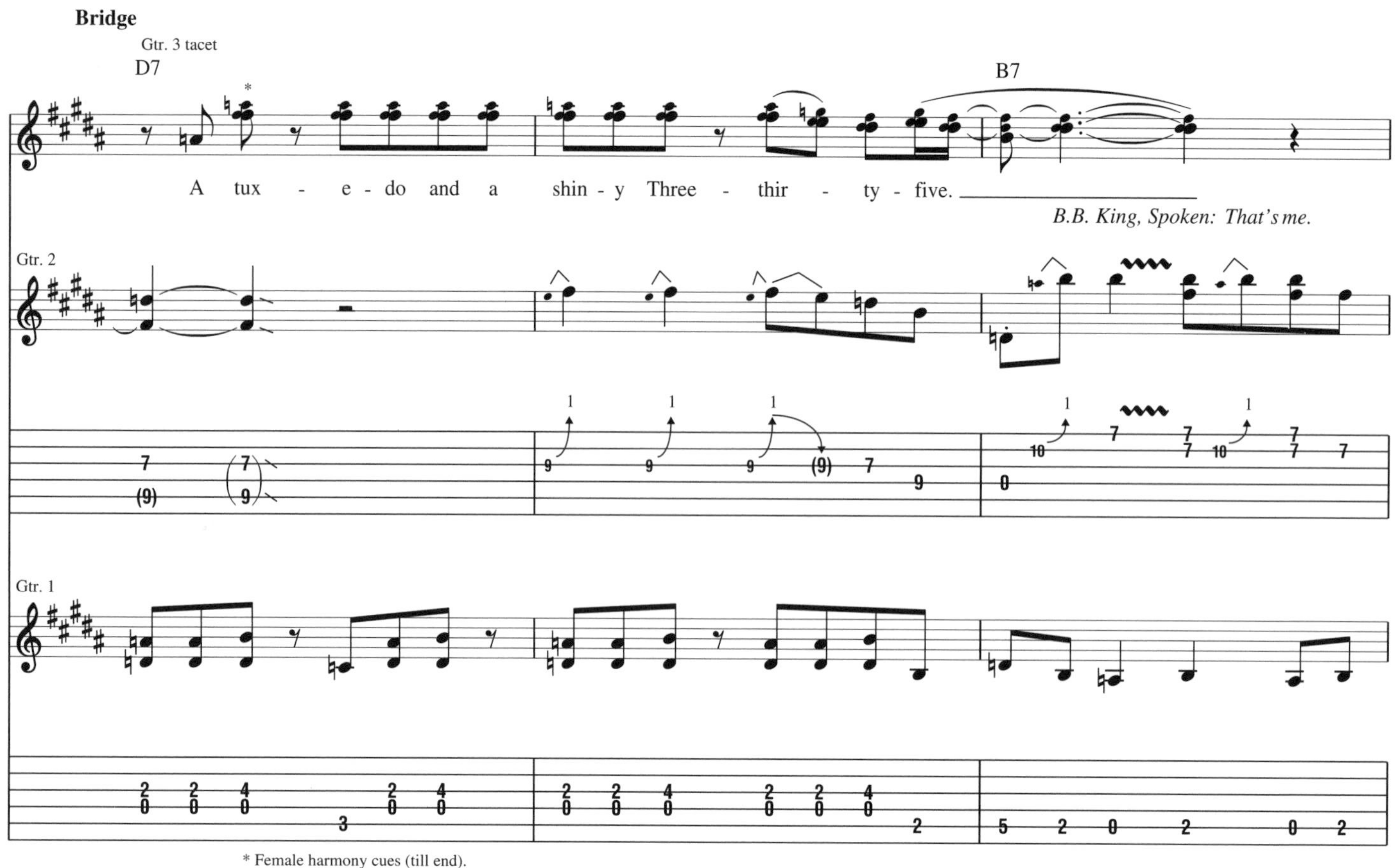

* Female harmony cues (till end).

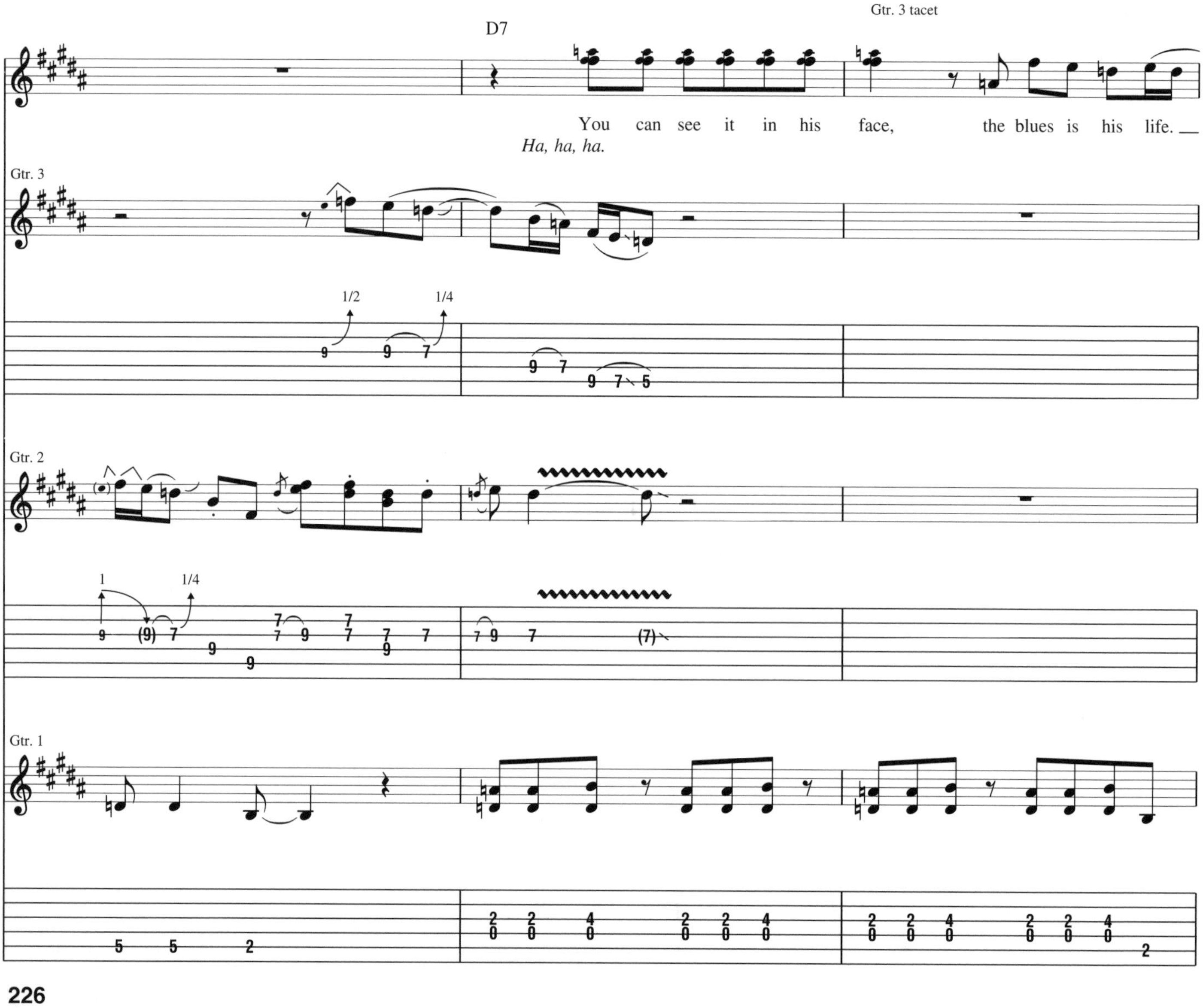

D7
Gtr. 3 tacet
You can see it in his face, the blues is his life.
Ha, ha, ha.
Gtr. 3
Gtr. 2
Gtr. 1

B7
G7
To - night, ev - 'ry - bod - y's
Gtr. 2
let ring
Gtr. 1
get - tin' their an - gel wings.
A7
And don't you know we're rid - in' with The
Gtr. 3
pp
Gtr. 2
let ring
w/ pick & fingers
Gtr. 1
let ring

Recitation
B7
King?
B.B. King, Spoken: I stepped out of Mississippi when I was ten years old,
with a suit cut sharp as a
razor, and a heart made of gold.
B7
I had a guitar hang-in' just about waist high,
Rhy. Fig. 3

Outro-Guitar Solos
Gtr. 3 tacet
Gtr. 1: w/ Rhy. Fig. 3 (till fade)
E
A7
B7
Well, don't you know we're rid - in' with The King?
and I'm gonna play this thing until the day I die.
Ha, ha, ha, ha.
Gtr. 2
Gtr. 1
End Rhy. Fig. 3
E7
A7
B7
Don't you know you're rid - in' with The King?
(Don't you know you're rid - in' with The King?
B.B. King, Spoken: You're ridin' with me daddy.
Gtr. 3
8va
loco
mf
Gtr. 2

E7 A7 B7

Don't ___ you know you're rid - in' with the King? ___
Don't you know you're rid - in' with The King? ___
You're in good hands, you're ridin' with me. *Yes, yes, you're ridin'*

grad. bend

8va loco

E7 A7

You're rid - in', you're rid - in' with The
You're rid - in' with The
with The King. *I wanted to say B.B. King, but you know who King is.*

B7

E7

King.

King.

Yes, you're ridin' with The King.

You're

You're

Yes, you are, you're ridin' with The King.

A7

B7

rid - in', you're rid - in' with The King.

rid - in', you're rid - in' with The King.

You're ridin' with The King.

Rid - in' with The

I'm a good chauffer too.

E7
A7
B7
King.
Rid - in' with The
King.
Don't you know you're rid - in' with The
King?
All of you girls, come on, you're ridin' with me.
That's alright Eric, you can ride with me
Begin fade
E7
A7
Rid - in' with The
King.
Rid - in' with The
You're rid - in', you're rid - in, you're rid - in' with The
too if you feel like it.
Yes, you're ridin' with The King.

B7 E7

King.
King.
You're ridin' with The King.

Rid - in' with The King.
I'm a good chauffer.

8va loco

1/2
19 19 14 (14) 12 9

1/4 1 1/4

A7 B7

Fade out

Don't you know you're rid - in' with The King?
Rid - in' with The King.)

8va

let ring

from Cream - *Disraeli Gears*

Sunshine of Your Love

Words and Music by Jack Bruce, Pete Brown and Eric Clapton

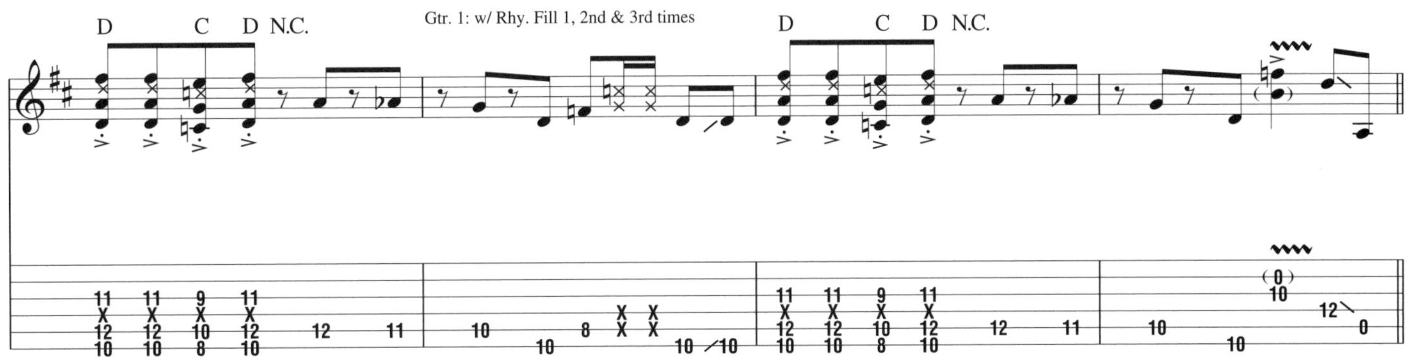
To Coda
D
C
D N.C.
Gtr. 1: w/ Rhy. Fill 1, 2nd & 3rd times
D
C
D N.C.

Chorus

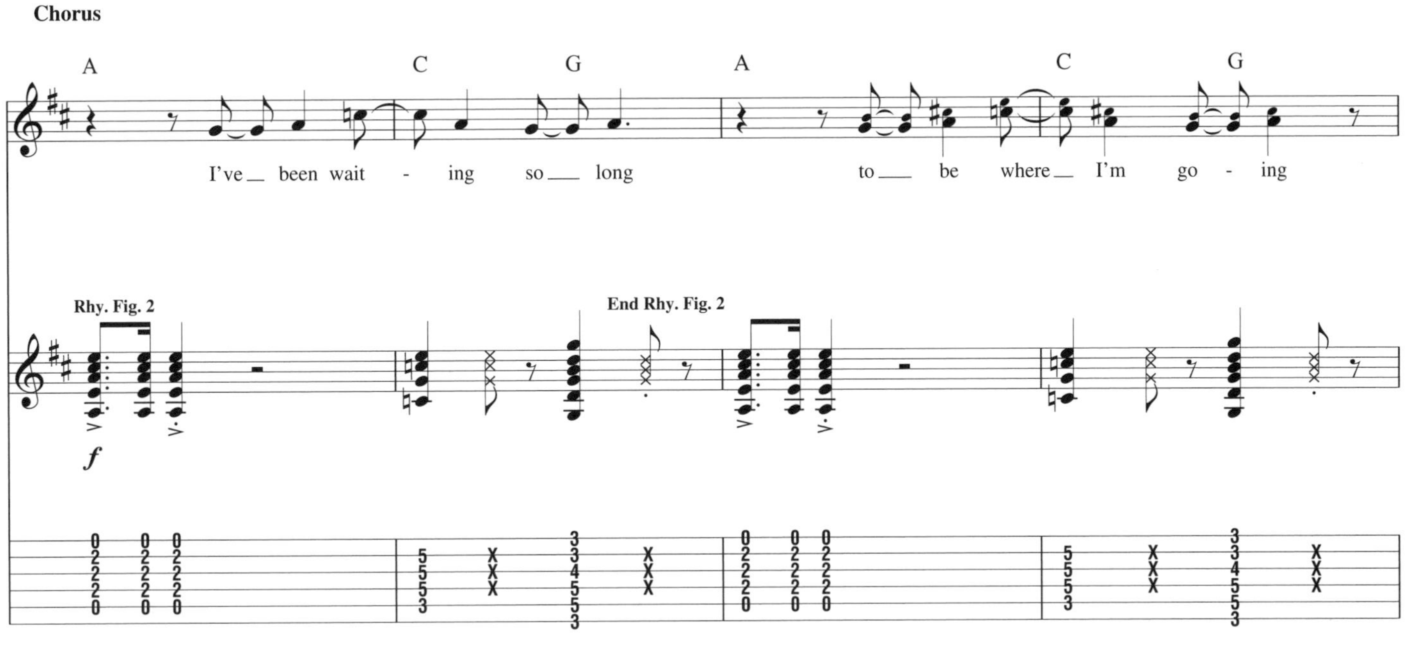
A
C
G
A
C
G
I've been wait - ing so long
to be where I'm go - ing
Rhy. Fig. 2
End Rhy. Fig. 2
f

Rhy. Fill 1
Gtr. 1

A
C/G
G
A
1.
in the sun - shine of your love.

D C D N.C.
2.
Guitar Solo
D C D N.C.
2. I'm
Gtr. 2 (dist.)
f
Gtr. 1
f

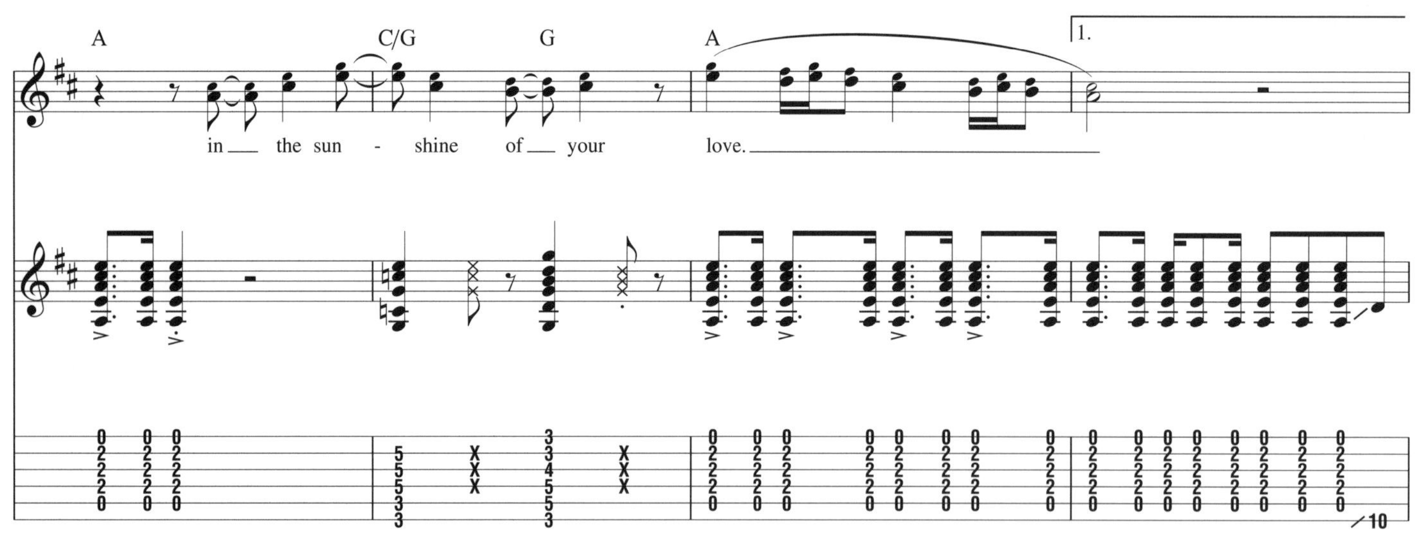

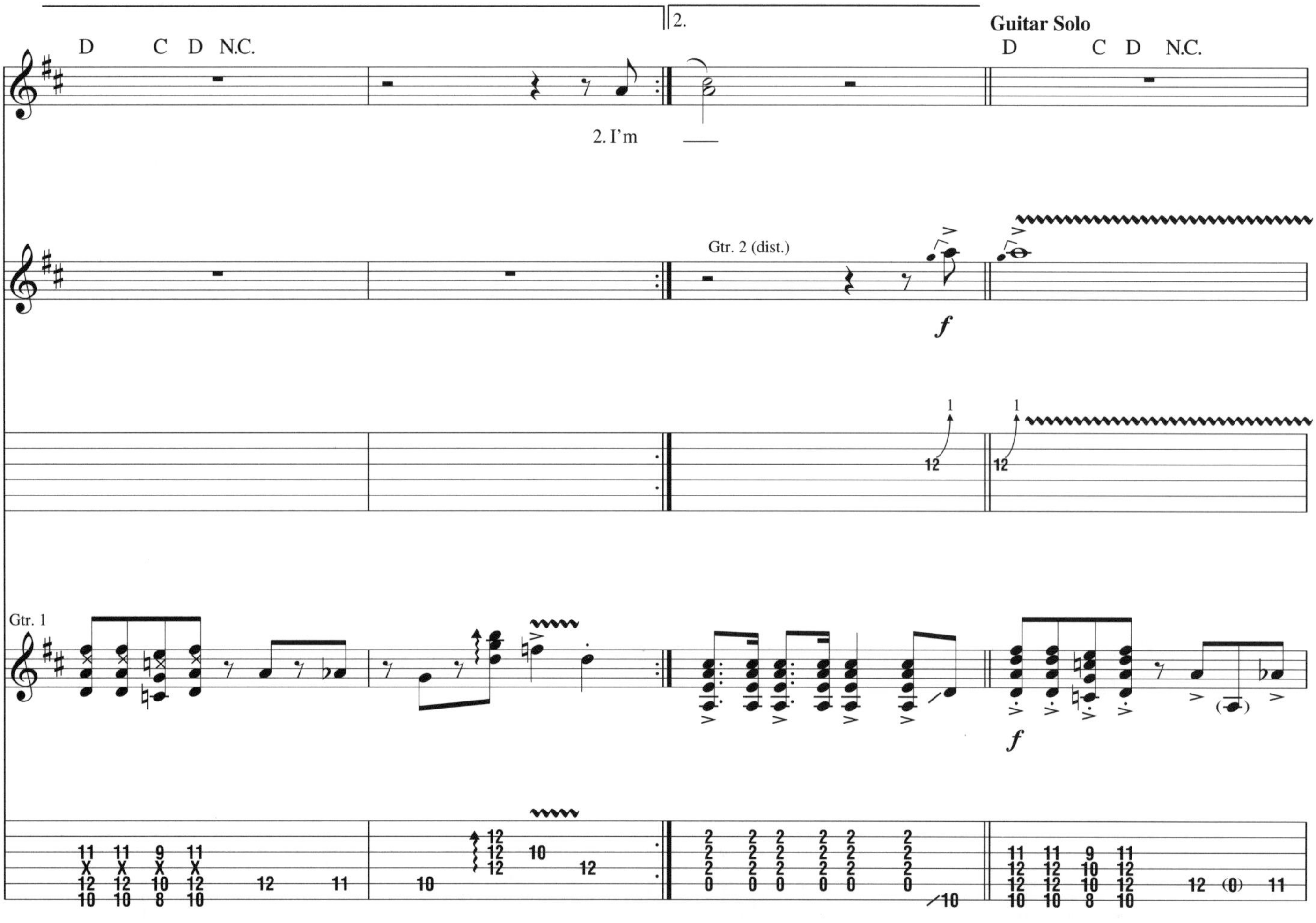

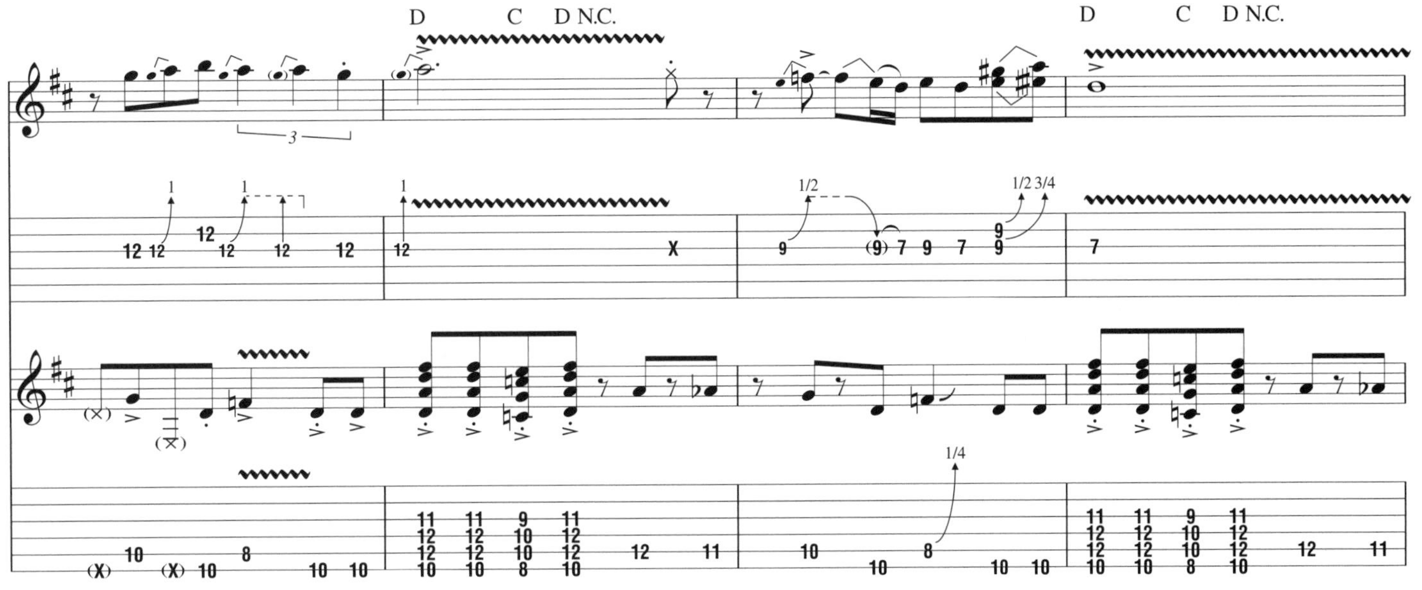
D C D N.C.
D C D N.C.

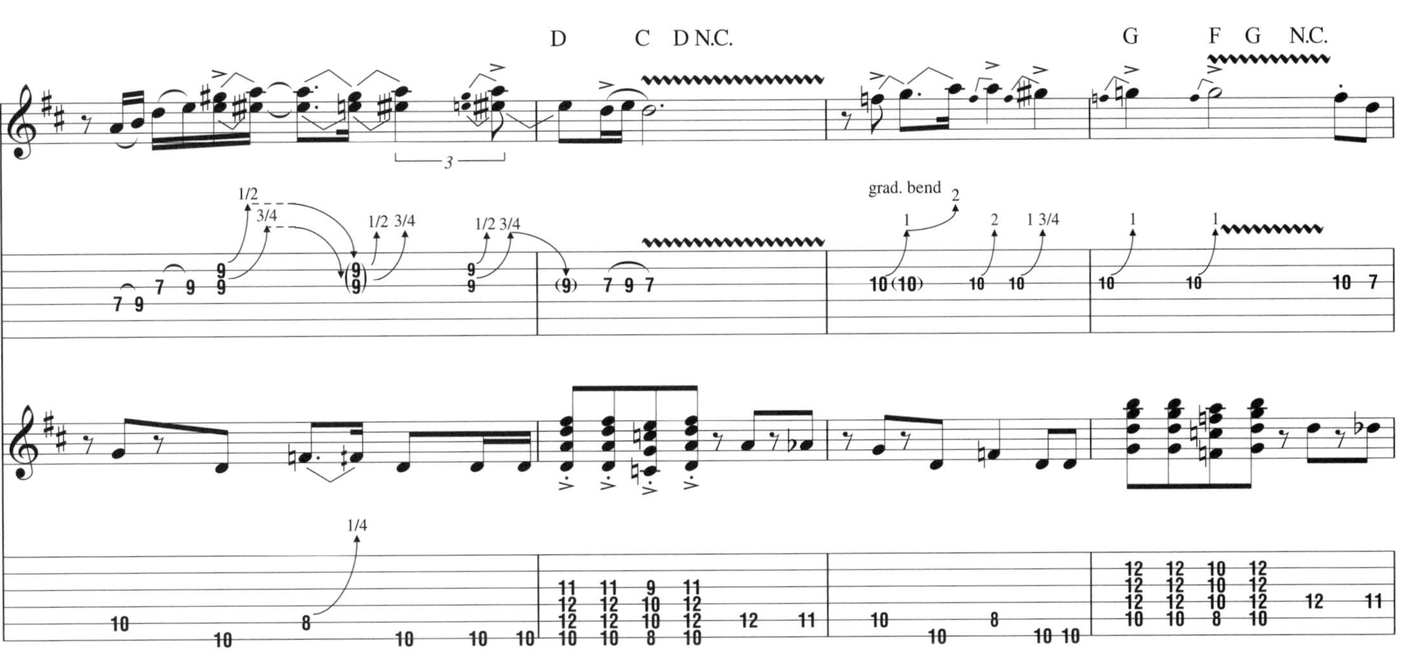
D C D N.C.
G F G N.C.
grad. bend

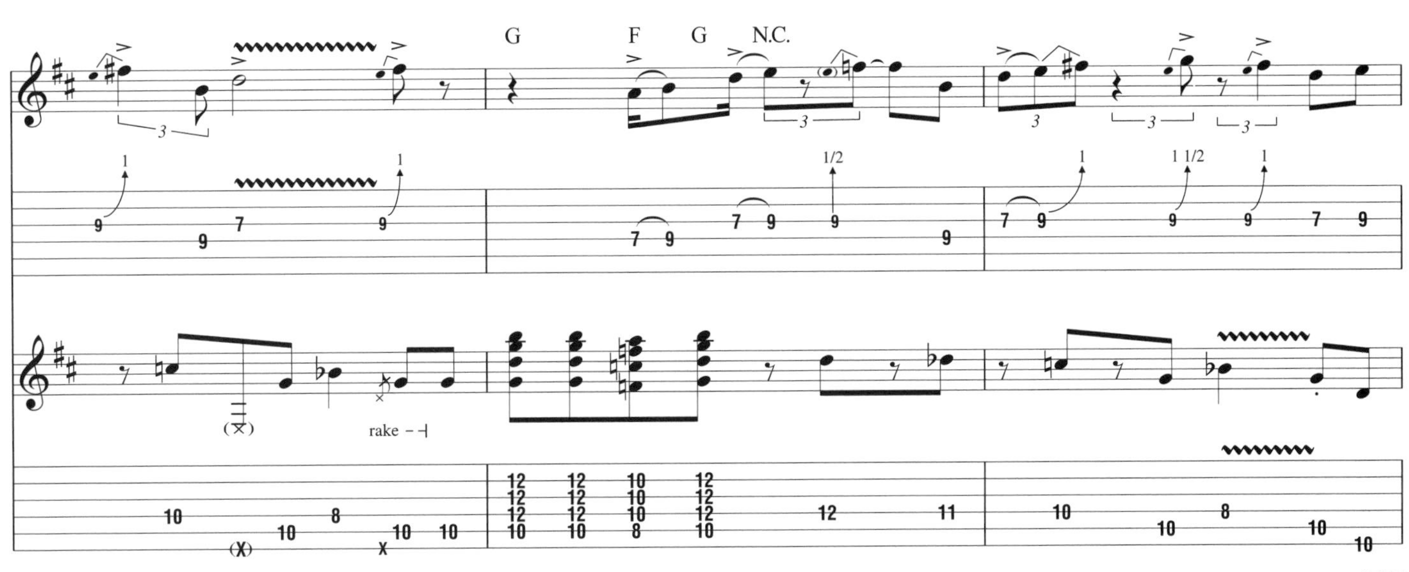
G F G N.C.
rake

D
C
D
N.C.
(cont. in slash)
G
F
A
C/G
G
Gtr. 1
Gtr. 2
10fr
8fr
A
C
G
A
C
G
A
D
P.M.
(cont. in notation)

D.S. al Coda
(take 2nd lyrics)
D
C
D N.C.
Gtr. 2 tacet
3. I'm
Gtr. 2
Gtr. 1

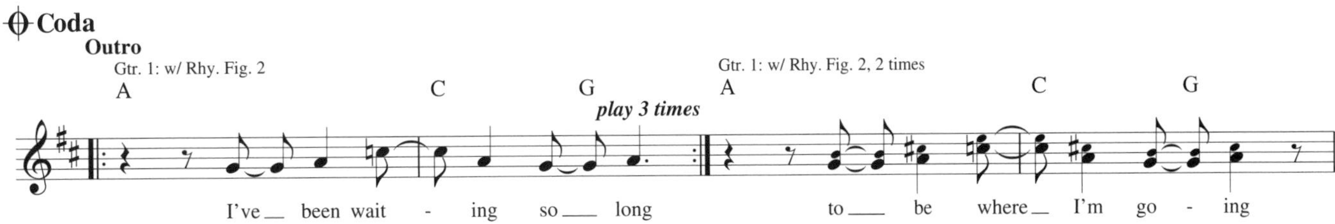
Coda
Outro
Gtr. 1: w/ Rhy. Fig. 2
A
C
G
play 3 times
Gtr. 1: w/ Rhy. Fig. 2, 2 times
I've been wait - ing so long
to be where I'm go - ing

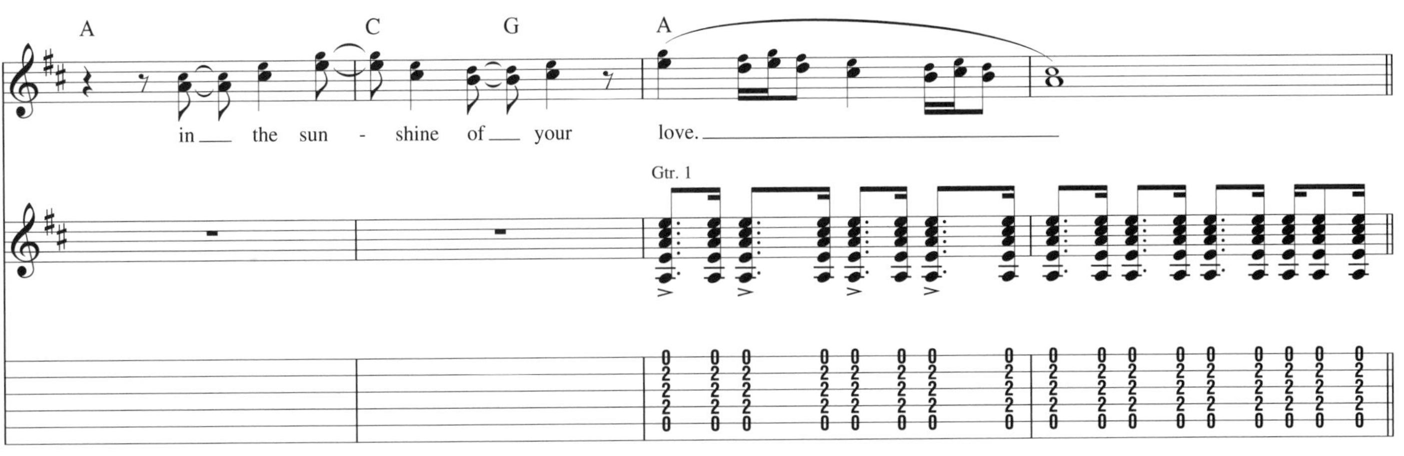
A
C
G
in the sun - shine of your
love.
Gtr. 1

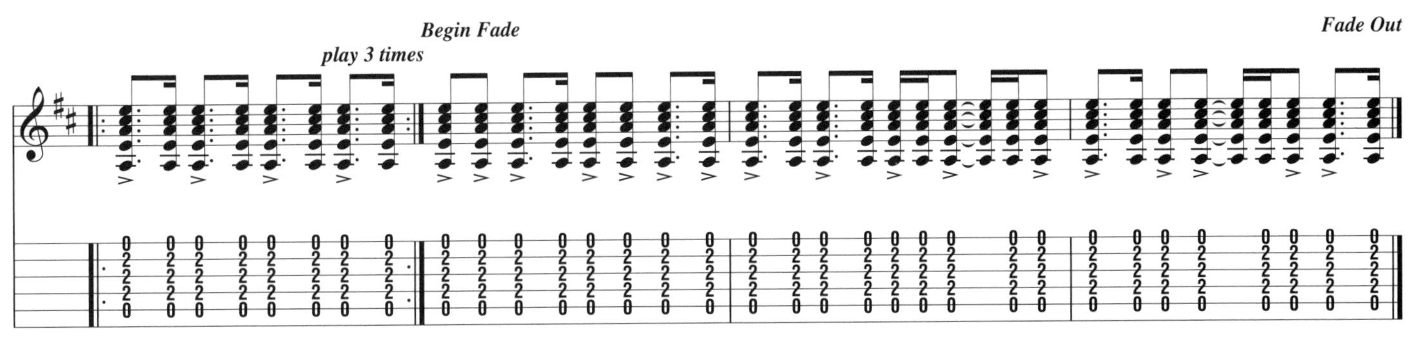
Begin Fade
play 3 times
Fade Out

from Eric Clapton - *Reptile*

Superman Inside

Words and Music by Eric Clapton, Doyle Bramhall II and Susannah Melvoin

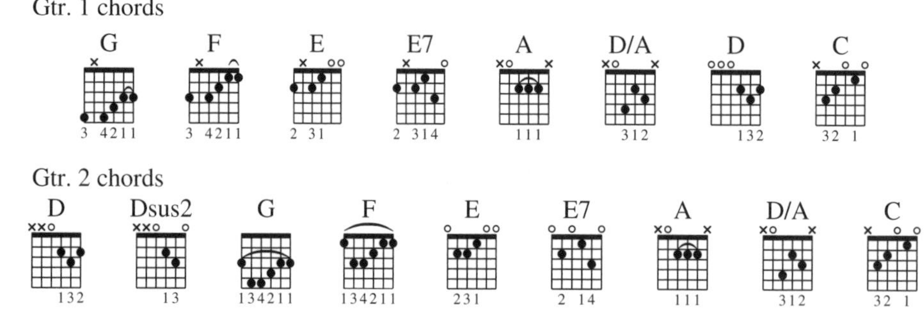

Gtr. 1: Drop D tuning:
(low to high) D–A–D–G–B–E

Gtr. 3: Open D tuning:
(low to high) D–A–D–F♯–A–D

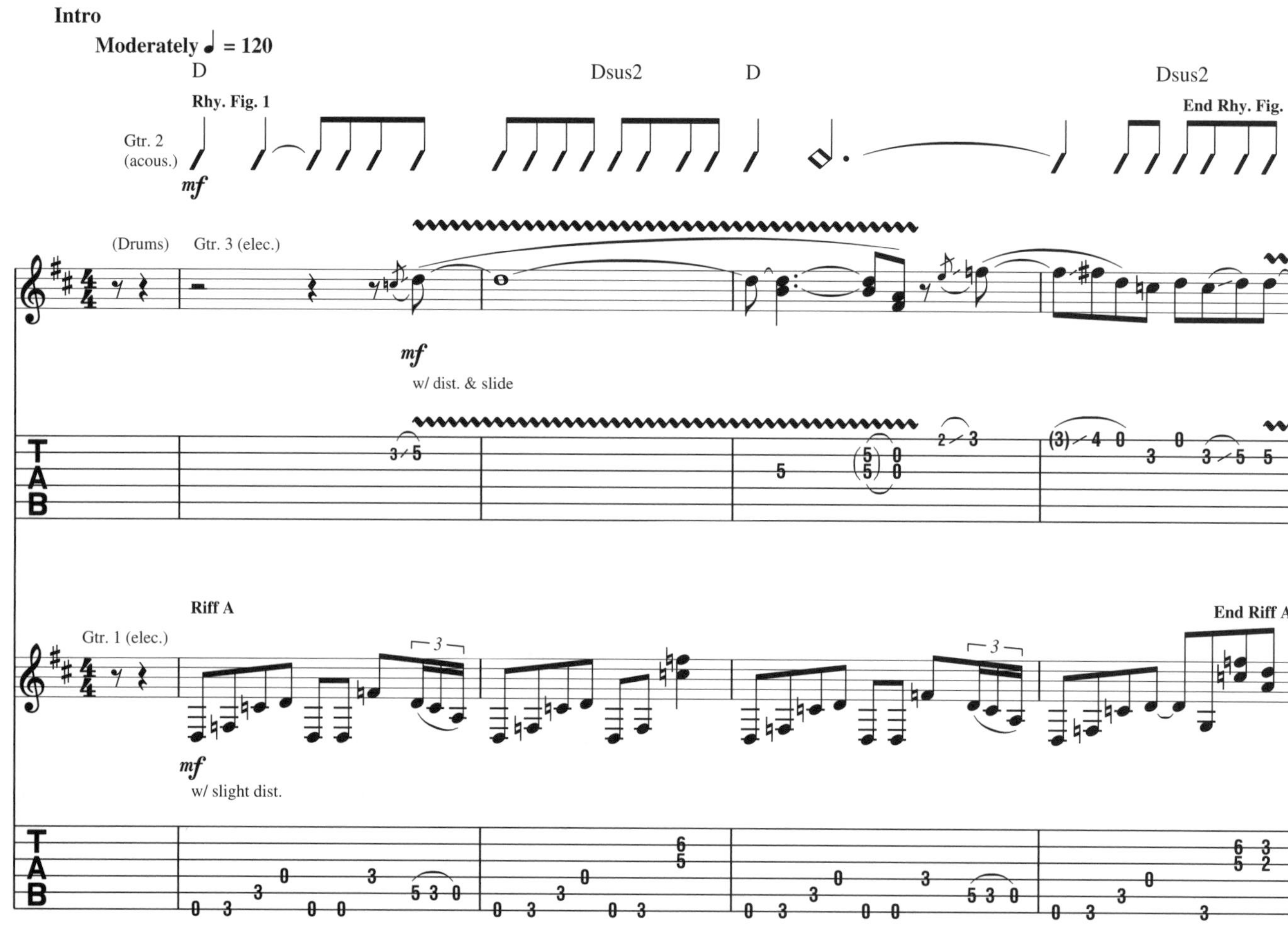

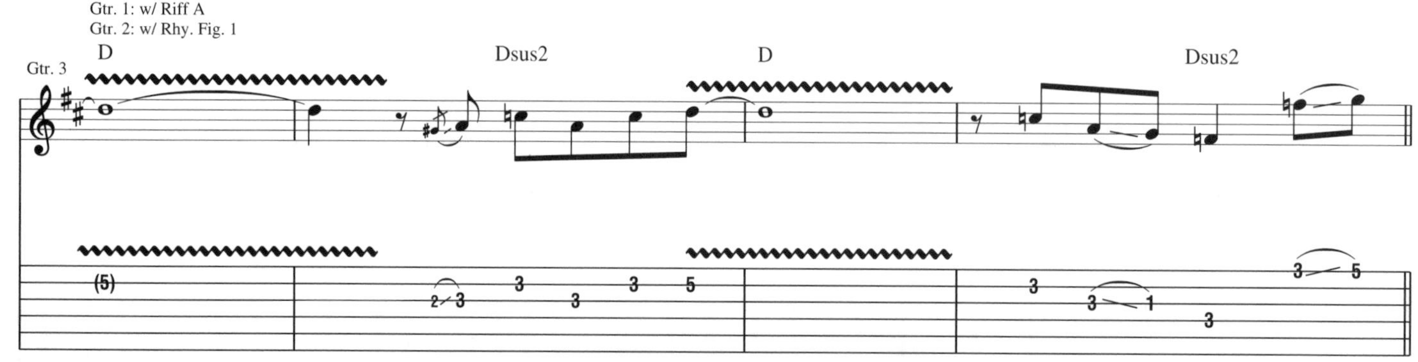

Verse
Gtr. 2: w/ Rhy. Fig. 1 (2 times)
D
Dsus2
D
Dsus2
1. Liv - in', lov - in; ain't gon - na waste my life
Gtr. 3
Gtr. 1
Riff B
1/2
D
Dsus2
D
Dsus2
sing - in' mu - sic. Some days the sun don't shine.
End Riff B
(cont. in slashes)
Pre-Chorus
G
F
Rhy. Fig. 2
Gtrs. 1 & 2
I don't wan - na be the one, the one that can nev - er say,
Gtr. 3

E
E7
A
D/A
End Rhy. Fig. 2
"I need to let it out." Won't you let me in?
Interlude
Gtr. 1: w/ Riff A
Gtr. 2: w/ Rhy. Fig. 1
D
Dsus2
D
Dsus2
Gtr. 4 (elec.)
mf
w/ dist.
fdbk.
1 1/2
*Vol. swell
Gtr. 3
Verse
Gtr. 1: w/ Riff B
Gtr. 2: w/ Rhy. Fig. 1 (2 times)
Gtr. 4 tacet
D
Dsus2
D
Dsus2
2. Give it all up, sur - ren - der thank - ful - ly.
Gtr. 3

Pre-Chorus

Gtrs. 1 & 2: w/ Rhy. Fig. 2
Gtr. 4 tacet

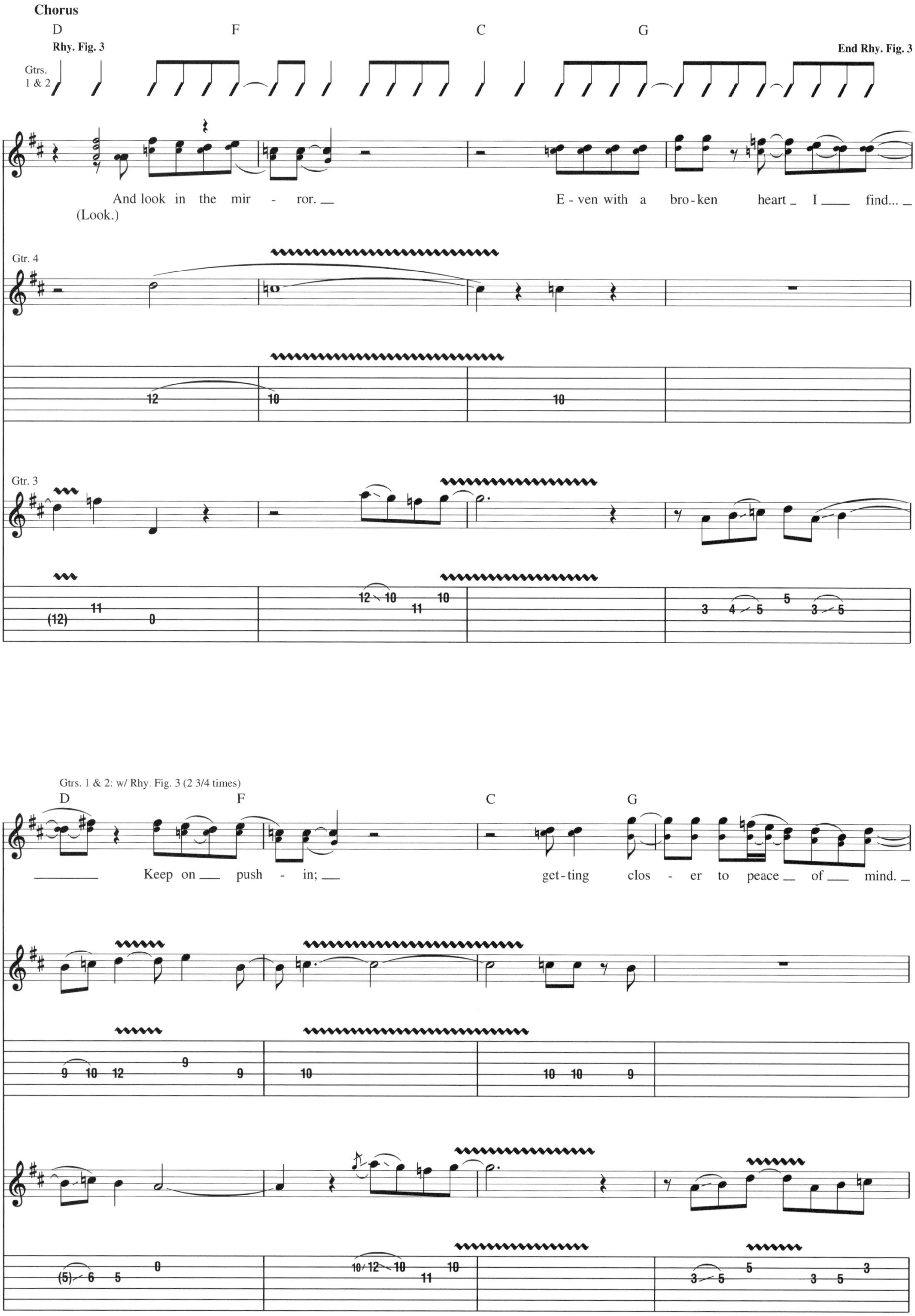

Chorus

D F C G

Rhy. Fig. 3 — End Rhy. Fig. 3

Gtrs. 1 & 2

And look in the mir - ror. (Look.) E - ven with a bro - ken heart I find...

Gtr. 4

Gtr. 3

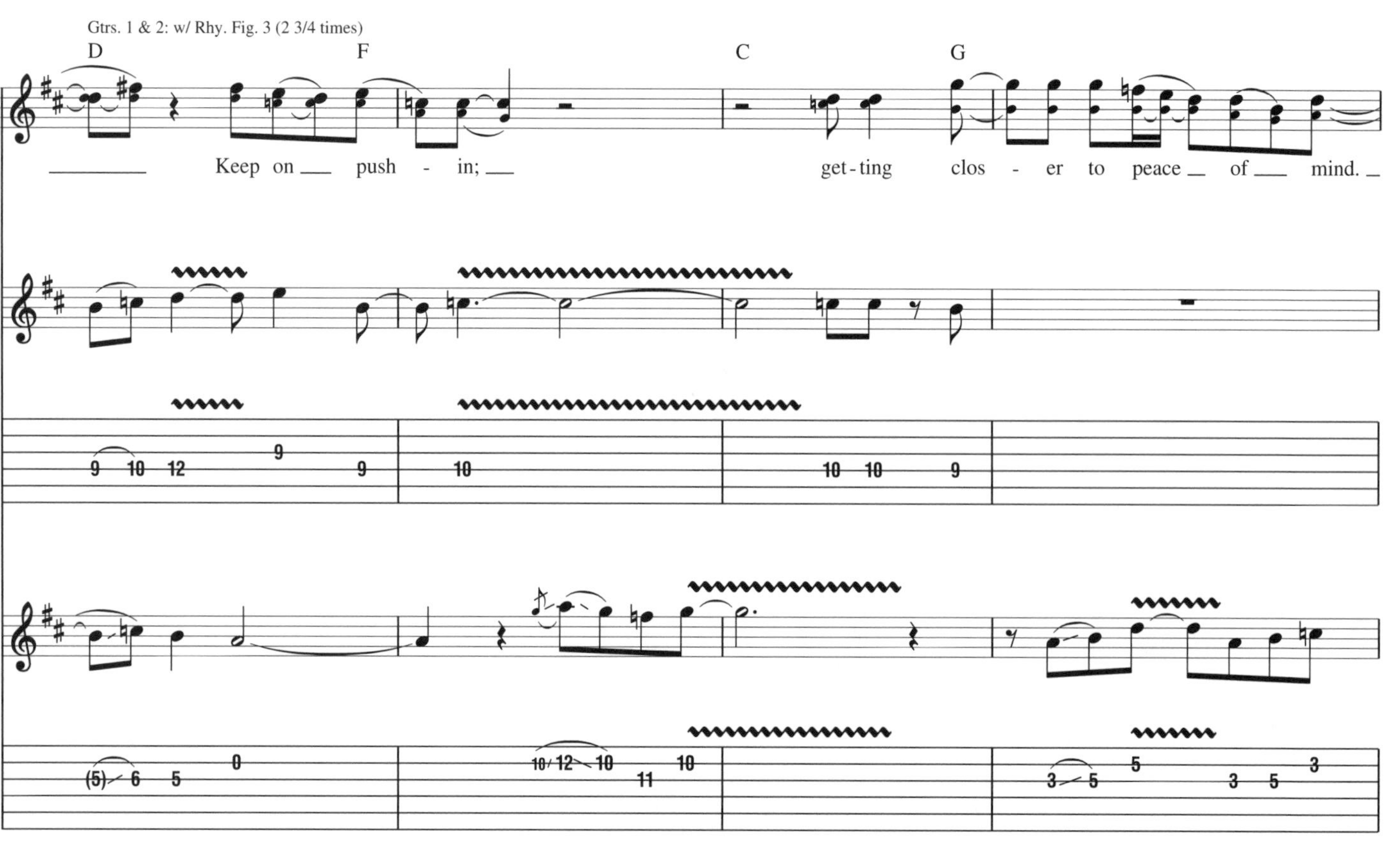

D
F
C
G
Look in the mir - ror.
(Look.)
E - ven with a
*Vol. swell
Gtr. 4 tacet
broken heart, I find living is so sweet.
Gtr. 3
Gtr. 1: w/ Riff A
Gtr. 2: w/ Rhy. Fig. 1
Dsus2
Rhy. Fill 1
End Rhy. Fill 1
Gtrs. 1 & 2
Now it's Su - per - man in - side.
(Su-per - man,

Verse
Gtr. 1: w/ Riff B
Gtr. 2: w/ Rhy. Fig. 1 (2 times)
Gtr. 4 tacet
D
Dsus2
D
Dsus2
Su - per - man __ in - side.) __
3. No more _ run - nin'; __ ain't gon - na hide a - way. _
Gtr. 4
Gtr. 3
D
Dsus2
D
Dsus2
I'm stand - in' __ out - side __ in the pour - ing rain. _
Gtr. 3
Pre-Chorus
Gtrs. 1 & 2: w/ Rhy. Fig. 2
Gtr. 4 tacet
D
Dsus2
G
'Cause I don't wan - na
8va
loco
Gtr. 4
P.H.
P.H.
P.H.
P.H.
Gtr. 3

F
E
E7
be the one, the one that can nev - er say, "I need to
Gtr. 3
let ring
A
D/A
let it out." Won't you let me in?
Chorus
Gtrs. 1 & 2: w/ Rhy. Fig. 3 (3 3/4 times)
D
F
C
G
And look in the mir - ror. E - ven with a bro - ken heart I find...
(Look.)
D
F
C
G
Keep on push - in'; get - ting clos - er to peace of mind.
(Keep on push - in'.)
Gtr. 4
Gtr. 3

D
F
C
G
Look in the mir - ror.
(Look.)
E - ven with a bro - ken heart, I find
1
13
5
10 12 (12) 10 11 10 10
0 0
3 5 5 3 5 0
D
F
Gtr. 4 tacet
C
Gtrs. 1 & 2: w/ Rhy. Fill 1
G
liv - ing is so sweet.
Now it's Su - per - man in - side.
1/2
1
2
13
(13)
5 0
10 12 10 12 10 11 10
3 5 5 3 5 0
Interlude
G
F
D
Gtrs. 1 & 2
(Su-per - man,
Su - per - man in - side.
Gtr. 3
5
5 7
(7) 4 3 4 5 3 5
3 0 3

G
F
Su - per - man,
Gtr. 4
*Vol. swell
Gtr. 3
D
C
Su - per - man in - side.
*Vol. swell

G
Chorus
Gtrs. 2: w/ Rhy. Fig. 3 (4 times)
Gtr. 4 tacet
D
F
C
G
And look in the mir - ror.
(Look.)
E - ven with a
Gtr. 3
Gtr. 3
Gtr. 4
divisi
D
F
bro - ken heart I find... Keep on push - in';
(Keep on push -

C
G
D
F
get - ting
clos - er to peace of mind.
Look in the mir -
- in'.)
(Look.)
Gtr. 4
Gtr. 3
Gtr. 4 tacet
C
G
- ror.
E - ven with a bro - ken heart I find
Gtr. 3
D
F
Gtr. 4 tacet
C
G
liv - ing is so sweet.
Now it's Su -
Gtr. 4
1/2
1 1/2
2 1/2
Gtr. 3

Outro
w/ Voc. ad lib (till end)
Gtr. 1: w/ Riff A (till end)
Gtr. 2: w/ Rhy. Fig. 1 (till end)
D
Dsus2
- per - man in - side.
(Su - per - man,
(Su - per - man.
Gtr. 3
Gtr. 4
Su - per - man in - side.
Su - per - man,
Su - per - man.
steady gliss.
*Slide positioned halfway between 3rd & 4th frets.

Dsus2
D
Dsus2
Su - per - man.
Su - per - man in - side.
D
Dsus2
D
Su - per - man.
Su - per - man,
Su - per - man in - side.
P.H.
Gtr. 4 tacet
Dsus2
Begin fade
D
Dsus2
Su - per - man,
Su - per - man.
Gtr. 3

D Dsus2 D Dsus2

Su-per - man in - side. Su - per - man, Su - per - man.

Gtr. 4

Gtr. 3

D Dsus2 D Dsus2 *Fade out*

Su - per - man in - side. Su - per - man.) Su - per - man.)

from Eric Clapton - *Unplugged*

Tears in Heaven

Words and Music by Eric Clapton and Will Jennings

A7/E
F♯7
F♯7sus4
F♯/A♯
Bm7
and car - ry on, 'cause I know I don't be - long
through night and day 'cause I know I just can't stay
D/E
To Coda
A
E/G♯
F♯m7
F♯m7/E
1.
D/F♯
E7sus4
E7
here in heav - en.
here in heav - en.
A
2.
Bridge
C
G/B
Am
Time can bring ya down,
D/F♯
G
Em
time can bend your knees.
Time can break your heart,

D/F#
G
D/F#
E
A/E
E7
have ya beg - gin' please,
beg - gin' please.
T
T
Interlude
A
E/G#
F#m7
F#m7/E
D/F#
A
E
A/E
E7
3
T
T
A
E/G#
F#m7
F#m7/E
D/F#
A
E
A/E
E7
T
T
Chorus
F#m7
C#/E#
A7/E
Be - yond the door
there's peace, I'm sure,
T

F#7 G#m F#/A# Bm7 D/E
and I know there'll be no more tears in heav-
A E/G# F#m7 F#m7/E D/F# E7sus4 E7
en.
T
A
Verse
A E/G# F#m7 F#m7/E
3. Would you know my name
T
D/F# A E A/E E7 A E/G# F#m7
if I saw you in heav- en? Would you be the same
T
T

D.S. al Coda
(take 1st lyric)
F#m7/E
D/F#
A/E
E
A/E
E7
if I saw you in heav - en?
T
Coda
A
E/G#
F#m7
F#m7/E
en.
'Cause I
T
Bm7
D/E
A
E/G#
F#m
know I don't be - long here in heav - en.
T
F#m/E
D/F#
E7sus4
E7
Freely
A
rit.
T
let ring

from Derek and the Dominos - "Tell the Truth" single
from Eric Clapton - *Crossroads*

Tell the Truth

Words and Music by Eric Clapton and Bobby Whitlock

Gtrs. 3 & 4: Open E tuning:
(low to high) E-B-E-G♯-B-E

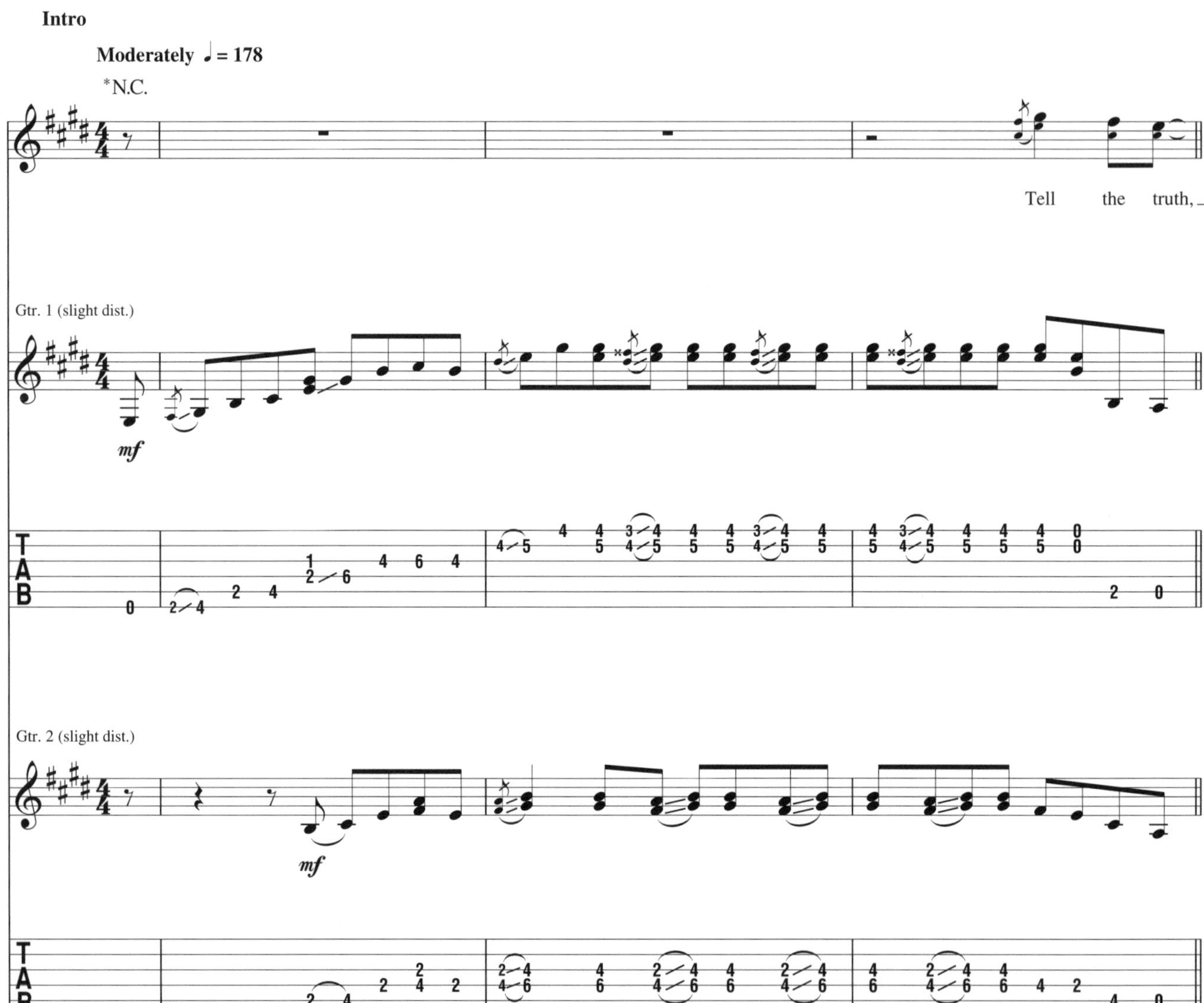

*Chord symbols reflect basic harmony.

 Chorus

A

tell me who's_ been fool - ing you?_

Gtr. 3 (dist.)

mp
w/ slide

let ring
let ring

Gtr. 4 (dist.)

mf
w/ slide

*Gtrs. 1 & 2

*Composite arrangement

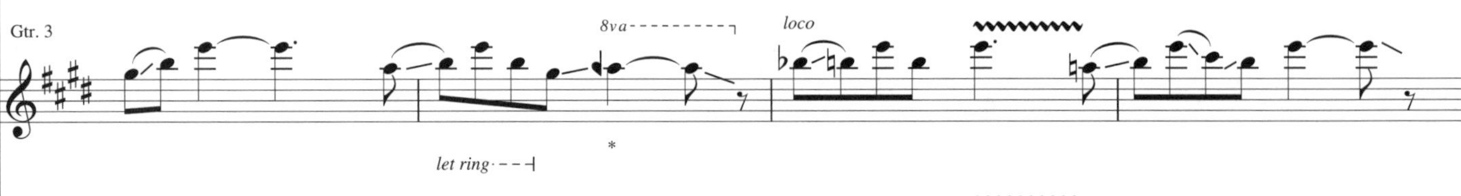

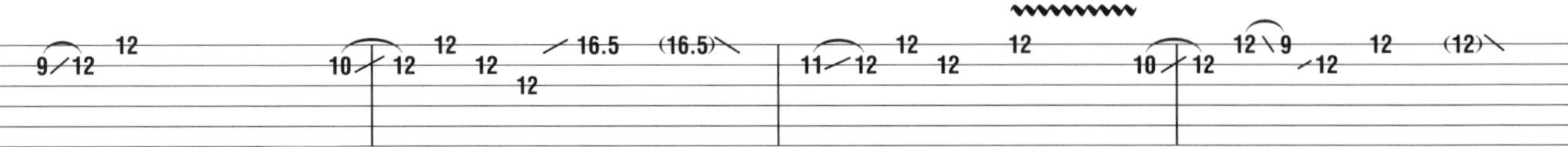

*Slide positioned between 16th and 17th frets.

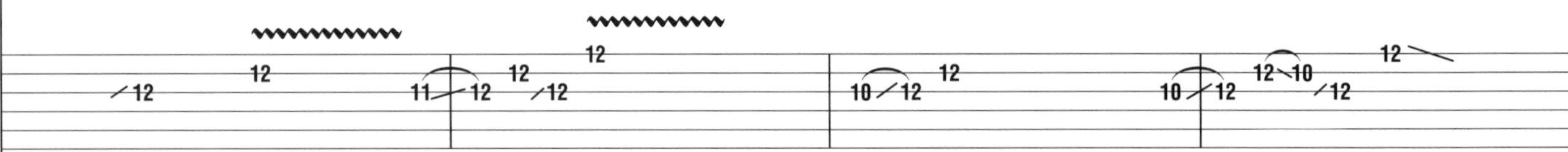

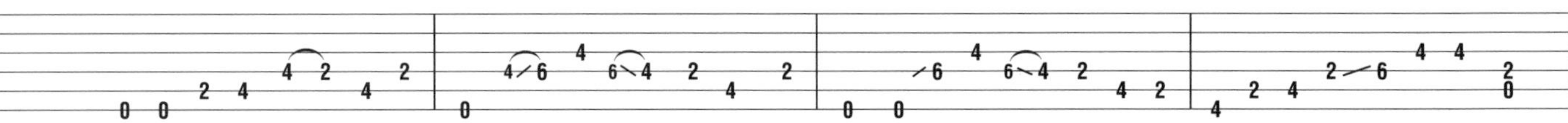

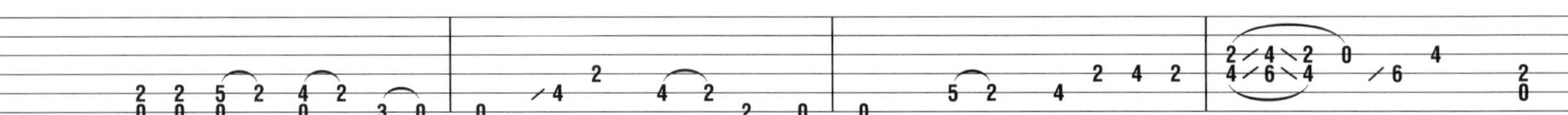

Who's
Gtr. 3
Gtr. 4
Gtrs. 1 & 2
B7
been fool - ing you?
let ring

Verse
N.C.
A
E
1. There you sit there, look-
2. It does-n't mat-ter just
3. Hear what I say 'cause ev-'ry
Gtr. 2
Gtrs. 1 & 2
Gtr. 1
divisi
A
E
A
in' so cool while the whole show is pass-ing you by. You'd
who you are or where you're gon-na end. Just
word is true, ya know I would-n't tell you no lie. Some-
let ring
let ring
let ring
let ring

E
G
D
bet - ter come to terms with your fel - low man soon 'cause
o - pen your eyes and take a look at your heart;
- times com - in' when it's gon - na be soon
the whole world is shak -
Rhy. Fig. 1A
Rhy. Fig. 1B
Rhy. Fig. 1
E
B
E
B
E
B
in' now, can't you feel it?

1.
G
D
B
N.C.
A new dawn is break - in' now, can't you see it?
End Rhy. Fig. 1A
let ring
End Rhy. Fig. 1B
End Rhy. Fig. 1
Gtr. 2
Gtr. 1
divisi
2.
To Coda
Interlude
B7
Tell the truth, - in' now, can't you see it? Can see
Rhy. Fig. 2A
Gtrs. 1 & 2
Rhy. Fig. 2

it yeah, I can see it, I can see it yeah, I can see
let ring
End Rhy. Fig. 2A
End Rhy. Fig. 2
C5
C♯7
it, can see it yeah, ooh,

G♯7
woof,
woof,
woo,
whoa.
let ring
Guitar Solo
A5
A♯5
8va
let ring
*Slide positioned between 16th and 17th frets.

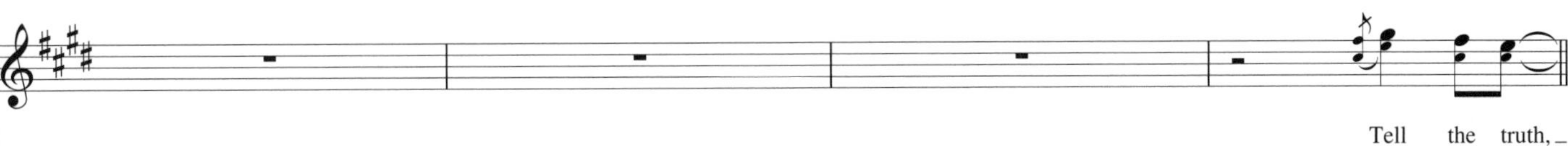
D.S. al Coda
(take 2nd ending)
B7
N.C.
Tell the truth,

8va
loco
Gtr. 3

Gtr. 4

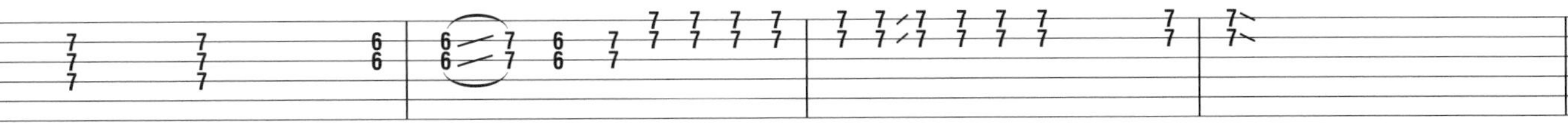

Gtr. 1

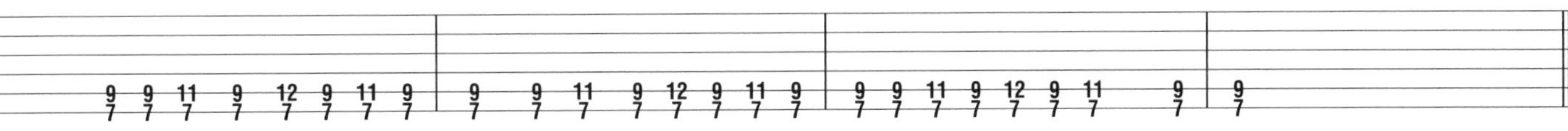

Gtr. 2

Coda

Interlude

Gtrs. 1, 2 & 4: w/ Rhy. Figs. 2 & 2A (4 times)

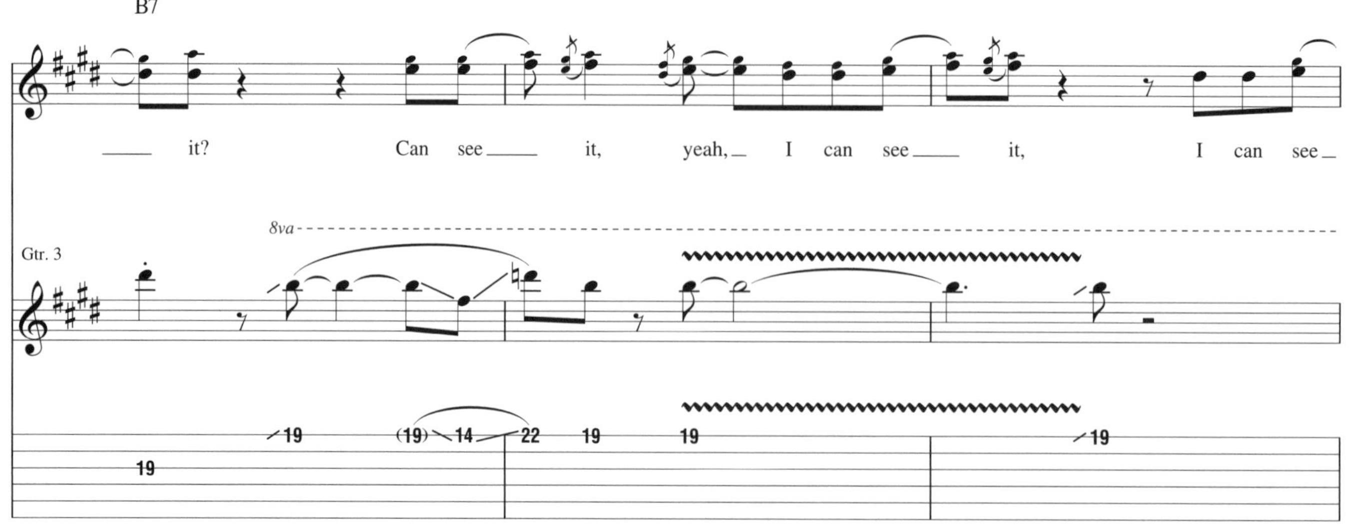

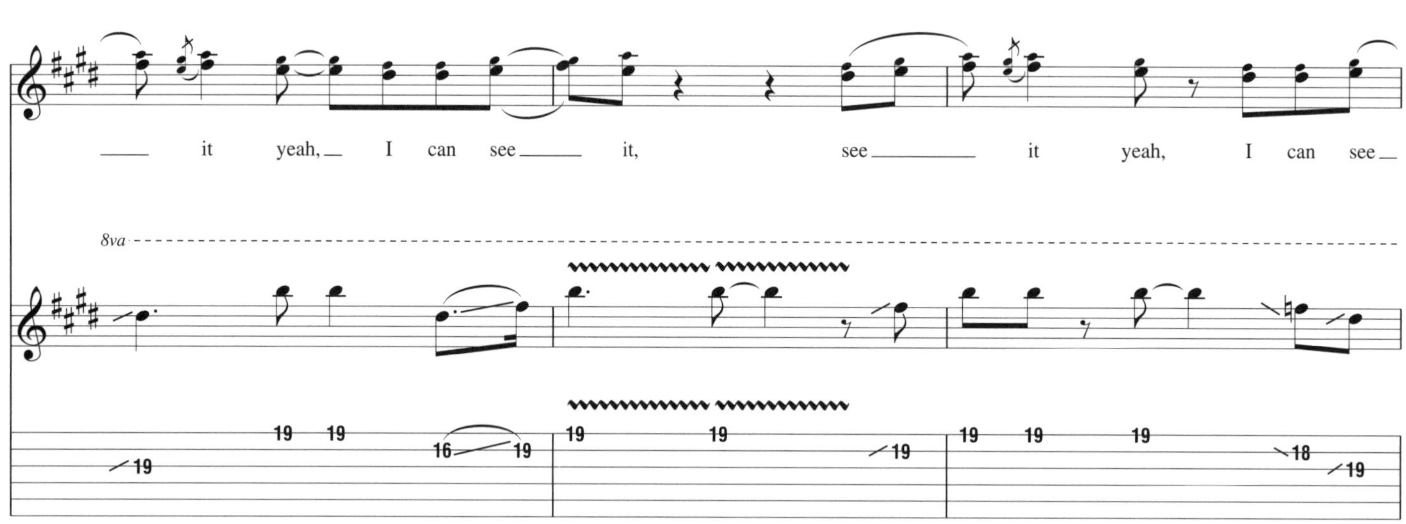

ooh, ooh, ooh, ooh, oo, oo,
8va
ooh, ooh, ooh, ooh.
8va
Gtrs. 1, 2, 3 & 4: w/ Rhy. Figs. 1, 1A & 1B
G
D
The whole world is shak - in' now, can't you feel
8va
E
B
E
B
E
B
G
D
it? Oh, can't you feel it now? A new dawn is break -

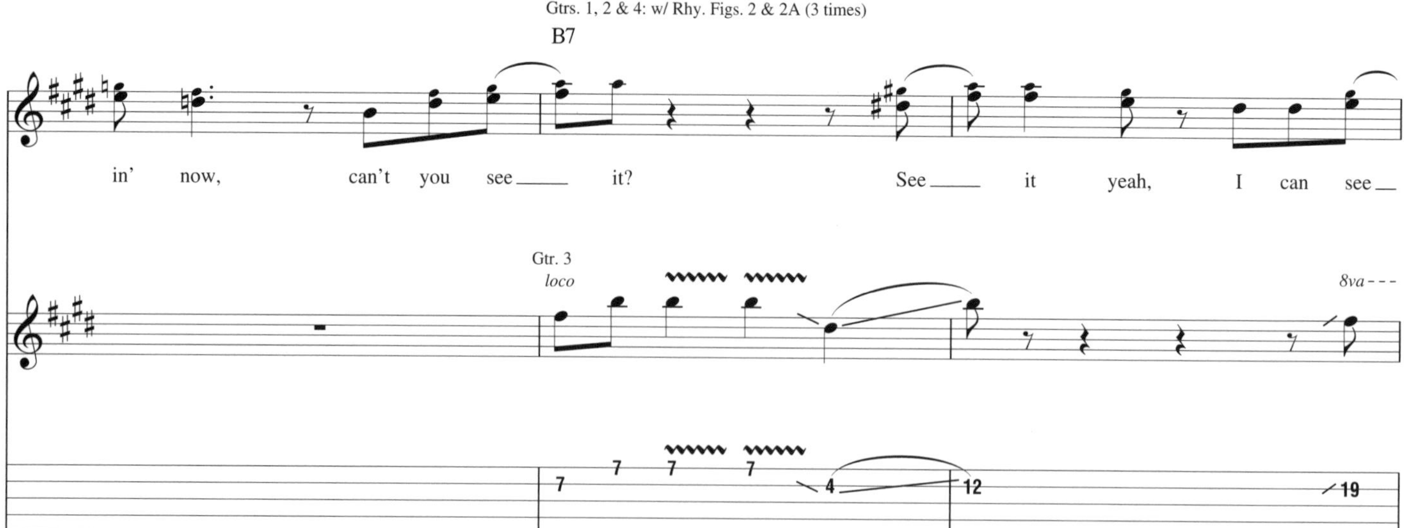
Gtrs. 1, 2 & 4: w/ Rhy. Figs. 2 & 2A (3 times)
B7
in' now, can't you see it? See it yeah, I can see
Gtr. 3
loco
8va
7 7 7 7 4 12 19
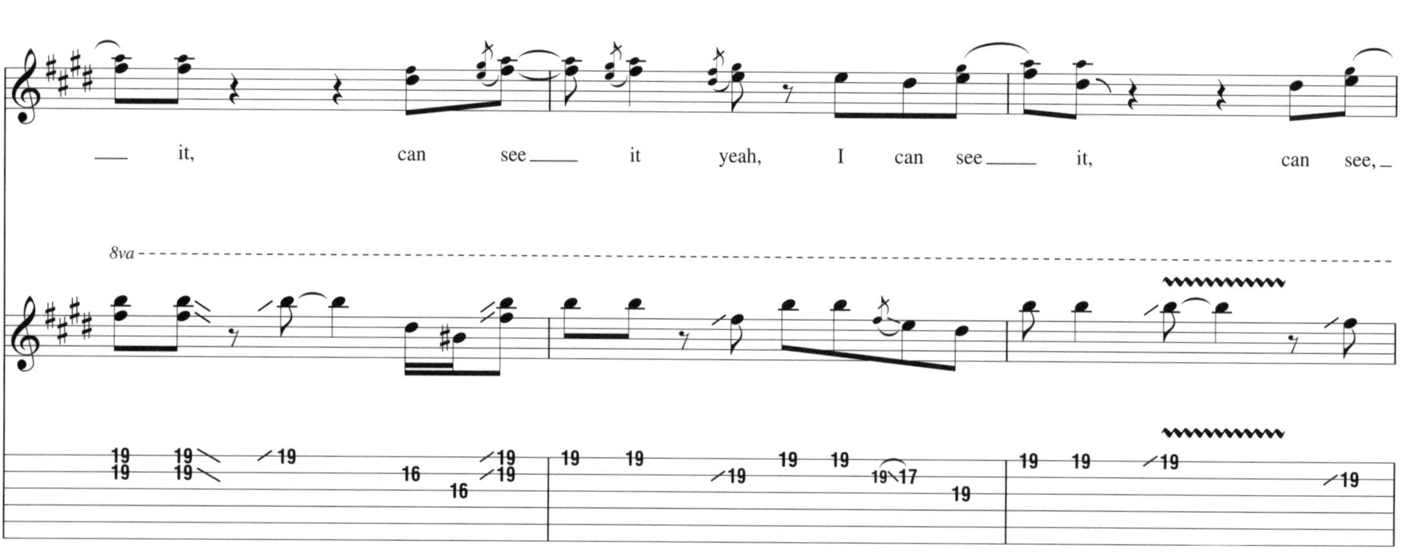
it, can see it yeah, I can see it, can see,
8va

it yeah, I can see it, see it yeah.
8va

G D E

8va

Gtr. 3

loco

steady gliss.

Gtr. 4

Gtrs. 1 & 2

from Eric Clapton - *Backless*

Watch Out for Lucy

Words and Music by Eric Clapton

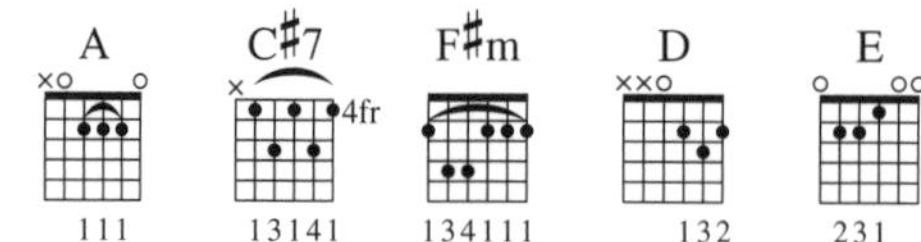

Intro

Moderately ♩ = 146 (♫ = ♩♪)

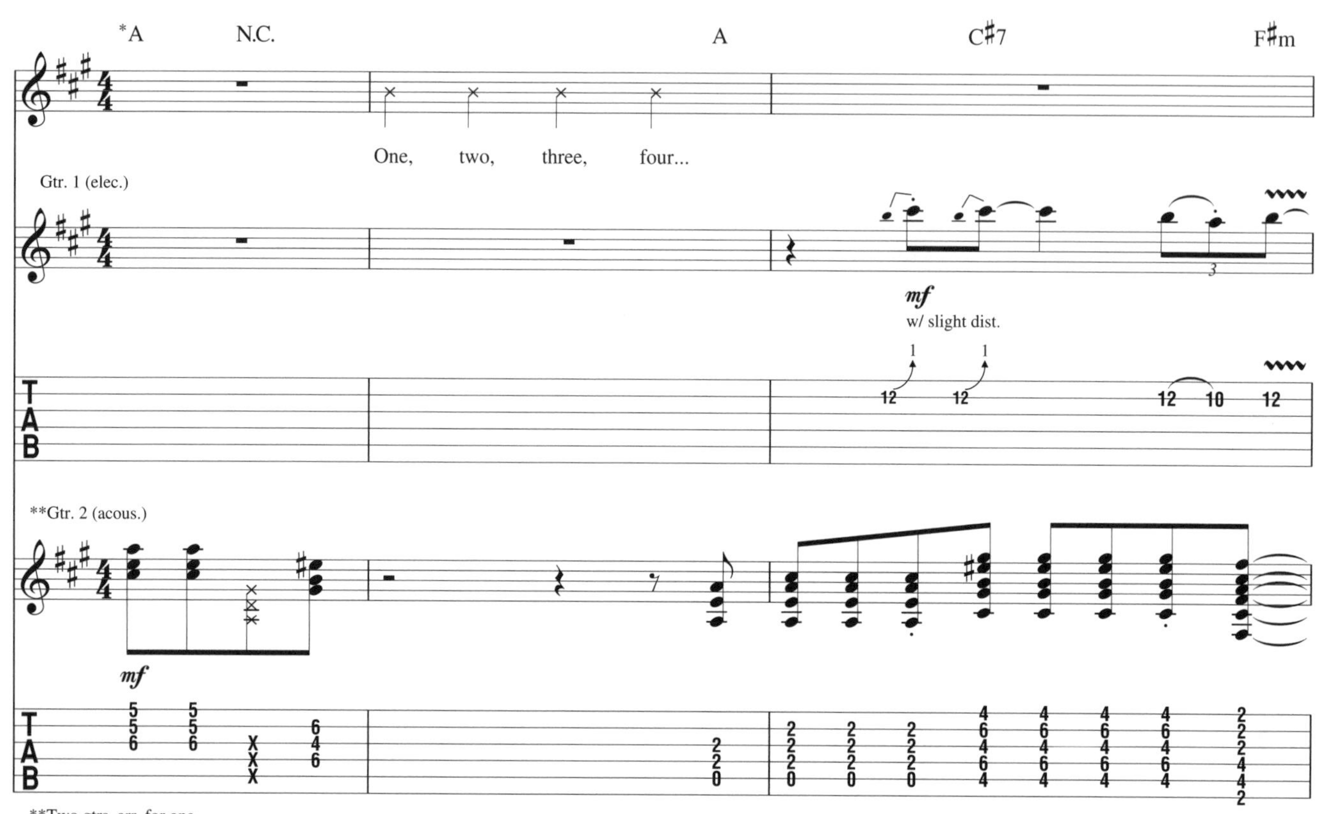

**Two gtrs. arr. for one.

*Chord symbols reflect implied harmony.

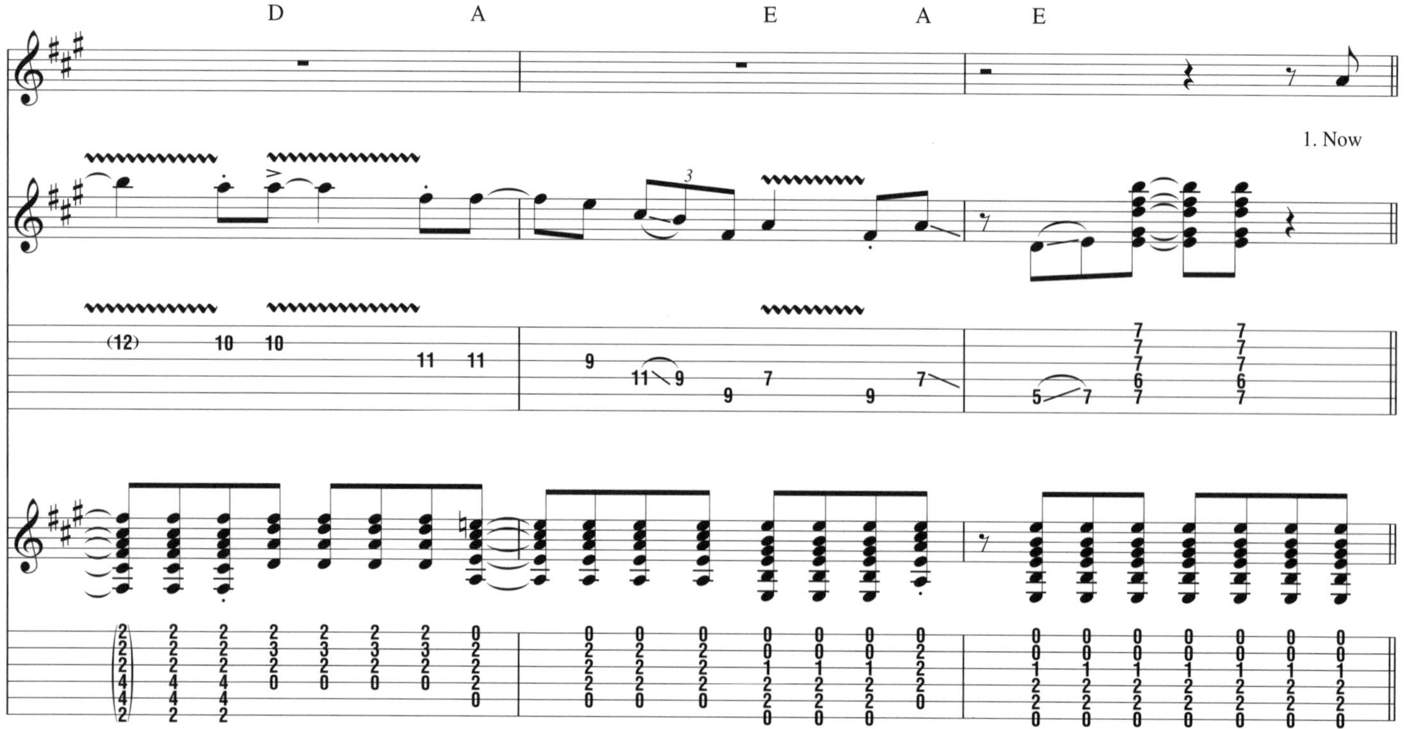

Verse
Gtr. 1 tacet
A
D
C♯7
D
my friend Bill was just a work - ing lad and he liked to have his fun.
Rhy. Fig. 1
A
E
D
He'd like to find a girl and get comf' - tab - le when his work -
Gtr. 2
E
F♯m
C♯7
- ing day was done. He would spend all his mon - ey on a Fri - day night,

D
A
F♯m
wake up in the morn - in' broke.
But he had a run in with lit - tle Lu -
C♯7
D
E
- cy then, be - lieve me that ain't no joke.
Gtr. 1
steady gliss.
Gtr. 2
End Rhy. Fig. 1
(cont. in slashes)
Chorus
A
C♯7
F♯m
D
A
C♯7
F♯m
Rhy. Fig. 2
Gtr. 2
Watch out for Lu - cy,
though she may look frail.
Gtr. 1

*Played as even sixteenth notes.

Verse

Gtr. 2: w/ Rhy. Fig. 1
A
D
C♯7
D
start - ed out work - in' in a ca - fé making mon - ey up on the side.
Gtr. 1
mp
mf
rake
1/2
A
E
D
She was free and eas - y, ev - 'ry - bod - y's friend, but she could-
rake
1/4
1/2
E
F♯m
- n't be sat - is - fied. So now up walks Bill with his cash
1
1/2
C♯7
D
A
in his hand, his heart up - on his sleeve. We
1/2

F#m
C#7
D
E
tried to warn him a - bout her ways, we nev - er did suc - ceed.
Chorus
Gtr. 2: w/ Rhy. Fig. 2
A
C#7
F#m
D
Watch out for Lu - cy,
A
C#7
F#m
D
A
E
F#m
though she may look frail. Say, "Ex - cuse me, Lu - cy, dar -
D
A
E
A
E
lin' don't you use me, I don't wan - na land in jail."

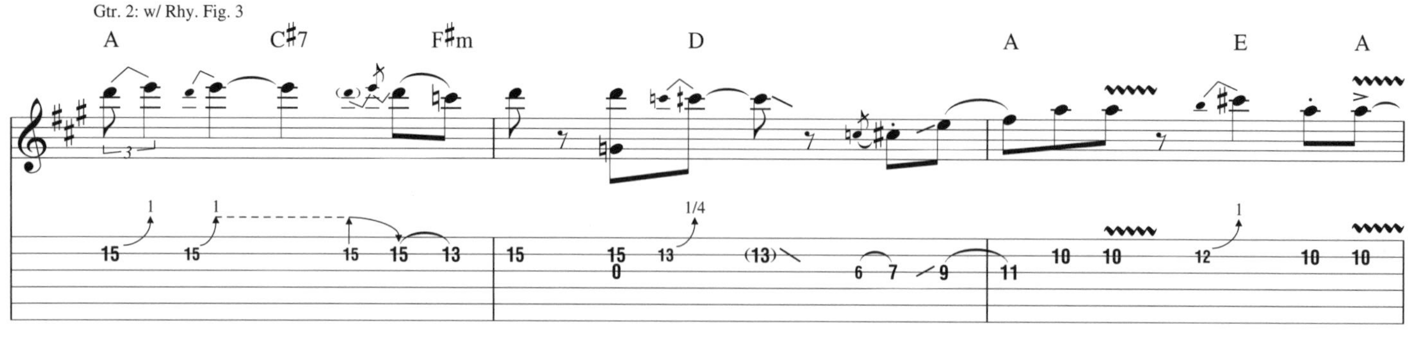

Gtr. 2: w/ Rhy. Fig. 3
A
C♯7
F♯m
D
A
E
A

Verse

Gtr. 2: w/ Rhy. Fig. 1
E
A
D
3. Well the trap was sprung for poor old Bill, you should - 've heard

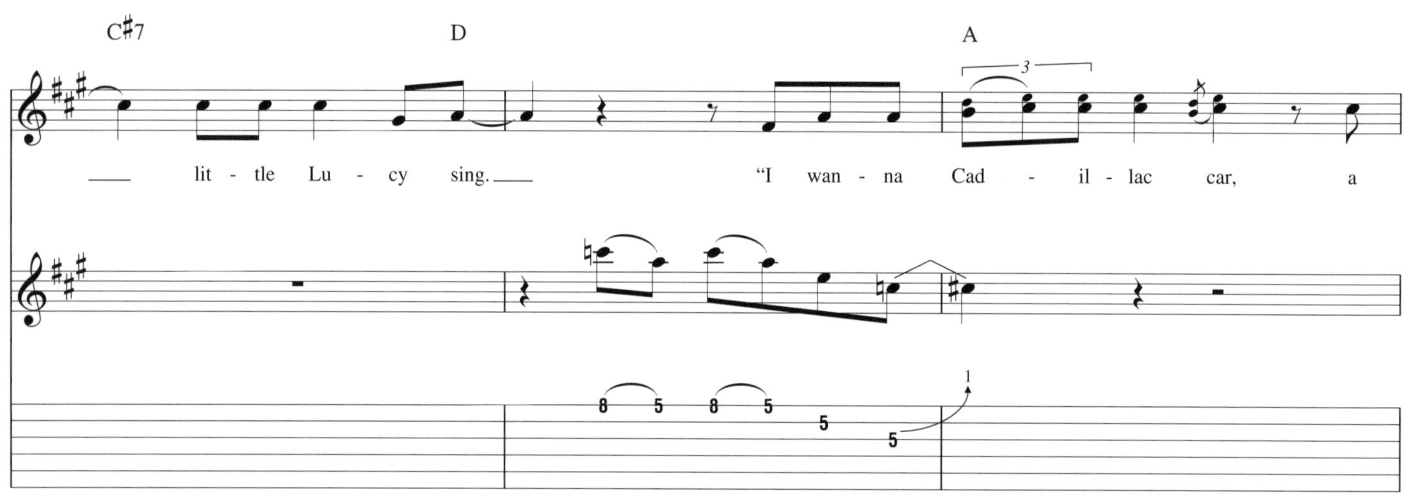

C♯7
D
A
lit - tle Lu - cy sing. "I wan - na Cad - il - lac car, a

E
D
E
beau - ti - ful home and a thou - sand dol - lar ring." They

F#m
C#7
D
A
found_ our he - ro in the gut - ter
with a dia - mond ring and a gun._
F#m
C#7
He'd done_ it for the love__ of Lu - cy
and
3/4
Chorus
Gtr. 2: w/ Rhy. Fig. 2 (till fade)
D
E
A
C#7
F#m
end - ed up on the run.___
Watch out___ for Lu -
D
A
C#7
F#m
D
- cy,
though she may look frail.____
Say, "Ex - cuse__

A E F#m D A E A
me, Lu - cy, dar - lin' don't you use me, I don't wan - na land in jail."
E A C#7 F#m D
Watch out for Lu - cy,
hold bend
A C#7 F#m D A E F#m
though she may look frail. Say, "Ex - cuse me, Lu - cy, dar -
1/2
D A E A E
lin' don't you use me, I don't wan - na land in jail."
1/4
let ring

Outro-Guitar Solo

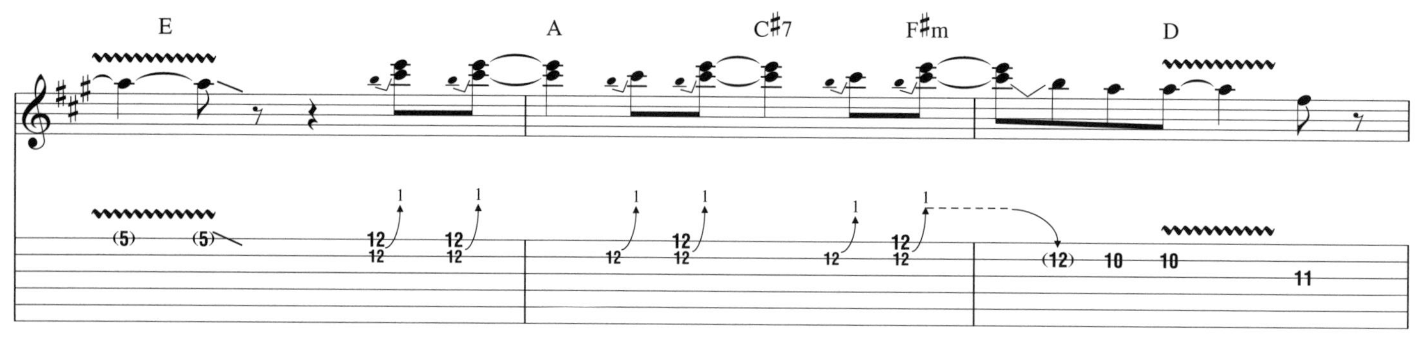
E
A
C♯7
F♯m
D

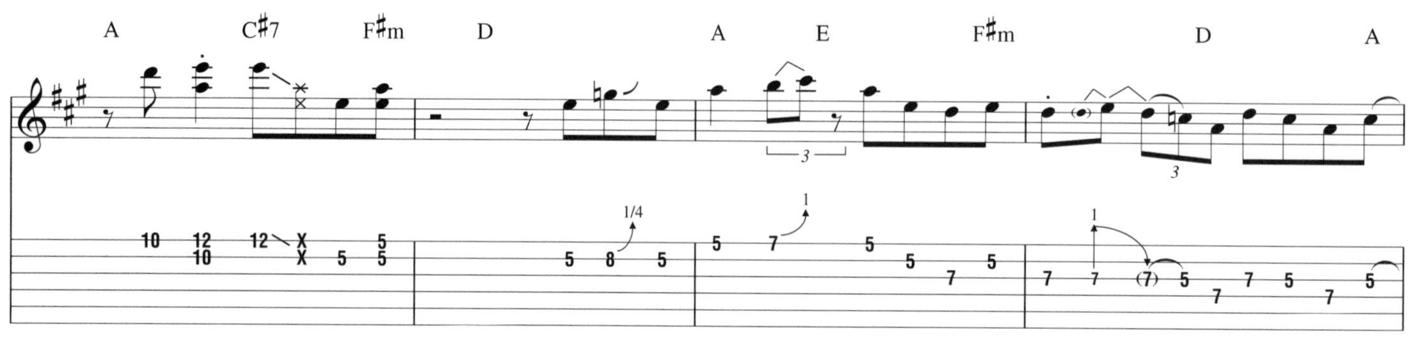
A
C♯7
F♯m
D
A
E
F♯m
D
A

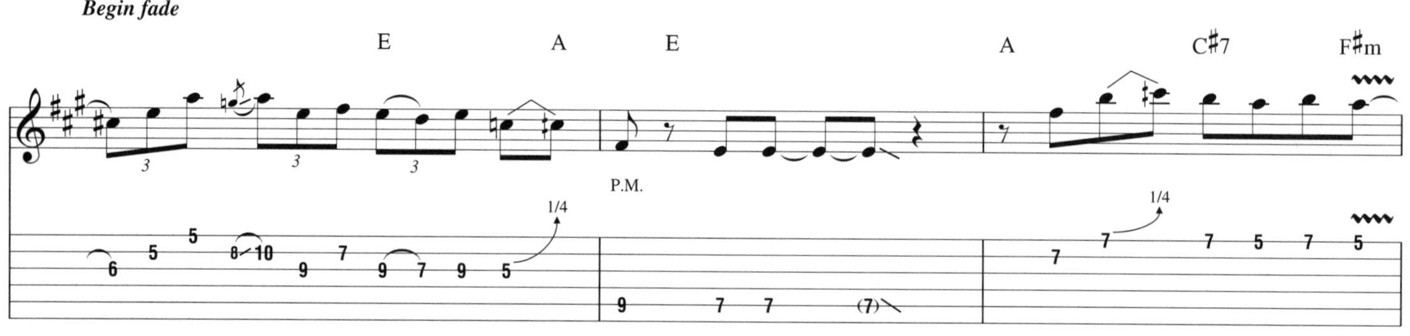
Begin fade
E
A
E
A
C♯7
F♯m
P.M.

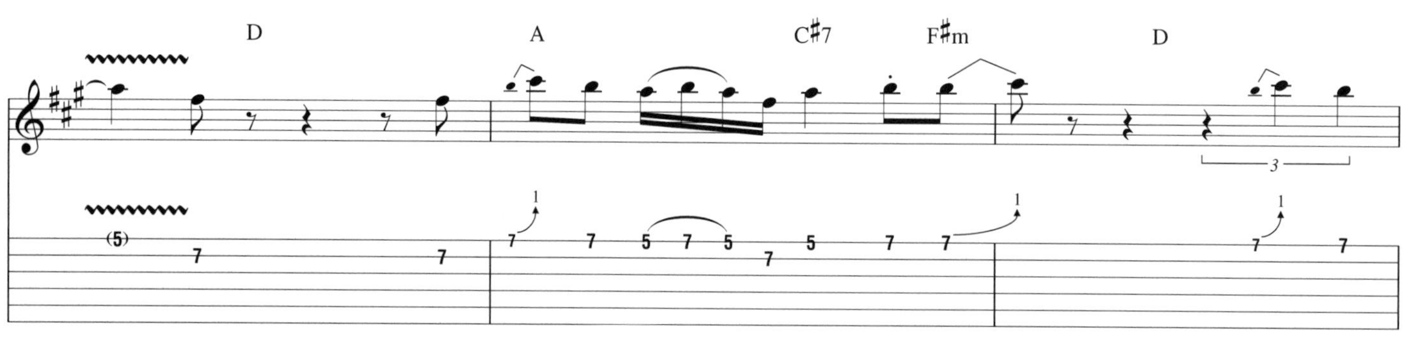
D
A
C♯7
F♯m
D

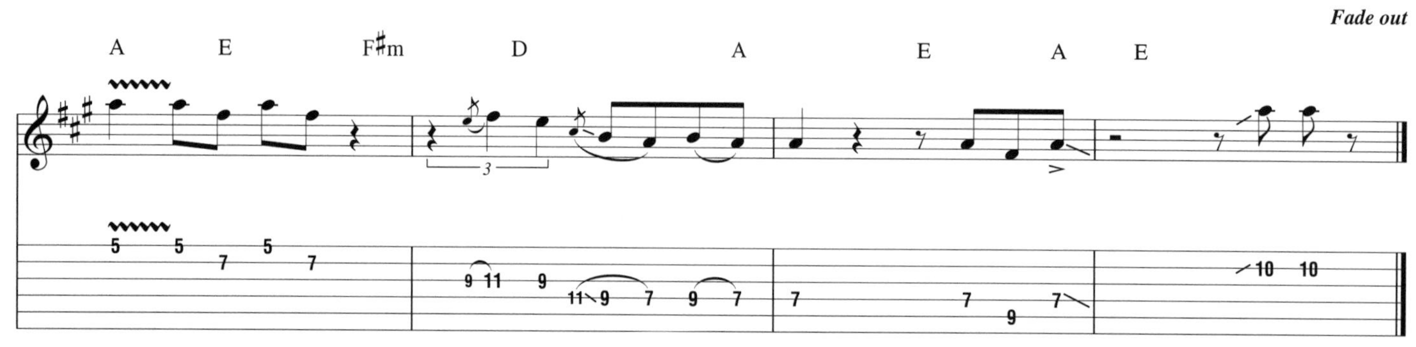
Fade out
A
E
F♯m
D
A
E
A
E

from Cream - *Wheels of Fire*

White Room

Words and Music by Jack Bruce and Pete Brown

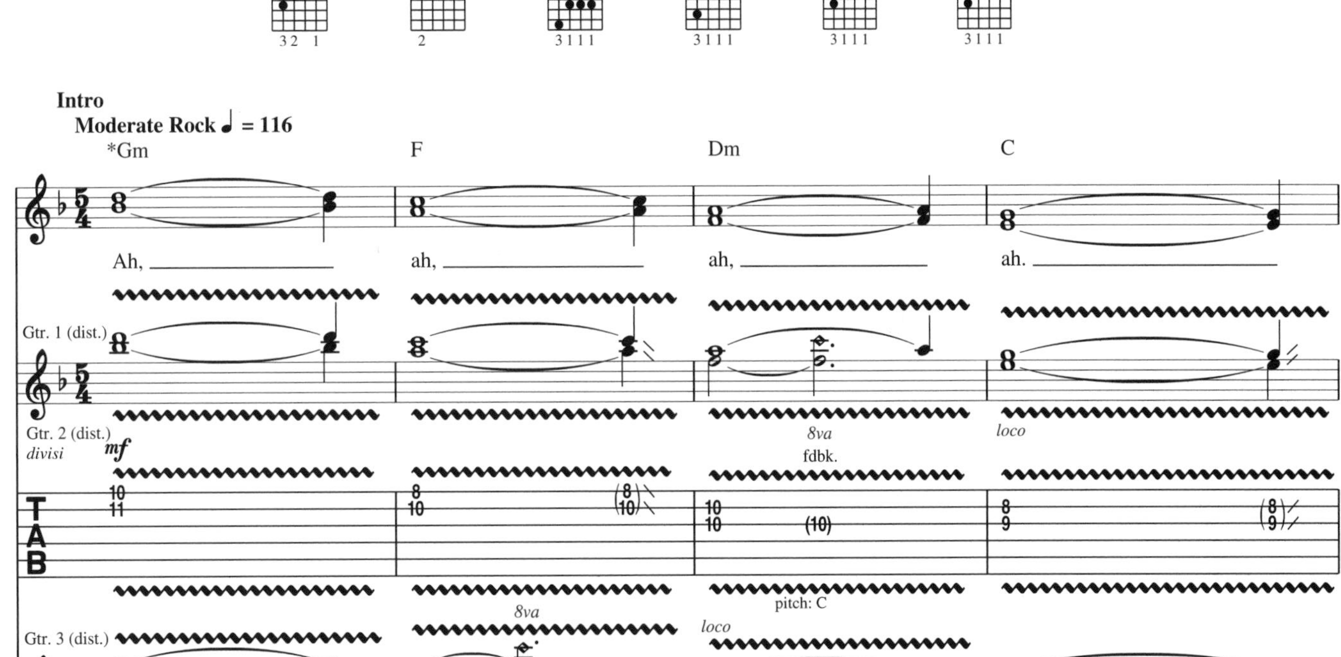

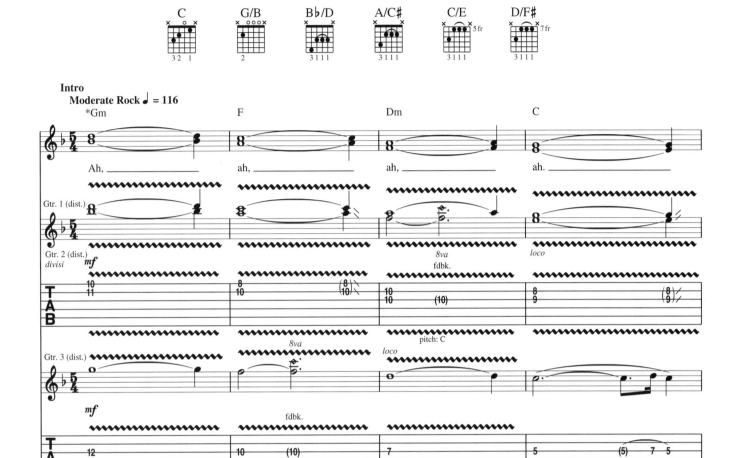

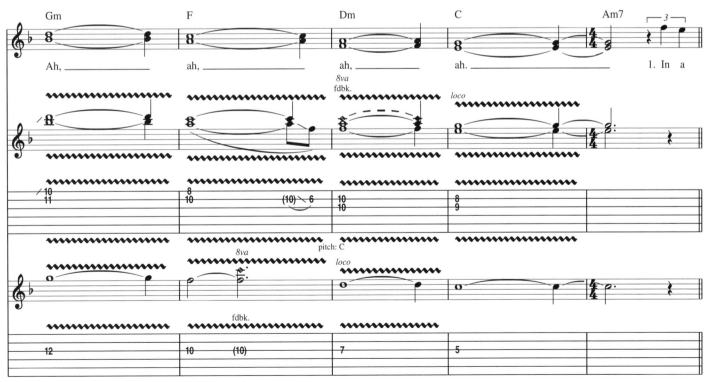

* Chord symbols reflect overall tonality.

pitch: C

Gm F Dm C Am7

Ah, ah, ah, ah.

1. In a

8va fdbk. loco pitch: C

Verse

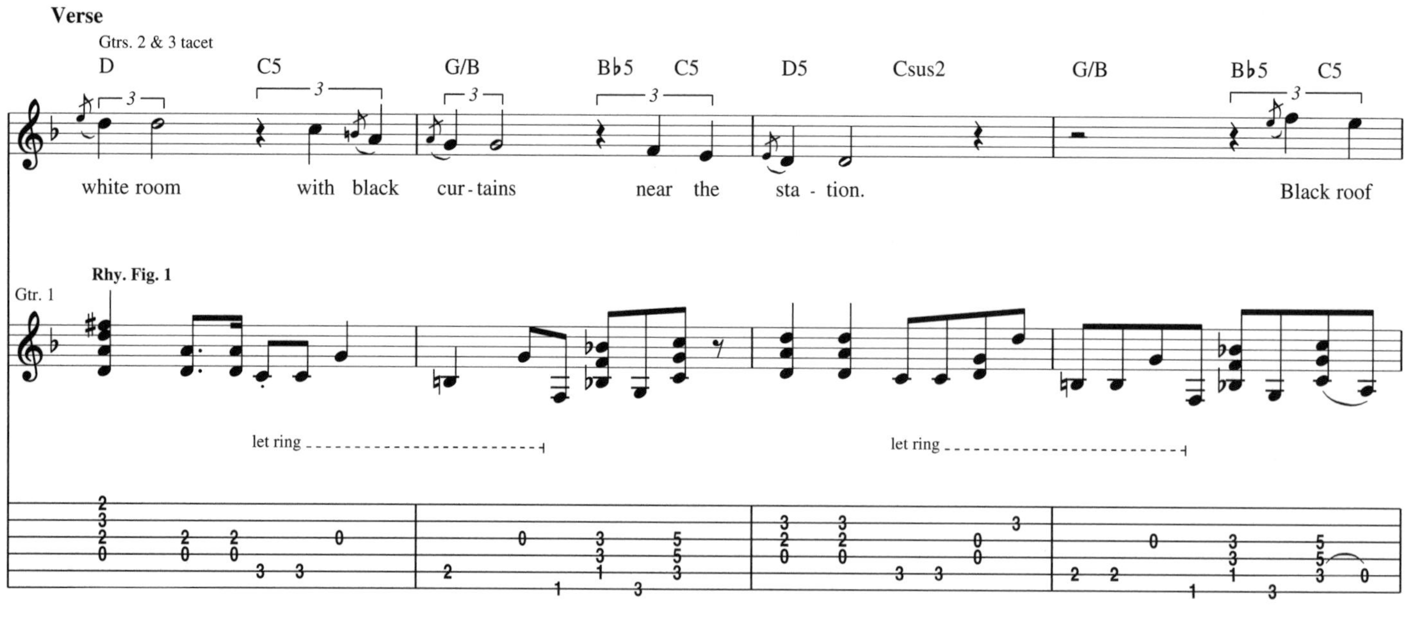
Gtrs. 2 & 3 tacet
D
C5
G/B
B♭5
C5
D5
Csus2
G/B
B♭5
C5
white room with black cur-tains near the sta - tion. Black roof
Rhy. Fig. 1
Gtr. 1
let ring
let ring

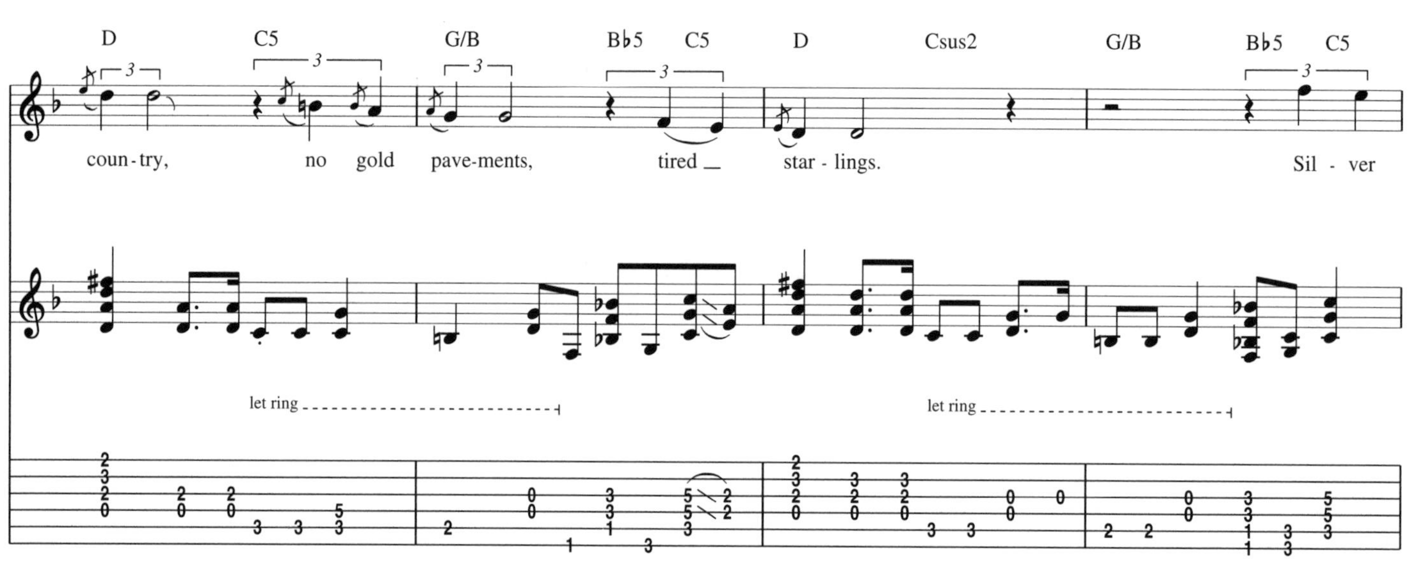
D
C5
G/B
B♭5
C5
D
Csus2
G/B
B♭5
C5
coun-try, no gold pave-ments, tired star - lings. Sil - ver
let ring
let ring

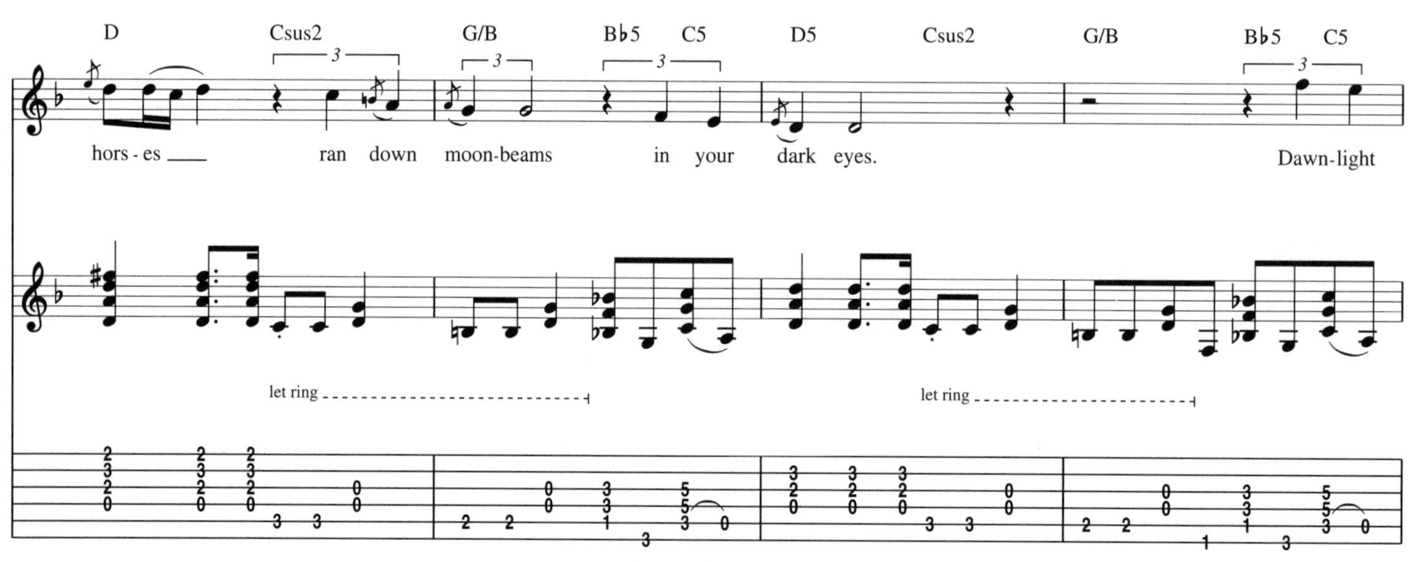
D
Csus2
G/B
B♭5
C5
D5
Csus2
G/B
B♭5
C5
hors - es ran down moon-beams in your dark eyes. Dawn-light
let ring
let ring

D Csus2 G/B B♭5 C5 D Csus2 G/B Gm/B♭
smiles on you leav - ing my con - tent - ment. I'll
End Rhy. Fig. 1
(cont. in slash)
let ring
let ring

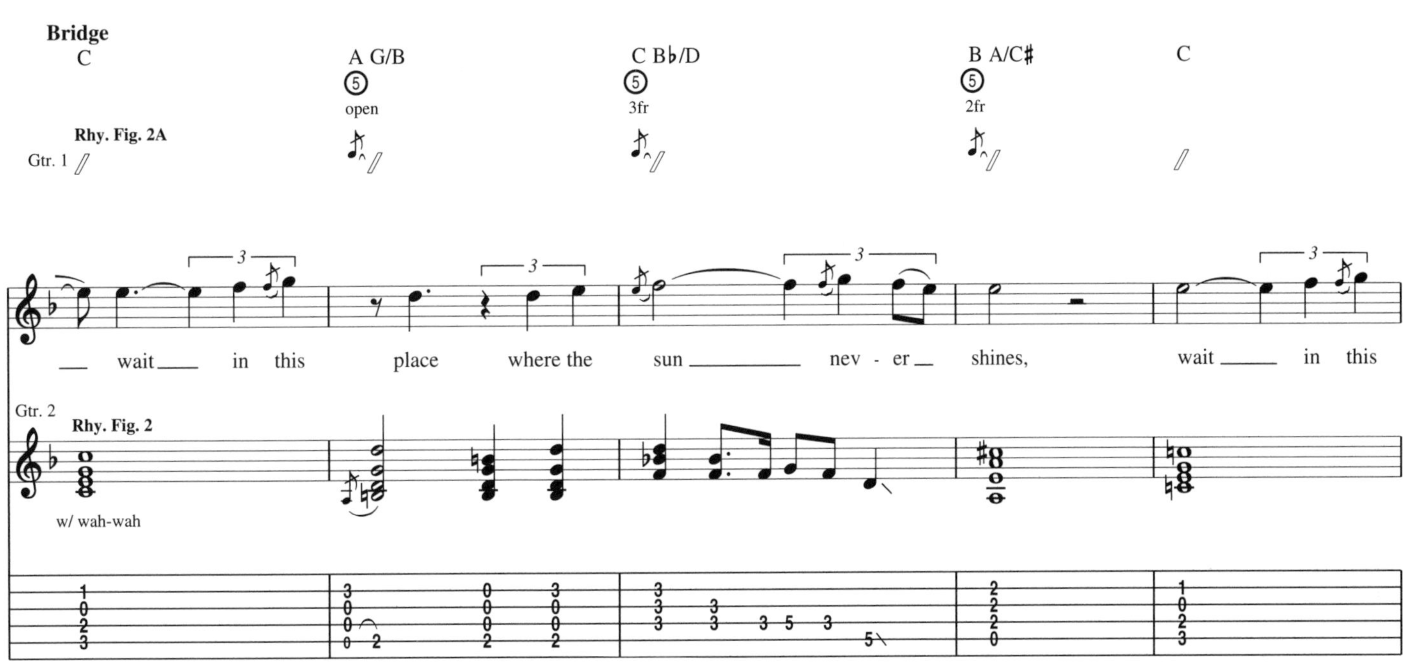
Bridge
C A G/B C B♭/D B A/C♯ C
open 3fr 2fr
Rhy. Fig. 2A
Gtr. 1
wait in this place where the sun nev - er shines, wait in this
Gtr. 2
Rhy. Fig. 2
w/ wah-wah

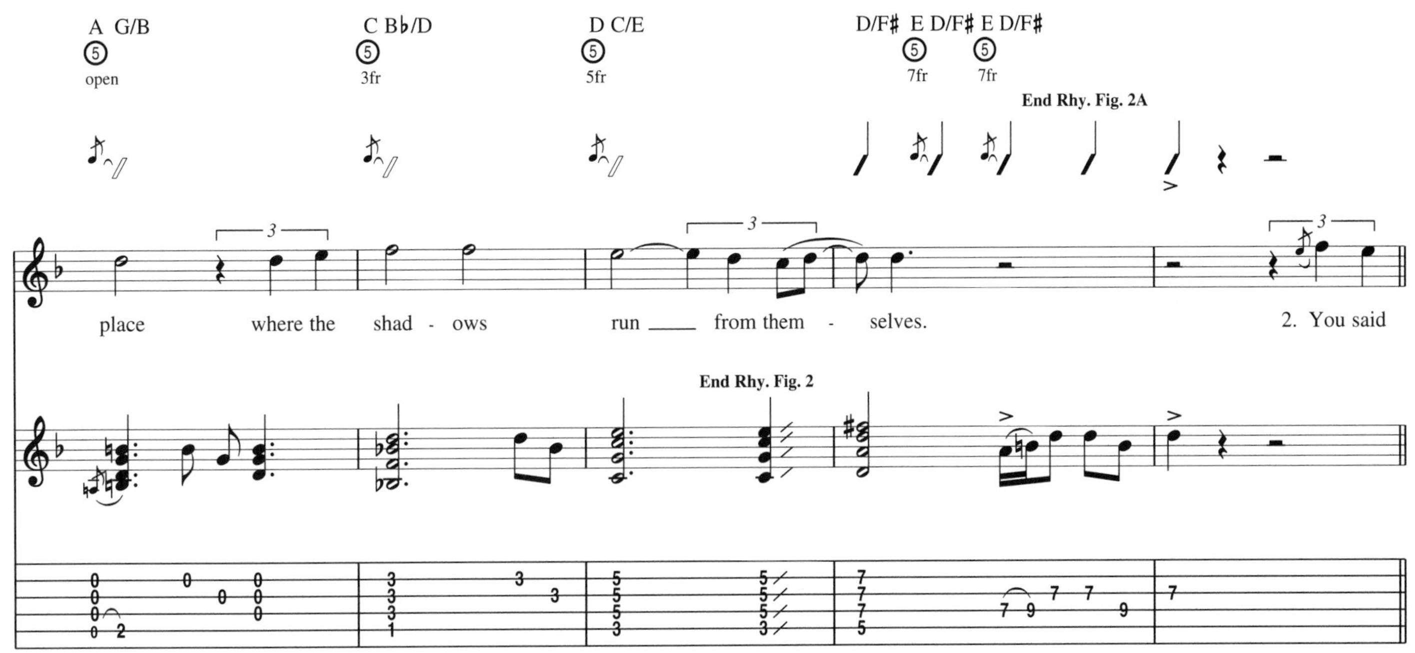
A G/B C B♭/D D C/E D/F♯ E D/F♯ E D/F♯
open 3fr 5fr 7fr 7fr
End Rhy. Fig. 2A
place where the shad - ows run from them - selves. 2. You said
End Rhy. Fig. 2

Verse

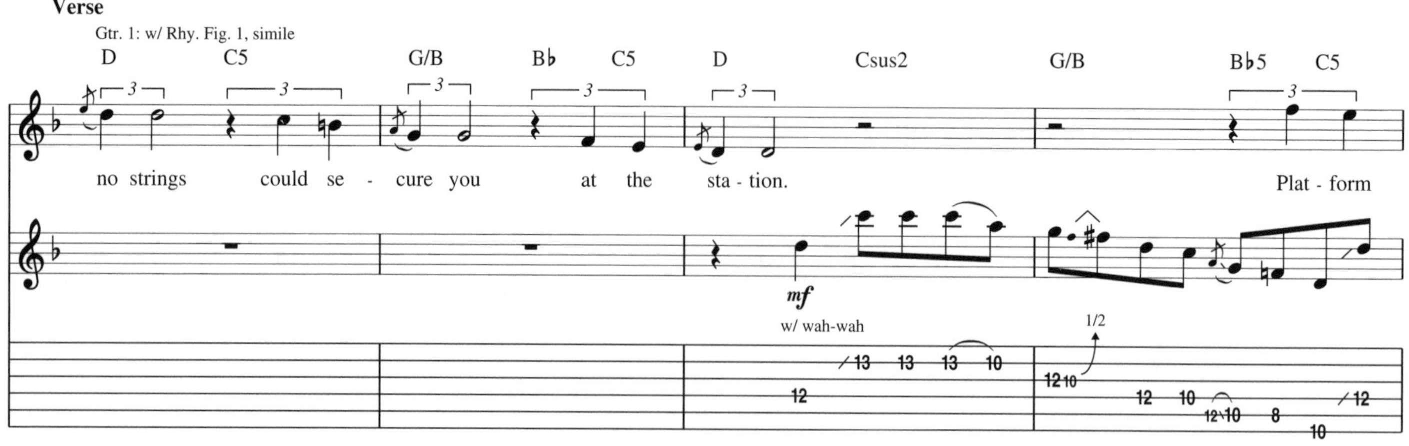
Gtr. 1: w/ Rhy. Fig. 1, simile
D C5 G/B B♭ C5 D Csus2 G/B B♭5 C5
no strings could se - cure you at the sta - tion. Plat - form
mf
w/ wah-wah
1/2

D C5 G/B B♭5 C5 D Csus2 G/B B♭5 C5
tick - et, rest - less die - sel, good - bye win - dows. I walked
full full full full full

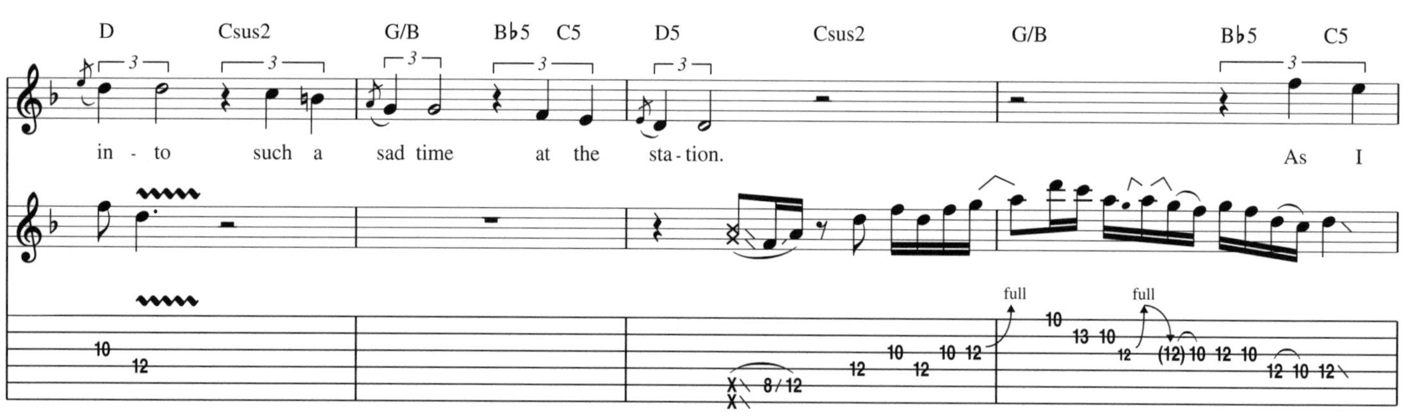
D Csus2 G/B B♭5 C5 D5 Csus2 G/B B♭5 C5
in - to such a sad time at the sta - tion. As I
full full

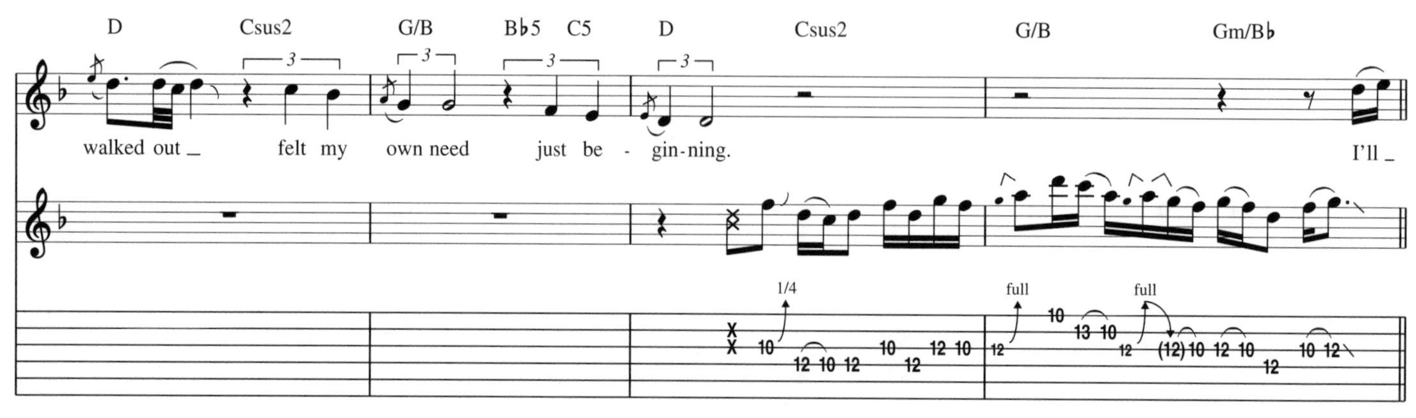
D Csus2 G/B B♭5 C5 D Csus2 G/B Gm/B♭
walked out _ felt my own need just be - gin - ning. I'll _
1/4 full full

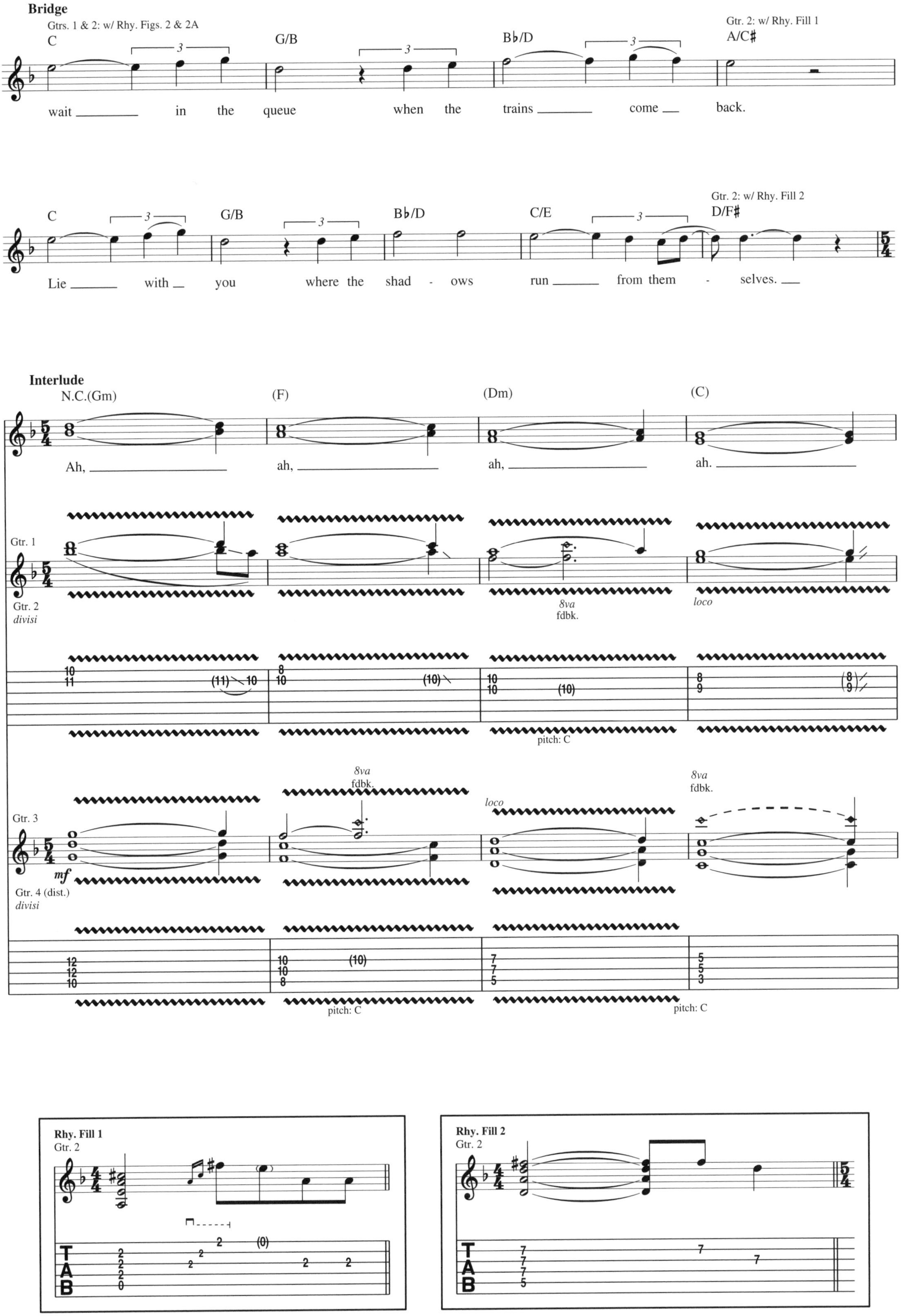

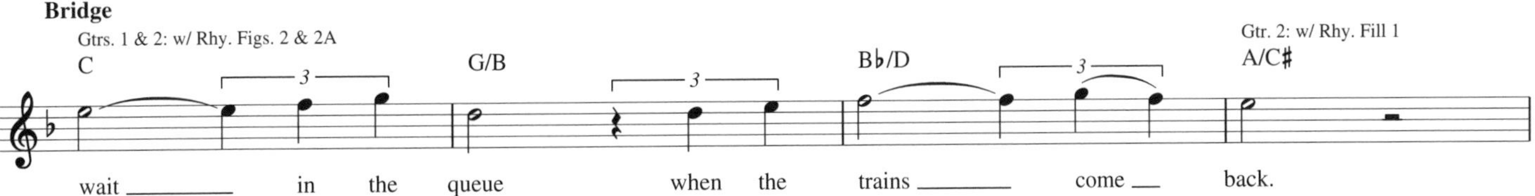

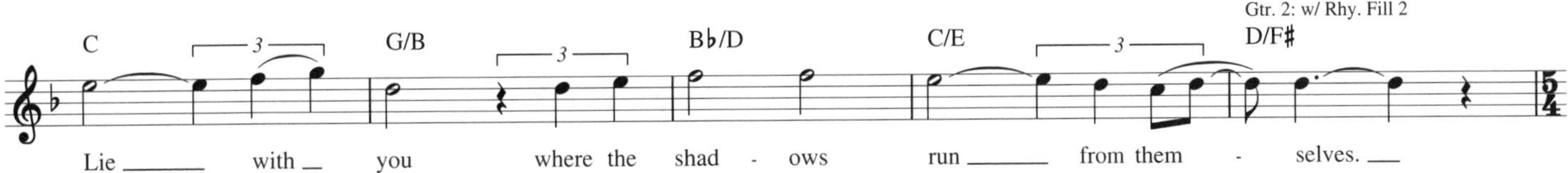

Interlude

N.C.(Gm) (F) (Dm) (C)

Ah, ah, ah, ah.

Gtr. 1

Gtr. 2 *divisi*

8va fdbk. *loco*

pitch: C

Gtr. 3

mf

Gtr. 4 (dist.) *divisi*

8va fdbk. *loco* *8va* fdbk.

pitch: C pitch: C

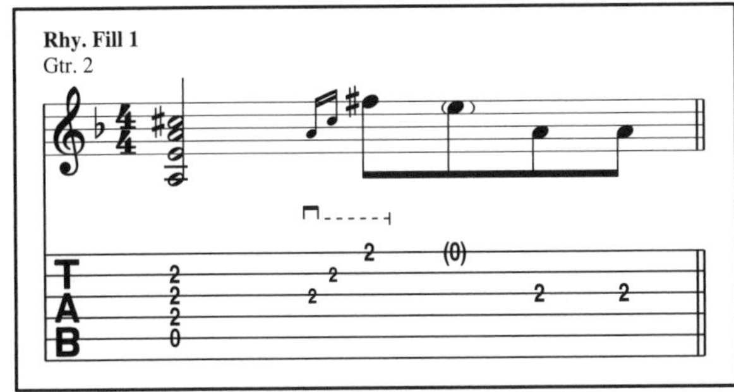

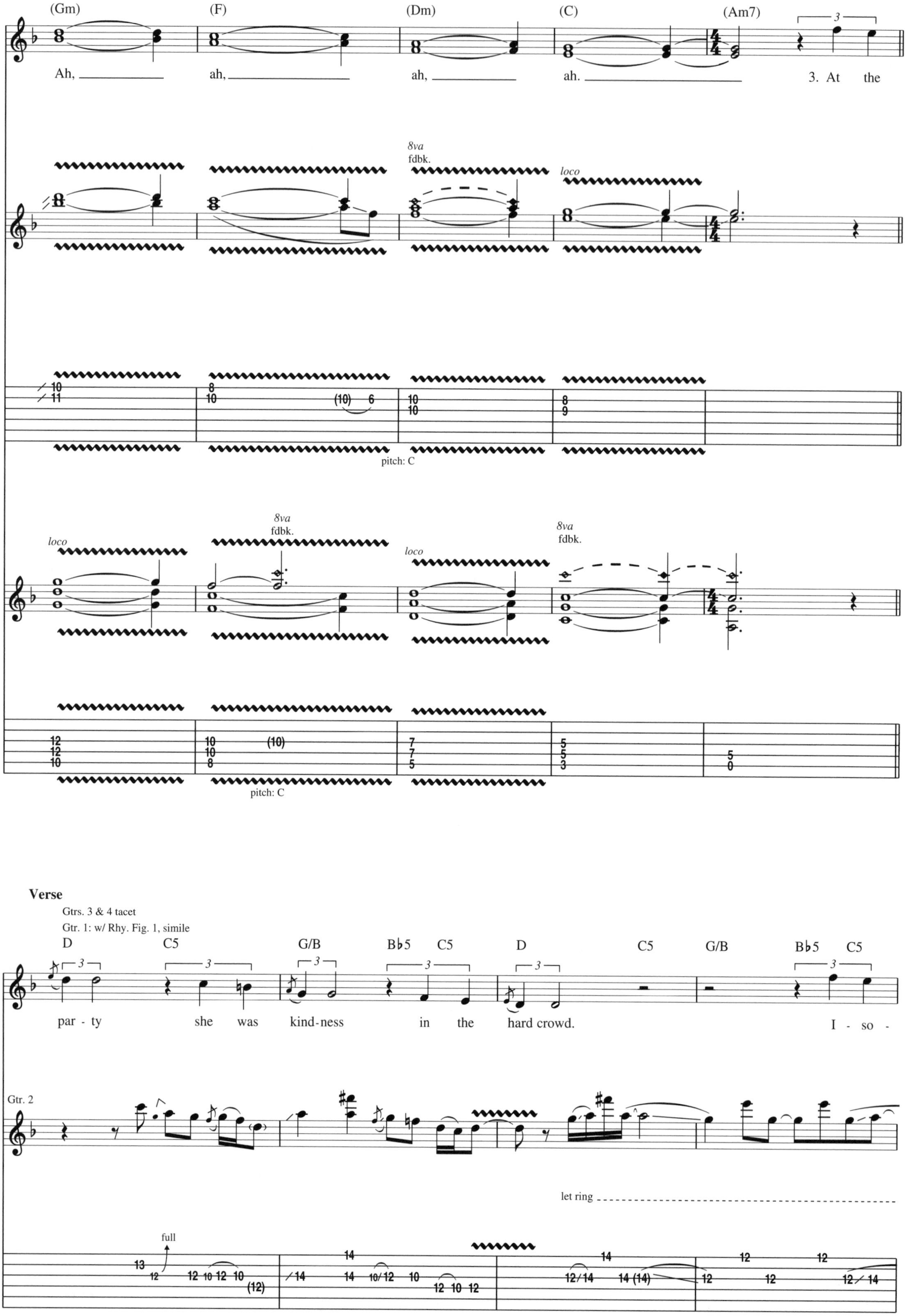

(Gm) (F) (Dm) (C) (Am7)

Ah, ah, ah, ah. 3. At the

8va fdbk.

loco

pitch: C

loco

8va fdbk.

loco

8va fdbk.

pitch: C

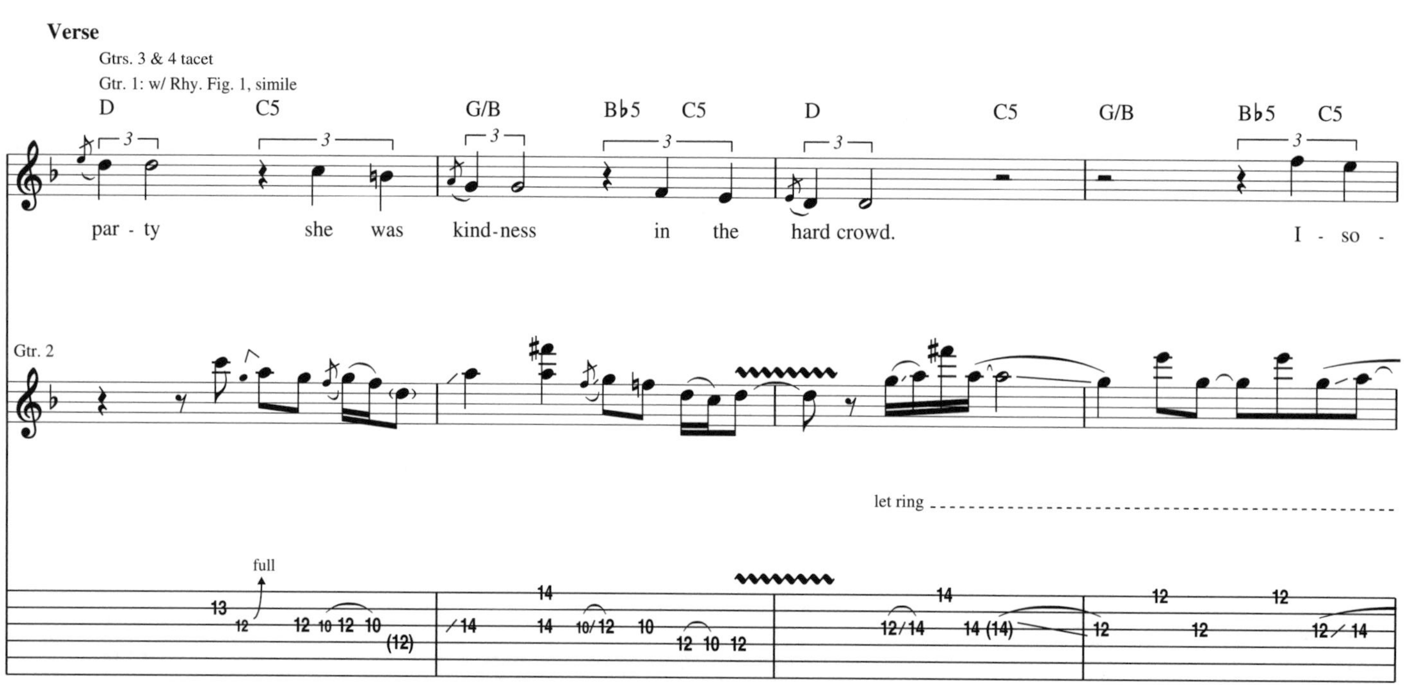

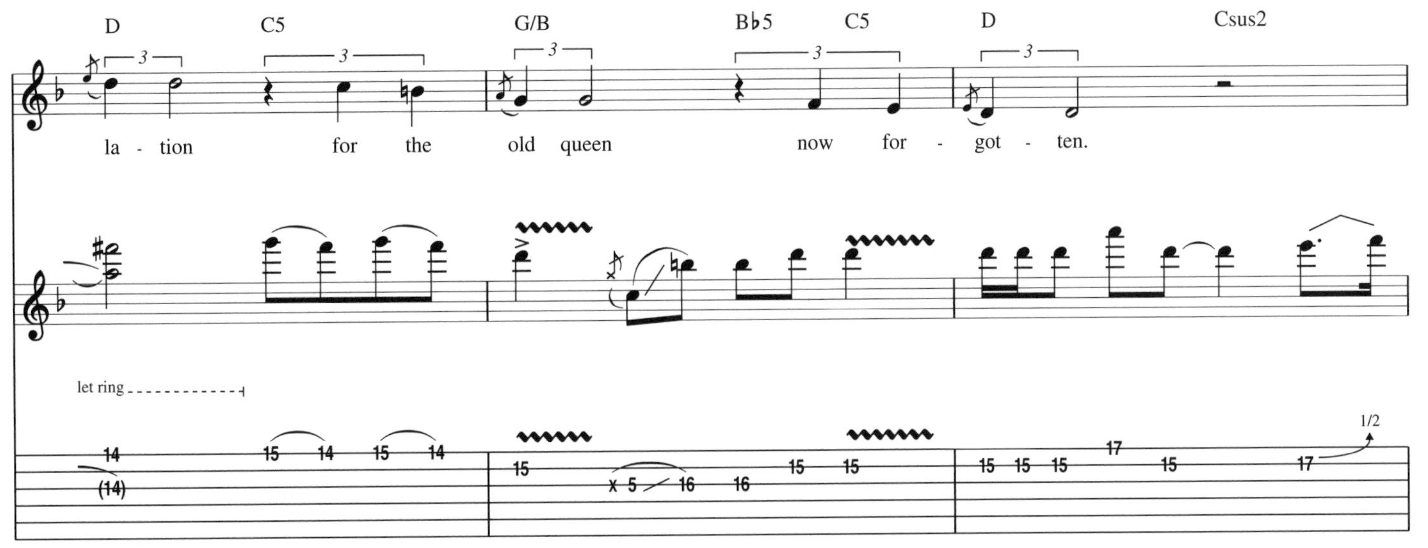
D
C5
G/B
B♭5
C5
D
Csus2
la - tion for the old queen now for - got - ten.
let ring
1/2

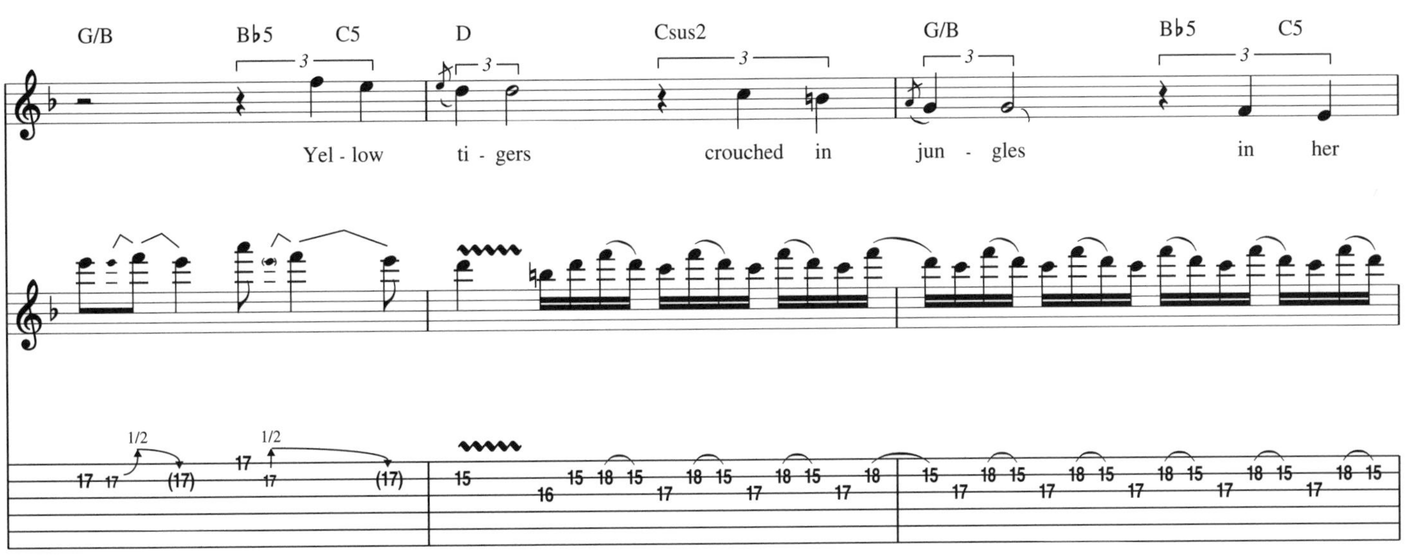
G/B
B♭5
C5
D
Csus2
G/B
B♭5
C5
Yel - low ti - gers crouched in jun - gles in her
1/2
1/2

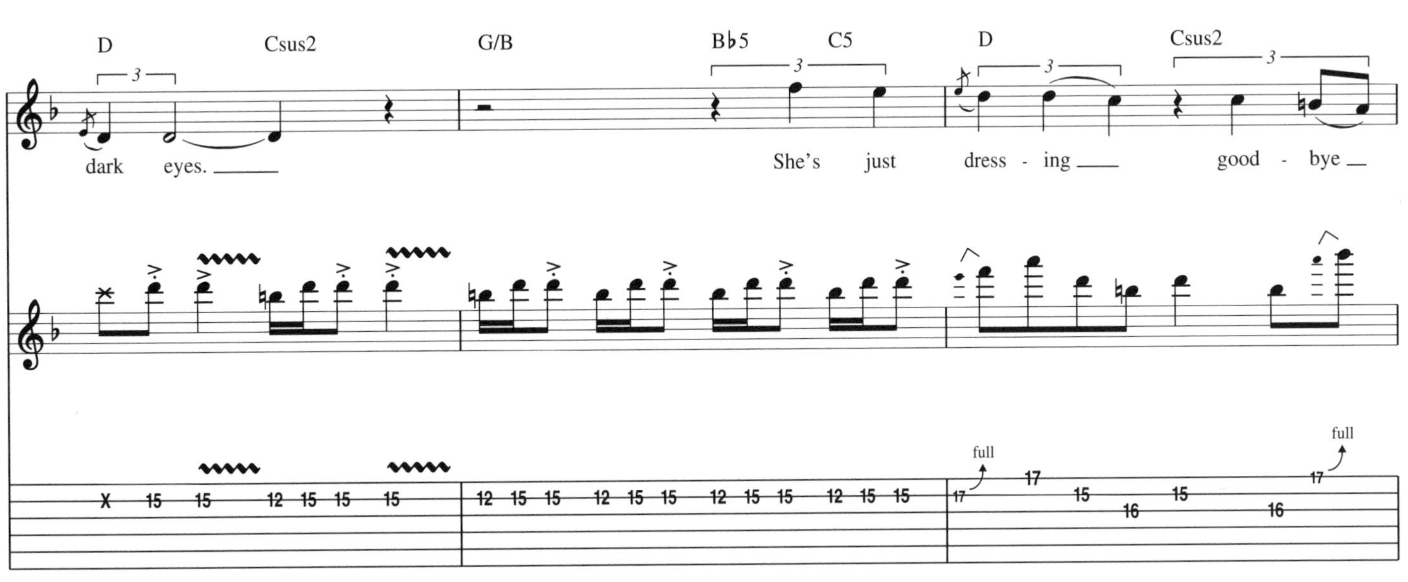
D
Csus2
G/B
B♭5
C5
D
Csus2
dark eyes. She's just dress - ing good - bye
full
full

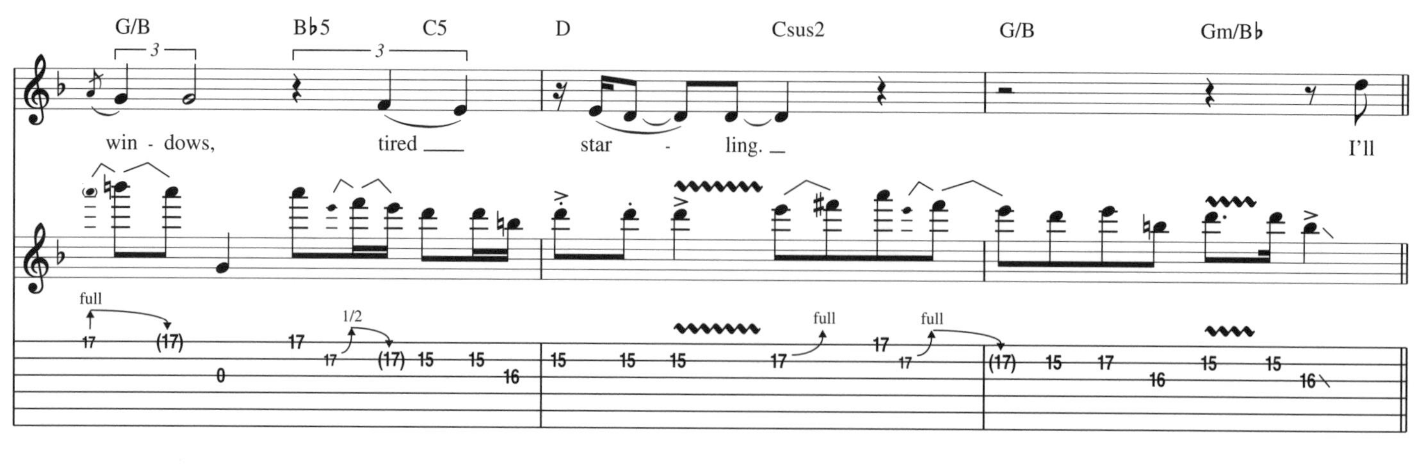

Bridge

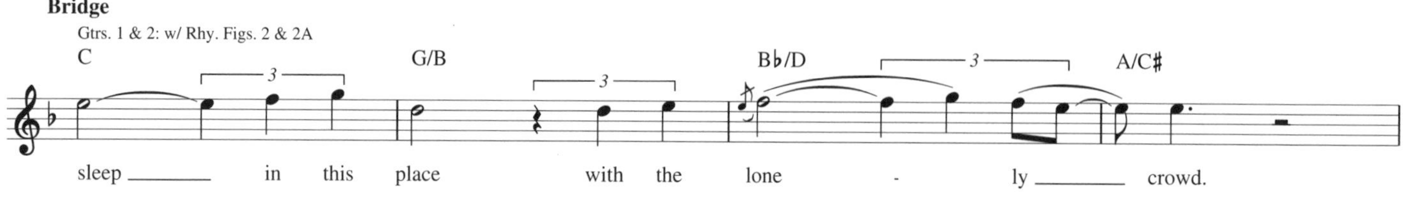

Interlude

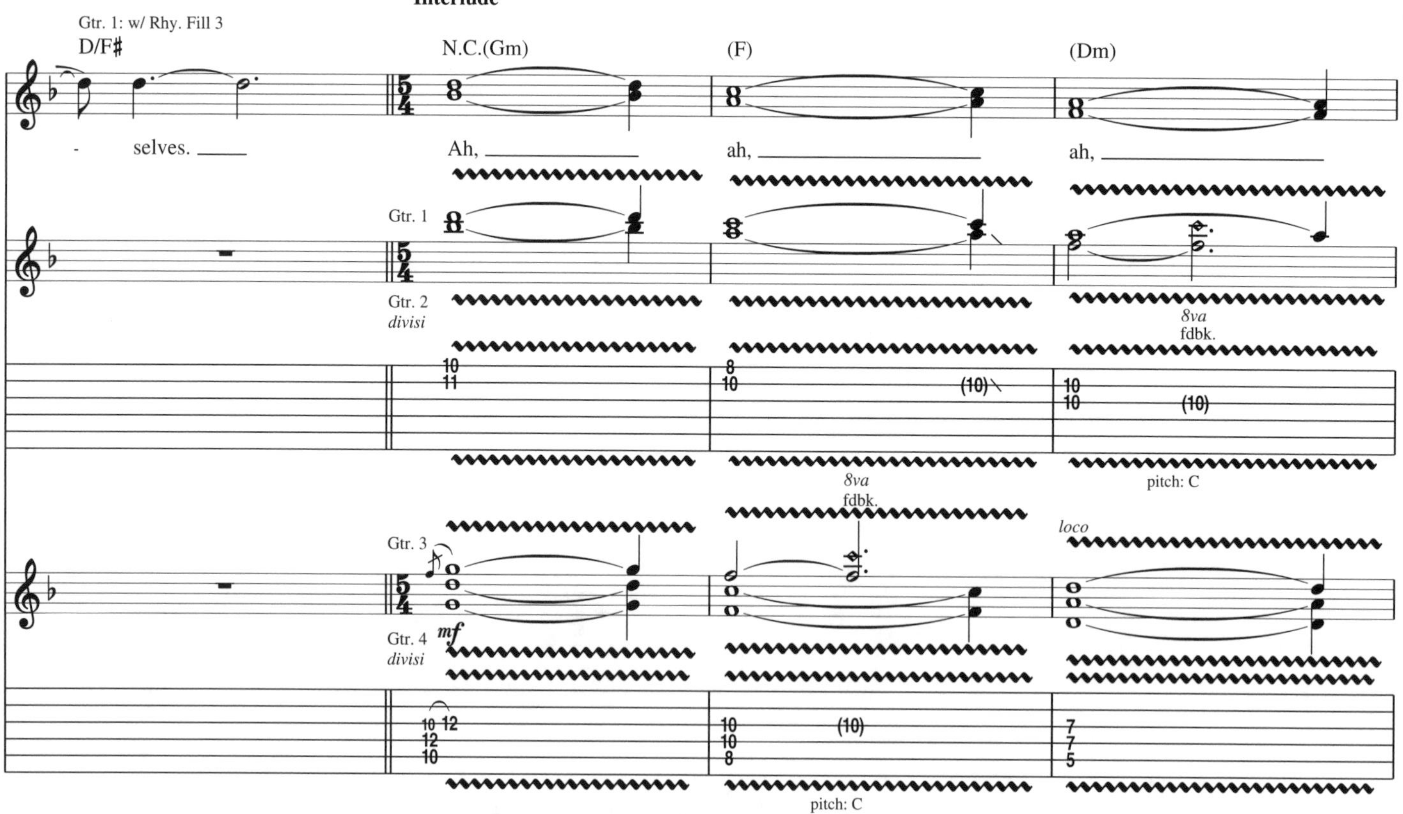

(C)
(Gm)
(F)
(Dm)
ah.
Ah.
ah,
ah,
loco
8va
fdbk.
pitch: C
8va
fdbk.
loco
pitch: C

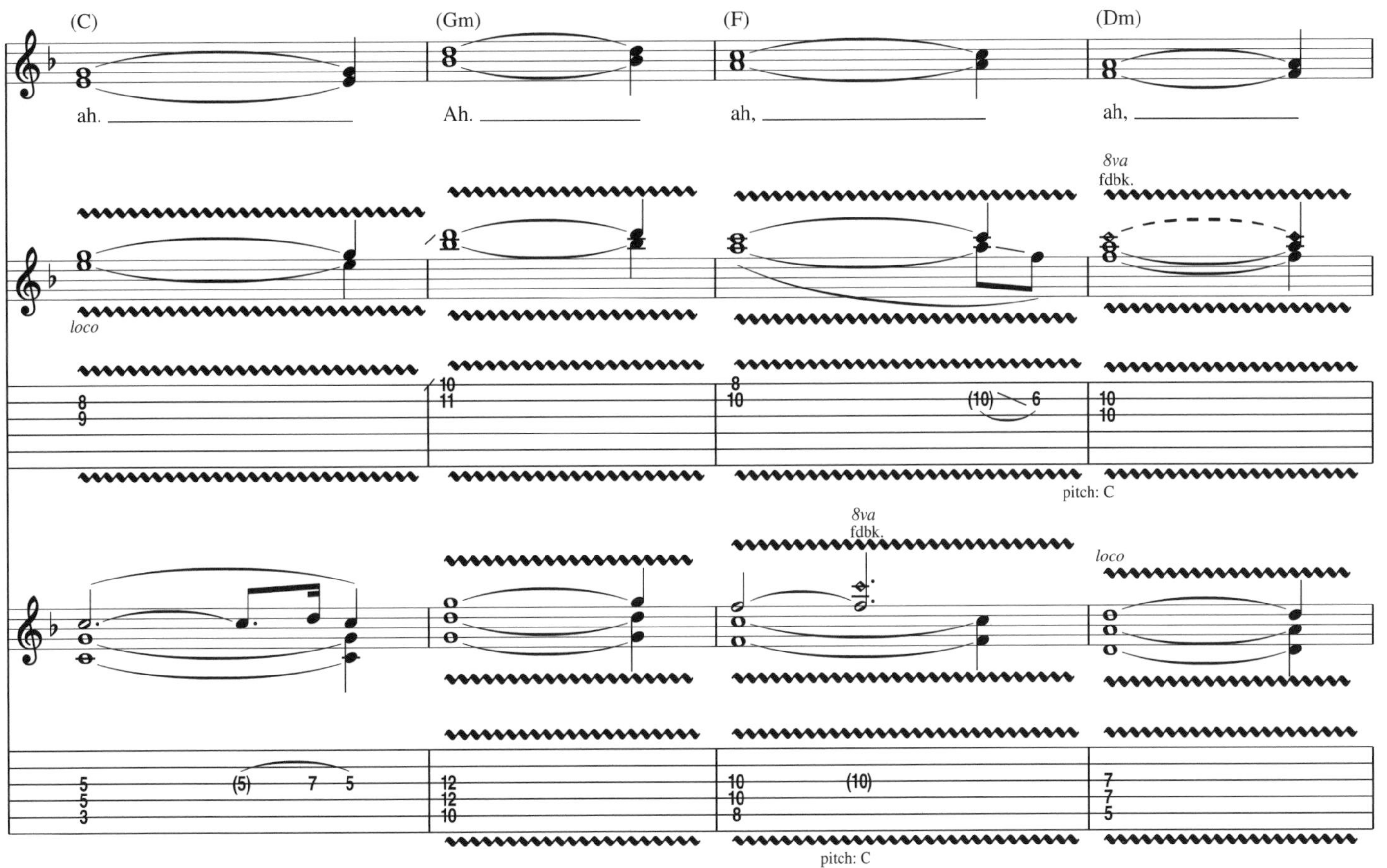

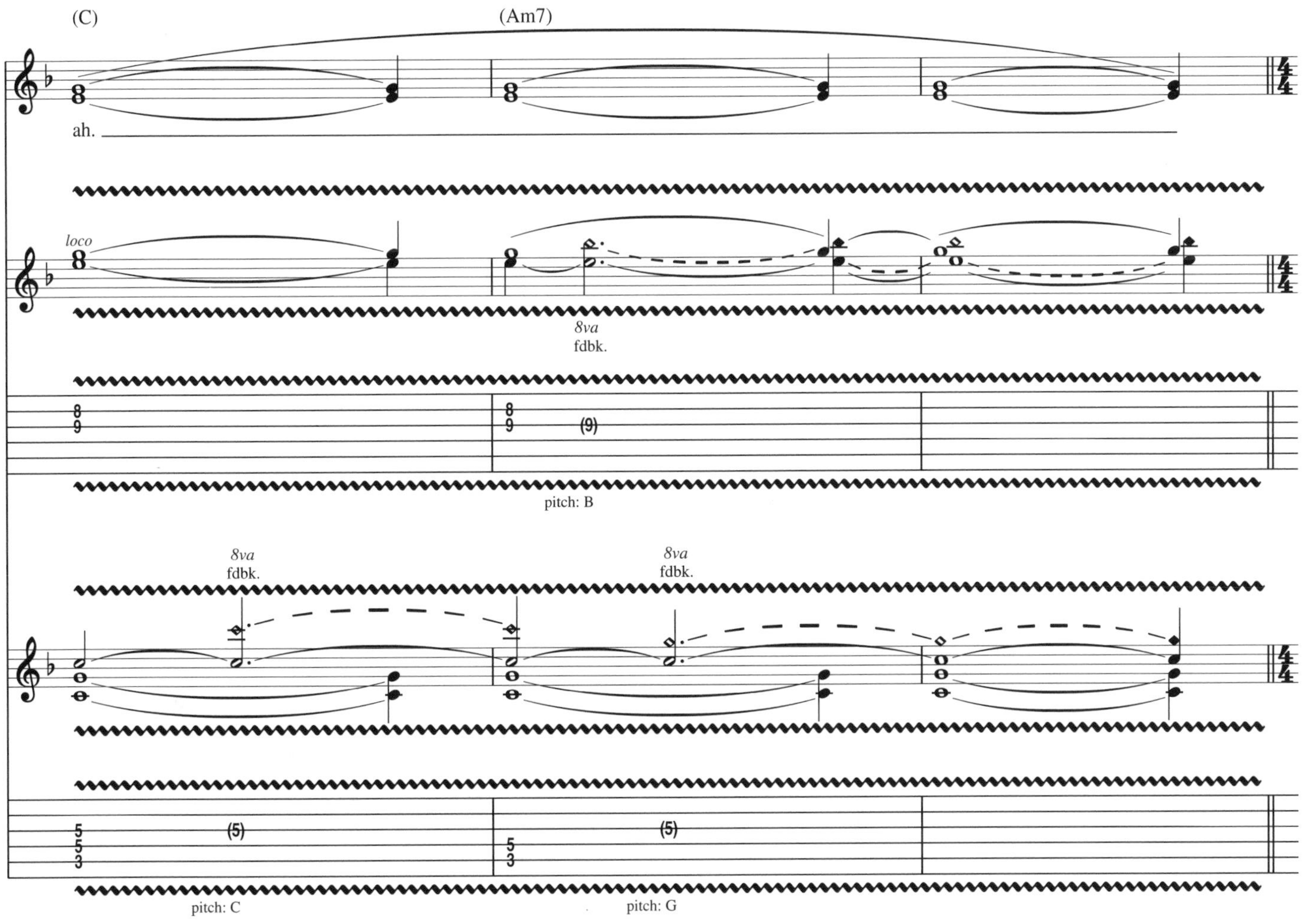

(C)
(Am7)
ah.
loco
8va
fdbk.
pitch: B
8va
fdbk.
8va
fdbk.
pitch: C
pitch: G

Outro-Guitar Solo

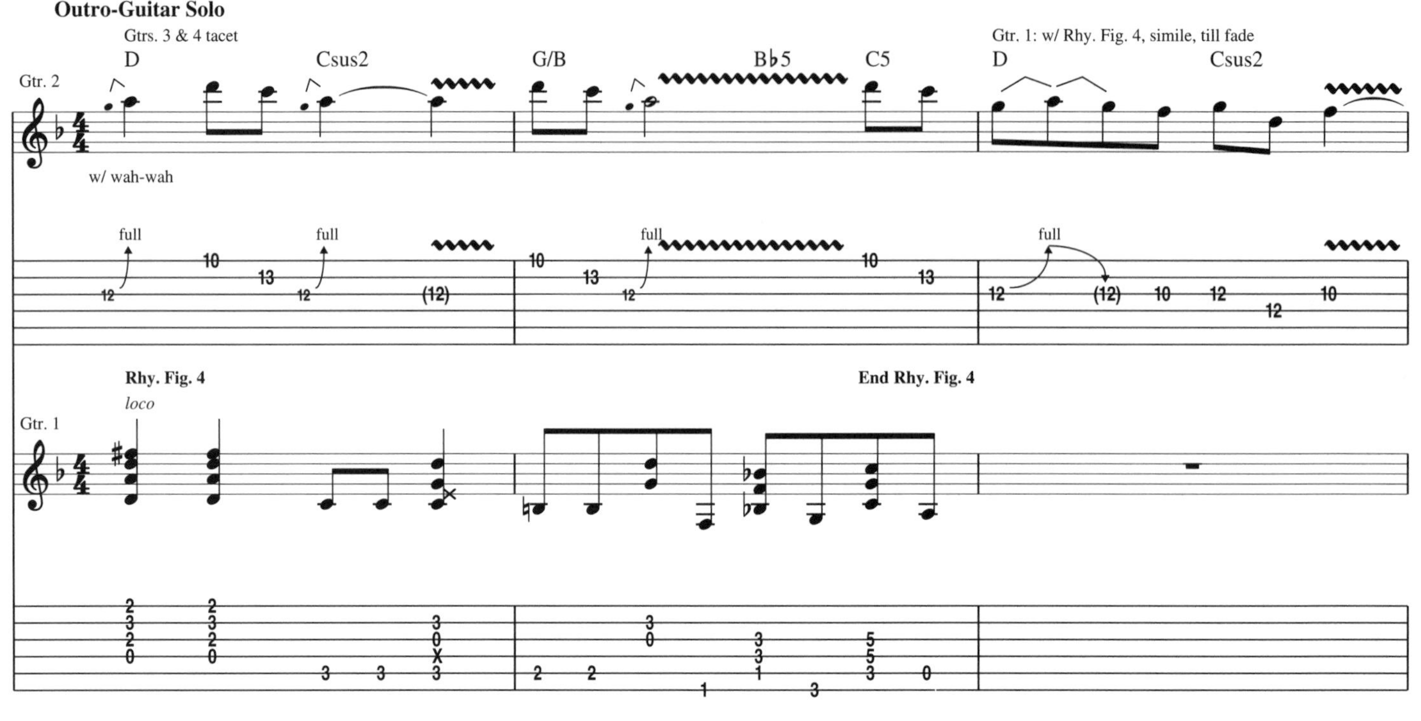

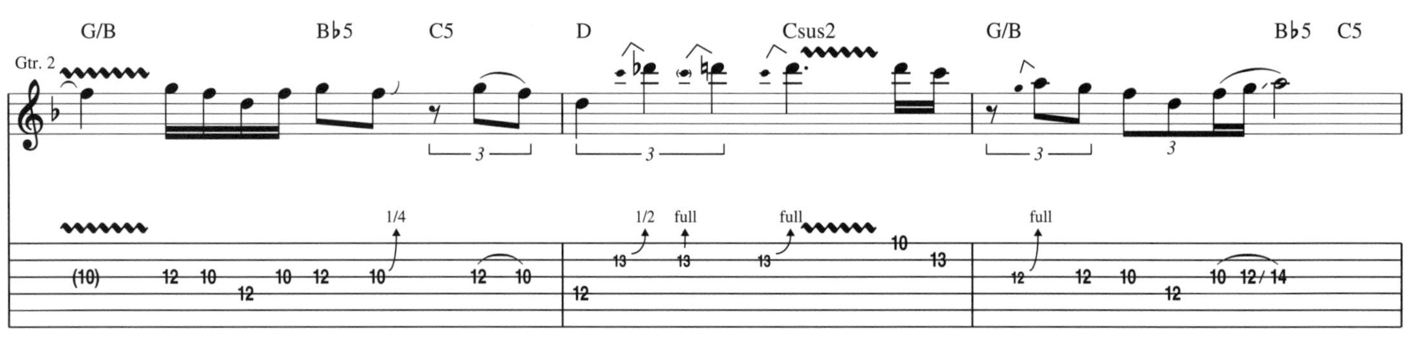

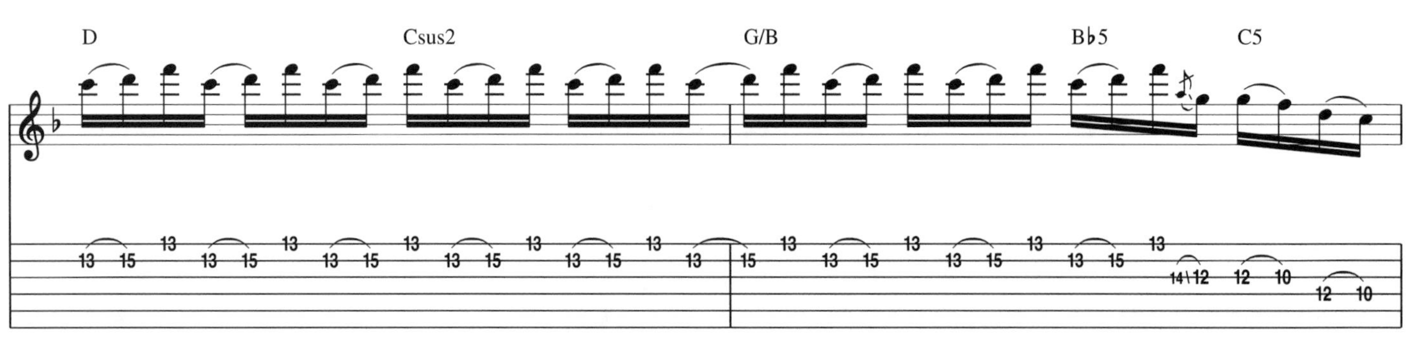

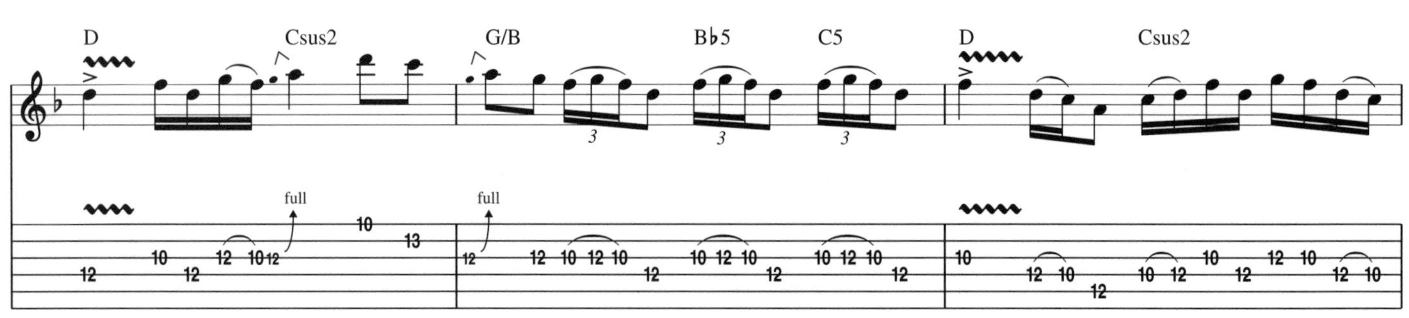

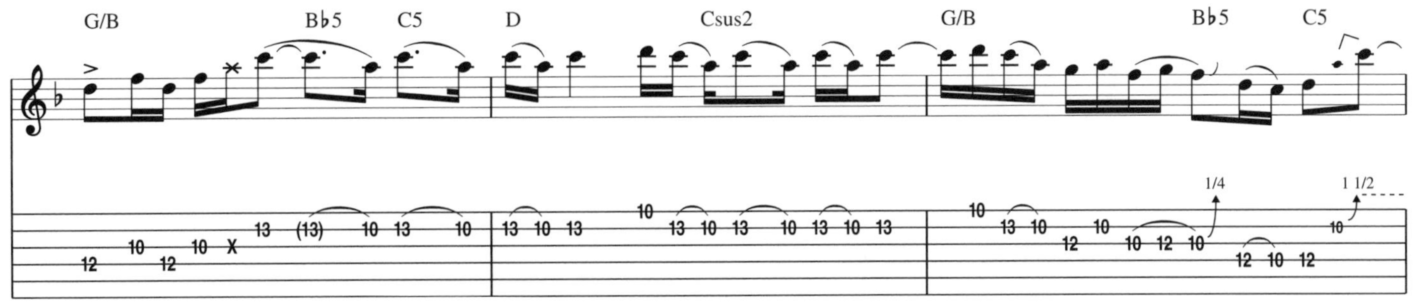
G/B
B♭5
C5
D
Csus2
G/B
B♭5
C5
1/4
1 1/2

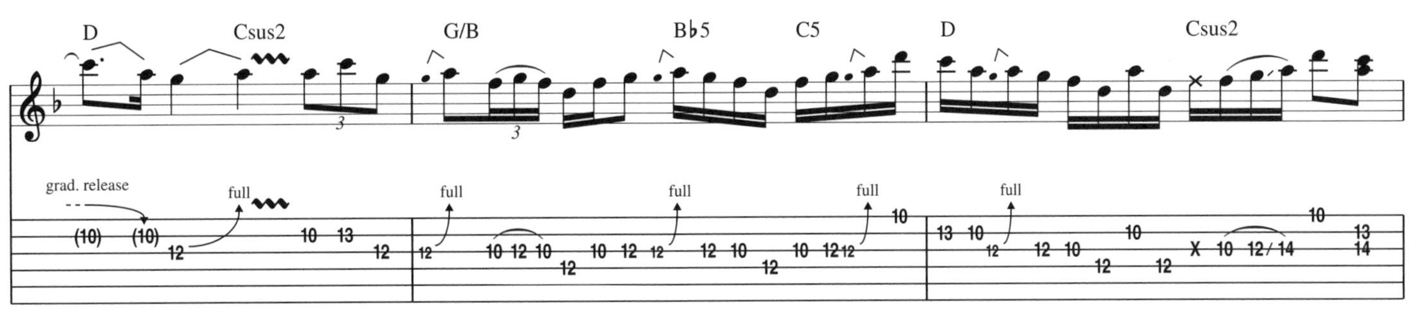
D
Csus2
G/B
B♭5
C5
D
Csus2
grad. release
full
full
full
full
full

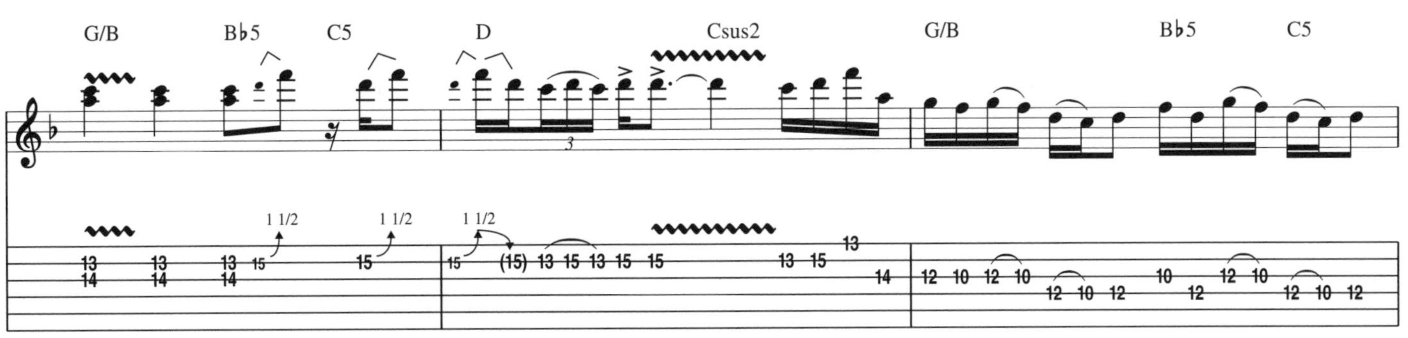
G/B
B♭5
C5
D
Csus2
G/B
B♭5
C5
1 1/2
1 1/2
1 1/2

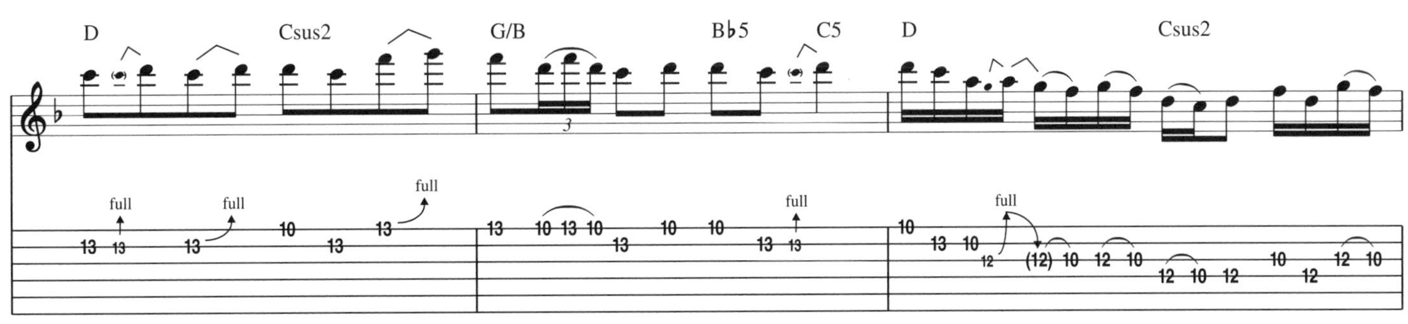
D
Csus2
G/B
B♭5
C5
D
Csus2
full
full
full
full
full

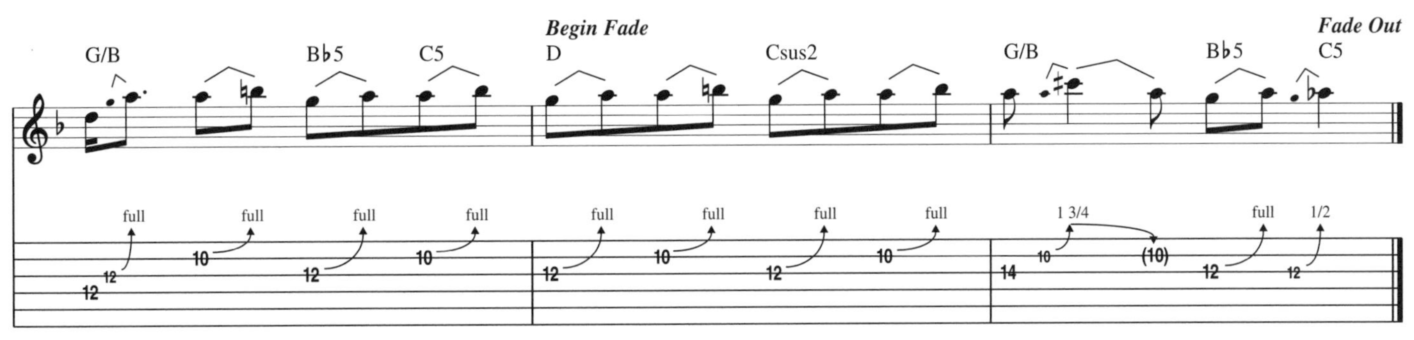
Begin Fade
Fade Out
G/B
B♭5
C5
D
Csus2
G/B
B♭5
C5
full
full
full
full
full
full
full
full
1 3/4
full
1/2

from Eric Clapton - *461 Ocean Boulevard*

Willie and the Hand Jive

Words and Music by Johnny Otis

Intro

Moderately w/ half time Bo Diddley Beat ♩ = 90

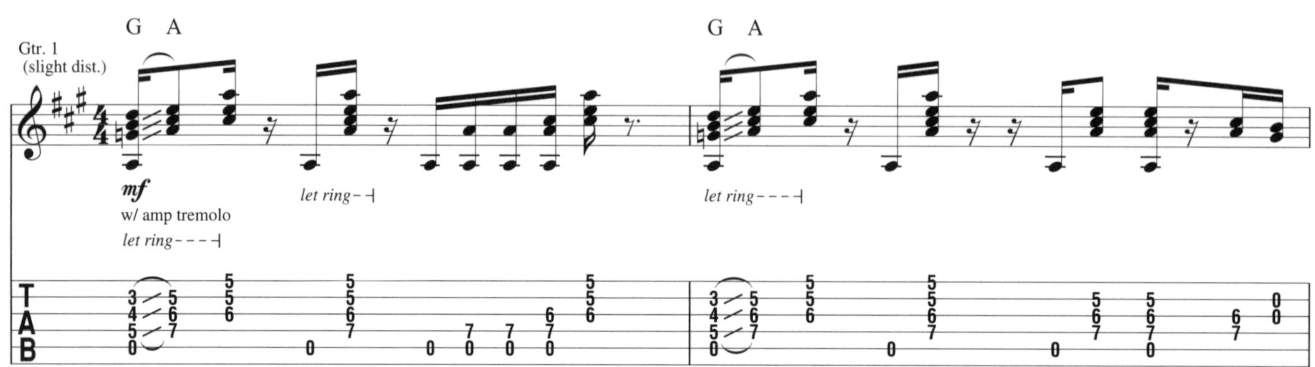

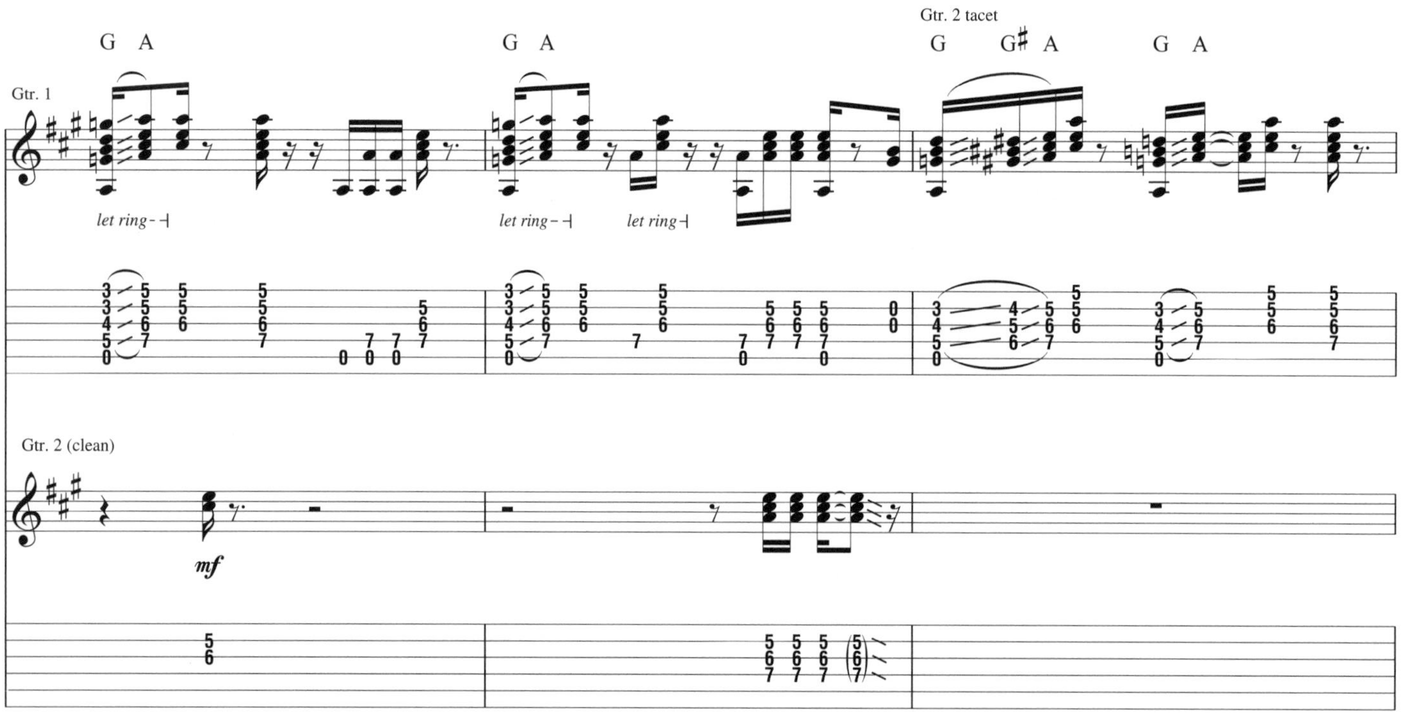

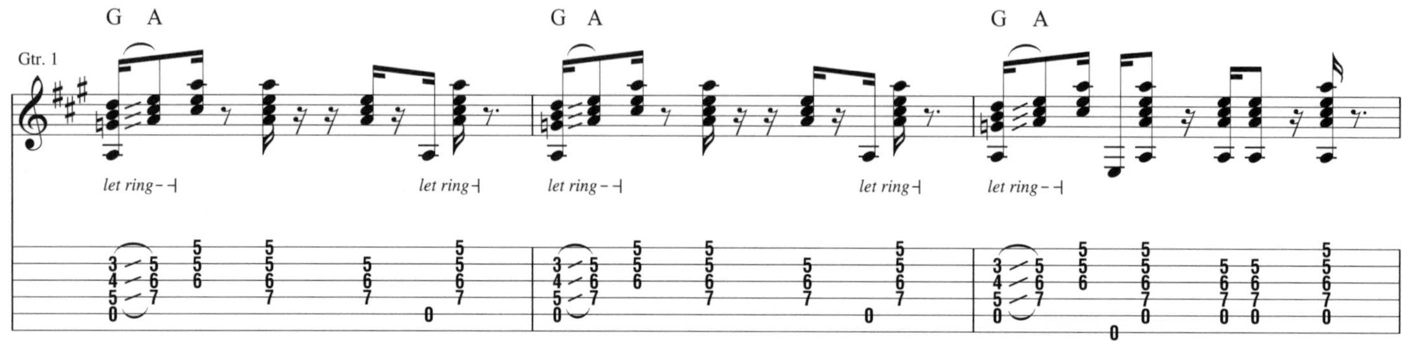

Gtr. 1
G A
G A
G A
let ring
let ring
3/4
1
1
1
1
Gtr. 2

Verse
G A
G A
G A
1. I know a cat named Way-out Wil-lie, got a
let ring
p
let ring
let ring

G A
D
cool lit-tle chick named Rock-in' Mil-lie.
He can walk and stroll and Suz-ie Q,
let ring
let ring

C D
A
G A
'n' do that cra - zy Hand Jive, too.
let ring
let ring
let ring

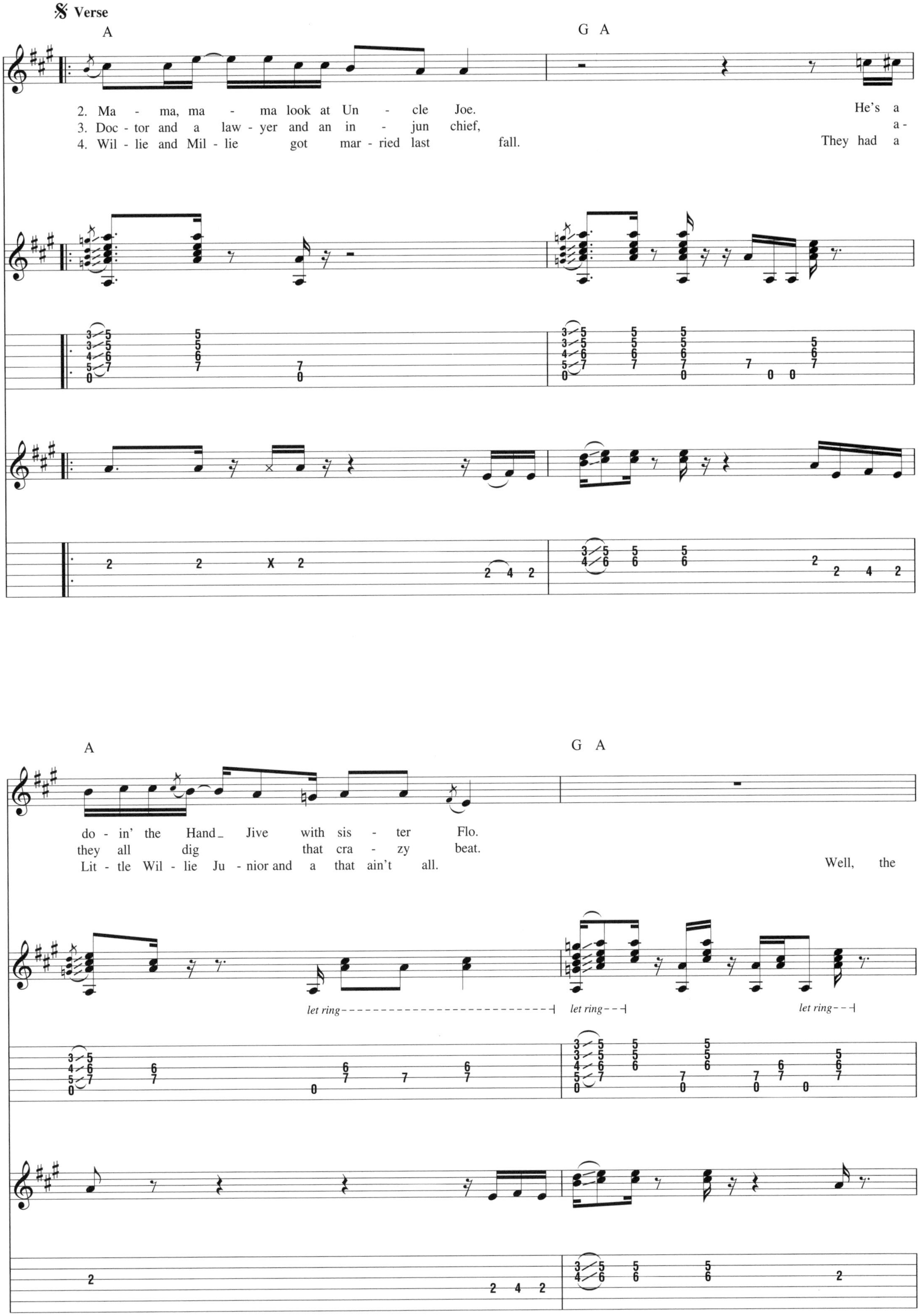

𝄋 **Verse**

A G A

2. Ma - ma, ma - ma look at Un - cle Joe. He's a
3. Doc - tor and a law - yer and an in - jun chief, a-
4. Wil - lie and Mil - lie got mar - ried last fall. They had a

A
G A
do - in' the Hand_ Jive with sis - ter Flo.
they all dig that cra - zy beat.
Lit - tle Wil - lie Ju - nior and a that ain't all. Well, the
let ring
let ring
let ring

D C D

Grand-ma gave ba - by sis - ter a dime, ah, to
Way-out Wil - lie give 'em all a treat when he
kids got cra - zy and it's plain to see, a

A G6 A6 A

do that Hand_ Jive one more time._
hit that Hand_ Jive with his feet._
do - in' the Hand_ Jive on T V.
Ah, Hand_

let ring

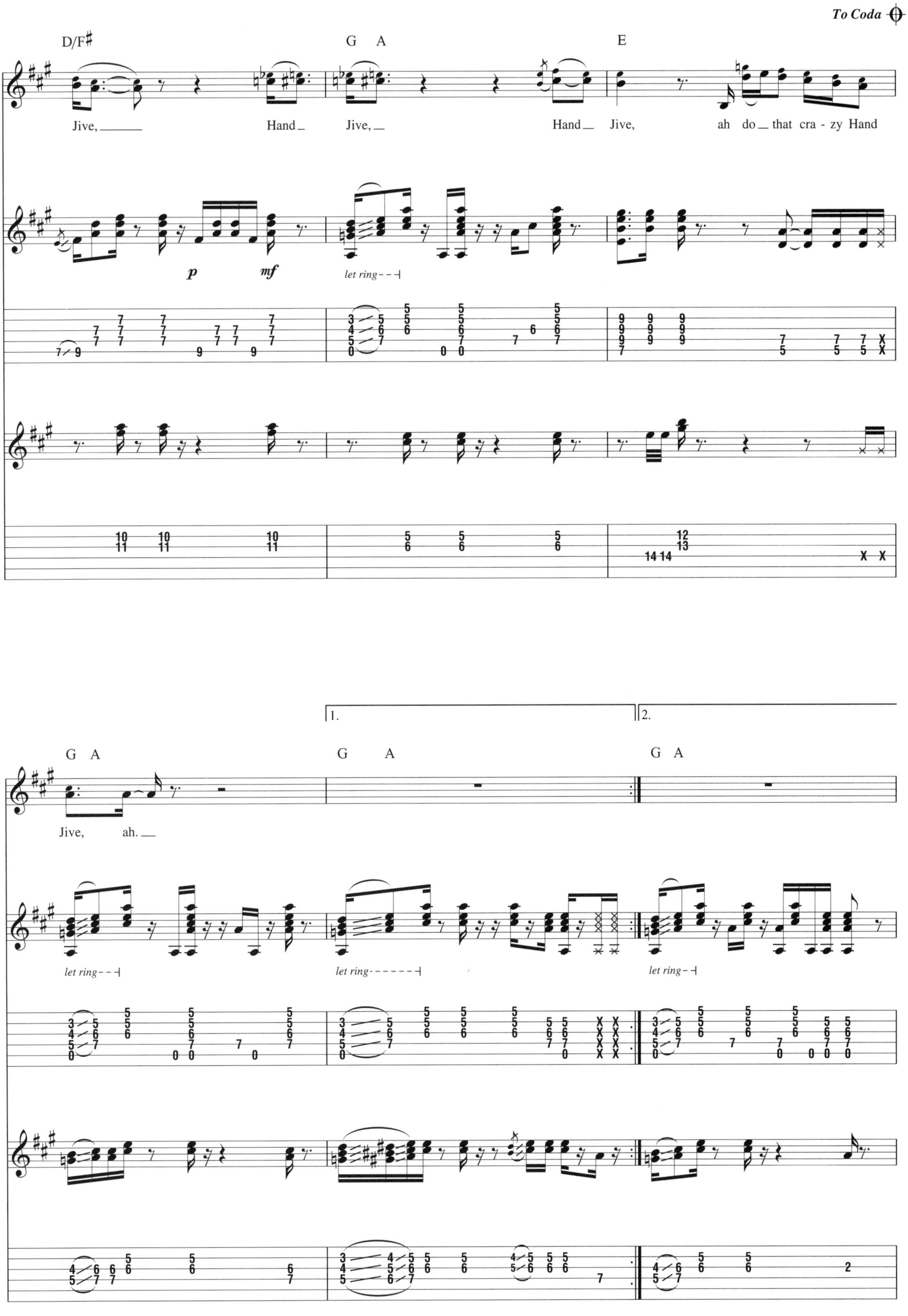

1. 2.

G A G A G A

Jive, ah.

let ring let ring let ring

Coda

D.S. al Coda

Outro-Guitar Solo

G A G A G A

Jive, ah, hey, hey.

let ring

F♯ A
G A
G A
let ring
let ring
G A
G A
G A
let ring
let ring
grad. bend
grad. bend
grad. bend
G A
G A
hold bend
grad. bend

G A
G A
grad. bend
let ring

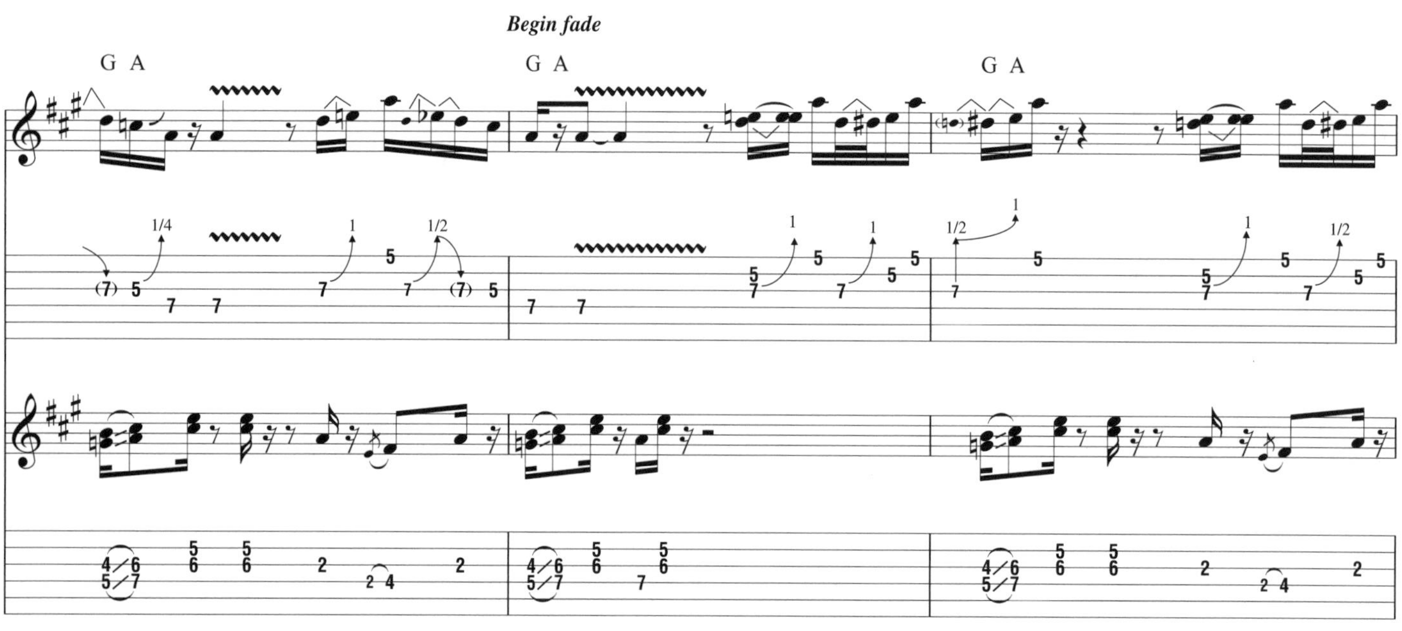
Begin fade
G A
G A
G A

Fade out
G A
G A
G A

from Eric Clapton - *Slowhand*

Wonderful Tonight

Words and Music by Eric Clapton

𝄋 **Verse**

Gtr. 3 tacet

G D/F♯ C/E D

1. It's late in the eve - ning. She's won-d'ring what clothes to wear.
2. We go to a par - ty and ev - 'ry - one turns to see.
3. It's time to go home now and I've got an ach - ing head.

simile on repeats

mp

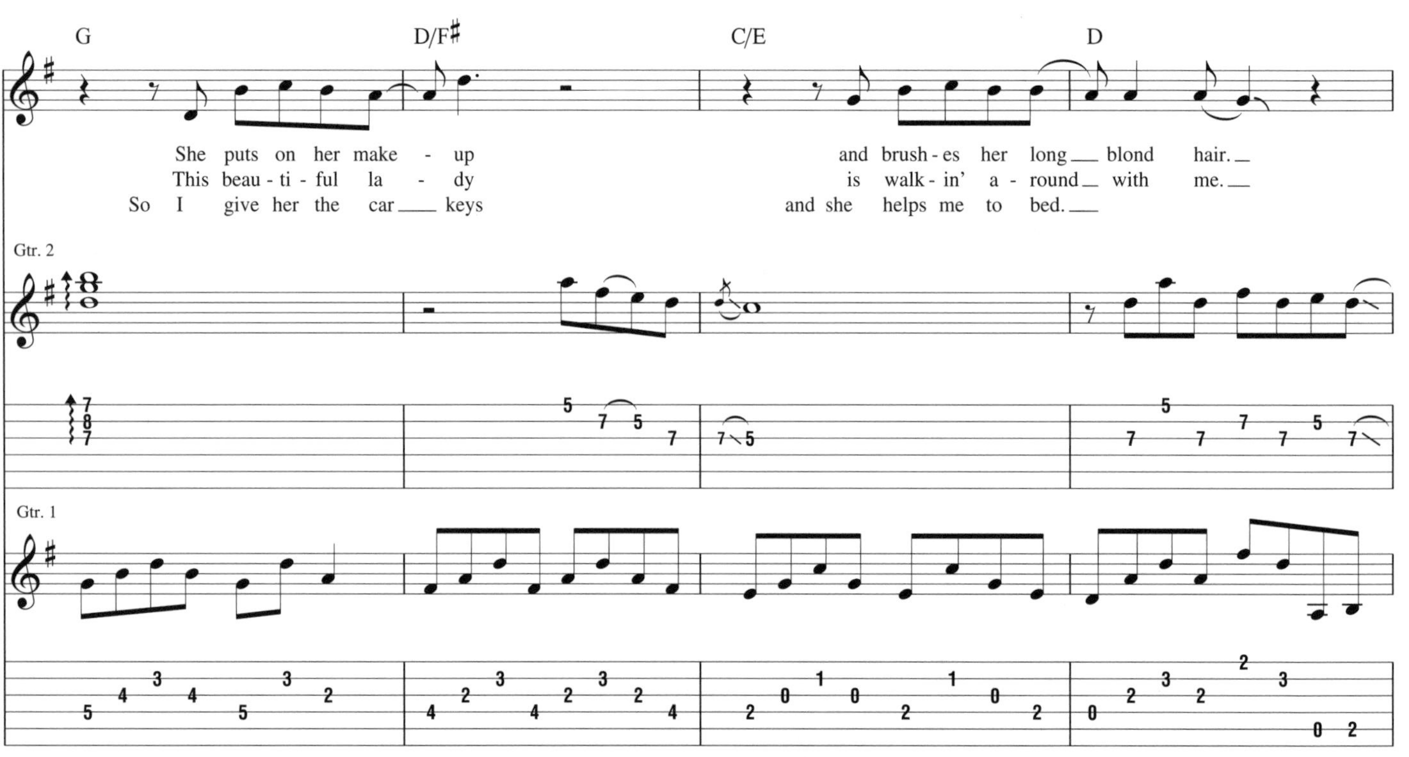

G D/F♯ C/E D
She puts on her make - up and brush - es her long blond hair.
This beau - ti - ful la - dy is walk - in' a - round with me.
So I give her the car keys and she helps me to bed.
Gtr. 2
Gtr. 1

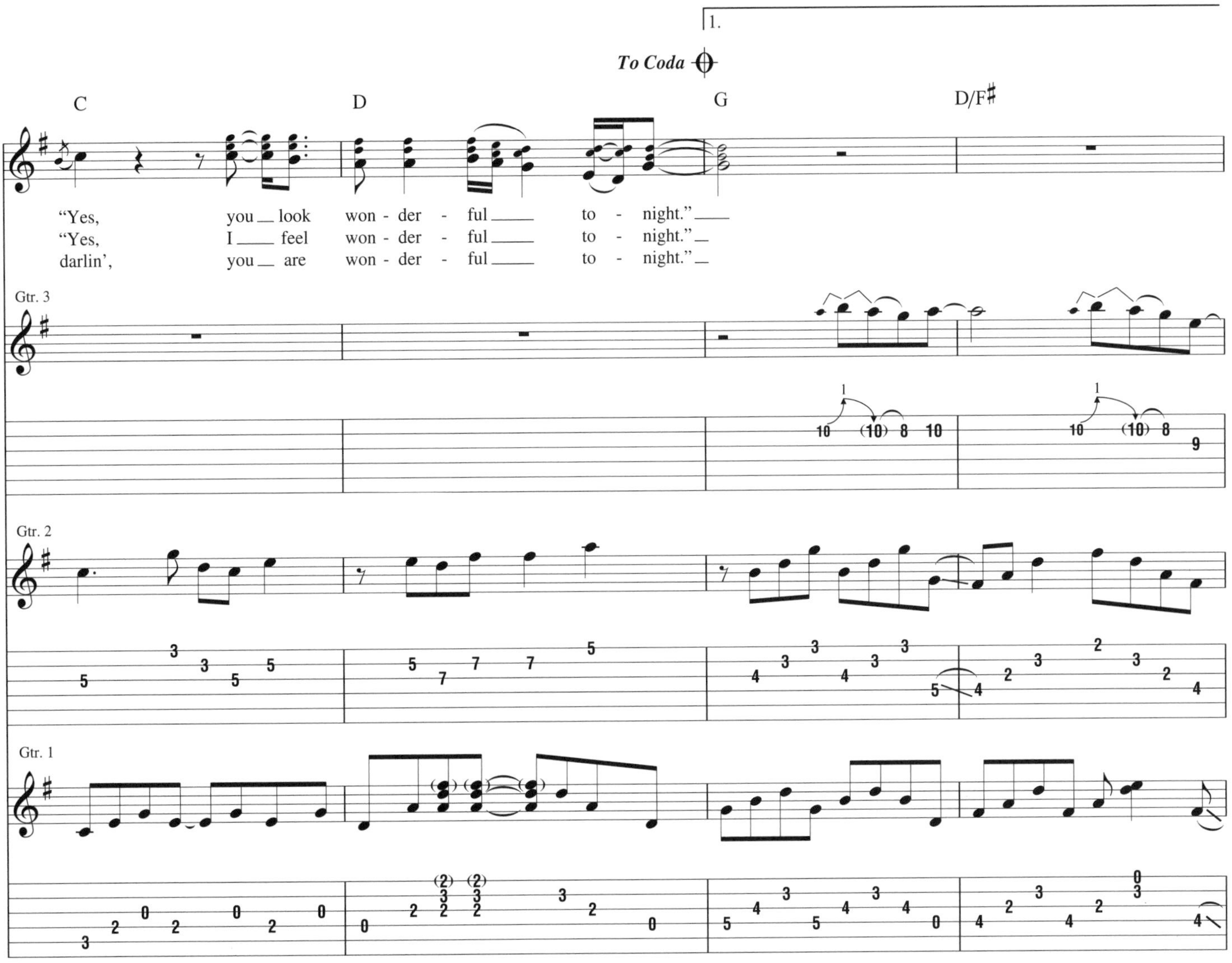

1.

To Coda ⊕

C D G D/F♯

"Yes, you __ look won - der - ful __ to - night." __
"Yes, I __ feel won - der - ful __ to - night." __
darlin', you __ are won - der - ful __ to - night." __

Gtr. 3

Gtr. 2

Gtr. 1

2.

C/E D G

Bridge

Gtr. 3 tacet

C D Csus2

I feel won - der - ful ___ be - cause I see ___ the love

(Oo, oo,

G
D/F♯
Em
C
light in your eyes.
And the won - der of it all
oo,
oo,
oo,
oo,
Gtr. 2
Gtr. 1

D
C
D
is that you just don't re - al - ize how much I love
oo,
oo,
oo.)

Interlude

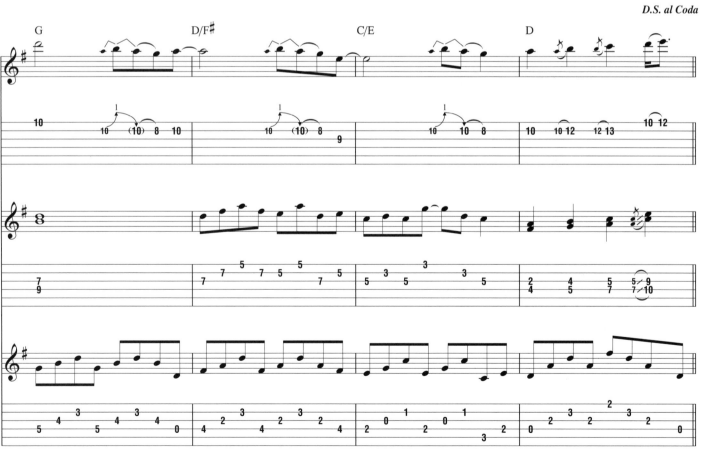

Coda

G D Em7 C

Oh my dar- lin', you are

1 3/4 1 10 (10) 10 (10) 8 9 7 9 7 9 7 5

* Played behind the beat.

Outro

D G D/F#

won - der - ful to - night.

1 1 hold bend

C/E D G

D/F♯ C/E D G

rit.

rit.

rit.